Gardening For Dummies, 2nd Edition

Cheat Sheet

W9-CCQ-998

Quick Pronunciation Guide to Common Plant Names

Abies	<u>aa</u>-bees
Acer	<u>aa</u>-sir
Betula	<u>bet</u>-you-la
Cercis	<u>kerr</u>-kiss (or "<u>sir</u>-sis")
Chamaecyparis	ka-mee-<u>qu</u>-pa-ris
Cotoneaster	ko-<u>tone</u>-ee-aster
Dianthus	dee-<u>anth</u>-us
Echinacea	ee-kee-<u>nah</u>-kee-a
Eleagnus	e-lee-<u>egg</u>-nus
Floribunda	flor-a-<u>bun</u>-da
Hemerocallis	hay-mee-row-<u>kay</u>-lis
Heuchera	<u>hew</u>-kee-ra
Lagerstroemia	law-ger-<u>strom</u>-ee-a
Lathyrus odoratus	<u>lay</u>-thi-rus
Lilium	<u>lee</u>-lee-um
Liquidambar	li-quid-<u>am</u>-bar
Liriope	lee-<u>ree</u>-o-pay (or "<u>lear</u>-ee-ope")
Muscari	mus-<u>kah</u>-ree
Parthenocissus	par-then-o-<u>kiss</u>-us
Quercus	<u>kwer</u>-kus
Raphiolepis	raf-ee-o-<u>lep</u>-is
Rudbeckia	rude-<u>beck</u>-ee-a
Trachelospermum	tra-kay-low-<u>sperm</u>-um
Trillium	<u>tril</u>-lee-um

Growing season by zone

Zone	Last Frost Date	First Frost Date	Typical # of Frost-Free Days
1*	Jun 15	Jul 15	30
2	May 15	Aug 15	90
3	May 15	Sep 15	120
4	May 10	Sep 15	125
5	Apr 30	Oct 15	165
6	Apr 15	Oct 15	180
7	Apr 15	Oct 15	180
8	Mar 10	Nov 15	245
9	Feb 15	Dec 15	265
10	Jan 20	Dec 20	335
11	Frost-free		365

*Susceptible to frost all year

The Basic Hand Tools of Gardening

Garden hose	Lawn rake
Hand trowel	Pruners
Stiff-tined rake	Shovel
Hoe	

. . . For Dummies: Bestselling Book Series for Beginners

Gardening For Dummies, 2nd Edition

Cheat Sheet

Made for the Shade

For those areas of your garden that receive limited sunlight, may we suggest the following shade-loving perennials and annuals:

Perennials

Bear's breech *(Acanthus mollis)* through zone 6

Bee balm *(Monarda didyma)* through zone 4

Bellflower *(Campanula portenschlagiana)* through zone 5

Bergenia *(Bergenia crassifolia)* through zone 4

Bleeding heart *(Dicentra spectabilis)* through zone 3

Columbine *(Aquilegia)* through zone 3

False spiraea *(Astilbe)* through zone 4

Globeflower *(Trollius)* through zone 3

Hosta *(Hosta)* through zone 3

Lady's mantle *(Alchemilla mollis)* through zone 3

Lungwort *(Pulmonaria)* through zone 3

Meadow rue *(Thalictrum)* through zone 5

Siberian iris *(Iris sibirica)* through zone 4

Annuals

Waxleaf begonia *(Begonia semperflorens-cultorum)*

Amethyst flower *(Browallia)*

Canterbury bells *(Campanula medium)*

Coleus

Impatiens

Lobelia

Monkey flower *(Mimulus hybridus)*

Forget-me-not *(Myosotis sylvatica)*

Flowering tobacco *(Nicotiana alata)*

Love-in-a-mist *(Nigella damascena)*

Scarlet sage *(Salvia splendens)*

Black-eyed Susan vine *(Thunbergia alata)*

Wishbone flower *(Torenia fourneiri)*

The Most Fragrant Plants

Arabian jasmine

Carnations

Chocolate cosmos

Common heliotrope

Dames rocket

Daphne

Flowering tobacco

Gardenia

Lilac

Michelia

Mignonette

Plumeria

Roses

Stock

Sweet olive

Sweet peas

Measurement Conversions

1 centimeter ≅ 0.4 inch

1 meter ≅ 39 inches ≅ 1.1 yards

1 kilometer ≅ 0.6 mile

1 liter ≅ 1.1 quarts

1 kilogram ≅ 2.2 pounds

1 gram ≅ 0.04 ounce

1 inch ≅ 2.5 centimeters

1 yard ≅ 0.9 meter

1 mile ≅ 1.6 kilometers

1 quart ≅ 0.9 liter

1 pound ≅ 0.4 kilogram

1 ounce ≅ 31 grams

Praise for Gardening For Dummies, 2nd Edition

"Despite the humorous title, *Gardening For Dummies* is a valuable book full of down-to-earth garden advice. I've been gardening most of my life, and I still found something new to learn in this well-organized book."
— Larry Sombke, public radio's *Natural Gardener*

"Creating a successful garden just got easier with the 2nd edition of *Gardening For Dummies*. It's packed with down-to-earth gardening advice that both novice and experienced gardeners will find useful."
— Doug Jimerson, VP, Editor-in-Chief, garden.com

"*Gardening For Dummies* offers the perfect map for a new generation of gardeners ... with this book and a little time practicing in the garden, you won't be a 'dummy' for long!"
— William Raap, President, Gardener's Supply Co.

Praise for Vegetable Gardening For Dummies

"This book contains all the basic requirements for the average American to plan and maintain a healthy and hardy vegetable garden. The chapters are comprehensive, witty, and easy-to-read. Planting and culture descriptions of individual vegetables are excellent with colorful descriptions and scrumptious recipes."
— Michael D. Orzolek, Prof. of Vegetable Crops, Pennsylvania State University

Praise for Flowering Bulbs For Dummies

"What a joy it is to have this book available to all gardeners. Bulb gardening has now been reduced to a simple pleasure."
— Dan Davids, President, Davids & Royston Bulb Co., Leading Flowering Bulb Wholesaler

"Flower bulbs are one of nature's close to perfect perennial plants. This book, with its easy, well-written style, covers just about every aspect of bulb gardening that the home gardener might encounter and should assure gardening successes with bulbs for all who read it!"
— Brent & Becky Heath, authors of *Daffodils for American Gardens*

Praise for Houseplants For Dummies

"Indoor gardening, quite an intimidating prospect for the brown-thumbed novice, comes alive under the user-friendly guidance of *Houseplants For Dummies*. Larry Hodgson has succeeded in making interior plantscaping accessible for both the novice and the seasoned professional."
— Matthew Gardner, President, California Interior Plantscape Association

"Finally — a book that takes the mystery out of how to keep houseplants alive! Even a veteran black-thumber will turn a shade of green after reading this concise, clearly presented houseplant primer. Following the right-on information presented in this book on how to take care of your houseplants when you're gone more than pays for the price of the book in saved plants."
— Steve Frowine, President, The Great Plant Company

"In my experience, the greatest success with plants comes with confidence. Larry Hodgson starts us off with a bang by demystifying common versus scientific names in a way that will make it easy for the gardener to feel at home. The analysis of home and self-analysis of the gardener in Chapter 2 are brilliant, and he goes on to simplify many of the other areas in which the beginner may fear to tread. The straightforward explanations, presented with a light touch, draw the reader in without taking away the pride of achievement that will come from filling the home with perfect plants."
— Derek Burch, Ph.D., Botanical and Horticultural Consultant

Praise for Lawn Care For Dummies

"I would recommend this book to anyone starting a new lawn or improving an existing one."
— Kevin N. Norris, Director, National Turfgrass Evaluation Program

"This is the one book you should have, keep handy, and use often!"
— Doug Fender, Executive Director, Turf Resource Center, Rolling Meadows, IL

Praise for Decks & Patios For Dummies

"Thorough and thoughtful, with plenty of solid, 'on the ground' advice. Bob Beckstrom will have you thinking like a landscape architect, a carpenter, a mason, an artist. If you're considering finally living to the limits of your lot line, this book is required reading: it's the guidebook to turning your yard into your favorite getaway destination."
— Bill Crosby, Editorial Director, ImproveNet

"This is an exceptionally complete guide. It treats decks and patios not as isolated projects but as features that should fit with the entire property, and it helps homeowners avoid later disappointments by covering details often overlooked in the eagerness to enjoy outdoor living. You know the book is thorough when it goes so far as to recommend that, before digging post holes by hand, you do some physical workouts!"
— Huck DeVenzio, Advertising Manager, Wolmanized wood

GARDENING FOR DUMMIES®
2ND EDITION

**by Mike MacCaskey
with Bill Marken
& the Editors of the
National Gardening Association**

IDG Books Worldwide, Inc.
An International Data Group Company

Foster City, CA ♦ Chicago, IL ♦ Indianapolis, IN ♦ New York, NY

Gardening For Dummies,® 2nd Edition

Published by
IDG Books Worldwide, Inc.
An International Data Group Company
919 E. Hillsdale Blvd.
Suite 400
Foster City, CA 94404
www.idgbooks.com (IDG Books Worldwide Web site)
www.dummies.com (Dummies Press Web site)

Library of Congress Catalog Card No.: 98-89730

ISBN: 1-56884-5130-2

Printed in the United States of America

10 9 8 7 6 5 4

1B/QY/QR/ZZ/IN

Distributed in the United States by IDG Books Worldwide, Inc.

Distributed by Macmillan Canada for Canada; by Transworld Publishers Limited in the United Kingdom; by IDG Norge Books for Norway; by IDG Sweden Books for Sweden; by Woodslane Pty. Ltd. for Australia; by Woodslane (NZ) Ltd. for New Zealand; by Addison Wesley Longman Singapore Pte Ltd. for Singapore, Malaysia, Thailand, and Indonesia; by Norma Comunicaciones S.A. for Colombia; by Intersoft for South Africa; by International Thomson Publishing for Germany, Austria and Switzerland; by Distribuidora Cuspide for Argentina; by Livraria Cultura for Brazil; by Ediciencia S.A. for Ecuador; by Ediciones ZETA S.C.R. Ltda. for Peru; by WS Computer Publishing Corporation, Inc., for the Philippines; by Contemporanea de Ediciones for Venezuela; by Express Computer Distributors for the Caribbean and West Indies; by Micronesia Media Distributor, Inc. for Micronesia; by Grupo Editorial Norma S.A. for Guatemala; by Chips Computadoras S.A. de C.V. for Mexico; by Editorial Norma de Panama S.A. for Panama; by Wouters Import for Belgium; by American Bookshops for Finland. Authorized Sales Agent: Anthony Rudkin Associates for the Middle East and North Africa.

For general information on IDG Books Worldwide's books in the U.S., please call our Consumer Customer Service department at 800-762-2974. For reseller information, including discounts and premium sales, please call our Reseller Customer Service department at 800-434-3422.

For information on where to purchase IDG Books Worldwide's books outside the U.S., please contact our International Sales department at 317-596-5530 or fax 317-596-5692.

For information on foreign language translations, please contact our Foreign & Subsidiary Rights department at 650-655-3021 or fax 650-655-3281.

For sales inquiries and special prices for bulk quantities, please contact our Sales department at 650-655-3200 or write to the address above.

For information on using IDG Books Worldwide's books in the classroom or for ordering examination copies, please contact our Educational Sales department at 800-434-2086 or fax 317-596-5499.

For press review copies, author interviews, or other publicity information, please contact our Public Relations department at 650-655-3000 or fax 650-655-3299.

For authorization to photocopy items for corporate, personal, or educational use, please contact Copyright Clearance Center, 222 Rosewood Drive, Danvers, MA 01923, or fax 978-750-4470.

is a trademark under exclusive license to IDG Books Worldwide, Inc., from International Data Group, Inc.

About the Authors

Michael MacCaskey: Michael MacCaskey began his college career as a creative arts student at San Francisco State University in 1969, but in the process became instead a passionate gardener. By 1976 he received a Bachelor of Science degree in ornamental horticulture from California State Polytechnic University, San Luis Obispo. Since then, he's had the good fortune to work for and learn from garden editors such as Walter Doty, Richard Dunmire, Joe Williamson, and Bill Marken. A second-generation Los Angeles native (zone 9), he was appointed Editor-in-Chief of Vermont-based *National Gardening Magazine* (zone 4) in 1994. Since then, he's been learning about gardening in a short-season, cold-winter region. His magazine writing has been honored by both the Western Magazine Publishers Association and the Garden Writers of America.

Bill Marken: Bill Marken is the editor of *Rebecca's Garden Magazine,* a new publication from Hearst Magazines Enterprises based on the popular television show. A lifelong resident of California, Bill served as editor-in-chief of Sunset, the *Magazine of Western Living,* from 1981 to 1996. Earlier in his career, he wrote for the magazine's garden section, pitched in on several editions of the best-selling *Western Garden Book,* and generally nurtured his interests in subjects related to gardening, landscaping, travel, and other aspects of the good life in the West. A vacation garden at 6,200-feet elevation gives him insight into cold-winter climates with 100-day growing seasons.

National Gardening Association: The National Gardening Association is the largest member-based, nonprofit organization of home gardeners in the U.S. Founded in 1972 (as "Gardens for All") to spearhead the community garden movement, today's National Gardening Association is best known for its bimonthly publication, *National Gardening* magazine. Reporting on all aspects of home gardening, each issue is read by some half-million gardeners worldwide.

For more information about the National Gardening Association, write to 180 Flynn Ave., Burlington, VT 05401 USA; or see its Web site at www.garden.org on the Internet.

ABOUT IDG BOOKS WORLDWIDE

Welcome to the world of IDG Books Worldwide.

IDG Books Worldwide, Inc., is a subsidiary of International Data Group, the world's largest publisher of computer-related information and the leading global provider of information services on information technology. IDG was founded more than 30 years ago by Patrick J. McGovern and now employs more than 9,000 people worldwide. IDG publishes more than 290 computer publications in over 75 countries. More than 90 million people read one or more IDG publications each month.

Launched in 1990, IDG Books Worldwide is today the #1 publisher of best-selling computer books in the United States. We are proud to have received eight awards from the Computer Press Association in recognition of editorial excellence and three from Computer Currents' First Annual Readers' Choice Awards. Our best-selling *...For Dummies®* series has more than 50 million copies in print with translations in 31 languages. IDG Books Worldwide, through a joint venture with IDG's Hi-Tech Beijing, became the first U.S. publisher to publish a computer book in the People's Republic of China. In record time, IDG Books Worldwide has become the first choice for millions of readers around the world who want to learn how to better manage their businesses.

Our mission is simple: Every one of our books is designed to bring extra value and skill-building instructions to the reader. Our books are written by experts who understand and care about our readers. The knowledge base of our editorial staff comes from years of experience in publishing, education, and journalism — experience we use to produce books to carry us into the new millennium. In short, we care about books, so we attract the best people. We devote special attention to details such as audience, interior design, use of icons, and illustrations. And because we use an efficient process of authoring, editing, and desktop publishing our books electronically, we can spend more time ensuring superior content and less time on the technicalities of making books.

You can count on our commitment to deliver high-quality books at competitive prices on topics you want to read about. At IDG Books Worldwide, we continue in the IDG tradition of delivering quality for more than 30 years. You'll find no better book on a subject than one from IDG Books Worldwide.

John Kilcullen
Chairman and CEO
IDG Books Worldwide, Inc.

Steven Berkowitz
President and Publisher
IDG Books Worldwide, Inc.

VIII
WINNER
Eighth Annual Computer Press Awards ≥1992

IX
WINNER
Ninth Annual Computer Press Awards ≥1993

X
WINNER
Tenth Annual Computer Press Awards ≥1994

XI
WINNER
Eleventh Annual Computer Press Awards ≥1995

IDG is the world's leading IT media, research and exposition company. Founded, in 1964, IDG had 1997 revenues of $2.05 billion and has more than 9,000 employees worldwide. IDG offers the widest range of media options that reach IT buyers in 75 countries representing 95% of worldwide IT spending. IDG's diverse product and services portfolio spans six key areas including print publishing, online publishing, expositions and conferences, market research, education and training, and global marketing services. More than 90 million people read one or more of IDG's 290 magazines and newspapers, including IDG's leading global brands — Computerworld, PC World, Network World, Macworld and the Channel World family of publications. IDG Books Worldwide is one of the fastest-growing computer book publishers in the world, with more than 700 titles in 36 languages. The "...For Dummies®" series alone has more than 50 million copies in print. IDG offers online users the largest network of technology-specific Web sites around the world through IDG.net (http://www.idg.net), which comprises more than 225 targeted Web sites in 55 countries worldwide. International Data Corporation (IDC) is the world's largest provider of information technology data, analysis and consulting, with research centers in over 41 countries and more than 400 research analysts worldwide. IDG World Expo is a leading producer of more than 168 globally branded conferences and expositions in 35 countries including E3 (Electronic Entertainment Expo), Macworld Expo, ComNet, Windows World Expo, ICE (Internet Commerce Expo), Agenda, DEMO, and Spotlight. IDG's training subsidiary, ExecuTrain, is the world's largest computer training company, with more than 230 locations worldwide and 785 training courses. IDG Marketing Services helps industry-leading IT companies build international brand recognition by developing global integrated marketing programs via IDG's print, online and exposition products worldwide. Further information about the company can be found at www.idg.com. 10/8/98

Dedication

We dedicate this book to new gardeners, individuals who sow a packet of seeds, plant a tree, or otherwise nurture a plant for the first time.

Authors' Acknowledgments

First we thank the Chicago staff of IDG Books Worldwide: Kathy Welton, publisher, and Holly McGuire, acquisitions editor. We especially thank Sarah Kennedy, former executive editor, for her support and enthusiastic promotion of ...*For Dummies* gardening books. Of the IDG team in Indianapolis, we thank senior project editor Kyle Looper who not only demonstrated excellent organizational and editorial skills, but great trust and patience as well. (A book this size and this complex is an act of faith as much as writing and editing!) We also thank Patricia Yuu Pan for her close reading and knowledgeable editing of the text. Thanks to artists Ron Hildebrand (most of the illustrations in the book) and Shane Kelly (USDA Zone maps) for their excellent work, and to IDG's Alison Walthall, Shelley Lea, and Brent Savage for their help with the color inserts. At NGA, thanks to President David Els President; Vice-President, Publishing, Larry Sommers; and the excellent magazine staff of Linda Provost, Shila Patel, Charlie Nardozzi, and Kim Mitchell. Special thanks to Second Edition contributors Karen E. Fletcher and Kathy Bond Borie, and to First Edition contributors Lynn Ocone, Vicky Congdon, Lance Walheim, Barbara Pleasant, Susan McClure, Robert Kourik, and Sally Williams. Thanks, finally, to technical editors and good friends Deb Brown, Denny Schrock, and Dick Dunmire for their consistently good advice.

Publisher's Acknowledgments

We're proud of this book; please register your comments through our IDG Books Worldwide Online Registration Form located at http://my2cents.dummies.com.

Some of the people who helped bring this book to market include the following:

Acquisitions, Editorial, and Media Development

Editors: Kyle Looper, Patricia Yuu Pan
(*Previous Edition: Melba Hopper*)

Acquisitions Editors: Holly McGuire, Sarah Kennedy

Copy Editors: (*Previous Edition: Diane L. Giangrossi, Diana R. Conover, William A. Barton*)

Technical Editors: Deborah Brown, John R. Dunmire, Denny Schrock

Editorial Manager: Leah P. Cameron

Editorial Assistants: Paul Kuzmic, Donna Love, Alison Walthall

Production

Project Coordinator: Regina Snyder

Layout and Graphics: Lou Boudreau, J. Tyler Connor, Angela F. Hunckler, Anna Rohrer, Brent Savage, Michael A. Sullivan

Illustrations: Ron Hildebrand, Hildebrand Design

Photography: D. Cavagnaro, McIntire/Crandall, Positive Images, Michael Thompson

Proofreaders: Christine Berman, Kelli Botta, Henry Lazarek, Rebecca Senninger

Indexer: Sharon Hilgenberg

Special Help

Maureen F. Kelly, Tim Gallan

General and Administrative

IDG Books Worldwide, Inc.: John Kilcullen, CEO; Steven Berkowitz, President and Publisher

IDG Books Technology Publishing: Brenda McLaughlin, Senior Vice President and Group Publisher

Dummies Technology Press and Dummies Editorial: Diane Graves Steele, Vice President and Associate Publisher; Mary Bednarek, Director of Acquisitions and Product Development; Kristin A. Cocks, Editorial Director

Dummies Trade Press: Kathleen A. Welton, Vice President and Publisher; Kevin Thornton, Acquisitions Manager

IDG Books Production for Dummies Press: Michael R. Britton, Vice President of Production and Creative Services; Cindy L. Phipps, Manager of Project Coordination, Production Proofreading, and Indexing; Kathie S. Schutte, Supervisor of Page Layout; Shelley Lea, Supervisor of Graphics and Design; Debbie J. Gates, Production Systems Specialist; Robert Springer, Supervisor of Proofreading; Debbie Stailey, Special Projects Coordinator; Tony Augsburger, Supervisor of Reprints and Bluelines

Dummies Packaging and Book Design: Patty Page, Manager, Promotions Marketing

◆

The publisher would like to give special thanks to Patrick J. McGovern, without whom this book would not have been possible.

◆

Contents at a Glance

Introduction 1

Part I: Getting Going with Gardening 7
Chapter 1: Just a Few Ground-Level Questions and Answers 9
Chapter 2: Zoning Out: What You Can and Can't Grow 17
Chapter 3: Planning Your Landscape 29

Part II: Color Your World 45
Chapter 4: Annuals... 47
Chapter 5: Perennials 61
Chapter 6: Bulbs 75
Chapter 7: Roses 87

Part III: Sculpting with Plants 105
Chapter 8: Trees and Shrubs 107
Chapter 9: Lawns and Ground Covers 129
Chapter 10: Vines 153

Part IV: At Ground Level 165
Chapter 11: Understanding and Improving Soil 167
Chapter 12: Raising Plants from Seeds 183
Chapter 13: Choosing and Planting Seedlings, Trees, and Shrubs 195

Part V: Caring for Your Plants 207
Chapter 14: Feed Me, Seymour! Watering, Feeding, and Composting 209
Chapter 15: A Snip Here, a Snip There: Pruning and Propagating 229
Chapter 16: Fighting Pests, Diseases, and Weeds 239
Chapter 17: Tools of the Trade 267

Part VI: Special Gardens 279
Chapter 18: Food Gardens 281
Chapter 19: Container Gardens 299
Chapter 20: Gardens for Birds, Bees, and Butterflies 317
Chapter 21: Gardening in Tight Spaces 325

Part VII: The Part of Tens 331
Chapter 22: Ten Quick Projects 333
Chapter 23: Perfumed Garden Flowers 343

Appendix A: Gardening Resources 351

Appendix B: Mail-Order Resources 367

Cartoons at a Glance

By Rich Tennant

page 45

page 165

"Something's about to die in your cactus container."

page 279

page 207

page 331

page 105

page 7

Fax: 978-546-7747 • E-mail: the5wave@tiac.net

Table of Contents

Introduction **1**

How to Use This Book.. 2
Part I: Getting Going with Gardening 3
Part II: Color Your World 3
Part III: Sculpting with Plants 3
Part IV: At Ground Level 4
Part V: Caring for Your Plants 4
Part VI: Special Gardens 4
Part VII: The Part of Tens 4
Part VIII: Appendixes 5
Icons Used in This Book 6

Part I: Getting Going with Gardening **7**

Chapter 1: Just a Few Ground-Level Questions and Answers **9**

How Do I Make My Plants Grow Rather Than Die?...................... 10
    Your climate and microclimates 10
    Sun or shade 11
    Soil and water 11
    Plants that are most at home in your garden 12
What Can I Use My Garden For? 12
Do I Have to Learn a Foreign Language? 13
    The fancy name 14
    Common names 15

Chapter 2: Zoning Out: What You Can and Can't Grow **17**

Plant Hardiness 18
The USDA Plant Hardiness Zone Map 19
The American Horticultural Society's Plant Heat-Zone Map 20
Length Counts: How Long Is Your Season? 21
Stretching Your Garden Season 22
Maximizing Winter Hardiness 27

Chapter 3: Planning Your Landscape **29**

Taking Stock of What You Have 30
Dreaming Up the Perfect Landscape 33
What Goes Where: Designing the Plan 36
    Using your space effectively 36
    Defining areas and ways to move through them 38
Creating a Final Plan 42

Part II: Color Your World 45

Chapter 4: Annuals 47
What's an Annual? 47
Getting Cozy with Annuals 49
    Some annuals are cool and some like it hot 49
    Areas where annuals live all year 50
    Sun and shade 50
How to Buy Annuals 51
What You Can Do with Annuals 52
    Playing with color 53
    Using shape, height, and structure 53
    Designing for fragrance 54
    Getting annuals together 55
    Containing annuals 56
Taking Care of Your Annuals 56
Our Favorite Annuals 57
    Cool-season annuals 57
    Warm-season annuals 59

Chapter 5: Perennials 61
What's a Perennial? 61
Beds and Borders 62
Designing a Perennial Border 63
    Beyond borders 64
Planting Perennials . . . and Afterwards 65
    Watering and feeding 65
    Pinching and pruning perennials 66
Our Favorite Perennials 68

Chapter 6: Bulbs 75
What Are Bulbs? 75
What You Can Do with Bulbs 76
When and How to Buy Bulbs 76
    Spring-blooming bulbs 77
    Summer-blooming bulbs 78
    Shopping tips 78
Planting Bulbs 79
Caring for Bulbs 81
Dividing and Propagating Bulbs 82
Bulbs in Containers 82
Favorite Bulbs 83

Chapter 7: Roses 87
Kinds of Roses 88
    Trying out hybrid teas 88
    Fun with floribundas 89
    Hail to the queen 90

Climbing high with roses 90
"Honey, I shrunk the roses!" 90
When a rose is a tree 91
Shrub roses 91
Landscaping with Roses 96
Buying Roses 97
Planting Roses 99
Fertilizing and Watering 100
The Mystery of Pruning 102
Other Rose Quirks 103
Helping Roses Survive Winter 104

Part III: Sculpting with Plants 105

Chapter 8: Trees and Shrubs 107

What Trees Can Do for You 107
Lower heating and cooling expenses 108
Make you look marvelous 108
Choosing the Right Tree 109
Don't Try This at Home 111
Our Favorite Trees 112
Rub-a-Dub-Dub, What's a Shrub? 117
What Shrubs Can Do for You 118
Our Favorite Shrubs 121

Chapter 9: Lawns and Ground Covers 129

Lawn Decisions 130
How big? 130
Which grass is for you? 131
Turfgrass short list 131
Putting in a New Lawn 134
Planting Lawn from Seed 134
Shopping for seed 135
How much seed to buy 135
Planting day 136
Planting Lawn from Sod 140
Buying sod 140
Laying sod 140
Planting Plugs and Sprigs 143
Care and Feeding of Lawns 143
Weeding 144
Mowing 144
Fertilizing 145
Tune-ups and face-lifts 146
Winter overseeding 146
Ground Covers instead of Lawns 147

Planting Ground Covers 147
Top Ground-Cover Choices 148
Over in the Meadow 152

Chapter 10: Vines **153**

Let's Play Twister 153
Using Vines Effectively 155
Don't let vines grow where they shouldn't 155
Provide sturdy support 155
Prune for healthy vines 156
Lean on Me 156
Choosing a Vine Support 156
Bamboo teepees 157
Chain-link fences 158
Metal trellises 158
Latticework trellises 159
Fan trellises 159
Plastic netting 159
Pillars 160
Wall-mounted supports 160
Arbors 160
Vines We Love 160
Annual Vines 162

Part IV: At Ground Level *165*

Chapter 11: Understanding and Improving Soil **167**

Clearing the Site... 167
Stripping sod 168
Other soil-clearing methods 169
Meeting Your Soil... 170
Soil texture.. 170
Soil structure... 172
One more big thing: Soil pH 174
Your soil, in detail 174
Improving Your Soil... 175
Exactly what do you add?.................................. 176
Changing pH.. 178
Adding nutrients.. 178
Green manure crops and cover crops 178
Loosening the Soil 179
Time for a tiller 180
Double digging 181
Simple raised beds 181

Chapter 12: Raising Plants from Seeds **183**

What Those Needy Seeds Need 184

Smart Shopping 184
Sowing Seeds Right in the Ground 185
A Dozen Easy Annuals to Direct-Sow 188
Starting Seeds Indoors 189
A Dozen Easy Annuals to Start Indoors 193

Chapter 13: Choosing and Planting Seedlings, Trees, and Shrubs ... 195

Buying and Planting Seedlings 196
Figuring Out Spacing for Transplants 196
Planting Seedlings, Step by Step 197
Container-Grown Trees and Shrubs 200
    Choosing container-grown trees and shrubs 200
    Transplanting trees and shrubs from containers 201
Bare-Root Planting 204
    Choosing bare-root plants 204
    Planting bare-root plants 205
Burlap-Wrapped Root Balls 205
    Choosing balled-and-burlapped plants 205
    Planting balled-and-burlapped plants 206

Part V: Caring for Your Plants 207

Chapter 14: Feed Me, Seymour! Watering, Feeding, and Composting 209

Watering Basics 210
    Getting water to your garden 210
    Determining the amount and frequency of watering 213
    Conserving water 215
Providing a Balanced Diet for Your Plants 216
Don't Compromise, Fertilize! 217
    Common fertilizer terms 217
    Kinds of fertilizers for various plants 219
    Organic fertilizers 220
Piling Onto the Compost Bandwagon 221
    From refuse to riches 222
    Bin there, done that! 223
    To build or to buy? 223
    Composting aids . . . who needs them? 225
    Heapin' it on 226
A-Mulching We Will Go 226
    Inorganic mulches 227
    Fertile mulches 227

Chapter 15: A Snip Here, a Snip There: Pruning and Propagating 229

Practical Pruning 229

How pruning affects plant growth 230
The kindest cuts 231
Pruning trees 232
Pruning in winter 234
Pruning in summer 234
Pruning tools 235
Down-to-Earth Propagating 236
Getting Plants for Free 237

Chapter 16: Fighting Pests, Diseases, and Weeds **239**

Preventing Bad Things from Happening 240
Identifying Damage 241
Insect Pests You're Most Likely to Encounter 243
Managing Pests 250
Encouraging "good" insects 251
Safe and effective pest chemicals 252
Preventing Plant Diseases 256
Solarization 257
A dozen dirty diseases: What to do 257
Least-toxic disease remedies 261
Controlling Weeds 263
Weed-control basics 263
Nontoxic herbicides 264
Ten common weeds 264

Chapter 17: Tools of the Trade **267**

Hand Tools 267
The magnificent seven tools 267
Hand-tool maintenance 268
Five more tools to buy 270
Powering Up Your Tools 270
Lawn mowers 271
Trimmers 274
Tillers and grinders 274
Where to Shop for Garden Tools 277
Nurseries 277
Other sources for tools and garden supplies 277

Part VI: Special Gardens *279*

Chapter 18: Food Gardens **281**

Planning a Vegetable Garden 281
Seasonal preferences 282
Choose the right location 284
Make the garden the right size 284
Designing the garden 284

Improving the soil 285
What to start with 286
It's all in the timing 286
Raise them right 287
Have a happy harvest 288
You Can't Go Wrong with These 288
What about Hybrids and Heirlooms? 289
Squeezing in Herbs 290
Is There Fruit in Your Future? 292
Six steps to a fruit tree harvest 293
Planning a fruit garden 294
Fruits for the home garden 294

Chapter 19: Container Gardens **299**
Choosing the Right Pots 299
Designing with Container Plants 302
Style points 302
One special plant 303
Combining plants in containers 304
How to arrange containers 304
Putting It All Together 305
Favorite Container Combos 307
Annuals all summer 307
Perennial accents 308
Delectable edibles 308
Container Plants for Four Seasons 309
A Primer on Soil for Pots 309
How to Plant Containers 312
Is Everybody Happy? 313
A fertilizing plan 313
What about repotting? 314

Chapter 20: Gardens for Birds, Bees, and Butterflies **317**
Making Birds an Offer They Can't Refuse 318
Beckoning Butterflies to Your Garden 320
Designing for butterflies 322
Mixing a butterfly cocktail 322
Catching up with caterpillars 323
Bees and Pollination 323

Chapter 21: Gardening in Tight Spaces **325**
Simple Pleasures 325
Details Make the Difference 326
Illusions of Grandeur 326
Finding Space Where It Doesn't Exist 327
Little Precious Gems 329

Part VII: The Part of Tens 331

Chapter 22: Ten Quick Projects 333
Cooking Up Herb Vinegars 333
Making Cut Flowers Last 334
Drying Flowers 335
Making a Flowering Centerpiece 336
Creating an Autumn Harvest Wreath 337
Forcing Narcissus Indoors 338
Creating a Water Garden in a Tub 338
Preparing a Salad Basket 340
Finding Treasures from Twigs 341
Cleaning Containers 341

Chapter 23: Perfumed Garden Flowers 343
Getting the Most for Your Whiff 343
Flowers Most Possessed with Scent 344
Fragrance after Dark 345
The Most Aromatic Herbs 346
Heavenly Scented Trees, Shrubs, and Vines 346
Best Bulbs for Fragrance 348
Redolent Roses 349

Appendix A: Gardening Resources 351
Books and Magazines about Gardening 351
Books 352
Magazines 355
Gardening Online 356
The World Wide Web 357
Where to look for answers 357

Appendix B: Mail-Order Resources 367
Bulbs 368
Flowers and Vegetables 369
Herbs 374
Fruits and Berries 375
Perennial and Specialist Plants 376
Roses 378
Tools and Supplies 379
Trees, Shrubs, and Vines 382
Water Garden Plants and Supplies 383
Wildflowers 384

Introduction

. . . .

*T*hanks to all the readers who made *Gardening For Dummies* one of the most popular gardening books of recent years. We're happy to say that several hundred thousand copies of the first edition have been sold since its publication in 1996.

Also, thanks to all our readers whose questions and comments prompted many of the changes and additions to this new edition. You'll notice extensive and significant improvements throughout the book: more color photos, updated climate maps, and the latest word on pest control and Web resources. We also reinforced and supplemented much of the basic information—compare the two books and you may not recognize a whole lot.

The more one learns about gardening, the more satisfying it is. As part of our learning process, we have published a number of other gardening books in the past few years: *...For Dummies* books on lawn care, decks and patios, perennials, roses, vegetables, bulbs, houseplants, annuals, container gardening, and landscaping. The expertise that went into all those books has clearly rubbed off here, and we tried to include as much of their pertinent information as possible.

With this book and all our others, we're going as quickly as we can to keep up with the rapidly increasing amount of gardening information and with the changes in gardening itself.

Think about how people once talked about gardens and gardening. For most folks, those terms usually meant a rectangular patch of ground — somewhere out back — where they grew a few vegetables or flowers. Gardens were practical, plain, and utilitarian.

But now, the word gardening signifies so much more. Gardening is all about a process that delights the eye and fuels the soul with a connection to the earth. As countless educators and community volunteers have learned, gardening is one of the quickest (and cheapest!) ways to reduce vandalism and crime, and to increase community pride.

As health-care workers have learned, gardening is good for the body. An hour or two of weeding, harvesting, or cultivating provides just the right kind of light exercise we all need.

Responsible gardening also does good things for the environment: materials get recycled and empty lots become community gardens, for example.

The point is, gardening has moved out of the vegetable patch and the flower bed. Gardening now encompasses our lives — if you have a yard, even a very tiny one, you are a gardener. If you have a sunny windowsill, you are a gardener. National surveys show that gardening has become the most popular, least exclusive hobby of all. Everybody is doing it.

As you read these very words, hundreds of hard-core horticulturists may be laboring over their beloved specimens. But millions of other people are simply enjoying their time outdoors and striving to make their little corner of the world more peaceful and beautiful — a better place to live. And that's what this book is about.

How to Use This Book

You have in your hands a gardening encyclopedia in miniature — all you need to know to get off to a good start. No matter what area of gardening interests you — growing roses or perennials or just cutting the grass — you'll find good advice here. And when you outgrow the level of information that we provide here, you can turn to the appendixes at the back of this book for pointers on where to look next, and to other *...For Dummies* books about related topics.

In every chapter, our basic goal is to give you the information you need to go out and plant or prune what you want. But novices aren't the only ones who will find this book useful. Gardening is such a huge topic that no one ever comes close to knowing everything about it. (That's one reason why gardening has become one of the most popular hobbies of all time.) If, for example, you are a seasoned rose grower but know almost nothing about starting a salad garden or pruning trees, you can find excellent advice in Chapters 18 or 15, respectively.

This book offers lists of plants that you can choose from to create a beautiful garden. We list the plants by the common name first, followed by the botanical name. The lists are alphabetized according to the botanical name.

For international gardeners, we've added approximate metric equivalents for plant heights, planting depths, and other pertinent measurements.

Part I: Getting Going with Gardening

Before you buy your first six-pack of flower seedlings in spring, you need to decide just where and when to start digging.

Chapter 1 begins at root level, guiding you through what your plants need to what you want from a garden.

Chapter 2 helps you determine which plants will grow in your climate.

Chapter 3 gets into the details of designing or planning a garden, with emphasis on making a rudimentary plan that you can refer to and refine later.

Part II: Color Your World

Here's where the real fun starts! This part is the heart of the book because, for most people, the essence of gardening is putting in colorful plants and watching them grow.

Chapter 4 tells you about those comets of the garden, flowering annuals.

Chapter 5 is about the colorful stalwarts, the perennials.

Chapter 6 deals with bulbs for all seasons — not just spring.

Chapter 7 covers the world's most famous flower, the rose.

Part III: Sculpting with Plants

Chapter 8 goes over the garden's skeleton — the trees, shrubs, and ornamental grasses that form your yard's foundation.

Chapter 9 discusses the plants of the horizontal plane (lawns and ground covers), while the vertical plane (vines) gets similar treatment in **Chapter 10**.

Part IV: At Ground Level

This section is the nitty-gritty of gardening— literally. The three chapters in this part are about working with soil and getting your plants started.

Chapter 11 helps you understand and improve your soil.

You find the basics of starting seeds in **Chapter 12,** and other plant-starting methods (seedlings, bulbs, and transplants) in **Chapter 13.**

Part V: Caring for Your Plants

In a nutshell, this section covers long-term garden maintenance.

Chapter 14 covers everything you need to know about the basics of plant care: watering, feeding, and composting.

Chapter 15 covers pruning, **Chapter 16** common sense pest control, and **Chapter 17** all those tools you need to accomplish as much as you'd like.

Part VI: Special Gardens

It's back to the fun stuff — plants and planting — in this section!

If you want to grow at least some of your own food, check out **Chapter 18.** In **Chapter 19,** discover what it takes to grow a garden in a container. In **Chapter 20,** you figure out how to achieve one of the most special gardens of all: the kind that's made with winged creatures in mind. Don't worry if you have just a small patch of yard; **Chapter 21** lets you in on some limited-space gardening secrets.

Part VII: The Part of Tens

No ...*For Dummies* book is complete without the Part of Tens, so we offer a compendium of expert tips for achieving interesting, low-care gardens. We collected some of our best ideas for you: ten quick garden projects **(Chapter 22),** and ten of our favorite fragrant plants **(Chapter 23).**

Appendixes

One exciting feature about gardening is the endless amount of information available on whatever aspect you find most compelling. The appendixes that we've compiled here are intended to help you in that effort.

Appendix A: Gardening resources

Just as this book can't possibly include all the plants that might grow in your garden, no book, even the biggest, fattest, most expensive ones, include more than a fraction of what you may want to know someday. That's why we believe so strongly in this section of resources. This appendix is the place to go if or when you want to know more about the following:

Gardening books and magazines. We recommend a few (including the book that you're holding right now) for your permanent library. But more important, we offer tips to help you choose the book or magazine that can serve you best.

Gardening online. Going online is often the quickest way to get your questions answered. We should know. The National Gardening Association has answered more gardening questions for longer than any other organization. In this appendix, you find some of our favorite gardening Web sites and automatic mailing lists. If you have any questions or comments after reading this book, you can contact us at nga@garden.org.

Appendix B: Mail-order gardening

The variety of plants, seeds, and tools that you can buy through the mail and have delivered the next day is astounding. Mail-order is the way to go, especially if you're looking for anything the least bit unusual. You can outfit your entire garden through the mail, from plants, to tools, to fertilizers, to ornaments.

Icons Used in This Book

 Suggests ways to save money.

 Points out ecological tips and ways to be earth-friendly.

 Flags information that even some experienced gardeners may not know.

 Marks tips that experienced gardeners live by.

 Offers international gardening advice and data.

 Demystifies gardening lingo. Although we've made this book as jargon-free as possible, you need to know some terms.

 Gives addresses and/or phone numbers for ordering special gardening equipment. (You can also find sources in the appendixes.)

 Watch out! Alerts you to avoid bad gardening experiences, including some that may cause injury.

Part I
Getting Going with Gardening

The 5th Wave   By Rich Tennant

"That should do it."

In this part . . .

You've probably heard about the green thumbs and the brown thumbs. Some people seem to have an almost magical ability to raise beautiful, healthy plants, whereas others seem to turn out only withering brown husks.

No matter which group you identify with, take note: Anyone can become a gardener. Like any other interest that's worth pursuing, gardening requires knowledge, experience, attention, and enthusiasm. If you're willing to dedicate some time and attention to gardening, you can move from the brown thumb camp into the green thumb camp. If you already consider yourself to have a green thumb, you undoubtedly know that gardening never ceases to surprise you, and you never finish learning.

Part I gives you a basic understanding of some of the key issues that gardeners face: what plants require in order to thrive, what you can do with your garden, how climate affects what you can grow, and how to take the space you have and maximize it.

Well, what are you waiting for? Get going!

Chapter 1

Just a Few Ground-Level Questions and Answers

· ·

In This Chapter

▶ Understanding what plants need from you

▶ Knowing what your garden can do for you

▶ Speaking the garden language

· ·

*1*f you want to learn more about gardening — and you must if you are reading this — just where do you start? We could start with some heavy-duty science, tossing around terms like *cotyledon, cambium,* and the ever-popular *pith.* Or we could start talking about beautiful gardens like critics of fine paintings — employing words like *composition, energy, focal point,* and such.

We don't mean to suggest anything but respect for scientists and artists. In fact, the chance to combine science and art is what draws many of us to gardening in the first place — especially if you throw in a little farming and a few old wives' tales (of course, you should or shouldn't plant sweet peas at the full moon).

All we really want to do here is to get you through a few basic principles of plant growth and garden planning so that you can rush out into the yard when the weather's right for planting and the soil is ripe for digging.

First, any questions?

How Do I Make My Plants Grow Rather Than Die?

Like other living things, plants have certain requirements for good health. For example, they require the right amounts of sunlight, moisture, and nutrients. Plants also need an equitable range of temperatures — neither too hot nor too cold.

When selecting plants, you can meet their requirements in one of two ways. The first involves selecting your favorite plants and then doing your best to alter the growing conditions at the planting site to meet their needs. You can change the growing conditions by adding sprinkler irrigation, incorporating fertilizer, hauling in fresh topsoil, pruning some trees, or covering plants with blankets in winter. But this is the backward approach.

A better way to make sure plants grow well — and need less care in the process — is to learn about the conditions at the planting site first and then choose plants that grow under those conditions. Of course, some of the plants that you want to put in are accustomed to conditions different from what you have in your yard, and those plants are going to need some attention to stay happy. But the better you match plants to the planting site, the longer the plants will live, the better the plants will look, and the less work (watering, pruning, fertilizing, and controlling pests) you'll have to do to care for them.

Your climate and microclimates

Matching a plant to a planting site needs to be done on both a large and a small scale. On a large scale, a plant needs to be adapted to the general climate of the area in which it lives. Can the plant withstand winter's low temperatures and summer's high temperatures? Is the annual rainfall enough to keep the plant alive, or will it need supplemental irrigation? Understanding your climate is a huge step toward successful gardening — Chapter 2, in fact, is devoted to climates.

On a smaller scale, can the plant grow well in the localized climate of your yard or the planting site? Smaller climates, called *microclimates,* can be quite a bit different from the overall climate of your area. For example, because of the shadows that your house casts, the northern side of your house is cooler and shadier than its southern side. Or a planting site located beside a white, west-facing wall can be several degrees warmer than the rest of the yard because of the reflected heat from the wall.

Sun or shade

All plants need light to grow properly. However, the amount of light that plants need varies.

Many plants require full sun for at least six to eight hours per day. Plants that don't get enough sunlight become *leggy* (long, spindly stems), as if stretching out for more light. Plants that don't get enough sunlight also tend to flower poorly.

Some plants prefer shady conditions for the entire day (or for at least part of the day). Many different types of shade exist, and each type of shade creates a different microclimate. For example, consider the area on the east side of your house. For at least half a day — in the morning — this area is sunny and warm. In the afternoon, the same area is shady.

The west side of the house is usually just the opposite — shady in the morning but hot and sunny in the afternoon. Heavy, all-day shade appears on the north side of the house, and filtered shade is found under trees. To further confuse the matter, shade can change with the seasons as trees lose their leaves and as the sun moves on the horizon. And in the hottest climates, some normally sun-loving plants prefer at least partial afternoon shade.

Note one obvious rule for gardening in the shade: Put *shade-loving* plants in the shade. Sun-worshipping plants just won't make it. Don't fret. Hundreds of incredible shade-loving plants (some with showy flowers and others with attractive foliage and form) are available to choose from.

To make matters just a little complicated, a plant's shade tolerance varies both by region and by specific garden conditions. For example, many plants that need full sun in cool northern climates (or in coastal areas) tolerate or require some afternoon shade when grown in warm southern climates.

Soil and water

The kind of soil in your garden — heavy clay or porous sand, for example — and soil moisture are closely related. Chapters 11 and 14 detail the importance of these two factors and the ways in which they affect plant growth. Those chapters also cover cultural practices such as tilling, watering, and fertilizing. Whether you see desert, snow, or palm trees when you look out your window, you can find plants that are well adapted to almost every situation. Wet, soggy clay soil is very difficult to correct, but certain plants can grow, and even thrive, under those conditions. Choosing plants to fit existing soil conditions is usually a great deal easier than altering the soil conditions themselves.

Plants that are most at home in your garden

Nothing epitomizes the principle of choosing plants appropriate to the site more than growing *native plants*. Natives are plants that grow naturally in a specific region or locality. Over hundreds (probably thousands) of years, these plants have become superbly adapted to the exact conditions of the areas to which they are native. In those areas or in similar areas, native plants grow with health and vigor and without the help of gardeners — abilities that make them very valuable as landscape plants.

Native plants are becoming very popular in many areas, particularly in arid regions of the western United States. Thirsty, non-native plants are impractical in these areas because they use too much of a precious resource — water. Local native plants can get by on what nature provides. And conserving natural resources always makes sense.

Using native plants also helps the native fauna — the birds, butterflies, squirrels, and other local animals — that depend on native plants for food and shelter.

Many retail nurseries can help you select native plants. Some mail-order catalogs also specialize in native plants, especially wildflowers. (See Appendix B for a full listing of gardening suppliers.)

What Can I Use My Garden For?

True, you can go buy plants and stick them in the ground — and let it go at that. But many of us want a "garden," which, by our definition, contains enough organization and space to allow room for growing plants plus other purposes — playing, relaxing, outdoor dining, entertaining, and more.

A garden can make your life more comfortable, healthier, more colorful, and more convenient. A garden lets you expand your living area to the outdoors, harvest fresh food, and pick your own flowers. Take a look at the different ways that a garden can enhance your life.

> ✔ **A private getaway.** Imagine taking a vacation in your own backyard or relaxing in a shady spot, secluded from the hustle and bustle of daily living. This dream can be yours, if you begin by creating a private area for your own pleasure.

- **A place for entertaining.** Whether you like large get-togethers with the extended family or business associates or a quiet dinner with a few friends, your garden can provide an ideal atmosphere. You need a few key ingredients to make your garden perfect for entertaining.

- **Don't forget Junior . . . or Spot.** Who will use your garden? Take into account children and pets — they have different garden interests than grownups.

- **Your own flower shop.** Cutting an armful of flowers from your own garden and bringing them indoors is so satisfying. If you like freshly cut flowers, be sure to leave space to grow your own. See Chapters 4 and 5 for more on flowers.

- **Harvesting the fruits of your labor.** One of the most delicious aspects of your garden is that it can produce wonderful vegetables, fruits, and herbs. You can grow gourmet produce, rare and special crops, and grow them organically.

- **A practical work area.** Being outdoors means more than fun and games. You may need a place in your yard to keep your garden tools, heating fuel tank, firewood, clothesline, or garbage cans. Organize all of these less-than-attractive outdoor necessities into the same out-of-the way location — a workstation separate from your entertaining and play areas. Ideally, the location should be handy, near the garage or drive-way, but far enough away from handsome views or gardens so that the workstation is not a distraction.

- **Take time to relax.** Anywhere that seems cozy and pleasant is a great place to put a sitting nook. The area doesn't have to be fancy, just a place for you to relax and, perhaps, watch the kids play. Start with a comfortable bench or chair and position it in shade beneath a magnificent oak, at the end of your vegetable garden, or at the back of your yard near the swing set. If you put in all-weather footing — gravel or mulch, for example — you can sit outside regardless of the soil conditions.

The possibilities for your garden are almost endless. Take some time to jot down everything you may possibly want in your yard. Chapter 3 shows you how to pull together all your needs and wishes in a garden plan.

Do I Have to Learn a Foreign Language?

The language spoken in gardening circles can be quirky. For example, dirt isn't just *dirt*, it's *soil*. Dirt is what you make mud pies with; it's the stain on your shirt. Soil, on the other hand, is full of promise and good nutrients. And some gardenholics tend to go on and on about plant names. You may catch them at the nursery asking, "Which Latin name is *most* correct, the old one or the new one?" or "What is the proper pronunciation for that plant?" Real garden snobs even get into heated debates about how to spell a particular plant name. Don't be too hard on these people. Not only can they not help themselves, but you may find yourself behaving the same way someday.

In other words, learning something about plant names helps you appreciate gardening more — and helps you get through this book.

The fancy name

The proper (scientific) *botanical name* of a plant consists of two parts, much in the same way that people have a first and a last name. However, in plant language, the last name comes first.

The most important name is the *genus* — the "Smith" of Joe Smith, if you will. (The genus name always begins with a capital letter when used as part of a multipart name.) A genus is a group of closely related plants. Just as in your own family, some of the plant cousins look a lot alike, while others don't bear much resemblance at all. Also like your family, some closely related individuals have very different comfort levels. One uncle lives in Phoenix, Arizona, and loves the heat. His sister thinks that Oxford, England, is quite warm enough, thank you very much. It's the same for plants.

The second name, the "Joe" part of Joe Smith, is the *species* name. The species name usually describes some feature of the plant or its preferred habitat, or serves as a tribute to whoever discovered the plant. But the species name is disguised in pseudo-Latin, of course, just to keep things interesting. Consider, for example, *Hosta undulata. Hosta* is the genus name. The species name, *undulata,* describes the undulating shape of the leaf.

The plain old-fashioned, natural species of some plants acquire new status in face of prodigiously hybridized plants — tulips, for example. In those cases, the norm for the plant is some kind of hybrid of indeterminate botanical origin. That's why when gardeners finally have in their gardens an actual natural, nonhybridized type of tulip they say something like, "And this is my species tulip." Gardeners are funny, aren't they? (In this book, we use the abbreviation *sp.* for *species.*)

Occasionally, a third name follows the species name — the *variety*. Varieties are members of the same species but are different enough to deserve their own name. Just as you may have one redhead in a family of brunettes, some plants are quite dissimilar to their siblings. For example, *Lychnis coronaria* bears magenta flowers. Her sister *Lychnis coronaria alba*, however, wears a white *(alba)* flower.

Another part of a botanical name is the "cultivated variety," or *cultivar.* Whoever discovered or created the plant decided that it was special enough to have its own name. And the cultivar is also special enough to be maintained by cuttings, grafting, line-bred seed propagation, or tissue culture. The cultivar name appears after the species or variety name. The cultivar name is the only part of the botanical name that isn't in italics but is always enclosed with single quotation marks. For example, a very nice form of *Lychnis coronaria* with a pink blush is called *Lychnis coronaria* 'Angel Blush'.

Common names

Of course, ordinary people don't go around using long Latin botanical names in everyday conversation. Instead, they use a sort of botanical nickname, called a *common name.* Common names are less formal and easier to pronounce than botanical names. They're also less precise. Just as your Aunt Norma calls you "pumpkin" and Uncle Bob calls you "Big Guy," many plants have several nicknames.

Often, the common name describes some distinguishing characteristic of the plant. For example, the plant called blue star has starry blue flowers. Sometimes, the origin of the name is lost in the mythology of a former time. Does anyone have a clue just who was the Susan of black-eyed Susan fame?

Finding that several unrelated flowers share the same common name isn't unusual at all. Unfortunately, regular English flower names are often just as silly as their highfalutin Latin cousins, if for different reasons. For example, two distinct plants share the name "mock orange," and at least five different plants go by "dusty miller." At least three unrelated perennials are called coneflowers: *Echinacea purpurea,* the *Rudbeckia* genus, and the *Ratibida* genus. On the other hand, many plants have no common name! Go figure.

The long and short of it is that you need to pay some attention to plant names — if only to avoid buying and planting the wrong plant.

Chapter 2

Zoning Out: What You Can and Can't Grow

In This Chapter

▶ Understanding which permanent plants can grow in your garden

▶ Looking at USDA Zones for plants' winter hardiness

▶ Getting to know the Sunset system

▶ Finding out about heat zones

▶ Creating frost-free days for annuals and vegetables

▶ Extending the growing season

▶ Maximizing winter hardiness

*E*ver hear the gardener's favorite pick-up line? It's "Hi, what's your zone?" If the response is neither stony silence nor a slap across the face, you're in luck — you've met another gardener. Now if someone has asked you this question and had no idea how to respond, this chapter is for you. But this chapter is also useful for anyone trying to decide which permanent plants — the trees, shrubs, ground covers, herbaceous perennials, and vines — to choose based on plant hardiness.

Why do you need to worry about zones with only permanent plants? These plants need to survive weather conditions that vary year-round in your garden: cool, wet weather; extreme heat or cold; and drought, for example. Year-round conditions are not an issue for most vegetables and similar annuals; these plants don't start growing until spring, and then they die in fall. What's important for annuals and vegetables is the *length* of that growing season, the number of days between frosts. (You read more about frost-free days later in this chapter.)

Plant Hardiness

Gardeners are keenly aware of the seasonal effects of temperature, particularly freezing temperatures, on the growth of landscape plants. Terms such as *cold hardy, frost hardy,* and *winter hardy* describe plants that can survive varying degrees of freezing temperatures without injury during winter dormancy.

Some very large and substantial plants curl their toes and turn mushy if exposed long enough to low temperatures. Imagine a banana tree thriving all summer in Duluth, Minnesota, and then imagine what happens to it in September. On the other hand, some plants can survive freezing, and even frigid, temperatures. Some escape the cold by hiding underground or under snow until spring. These plants include the bulbs and many perennials. Others, such as hardy trees and shrubs, undergo metabolic changes between summer and winter.

The genetic capacity of a plant to acclimate determines cold hardiness. When plants acclimate, they transform themselves from a nonhardy to hardy condition that allows them to withstand freezing temperatures. But absolute temperature, as devastating as its effects can be, is not the only criterion of hardiness. Many plants are not injured in winter by minimum temperatures, but in spring and fall as they adjust to changing weather. At those times, while not growing at full tilt, plants are not fully hardy either. So you can see that determining where and when a plant is hardy can be complicated. Temperatures are crucial, but so are a region's climate patterns and how the plant responds.

Winter injury is easy to diagnose when you see lots of brown leaves on an evergreen plant, injury or death of flower buds, or splitting bark. But sometimes damage from winter temperatures is difficult to see, manifested only in delayed bud development or slightly reduced growth.

Perhaps the safest course to ensure plant adaptability is to grow plants native to your particular region. Such plants most likely have the constitution to survive in your garden. And for the most part, local nurseries stock only plants that are known to survive in their region. However, plants don't stay in their regions of origin any more than gardeners do. Plants native to China, Siberia, or Mexico thrive alongside each other in many U.S. gardens. Furthermore, a gardener in California may want to grow a plant native to the Great Plains. New plants that no one knows a lot about constantly debut on the retail market, and gardeners always want to experiment. In these cases, gardeners need some way to compare their gardens' climates with the climate where the plant grows well. Zone maps play a critical role here.

Most often, when people refer to their growing zone they're talking about which USDA zone they live in.

The USDA Plant Hardiness Zone Map

The U.S. Department of Agriculture's Plant Hardiness Zone Map — last updated in 1990 — is the most widely used hardiness zone map. The map has been so useful for gardeners in the United States that the system has been extended to other regions, such as Europe. The USDA zone map is the one most gardeners in the United States rely on, and the one that *National Gardening* and most garden magazines, catalogs, and books currently use. Turn to the Landscaping color section of this book to see this map.

The chill factor

The USDA zone map divides North America into zones based on the average annual minimum temperature. Each zone is 10°F (–12°C) warmer (or colder) in an average winter than the adjacent zone.

North America encompasses 20 zones, numbered 1 through 11. (Zones 2 through 10 are subdivided into *a* and *b* regions where average minimum temperatures differ by 5°F, or –15°C. We don't include the subzones in this book because these designations exist only for North America.) Western Europe has 10 zones (numbered 1 through 10).

These zone maps link regions that share an average winter minimum temperature. For instance, typical winters in Colorado Springs, Colorado; Albany, New York; and Prague, Czechoslovakia, reach –20°F (–29°C), so each city is in USDA Zone 5. This is not to say that the climate in these distant cities is the same or that the same plants grow well in all three cities. But the average winter minimum temperatures are very similar, and that is one of the key factors that determine plant survivability.

All the plants in this book bear the code for a USDA hardiness zone. If you live in one of the plant's recommended zones, you have some assurance that the plant is hardy enough to survive winter.

USDA zone shortcomings

Unfortunately, no zone map is perfect, and the USDA hardiness map is no exception. In the eastern half of North America, the USDA map doesn't account for the beneficial effect of a snow cover over perennial plants; the regularity or absence of freeze-thaw cycles; or soil drainage during cold periods. Other factors that determine plant survival that this zone map can't accommodate include the amount and distribution of rainfall (or availability of irrigation water), and soil conditions.

Sunset zone information for westerners

Average minimum temperature, as depicted in the USDA zone map, isn't the only factor that determines which plants grow in particular locations; but it is a fairly accurate predictor in many regions. In western North America, however, the weather comes in from the Pacific Ocean and becomes less marine (stable) and more continental (subject to wide swings) as it moves from mountain range to mountain range. In these areas, summer heat, the amount and duration of precipitation, humidity, seasonal winds, and number of sunlight hours affect plant hardiness as much (or more) as winter cold.

If you live in western North America, we suggest that you check out the zone maps featured in the *Sunset Western Garden Book* (Sunset Publishing Corp.). This zone system is based on what plants grow where rather than on a single feature of climate, such as minimum temperature. Many garden experts have contributed to the Sunset zone maps over the years, so these zones reflect the plants that thrive there. You can also check out this zone system at Sunset's Internet site, www.sunsetmag.com/Magazine/MagazineFrame.html.

In the western United States (west of the 100th meridian, which runs roughly through the middle of North and South Dakota and down through Texas, west of Laredo), the USDA map is even less useful. The key problem is the map's absolute reliance on average winter minimum temperature — a system that can equate regions of climates that differ in every way but temperature, such as San Diego and Florida. If you live in the West, try to have a copy of the Sunset Western Climate Zone Map handy. Check out this chapter's sidebar, "Sunset zone information for westerners," to find out more about the Sunset system.

The American Horticultural Society's Plant Heat-Zone Map

The significance of winter's lowest temperatures decreases as we shift from places where winter freezes can kill many plants to areas where freezes merely mean frost on lawns and windshields. Obviously, winter lows above 20°F (–6.6°C), and especially lows in the high 20s, are much less damaging than lower temperatures. But on the other hand, areas with mild winter temperatures often have soaring summer temperatures. Gardeners have discovered that summer high temperatures can limit plant survival just as surely as winter low temperatures.

In 1997, the American Horticultural Society published a zone map that accounts for a plant's adaptability to heat. Called the *AHS Plant Heat-Zone Map* (or the *Heat Map*), this 12-zone map of the United States indicates the average number of days each year when given regions experience temperatures of 86°F (30°C) or higher. According to the AHS, 86°F is the temperature at which many common garden plants begin to suffer damage from heat. The zones range from summer cool zone 1 (one day or less at 86°F or warmer) through hot summer zone 12 (210 days or more per year).

The AHS heat zone map is still new and not widely published. To find out more information about the map, head to http://members.aol.com/gardenahs/heat.htm on the Internet. You can also buy your own color poster of the AHS map for $15. To order, call the AHS at (800) 777-7931, ext. 45.

Length Counts: How Long Is Your Season?

You can grow most vegetables and annual flowers anywhere! Some of the largest, most beautiful vegetables we've ever seen were from avid gardeners in Alaska. If you can grow vegetables where the sun doesn't shine for six months of the year, you know they are easy to grow.

Which USDA zone you live in isn't as critical for vegetable growing as it is for fruits, perennial flowers, trees, and shrubs. When it comes to vegetables and other annuals, the length of your growing season is much more important.

A *growing season* consists of the *average* number of days between frosts. Sometimes you hear "growing season" referred to as "frost-free days." Some vegetables are very quick to grow and mature, so they require relatively little time. Others need a long growing season. Usually, seed packets or garden catalogs show a number along with the phrase "days to harvest" or something similar. This number is a rough guide to how long a season that particular vegetable needs to mature. Of course, it would make no sense for us here in Burlington, Vermont, to grow a vegetable that requires 200 frost-free days to mature, like jicama for instance. It'd never have a chance! Likewise, to grow many kinds of tomatoes to maturity here, we need to start seeds indoors before the last frost. This early start means 1- to 2-month-old plants are ready for planting as soon as the danger of frost passes. Table 2-1 shows USDA zones and typical frost-free days.

You can read a lot more about the needs of specific vegetables and growing seasons in *Vegetable Gardening For Dummies* by Charlie Nardozzi and the Editors of the National Gardening Association (IDG Books Worldwide, Inc.).

Table 2-1	Typical Number of Frost-Free Days by USDA Zone (Northern Hemisphere)		
Zone	*Last Frost Date*	*First Frost Date*	*Typical Number of Frost-Free Days*
Zone 1*	June 15	July 15	30
Zone 2	May 15	August 15	90
Zone 3	May 15	September 15	120
Zone 4	May 10	September 15	125
Zone 5	April 30	October 15	165
Zone 6	April 15	October 15	180
Zone 7	April 15	October 15	180
Zone 8	March 10	November 15	245
Zone 9	February 15	December 15	265
Zone 10	January 20	December 20	335
Zone 11	Frost-free		365

Susceptible to frost all year

As a general rule, if you plant your tomatoes, cucumbers, and watermelons in May or June and your broccoli, lettuce, and peas a month or so before that, you're doing okay.

Stretching Your Garden Season

When you live in a northern climate, you deal with a short growing season. If you want to increase your garden bounty, you need to squeeze in a few extra weeks of plant growth earlier and later in the year. By using some of the techniques described here, you can enjoy the advantages that gardeners have in one or two zones milder.

Planting earlier in the year

Gardeners are master manipulators and have devised all sorts of ways to get a jump on spring. The first simply is to plant early. Here's how to get away with fooling Mother Nature:

✔ **Start plants indoors.** Cool-season plants, such as snapdragons or lettuce, tolerate light frosts. Start them indoors, timed so that they are ready for transplanting about three to four weeks before the average last frost date.

You can start frost-tender plants — such as marigolds — early, too. Plan to transplant them under protective cover (described in this section) about two weeks before the average last frost date.

✔ **Use a cold frame.** A *cold frame* speeds seed germination and shelters plants from frost. The frame is a bottomless box, usually constructed from wood. The structure has a slanting, tight-fitting top made of old windows or other transparent or translucent materials such as plastic or fiberglass. A typical frame is approximately 3 feet wide and 6 feet long (1 x 2 m) with an 18-inch-high (30 cm) back sloping down to 12 inches high (46 cm) in the front. (See Figure 2-1.)

Place the frame outdoors, over a garden bed or against the south wall of your home. Orient the frame so that it slopes to the south. The sun warms the air and soil inside, creating a cozy environment for plants. Sow seeds for transplants directly in the cold frame. (Or grow crops such as radishes, spinach, beets, and lettuce to maturity in the frame.)

Prop the top open during the day for ventilation and lower it at night to conserve heat. If you can't check the frame regularly, consider buying a thermostatically controlled vent opener as insurance against cooking or freezing your plants.

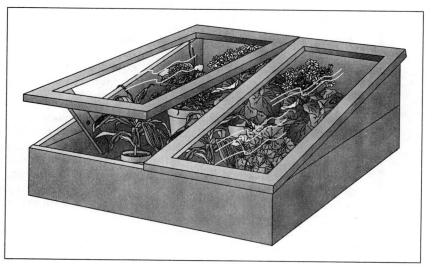

Figure 2-1: Use a cold frame to protect young plants in early spring.

If you like the idea of a cold frame but want even greater temperature control, consider a *hot bed*. This device is essentially a cold frame with a heat source (commonly electric heating cable) to warm the soil. The cable usually includes a built-in soil thermostat preset for about 75°F (24°C), ideal for germinating most seeds. You can find cable with a thermostat and plug sold by wattage and length.

When tender plants are ready for the garden, you need to protect them from frost. Here's a rundown of useful frost guards:

- ✔ **Use hot caps.** These devices are individual covers that work like miniature greenhouses. Hot caps can be homemade or store-bought. To make your own, cut the bottom out of a plastic gallon milk jug. Anchor it in the ground with a stake and leave the cap off so that your plant doesn't bake inside. Commercially produced hot caps are made of translucent wax paper, plastic, or fiberglass.

- ✔ **Set up a water-filled cloche.** A couple of different kinds are available, one with thin plastic, flexible walls and one with heavier, stiff walls. In both cases, you fill the walls with water. During the day, the water absorbs solar heat. As the water cools down at night, it releases heat slowly, protecting the plant inside from temperatures as low as 16°F (–9°C). Use cloches to protect seedlings from late spring frosts.

- ✔ **Use row covers.** Drape lightweight synthetic fabrics, called *floating row covers,* over the plants. The covers let light and water pass through while protecting plants from temperatures as low as 24°F (–4.5°C), depending on the fabric used. The fabrics are available in a variety of widths and lengths. (See Figure 2-2.)

  Row covers of slit plastic are cheaper but usually require more work because they need support from hoops or a frame. You also have to pull the plastic aside to water. Plastic covers create higher daytime temperatures than fabric, which may be advantageous when you're trying to give heat-loving plants like peppers a boost in cool weather.

- ✔ **Recycle junk from your house.** Every so often, an unexpected late spring frost catches you off guard. Usually, the frost prediction comes about the time green, tender, young plants dot the garden. To save plants, rummage around for anything that may protect them without crushing them. Cardboard boxes, old sheets, empty buckets, or even newspaper spread over the plants lend a few degrees of protection. Just remember to remove the stuff the following day or the plants may bake.

In addition to providing frost protection, serious cold-climate gardeners often warm the soil in early spring before planting. They spread a soil-warming, plastic-type mulch over the soil surface and cut holes in it for the transplants. After planting, they protect plants with floating row covers.

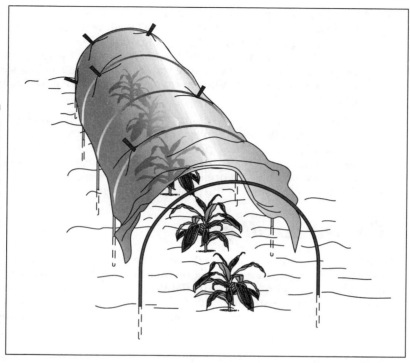

Figure 2-2:
Lay lightweight row covers directly over seedlings or support them with wire hoops. Plastic row covers develop more heat and must be vented.

Clear plastic traditionally has been the mulch of choice for heating the soil, but weeds really thrive under it. Now you can use a new high-tech option called *IRT mulching film*. This green film heats up the soil as well as clear plastic does, but blocks the portion of the light spectrum that supports weed growth. (Clear plastic is still the best to use if you want to *solarize* or heat the soil sufficiently to destroy insects, fungi, and weed seeds. This technique is most effective in hot summer regions that have many consecutive sunny days.)

Gardening beyond autumn

Now that you have a jump on spring, consider these tips on foiling the first frosts of autumn:

- ✔ **Cover up again.** You often can face an occasional light frost before the first big killer. On those crisp, clear evenings when a light frost is forecast, throw a few bedsheets or floating row covers over tender crops. With a little effort, you can prolong the harvest of summer crops.

✔ **Spray on frost protection.** What if you forget — or are just too tired — to cover up crops on a chilly evening? Well, you have a second chance to save them (after you've rested, of course). Turn on your garden sprinkler during the late-night hours (as soon as the temperature drops below 33°F, or 0.5°C). Leave the water on until the sun has warmed the air up above freezing. A fine spray of water is more effective than large water droplets.

✔ **Plant again.** Cool-season plants tolerate frost. You can plant a second crop of many flowers and vegetables in mid-to-late-summer for a late autumn or winter. These plants grow quickly in the still-warm soil of summer and start maturing about the time tender crops are declining. Kale (both edible and ornamental), beets, chard, pansies, and turnips are among the stars of the post-frost harvest.

Gardening all year

Frost is the culprit that usually dictates the beginning and end of the gardening season. Planting dates revolve around the first and last average frost dates. If you don't know the dates for your area, ask a nursery professional or call your extension office. The extension system phone number is usually listed in the phone book among the state university numbers or under *Extension* in the business section.

In mild-winter regions, where an occasional light frost is as bad as it gets, the best way to stretch the season is to keep on gardening right through winter. Winter gardening has many benefits: Pest and disease problems are fewer; you don't have to water much, if at all; and winter crops are varied, nutritious, and delicious. In addition to the cool-season vegetables (see Chapter 19 for more on vegetables), annual flowers such as pansies, calendula, stock, and primrose thrive in winter. Autumn is prime planting time for winter gardening, although you can plant some crops, such as lettuce and beets, in succession through the winter.

If you want to reap every last tomato in autumn but don't want to hassle with protecting individual plants from frost, you have a couple of other options:

✔ Pick your green tomatoes right before the first frost. Arrange them in a single layer on a shelf or table and cover them loosely with newspaper. Check frequently for ripeness and toss any that start to rot.

✔ When frost is predicted, cut or pull your plants and pile them together. Cover the pile with plastic. The tomatoes will continue to ripen.

One strategy for getting ripe tomatoes, eggplants, peppers, and melons before the frost gets them is to grow what are called *short season* or *early* varieties. These plants mature more quickly than their "long season" relatives. An 'Ichiban' Japanese eggplant, for example, takes only 61 days to mature, whereas the Italian heirloom, 'Rosa Bianca', takes 75 days.

Maximizing Winter Hardiness

You may be better off if you stick with plants that are known to be hardy in your area. If you do, you don't have to fuss with various measures intended to help plants survive. But gardeners often experiment, or perhaps you just want to grow a particular plant that is not reliably hardy in your area. In such cases, you may have to take some special steps to protect the plant against the winter cold.

Gardeners can, to some degree, help plants adapt to winter. For instance, reduce the amount of nitrogen fertilizer applied after mid-July and stop all fertilization by late summer. Also, do everything you can to ensure that your plants enter the autumn season healthy but not growing too fast.

Make sure the soil in which evergreens are growing is well-watered in mid to late autumn, before the soil freezes. If the landscape where evergreens are located is in a dry site, sandy soil, or under the overhang of a roof, also make sure the soil is well-watered in midwinter if the temperature is above freezing.

Here are some other steps you can take to decrease the likelihood of winter injury to plants:

- ✔ **Plant on the north side.** Choose a location for marginally hardy plants with a northern or eastern exposure rather than south or southwest. Plants facing the south are more exposed to the sun on warm winter days and thus experience greater daily temperature variation.

- ✔ **Mulch.** Apply a layer of mulch, 3 to 4 inches (7.5 – 10 cm) deep, after the soil freezes to keep the soil cold rather than protect the soil from becoming cold. This practice reduces injury from plant roots' *heaving* (coming out of the soil) because of alternate freezing and thawing. Plants that benefit from this practice include perennials, alpine, rock garden plants, strawberries, and other shallow-rooted plants. A mulch maintains a more even soil temperature and retains soil moisture.

  Apply bark products, composts, peat moss, pine needles, straw, hay, or any one of a number of readily available materials from the local garden center. You can prop pine boughs (or remains from Christmas trees) against and over evergreens to help protect against damage by wind and sun.

- ✔ **Wrap with twine.** Plants such as arborvitae, juniper, and yew often suffer damage from the weight of snow or ice. Prevent plant breakage by fastening heavy twine at the base of the plant and winding it spirally around and upward to the top and back down in a reverse spiral. This technique is more necessary as plants become larger and begin to open at the top. Be certain to remove the twine during the growing season.

✔ **Use burlap screen.** Stretch a section of burlap around three stakes to protect young or not fully hardy plants from the south, west, and windward exposures.

A burlap wrap with stakes protects plants from the drying winter sun and wind and drift from deicing salts applied to drives and streets. Wrap most of the plant, but leave some of the top of the plant exposed. Evergreen plants need light, even in winter.

✔ **Prevent drying.** Narrow and broadleaf evergreens lose moisture through their leaves in winter. Plant roots can't absorb moisture from the soil in winter because the soil may be frozen and therefore cannot replace the moisture the leaves lose. The foliage desiccates, turns brown, and may drop. This can be serious with evergreen azalea, holly, boxwood, and rhododendron. Make sure that evergreens are properly watered throughout the growing season and into the fall. Decrease watering slightly in fall to encourage hardening off, and then water thoroughly in October and continue until soil freezes.

✔ **Prevent animal damage.** Some landscape plants, especially during a time when there is an extended period of snow cover, become a food source for rabbits, mice, or voles. When their normal food supply is covered with ice or snow, rodents turn to the bark and young stems of apple, flowering crabapple, mountain ash, hawthorn, euonymus, and viburnum, among others. If the animals chew the bark completely around the plant and cause it to girdle, the plant may die. In *girdling*, the all-important living cells of woody plants are just under the bark. If these cells are damaged or destroyed, the water and nutrients flowing between the plant's roots and leaves become impeded or stop completely. Partial girdling creates wounds for borers and disease organisms to enter, and weakens the plant itself.

Protect stems and trunks of these plants in late autumn with plastic collars cut in a spiral fashion so that they can slip around tree trunks. Spray or paint trunks, stems, and lower limbs with rodent repellents. A number of these materials are available in most garden centers. Repeat the application at least once during a warm period in midwinter. Mixing the repellents with an antitranspirant often results in extended effectiveness of these products. If you use any kind of long-lasting wrap, be sure to remove it come spring.

Chapter 3
Planning Your Landscape

- -

In This Chapter

▶ Taking inventory of your property

▶ Making your wish list

▶ Drawing up the plan

▶ Controlling costs

- -

*W*hether your land consists of a new bare-dirt lot, an overgrown jungle of a garden, or any situation in between, your property is the canvas upon which you create your garden masterpiece — your place to relax, entertain, welcome visitors, watch your children play, hold backyard barbecues, and so on. The sum of your work on the grounds surrounding your home — including the hardscape (patios, decks, walks, and so on) and plantings — is your home's *landscape*. A good landscape not only adds value to your home, it can also solve problems such as bad views, noise, and lack of privacy.

We strongly recommend that you start your landscape with a plan. Most gardeners benefit from precisely planning a design on paper, but a loose mental plan may suffice. In any case, the goal is to figure out the best ways to maximize your outdoor space. Base your decisions on what looks good to you, how you plan to use the space, how much maintenance you want to do, and what you can afford. This chapter should give you enough information to assess the strengths and weaknesses of your site, create a plan for a landscape that suits your lifestyle, and, hopefully, accomplish your landscape as inexpensively as possible.

Your landscape is a large investment of your time and money, so you may want to call in a landscape architect or designer to give you advice or to draw up a plan for you. You can even show the professional your own plan and ask for suggestions or confirmation of your good sense. You can also pick up many more tips and tricks on the art and science of landscaping in *Landscaping For Dummies* by Philip Giroux, Bob Beckstrom, and the Editors of the National Gardening Association, published by IDG Books Worldwide, Inc.

Taking Stock of What You Have

The results of your landscaping work depends, to some extent, on what you have to work with, so you should begin your landscape plan by assessing the current condition of your property. This up-front *site analysis* is an integral part of planning a landscape. You should try to take into account issues such as the following:

- **Your property's strengths and weaknesses.** Does your property have good drainage or poor drainage? Do you have a private area that catches the prevailing breezes in summertime? Does your property have good soil, poor soil, or a combination? Do you want to accentuate or hide any views?

- **Problems that need solutions.** Do you want to cut off the view of nosy neighbors with a privacy hedge? Do you want to create an out-of-the-way area to make a compost pile to recycle your lawn clippings and raked leaves? (See Chapter 14 for more information on composting.) How much time and energy are you willing to put into maintaining your property?

- **Personal likes and dislikes.** Does your taste run to the calm and serene or to the colorful and wild? Do you want a brick patio with room for dozens of guests? Or would you prefer a vegetable garden with enough tomato plants to feed the neighborhood all summer and still leave plenty of canning work to keep you busy and exhausted? And, if you have children, where do you want them to play? View plenty of other landscapes to help determine your preferences: Go on garden tours, peek into neighbors' yards, visit arboretums, and look through books and magazines.

Start your site analysis by penciling in a rough drawing of your property on a large piece of paper (at least 8½ by 11 inches or 22 x 28 cm). Be sure to include important existing features of your property such as your house (including windows and doors), sidewalks, driveway, and permanent structures. Remember to add general compass directions to your sketch. The sketch doesn't have to be very precise at this stage.

Place your drawing on a clipboard and walk around your house and yard at different times of the day. Note the following:

- **Existing plants.** Draw in plants, such as large trees, that you may want to preserve.

- **Sun and shade.** Note areas that are sunny or shady and at what times of day. This information helps you match plants with appropriate light conditions, and it may also give you ideas about creating a more comfortable living space. Sunlight changes direction and intensity dramatically by seasons. For example, in midsummer, the south and west sides of the house are sunniest and warmest. If you live in a cool summer area, you may want to take advantage of the warmth in those areas, but if you live in a hot summer area, these may be places where you want shade trees or arbors.

✔ **Views.** Note the good and bad views that you may want to preserve or block. Good views are easy to recognize, but what about the neighbors' views of your yard or your view of theirs? And if you put in a raised deck, what will you see then? Are utility poles visible?

✔ **Prevailing winds.** Mark down strong winds that you may want to buffer or redirect.

✔ **Slope and drainage.** Draw in some arrows that give you a rough idea of the contour of the land. Sloping ground or uneven terrain can become an interesting part of a landscape, especially if accentuated with walls or dry streambeds. But sloping ground also can present erosion or drainage problems that can threaten your house or yard. Record any areas that seem overly wet or where moss or algae grows. Watch where excess rainwater flows. Some plants not only live in wet or soggy soil but also thrive in it; these are the plants you find in bog and water gardens. Drainage problems are sometimes complicated; consider consulting with a landscape architect or engineer who has experience with water drainage problems.

✔ **Soil.** The soil in your yard provides nutrients, moisture, and support for plants. But soil types differ, sometimes even within the same property. Soils come in a huge range of textures and pH levels (the measure of acidity or alkalinity) and contain different amounts of organic matter, nutrients, and moisture. See Chapter 11 to find out more about soil characteristics so that you can choose plants that will thrive in your garden.

✔ **Interesting natural features.** If you're lucky enough to have rock outcroppings or a small stream, they can become special landscape features.

✔ **Noise, smells, lights.** Open up all your senses and then write down anything else you notice — lights at night, noise from next door, and even unpleasant odors. You may be able to do something about them.

✔ **Views from indoors.** When you look out windows, what do you see: a nice view of the yard, or the neighbor's back porch? Who can see into your home via the windows from the street or next door? Does sunlight blaze through the windows, heating the house in the afternoon? Or is it pleasant light, cast on the kitchen table as you drink coffee in the morning? Do car lights, street lamps, or signs shine in the windows at night?

To help you organize the different areas of your yard, you can draw *goose eggs*. Drawing a goose egg doesn't mean that you draw a complete blank (I just don't know what to do with this yard!); it refers to penciling in somewhat circular areas that you think works well for specific purposes, as shown in Figure 3-1. After you finish the first goose egg, draw several more to consider alternatives and decide which works best.

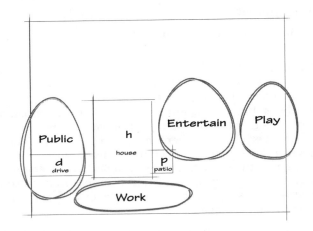

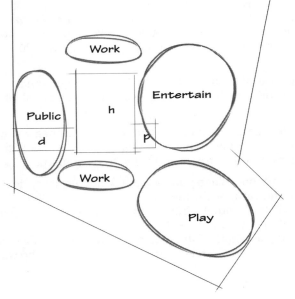

Figure 3-1: The shape of your property doesn't determine how you use it. In these examples, two differently shaped properties are organized similarly.

Most houses have a front yard, a back yard, and two side yards. To divvy up your list of outdoor wants and needs — eating, playing, sitting, and such — think of which activities you do in which areas.

Don't forget to use your property's natural strengths to your advantage. No doubt you already know the location of the best flat lawn for that pitch-and-catch area. You also know the most discreet place to hide the compost heap and trashcans. You know which neighbor will hate having a view of the dog run from his bedroom window. You know where the sun beats down on late summer afternoons — perfect for the herb garden — and where the neighbor's oak tree casts a cool pool of shade.

Dreaming Up the Perfect Landscape

To get the most from your property, you need a design that meets the needs of your lifestyle. A good way to start is to develop a wish list of everything that would go into the garden of your dreams. (Consider money to be no object; you can always come back to reality later.) Be sure to imagine members of your family enjoying the areas. Take a look at some of the things you can add to your wish list:

✔ Enough lawn for the kids to play catch

✔ A flower cutting garden

✔ A spacious deck or brick patio

✔ Lighting for night-time entertaining or for accenting special landscape features

✔ A gazebo, arbor, or pergola

✔ A lush vegetable garden or fresh herb plot

✔ A privacy hedge to keep out nosy neighbors

✔ A tool barn or potting shed

✔ A place where butterflies, birds, and cute little critters come to visit

✔ A private retreat with a bench or hammock where you can get away to read *Gardening For Dummies,* 2nd Edition

✔ A fenced-in dog run

✔ A swimming pool or spa

✔ A pond for water gardening or fish

✔ A compost pile to recycle your lawn clippings and raked leaves

✔ A rose garden

- ✔ A fruit orchard
- ✔ A bulb garden where flowers announce the start of a new season
- ✔ A scented garden that comes alive with various fragrances
- ✔ A barbecue big enough to roast a pig on

Who will use your yard?

Design your landscape so that it gets maximum utility and provides plenty of enjoyment. Make sure you think about issues like the following:

- ✔ If you have young children, safety, as well as fun, is a consideration. A swing set in a fenced backyard makes sense. You may also want to think about a storage area for all those toys.
- ✔ Older children can probably make use of the front lawn.
- ✔ Perhaps you can keep the back lawn smaller so that you have room for a big vegetable garden.
- ✔ Do you barbecue enough to warrant a built-in grill placed as close to the kitchen door as possible? How about an outdoor sink?
- ✔ What about Fido? Better put in a dog run or who knows what he'll do to the new landscape.

When will you use your yard?

Think about the time of day and the time of year in which you plan to use your yard. Consider the following tips when planning your landscape and when you'll use it most.

- ✔ If you plan to be outdoors after work in the late afternoon, where will you be most comfortable at that time of day? Maybe that shady spot under the big oak tree out back. . . . On the other hand, if summer sunshine heats up the patio area, maybe you need an overhead structure for shade, or you can plant shade trees instead.
- ✔ If you like to use the garden at night, good outdoor lighting is a must.
- ✔ If you like to be outside during the rainy season, a covered patio would be nice.
- ✔ If bugs like the garden at the same time as you do, a screened-in patio cover can keep them at bay.

What's your neighborhood like?

Most neighborhoods have a certain character created by similar landscapes and homes. Large lawns and deciduous shade trees tie together many northern neighborhoods. Pines unite neighborhoods in the southeast. In the southwest, front yards often consist of native desert plants, without a patch of green lawn in sight.

When you dream up your new landscape, remember to keep any regional or neighborhood character in mind. Try not to be so different in your landscaping that you disrupt the overall continuity of the community, particularly in the front yards, which often tend to blend together. (You can probably go wild in the backyard.) This advice is practical, not a plea for conformity, because a new landscape that resembles what already exists in your neighborhood looks best. On the other hand, if you have a vision and you're sure it is the look you want, then deviating from a neighborhood style is perfectly okay (codes and covenants notwithstanding).

Then there's that thing called "resale value." Lots of people find themselves landscaping simply to enhance the street appearance of their home for potential buyers. If you're landscaping for resale, play it safe. Take cues from neighboring yards.

Matching your garden to the historical or cultural heritage of your neighborhood, house, or hometown is an easy jumping-off place. Consider an old-fashioned Grandma's garden for a charming small-town cottage, a naturalistic blooming desert for a southwestern adobe, or a lush English perennial border for a Tudor showplace.

How much maintenance are you ready for?

Landscape maintenance is an ongoing event that can guarantee success or failure. You can design low maintenance into a landscape, as follows:

- ✔ Create a yard with lots of hardscape and very little planting.
- ✔ Avoid overplanting or using fast-growing plants that get too large for their space. Such plants require more pruning and replanting later.
- ✔ Use low-maintenance perennials or flowering shrubs instead of annuals. Annuals add areas of brilliant color, but you will need to replant the beds every year.
- ✔ Plant ground covers instead of a lawn if you're unwilling to mow your lawn weekly. (But keep in mind that getting the ground cover thick enough to choke out weeds takes effort, too.)

intenance masonry rather than wooden landscape elements.
to build wooden landscape elements like decks and fences,
: to paint or apply preservatives every two to three years.
ising pressure-treated lumber for ground-contact situations
: plastic wood look-alikes for fences and decking.

automated irrigation system (as explained in Chapter 14),
n water even when you're out of town. If you don't have an
ed system, then you must water everything by hand or move
rs around your property.

What Goes Where: Designing the Plan

After adding the elements from the wish list to your sketch, you may want to create a more accurate and specific site analysis, drawn exactly to scale. (Check out this section's sidebar, "Making a scale drawing of your property.") You can get exact dimensions of your property from the plot or the building plan developed when your house was built. If you can't find a plan, ask at your municipality's building or zoning department.

The plot plan shows the shape and size of your property as well as the location of your house. The plan saves you from having to fight your way through perimeter thickets to measure yard dimensions. Make a dozen photocopies of your original plot plan so that you can try out different schemes and record your ideas.

Figure 3-2 is a sample of what your site analysis might look like after you transfer the details of your inventory to the plot plan.

Using your space effectively

Make sure that you think of the whole outdoor property as living space. Overcoming the traditional approach — backyards are where we actually live, front yards are for show, and side yards are mostly ignored — can be difficult. Why not make your entire landscape your living area? The following are some off-the-beaten-path ideas that allow you to make good use of your front and side yards:

> ✔ **Front yard.** If you shield the front yard with walls of greenery or a privacy fence, then you can do what you like with your front yard. If that's a bit bold for you, consider at least moving some of your ornamental garden beds to the front instead of having only the boring, old, look-good lawn. If you're inspired to plant a prairie or a naturalistic woodland out front, talk to the neighbors first so that they know what you're doing, and keep paths well groomed so that the landscape looks guided instead of frighteningly wild.

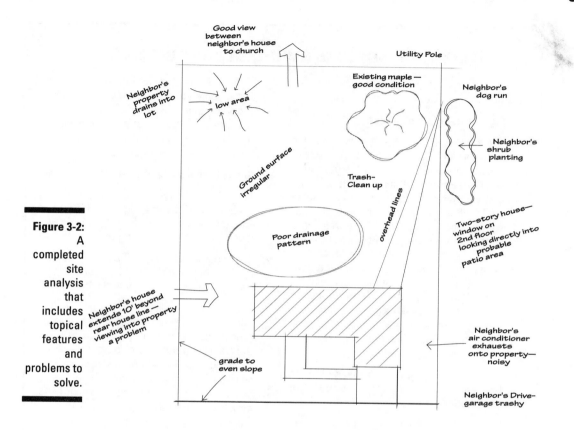

Good view between neighbor's house to church

Utility Pole

Existing maple — good condition

Neighbor's dog run

Neighbor's property drains into lot

low area

Neighbor's shrub planting

Ground surface irregular

Trash-Clean up

overhead lines

Figure 3-2: A completed site analysis that includes topical features and problems to solve.

Poor drainage pattern

Two-story house— window on 2nd floor looking directly into Probable patio area

Neighbor's house extends 10' beyond rear house line — viewing into property a problem

Neighbor's air conditioner exhausts onto property— noisy

grade to even slope

Neighbor's Drive-garage trashy

Many communities' home-owner's associations have restrictive covenants that very much narrow your landscaping options. Be sure to check before embarking on any do-it-yourself makeovers.

Backyard. You don't always need to relegate your vegetable patch to the backyard. You can put your vegetable plants wherever the light, soil, and convenience are best. A well-tended patch, planted in an interesting design of diagonals or squares that intersperses veggies with flowers and herbs has a lot of curbside appeal.

✔ **Side yard.** Side yards are often narrow, sometimes shady, and they're usually seen as nothing more than a thruway from the front yard to the back. Give yourself reason to linger in your side yard by mounting a hammock or adding a bench. If your side yard is sunny, it can be the perfect place for a strawberry patch or a row of raspberries. Or add a surprise to be discovered — such as a whimsical garden ornament.

Making a scale drawing of your property

If you don't have a plot plan, consider these tips for drawing your property to scale.

✔ **Start by using graph paper.**

The easiest kind of graph paper has five squares per inch of paper space, which allows you to easily record the garden in units of 5 and 10 — that is, 1 inch (2.54 cm) can equal 5 or 10 feet (1.5 or 3 m). Some kinds of graph paper come with four squares per inch, which requires more mathematical manipulating. In that case, 1 inch (2.54 cm) can equal 4 or 8 feet (1.2 or 2.5 m). Graph paper also comes in a variety of sizes. The standard 8½ x 11-inch (22 x 28 cm) paper may not be large enough to accommodate an entire landscape. You can find oversized graph paper, as large as 17 x 22 inches (43 x 46 cm), at better office or art supply stores.

✔ **Find a proportional scale that's suitable for your drawing and landscape complexity.**

If you want a simple landscape planted with trees and shrubs, you can make 1 inch (2.54 cm) of plan space represent 8 or 10 feet (2.5 or 3 m) of landscape space. But, if you want complicated flower, herb, and vegetable gardens, you can include more detail on your plot plan by making 1 inch (2.54 cm) represent 4 or 5 feet (1.2 or 1.5 m) — even less if necessary.

✔ **Always use a measuring tape to calculate distances.**

Eyeballing or estimating is not precise enough. At the minimum, you need a 50-foot-long (15 m) measuring tape.

✔ **Start your measuring in the front yard, recording the length and the width. Then measure the side yards and the backyard.**

The front yard ends at an invisible line that cuts across the width of your property and runs along the front of your house. Draw the front yard perimeters on the plan. For example, if you measure the front yard as 50 feet (15 m) long and wide and you use a scale of 5 feet (1.5 m) equals 1 inch (2.54 cm), then your front yard will be a 10-inch square (25 cm) on your plan. Do the same for the side yards and backyard.

Defining areas and ways to move through them

Try to imagine decorating your living room if it had no walls. You'd have a hard time putting your furniture in the right place. Outdoor living rooms work the same way, except now you need to figure out where to put the flower bed instead of the sofa bed.

Structures and plantings can define the boundaries of your landscape, creating "walls" to set off different areas of your garden. For example, surround your herb garden with a hedge of lavender and install a gate at the entryway. Add a lattice screen to your deck or patio and grow flowering vines on it if you need a bit of privacy. See Chapters 8 and 10 for more suggestions on shrubs, trees, and vines to use for privacy.

After you establish the perimeters of your garden, turn your attention to the pathways. Make the walkways simple and practical. Your kids and your dog will want to get to the sandbox or the front door in a beeline. You'll also want an easy-access, straight-arrow path for getting to your car in the morning or for lugging in groceries after work. Plan a wide, flat, solid path to trundle wheelbarrows full of compost, manure, grass clippings, and other goodies.

Exercise your artistic side by planning pleasure routes through the rest of your landscape. Guests at your patio party can enjoy wandering along paths that go through flower beds and greenery. When you start playing with paths, you'll find that they're a great design trick for making your garden seem bigger. Obscured by shrubs, ornamental grasses, or other tall plants, paths can double back, twist and turn, and proceed for much longer than you'd think in a limited space.

The width of paths affects the speed at which people walk them. Wide paths are not only practical for two people to stroll along side-by-side, the width encourages lingering. Narrow paths make our feet speed up.

Paths don't have to be made of paving materials. A swath of lawn that wends through garden beds is as much a path as that beautiful brick herringbone you lay through the herb garden.

If you plan to include fenced areas in your landscape, make sure they don't block access to other parts of the yard. Include gates where they make sense, or leave sections open for easier access.

The hardscape

Patios, decks, walkways, fences, trellises, gazebos, and other hardscape elements of your landscape are just as important as the plants. Make your hardscape elements as attractive as your planting beds. Remember that you'll be looking at these structures unadorned in the off-season, when leaves are down and plants are dormant. Soften the hardscapes in all seasons by planting woody shrubs, vines, ornamental grasses, and trees nearby.

Shopping for hardscape materials is not for the budget-squeamish. Luckily, you can use some tricks to come up with a beautiful hardscape without breaking the bank. Scavenging materials is one of the finest arts in the home landscaping spectrum. Keep your eye out for demolition sites, dumps, and other likely bonanzas. (But don't assume that construction debris is headed for the dump. You run into lots of us recyclers these days. Remember to always ask permission before loading your pickup truck.) Most contractors are happy to give you their refuse so that they don't have to pay to put it in a landfill.

Designing with repetition and unity

Unity refers to the overall feeling that a landscape creates a whole greater than the sum of its parts. In a unified landscape, the eyes and feet of visitors flow from one part to another. Clearly defined pathways are a first step toward unifying your landscape.

Repetition refers to a theme or element that crops up in different parts of your landscape. Repetition and unity go hand-in-hand — repeating elements often helps create a feeling of unity in your landscape.

Repetition of hardscape materials — including brick, wood, stone, concrete, wood chips, and fencing — is a simple way to give your garden a unified look, even if the areas are distinctly different. Man-made materials carry great weight in the landscape, because they draw our human eyes like a magnet. If your hardscape materials match the style of your garden, you can quickly unify the various elements of your landscape. For example, you can use a single section of diagonal, framed lattice to support a climbing rose along the wall of your house. Attach a few sections to form an L-shape to shield the compost pile from view; or add three or four linked sections to serve as a privacy screen along the patio.

Repeating shapes helps pull elements together, too: curved outlines of beds, undulating paths, and mounds of plants; or yardstick-straight bed edges, spiky plant forms, clipped hedges, and vertical-board fences.

Repetition of plants themselves is another way to achieve unity. Sticking the same plants here and there is an easy trick. Simply repeat backbone plants that perform well most of the year — like hostas, evergreens, groundcovers, and shrubs — to tie your garden areas to each other.

Repeating colors also helps to unify your landscape. Plant clumps of yellow flowers in various beds, pots, or plantings across your back yard, and you'll find that your eye travels from one patch of yellow to the next in a satisfying way. You can combine colors of plants with colors of the house or hardscape, too, for unity's sake.

Frugal substitutes are fun to come up with and can give you even more satisfaction when you gaze upon your finished work. Jog your ingenuity with these starters:

- ✔ Instead of making a stone wall out of expensive fieldstone, stack chunks of old concrete sidewalk.

- ✔ Can't afford an all-brick walkway? Use a strip of brick (one or two bricks wide) along the sides and fill the center with inexpensive concrete or pavers. Edge with landscape timbers for a finished look.

- ✔ Dress up plain gray concrete with dyes. Or use the small stones called *aggregate* in the mix so that the finished surface has a pleasant pebbly look.

- ✔ Customize your patio by making your own art pavers for corners and accents. Make handprints, press in and peel off leaves to make impressions, or stud with bits of colored glass for a one-of-a-kind look.

- ✔ Visit architectural salvage dealers for real buys on fencing, arbors, ironwork, and neat decorative touches.

- ✔ Brick from buildings will deteriorate in the garden, but unless you're laying miles of paths, it can be a fine and frugal choice until you can afford the heavy-duty, high-fired exterior grade you want.

The plants

Plants come in a rainbow of sizes, shapes, and colors. (For information about how to use specific plants, see Chapters 4 through 10.) Some characteristics point out architectural highlights. Others are as handsome as sculptures. Some harmonize; others contrast. Consider the varying design characteristics of plants before you finish your design.

- ✔ **Size.** The tallest trees can frame or shade your house or sitting area. Medium-tall plants, such as tall shrubs and small ornamental trees, can provide height in a small yard or function as screens. Medium-sized shrubs can help blend the house into the landscape. If you're planting shrubs around the foundation, stick with plants that are naturally dwarf, not growing much over 3 feet (1 m) tall, so that they don't overwhelm the site, block windows, or require regular pruning. Smaller plants — flowers, vegetables, low shrubs — can fill in openings between larger plants.

- ✔ **Form and shape.** Plants come in a variety of shapes that you can blend and balance for maximum beauty. A conservative way to start your landscape is to use a majority of rounded shapes, accented occasionally by other forms such as the following:

  - *Horizontally spreading plants,* such as junipers and native dogwoods, blend strongly vertical architecture — including the corners of your house — into the landscape.

  - *Upright or spiky plants,* such as columnar arborvitae, stand out like exclamation points. Avoid the cliché of using these on either side of your entry; choose low-growing plants instead.

  - *Low and spreading plants* such as creeping junipers and ivies cover the ground like a carpet, filling space with greenery to help tie the landscape together.

- ✔ **Texture.** Some plants, such as oak leaf hydrangea and sheared yew, have a bold, eye-attracting texture because of large leaves, dense branching, or a dark appearance. These plants are strong and can stand on their own or visually anchor a garden bed. But too many bold plants can look somber or overwhelming.

Other plants, such as Shasta daisies and spiraeas, have medium texture with moderate-sized leaves, average shapes, and a moderately loose growth habit. These plants look comfortable in the garden but, without other textures, can become boring.

Fine-textured plants, such as astilbe and flax, have small or finely cut leaves or open, fine-stemmed shapes that allow light to shine through. These plants can be intricate and invite a closer look but can also appear insubstantial and, in large quantities, chaotic.

✔ **Color.** Plants provide color with their foliage, flowers, berries or cones, or even stems, as in the case of red-twig dogwood. Choose a color scheme that emphasizes one color in addition to green. Make sure that the color looks good with your yard's hardscape — for example, pink flowers are attractive near a red brick walk. And drop in small amounts of different colors as accents. You may have a small garden of blue or purple flowers with highlights of yellow. Hot colors, such as yellow, orange, and red, are strong and work well in a large yard or a faraway bed. Cool colors, such as blue and purple, recede and are best used in a small yard or a close-up bed.

✔ **Order.** Your garden needs dominant features with similar characteristics — plants of like shapes, sizes, textures, or colors — to create a sense of order. One way to achieve order is to mass identical varieties into natural-looking groups. But you also need some variety or accent, which you achieve by adding plants with different characteristics.

Creating a Final Plan

Think of your final plan as a tool to help determine the price tag of this project, to establish your priorities, and to ensure that all those separate parts of your landscape — the barbecue pit, the meditation pool, the children's area — are present and accounted for.

You can use copies of the plot plan to start your landscape design, sketching in existing landscape features that you intend to keep, using your site analysis as a reference point. If you can't find your plot plan, you need to measure your entire yard. Either way, make your plan to scale so that it gives a precise representation of your yard. See the sidebar in this chapter, "Making a scale drawing of your property," for tips on drawing to scale.

On paper, you can eliminate the existing features that you no longer want — you'll create a blank slate on which to draw new features. You can adapt, change, and reorganize with a flick of an eraser. To help you visualize your new yard, make tracing paper overlays to show different scenarios for your landscape, moving your patio behind the garage or close to the kitchen door, for example. Set overlays on top of the original plot plan and secure them with masking tape so that they're easy to move and change. Other overlays can show the color of the garden as it changes by season or the size of trees and shrubs as they grow.

Follow these steps to create a final plan (assuming you have a plot plan).

1. **Take the graph paper and measuring tape out into the yard with you.**

   Note on the paper which directions are north and south and the scale you're using.

2. **Plot each landscape feature that you intend to keep.**

   Find its depth in the length of the yard by measuring from either the house or the street. Make a pencil mark to show its location. Then measure its distance from the side of the property. Move the pencil mark to indicate the correct spacing from the side property line.

   If the landscape feature is a tree, measure the limb spread of the tree and indicate it with a circle around the mark. If the tree is young, you may want to use a dotted line to show the ultimate shady, mature spread.

   If you plan to eliminate existing features, don't bother to sketch them in. Not including them saves you time and trouble as you plan new developments for your yard.

3. **After you pencil in the entire yard, check the accuracy of the drawing.**

   When you eyeball the plan and look at the yard, does it appear that everything is in the right place? Pull out your measuring tape and check several sample distances. Redraw as necessary.

4. **Add new features and plants.**

   Draw in the plants and areas for all those special activities you will enjoy eventually. Add any paths you have planned, drawing lines to indicate their shape and width. Draw in fences, arbors, hedges, a patio or deck, and other elements you've chosen. After you have all the parts of the design in place, feel free to ink over your pencil lines with different colored markers; you can see at a glance which lines are paths, which are fences, and so on.

Using your computer

A number of landscaping software programs are now available that can help you design your dream landscape. After you have your scale plot plan, you can input it into your computer and develop your design electronically.

Using landscaping software

- ✔ Saves you the time and trouble of drawing all changes and updates by hand.
- ✔ Lets you explore the way a landscape may look when viewed from different angles, at different times of the year, or at any time in the future.
- ✔ Helps your decision-making. The software may include a detailed plant encyclopedia. You may be able to indicate your landscape needs and have the program select suitable plants.

One example of landscaping software is *Complete LandDesigner* (Windows 95) from Sierra Online. Phone 800-757-7707 or try www.sierra.com on the Internet. This full-featured program includes an extensive plant database provided by White Flower Farm. The package costs about $50.

Field testing

If you want more of a real-life picture of what your landscaping will look like, go outside and play make-believe:

- ✔ Outline paths with a water hose or rope, or sprinkle a path of flour or ground limestone so that you can see the direction paths take.
- ✔ Put lawn chairs where you want to add shrubs or young trees.
- ✔ Pound tomato stakes into the ground to show the future homes of roses or large perennials in your flower beds.
- ✔ Rake leaves or straw into the outlines of your new beds.
- ✔ Use a step ladder as a good fool-your-eye representation of an arbor.

Part II
Color Your World

The 5th Wave
By Rich Tennant

©RICHTENNANT

"Well, Roger wanted to design the garden, and, of course, I _knew_ he was a paleontologist, but I had no idea..."

In this part . . .

Of all the wonderful benefits that flowers bring to a garden, their vibrant and beautiful colors mean the most to us. We get excited just thinking about mixing and matching flowers of different colors to create striking effects, but actually seeing them is the real payoff.

Think of your garden as your canvas, and the colors of the various annuals, perennials, flowering bulbs, and roses as your palette. Now stretch out with your imagination: Can you see that little clump of yellow over there? Can you see those purple bunches here and there? How about splashes of red in the corners and there in the middle?

In this part, we tell you about our favorite annuals, perennials, flowering bulbs, and roses. Enjoy the colors!

Chapter 4

Annuals

• •

In This Chapter

▶ Understanding annuals and their needs

▶ Buying annual plants

▶ Using annuals' color, shape, and fragrance in your garden

▶ Taking care of your annuals

▶ Looking at favorite annuals

• •

> Annuals are the workhorses of the flower garden. If you want color, if you want your garden to be bright and showy, and if you want your garden to look good right from the start, annuals are the answer.

What's an Annual?

Annuals are the shooting stars of the garden universe. They burn brightly indeed, but briefly.

To be technical for a moment, an *annual* is a plant that undergoes its entire life cycle within one growing season. You plant a marigold seed in May, the seedling sprouts quickly, it starts blooming in July, frost kills it in October, seeds scatter and (we hope) sprout the next spring to start the process again. Figure 4-1 shows the life cycle of an annual.

In some instances, however, our definition of annual gets a bit dicey. Annuals and *perennials* (which we formally introduce in Chapter 5) have a way of overlapping — in definition, as well as in the garden. Some perennials act like annuals when you grow them in cold climates. Geraniums, for instance, may not survive the month of May in Minneapolis or another climate with late frosts but will live for years in Southern California. You find perennials that act like annuals listed as annuals in this book.

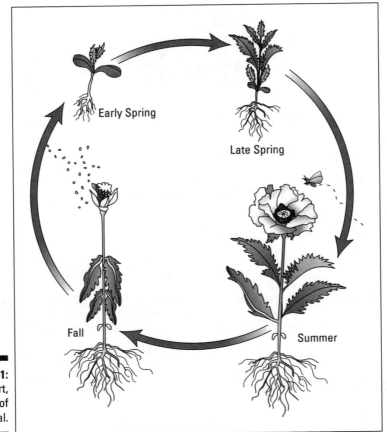

Figure 4-1:
The short,
happy life of
an annual.

Because annuals grow so easily and quickly — and are so popular — you can find an overwhelming number of varieties. Plant breeders have been busy with annuals for more than a hundred years, and look what they've done: A plant that in nature had yellow flowers with four petals may now produce a bloom with 16 white petals.

Many of the breeding efforts have gone into producing smaller, more compact plants (dwarfs). You can also find annuals developed to trail from hanging baskets (trailers). You can also find an amazing array of flower types, as described here:

✔ A *single* flower, the type most often found in nature, has a single layer of petals.

- ✔ A *double* flower has additional layers of petals.
- ✔ A *fully double* flower has many layers of petals.
- ✔ A *bicolor* flower has two prominent colors in its petals.
- ✔ A *star* flower has a color pattern in the petals that is remarkably star-shaped.
- ✔ A *picotee* flower has petal tips in a color different than the rest of the petal.

Getting Cozy with Annuals

Absorb a few facts about your area's climate and seasons, plus some of your own garden's idiosyncrasies, and you can make much wiser selections at planting time. Most important are some key dates, like when the danger of frost is past in spring and when frost is likely in fall. If you live where winters are essentially frost-free, you need to know when the seasons shift — allowing you to plant either warm- or cool-season annuals. Such know-how is easy to get, either from your local nursery, cooperative extension service, or from the chapter about climate in this book, Chapter 2.

Some annuals are cool and some like it hot

Depending on their origin and what's been bred into them, annuals prefer one of two growing conditions.

- ✔ *Cool-season annuals* perform best in mild temperatures (about 70°F, or 21°C), cool soil, and when days are short. In most parts of the United States and Canada, these conditions are typical in early spring and early fall. These annuals also do well when temperatures are similarly mild all summer in mountain regions or along the coast and in areas to the far north.

  Cool-season annuals can withstand frost. Some types are quite hardy and in many areas are actually perennials. Hot weather and long days cause cool-season annuals to set seeds, thus ending the bloom season. Examples of cool-season favorites are calendula, pansy, and snap-dragon. Usually, you can safely plant cool-season annuals in early fall or a few weeks before the average date of the last spring frost in your area.

> ✔ *Warm-season annuals* thrive in hot summer weather. Most of these annuals are tender — freezing temperatures can damage or even destroy them. Warm-season annuals include celosia, impatiens, marigold, vinca rosea, and zinnia. Plant warm-season annuals after the date of your last frost, when soil and air temperatures are warming up. These plants peak in midsummer.

Areas where annuals live all year

In a number of locations, you can grow annuals throughout the entire year. Winter temperatures in these climates rarely drop much below freezing, including much of California (except for higher elevations regions), low elevations of the Southwest (such as Palm Springs and Phoenix), and much of the Gulf Coast and southern Florida. On the USDA zone maps in the color section of this book, such regions are zone 10 and parts of zone 9.

In those kinds of mild-climate regions, you can plant cool-season annuals such as pansies and Iceland poppies in late summer or early fall (after summer cools off). Blooms may appear before Christmas and peak in late winter and early spring. After growth and flowering slow down in spring, replace the plants with warm-season annuals.

Truly tropical climates such as those in Hawaii and south Florida are in a separate category and have their own special rules for growing annuals. After all, in these zone 11 regions, gardeners grow tomatoes in winter! If you live in such a unique region, most of this chapter will still be a useful guide. But it's a good idea to double-check with local nurseries for exact timing.

Sun and shade

Most annuals are sun worshippers. After all, to grow and live as quickly as they do, their leaves need to collect all the energy they can, especially early in the season. Here's where it pays to be an observer: Watch how the sunlight falls in your garden and use that information to decide which annuals to plant and where to plant them.

Most annuals need about five to seven hours of direct sunlight during the middle of a summer day. If a spot in the garden gets its five to seven hours of sunlight during the morning or late afternoon when the sun is not as intense, most annuals aren't going to prosper. On the other hand, if you live where the midday sun is particularly intense, even sun-loving annuals will benefit from some shade during that time. But for most of us, the best idea is to plant shade-lovers such as impatiens or begonias in those areas instead.

Watch the pattern of sun and shade in your garden. The patterns change with time and the seasons, as the sun moves higher and lower in the sky, as trees grow taller and develop and lose leaves, and as neighbors build or tear down buildings.

How to Buy Annuals

You have three choices when it comes to planting annuals.

✔ Sow seeds directly where the plants are to grow and bloom.

✔ Start seeds indoors and transplant seedlings to the garden later.

✔ Start with transplants of varying sizes (from small plants in six-packs to larger ones in gallon cans). Most often, buying transplants from local nurseries is the easiest approach. You can also buy transplants of annuals by mail and, in doing so, enjoy more choice.

Starting annuals from seeds offers a couple of big advantages:

✔ You save money if you're doing a lot of planting.

✔ You get a much bigger choice than with seedlings sold at the nursery.

A nice thing about buying transplants at the nursery is that many annuals can give your garden instant color because they are already in bloom. Nursery transplants come in a wide assortment of package sizes, from four-packs to gallon size, as shown in Figure 4-2.

We describe techniques for each planting method — seeds in Chapter 11, and seedlings in Chapter 12 — so transplant yourself to those chapters for the scoop.

Many plants that bloom easily from seed can reseed themselves and come back year after year on their own. Most annual wildflowers reproduce themselves this way. Toward the end of the season, let annuals such as alyssum, calendula, cosmos, forget-me-nots, marigolds, pansies and violas, sunflowers, vinca, and zinnias go to seed for a garden full of *volunteers* next season. Such volunteers won't necessarily be exactly the same as last year, especially if they are seeds of hybrid varieties. For instance, the colors of the volunteers may fade or revert to the common color. But unless you're a really expert gardener who wants a particular variety, these mongrel volunteers are just as good.

Pulp pot

Gallon can

Figure 4-2:
Annuals
come in a
variety of
nursery
containers.

Inch pot

Six pack

What You Can Do with Annuals

Inexpensive, fast-growing, and long-blooming, annuals are perfect plants to have fun and experiment with. Try out wild color combinations, carpet an entire bed, or fill pots to overflowing. Make a hideous mistake (perhaps red and lavender together makes your dog howl) and you may even have time to replant during the same growing season.

Annuals are versatile and just about foolproof. You don't need to be born with a silver trowel in your hand to achieve some beautiful effects in your yard:

✔ Plant entire beds and borders in swaths of color.

✔ Create a combination of annuals for your pots and window boxes that blooms all summer long.

> ✔ Mix annuals into borders of trees, shrubs, and ground covers to add seasonal color, fragrance, and texture.

Playing with color

Try different combinations of color to find what you most enjoy in your garden. Experiment with mixing colors, and trust your own eye. One gardener's favorite combination, such as purple petunias with scarlet geraniums, may be another gardener's worst color-clash nightmare.

Also remember that a great many plants now come with multicolored-leaves (known as *variegated* in the trade), which creates a tapestry of color and pattern even when the plant is not in bloom. Yellow-foliaged plants, or those with leaves splotched in cream or white, can brighten a dark corner as effectively as white flowers. Such foliage gives the effect of dappled sunshine on leaves. Coleus are the classic foliage plants, with leaves mottled in every color from near black, to lime green, white, and bright fuchsia pink.

An easy way to deal with color is to think of all colors as falling within the ranges of *hot* or *cool*. Hot colors, such as yellow, orange, bright purple, and red are lively and cheerful. Most cool colors, such as pink, blue, lavender, and cream, blend well together, creating a feeling of harmony and serenity.

Using shape, height, and structure

A plant's form is every bit as important as its color and too often overlooked.

Need an almost instant privacy screen from neighbors? Annuals offer the perfect remedy. Annuals can add height to a garden, with towering sunflowers creating screening, or providing color at the back of the border. As you hike in the woods, notice how nature layers plant heights: tall trees, small or *understory* trees, large shrubs, ferns, and then ground cover plants that carpet the forest floor. Such complexity pleases the eye; you can blend annuals with other plantings to create this same effect in your garden beds. Use different heights, from a tall sunflower or ornamental corn to diminutive sweet alyssum.

No rule exists about planting the shortest flowers in front, with the taller in back! Tall, airy annuals, such as *Verbena bonariensis,* with its skinny branches topped with tiny purple flowers, work as *scrim* plants. The garden is meant to be viewed through airy scrim plants planted in the foreground, adding a new focus or perspective to the other plantings.

Texture adds another element to the garden. The droopy, chenille-like softness of love-lies-bleeding *(Amaranthus)* adds a striking note to a planting scheme, while the feathery foliage of love-in-a-mist *(Nigella)* can knit together varied plantings in the front of a border. Frilly China asters or the soft seed heads of annual grasses add fluff and interest. The spiky spires of foxglove or the candelabra-like heads of woodland tobacco *(Nicotiana sylvestris)* accent the more rounded forms of lower growing annuals, perennials, and shrubs.

Designing for fragrance

Of all the senses, smell most strongly evokes memory. The strong perfume of sweet peas, or the spicy smell of nasturtiums can bring back an acute longing for a favorite garden from the past.

The flower fragrances you prefer are as personal as the perfume or aftershave lotion you choose to wear. Plant generously so that you have plenty of flowers and leaves to pick for bouquets and bowls of potpourri. Even a few sprays of the unassuming common mignonette *(Reseda odorata)* can scent a room or front porch. As a rule, choose the more old-fashioned varieties of flowers, which usually tend to be more fragrant than modern hybrids; you may need to order seed packets to find the older, most strongly scented varieties.

The best way to find such old-fashioned, heirloom varieties is to study the catalogs of seed companies that make a specialty of them. Check Appendix B in this book and read the descriptions of the seed companies until you find the ones that include heirloom flowers.

Remember to add a few fragrant blooms to every pot, window box, or hanging basket. Concentrate sweet-smelling flowers near walkways, entries, patios, and decks so that you and your guests can enjoy them often. Some plants don't waste their scent on the daylight hours; they reserve their allure for night-flying moths and their pollinating ways. For instance, flowering tobacco *(Nicotiana)* and the moonflower vine release their sweet scent on the evening air and, so, are an ideal addition to planting beds or pots near bedroom windows or on patios that you use in the evening.

Here are some favorite easy-care annuals that add fragrance to the garden:

- ✔ **Heliotrope.** Dark, crinkly leaves show off vanilla-scented purple or dusky-white flowers.

- ✔ **Mignonette.** This little plant is easy to grow from seed and has an amazingly strong, sweet fragrance.

- **Nicotiana, or flowering tobacco.** The white flowers have a nearly tropical scent that is particularly strong in the evening.
- **Night-scented stock.** This old-fashioned, early blooming favorite has the scent of cloves.
- **Scented-leafed geraniums.** Fuzzy, splotched, and streaked leaves come in a wide variety of scents, from chocolate, to cinnamon, lemon, and mint.
- **Sweet alyssum.** Masses of tiny, scented flowers make this a favorite edging plant.
- **Sweet peas.** A childhood favorite for many people, the older varieties of sweet peas retain the sweetest of scents all day long.
- **Sweet William.** Gardeners have grown this plant since Elizabethan times for its spicy, sweet fragrance.

Getting annuals together

For the brightest blast of color, plant annuals en masse. Low-growing types usually work best for this type of planting, and you can go with just one color or mix a number of colors. The important consideration is to plant many annuals and plant them close (usually 6 to 8 inches apart). Start with six-packs and space the transplants evenly in staggered rows. (See Figure 4-3.) The plants grow quickly and fill in the spaces to give you a solid bed of bright color.

If you prefer a less-regimented look, try mixing many different types of annuals together in one bed. In general, keep the lower-growing plants in front and the taller ones in back, but no hard rules about plant placement exist. Keep to a particular color scheme, such as mixing only complementary colors, or you can go with whatever color scheme you like.

Figure 4-3:
Plant annuals in staggered rows, evenly spaced, for a bed of color.

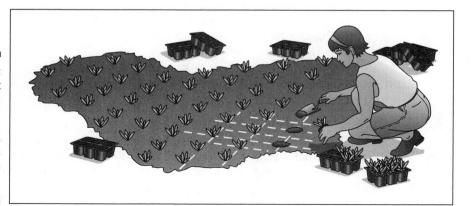

Low-growing annuals, such as ageratum and lobelia, are very useful as edgings. You can plant these low-growers along walkways or in front of other annuals, in front of perennials, or even in front of flowering shrubs, such as roses.

Containing annuals

Flowering annuals are especially at home in containers, making it easy for you to insert a touch of color into visible, highly used areas. Match the plant's habits with the pot. Spreading annuals, such as alyssum, cascade over the sides of containers and look really nice in hanging baskets or window boxes. Lower-growing, compact varieties usually are most suitable for container growing, but you can use taller types as well. By planting many pots with many different annuals, you always have some at peak bloom to put in your most visible spots, such as porches or patios. For details on growing plants in containers, see Chapter 19.

Taking Care of Your Annuals

Maintenance, especially proper watering, greatly affects how annuals behave. Unlike many plants, annuals aren't forgiving if they don't get the water they want when they want it. Fast, consistent growth is critical with annuals. If plant growth stalls, you may lose a good part of, if not all, of the blooming season.

Watering requirements vary with the weather, seasons, and garden conditions. (You knew we were going to say that!) Take a look at these ways to tell when your annuals need water:

- **Study your plants.** When an annual starts to dry out, the leaves look droopy, start to wilt, and may lose their bright green color.

- **Dig in the ground.** Annuals don't have time to reach down deep in the soil. Most need water when the top 2 or 3 inches (5–7.5 cm) of soil dry out. Dig around with a small trowel or shovel to check how moist the soil is.

Fertilizer is also critical for first-rate blooming. For best flowering, you want to keep plants growing vigorously, never stalling. Here's a simple fertilizer program that works for most annuals in most gardens:

- When you are preparing the planting bed, spread a complete, granular fertilizer evenly over the bed at the rates recommended on the package. Use a fertilizer with a ratio of 10-10-10 or 5-10-10. Work the fertilizer into the soil along with a 2- or 3-inch (5–7.5 cm) layer of organic matter.

- Every four to six weeks during the growing season, fertilize again with a similar ratio of fertilizer but in liquid form.

The other essential step is deadheading: Cut or break off flowers as they fade. Doing so encourages the plants to produce even more blooms because the plant doesn't expend energy producing seeds.

Our Favorite Annuals

Everyone has his or her favorite flowers, and we have quite a few ourselves. This section lists some of the most reliable, colorful annuals. We divide the list into cool-season and warm-season types.

Cool-season annuals

Our favorite annuals for cooler climates or for cooler seasons include the following:

- **Snapdragon.** *Antirrhinum majus.* These plants produce wonderfully colored spikes of white, yellow, orange, red, purple, and multihued flowers. The common name comes from the hinged blossom, which opens and shuts like jaws when you squeeze the sides. Varieties range from 12 to 36 inches (30 cm–1 m) high. Plant them in full sun from transplants.

- **Flowering cabbage or kale.** *Brassica* species. These vegetable relatives look very much alike. Their value lies in their brightly colored, ruffled, or frilly foliage arranged in a head like a cabbage. The foliage is usually green with purple, pink, or white markings. Plants grow 12–18 inches (30–45 cm) high. Plant in full sun from seed or use transplants.

- **Pot marigold.** *Calendula officinalis.* Yellow or orange (or sometimes white) daisylike flowers highlight this easy-to-grow annual. Pot marigold is a nice cut flower. The compact plants reach 12–30 inches (30–45 cm) high. Plant in full sun from seed or use transplants.

- **Dusty miller.** *Centaurea cineraria.* One of the most valuable gray-foliaged plants, Dusty miller is useful for highlighting other colors. This plant, which is perennial in mild climates, makes other garden plants look better and brighter. Yellow flowers appear in summer, starting when the plant is in its second season. The plants have finely cut leaves and a mounding habit; they grow to about 18 inches (46 cm) high. Plant in full sun from transplants. *Senecio cineraria* is another gray-foliaged plant that grows slightly taller (to about 2$\frac{1}{2}$ feet, or 75 cm, high) than *Centaurea cineraria.*

- **Larkspur.** *Consolida ambigua.* Delicate spikes of spurred flowers come in pastel shades of white, blue, pink, and purple. Larkspurs grow 12–48 inches (30 cm – 1.2 m) high, depending on variety. The plants are easy to grow from seed and do best in light shade.

- **Chinese forget-me-not.** *Cynoglossum amabile.* Wispy clouds of tiny, deep blue, pink, or white flowers accent this classic for shady gardens. Chinese forget-me-nots grow 12–18 inches (30–45 cm) high. The plants are easy to grow from seed and reseed readily. *Myosotis sylvatica,* the common forget-me-not, is very similar and is equally good in shady gardens.

- **California poppy.** *Eschscholzia californica.* The much-loved California wildflower grows easily from seed (and they reseed readily). California poppies bloom mostly in shades of yellow and orange (or sometimes white). The plants reach 10–24 inches (25–60 cm) high. Grow in full sun.

- **Sweet peas.** *Lathyrus odoratus.* Intensely fragrant blooms make this a much-loved annual. The vining plant comes in single colors and multicolors — almost every hue except true blue and green. Sweet peas make a wonderful cut flower. Most varieties need support such as a fence or trellis. However, bushier, low-growing types, such as 'Little Sweetheart', do not need supports. Plant in full sun from seed.

- **Annual chrysanthemum.** *Leucanthemum paludosum* (Also listed as *Chrysanthemum p.).* Grow this glorious miniature bloomer from seeds or transplants. Small, white-and-yellow daisylike flowers cover the plant. Annual chrysanthemums grow best in full sun and reach 12–18 inches (30-45 cm) high.

- **Sweet alyssum.** *Lobularia maritima.* This ground-hugging (usually under 6 inches, or 15 cm, high) annual covers itself with tiny, bright white, purple, or pink blooms. Alyssum flowers best in cooler weather and is quite hardy, but it often blooms into summer, too. Alyssum is one of the finest edging and container plants. This plant is easy to grow from seed and reseeds readily. Plant in full sun.

- **Stock.** *Matthiola incana.* Intense, spicy scents make stock one of the most deliciously fragrant annuals. Depending on variety, flower spikes reach 12–30 inches (30–75 cm) high in shades of white, pink, purple, and red. Stocks are best started from transplants. Grow in full sun.

- **Geranium.** *Pelargonium* species. These old-time favorites are often used as perennials in mild-winter climates. Geraniums have huge clusters of white, pink, red, purple, orange, or bicolored flowers in spring and summer. The plants grow 8–36 inches (20 cm – 1 m) high; some have variegated leaves. Start geraniums from transplants and grow in full sun to light shade.

- **Primroses.** *Primula* species. Primroses are perennials in many mild climates, but usually grown as annuals. Brightly colored flower clusters rest atop straight stems that seldom reach more than 12–18 inches (30–46 cm) high. Many colors are available to choose from. Fairy primrose, *P. malacoides,* produces airy clusters of white, pink, and lavender blooms above hairy leaves. English primrose, *P. polyantha,* has brighter, often multicolored flowers above deep green, crinkled leaves. Plant in full to partial shade and start with transplants.

- **Nasturtium.** *Tropaeolum majus.* This sprawling annual has neat, round leaves and bright orange, yellow, pink, cream, or red flowers. Nasturtiums grow about 15 inches (38 cm) high on the ground, but the plants can climb up to 10 feet (3 m) when given proper supports. Nasturtiums are easy to grow from seed; plant in full sun or light shade.

- **Pansies and violas.** *Viola* species. These flowers often resemble colorful little faces. Imagining prettier flowers than pansies and violas is hard. These annuals bloom in almost every single color and multicolor except green. Pansies have slightly larger (but fewer) blooms than violas. Both feature neat, compact plants that seldom grow more than 8 inches (20 cm) tall. You can grow pansies and violas from seed, but transplants are more common. Plant in full sun or light shade.

Warm-season annuals

Ah, summertime . . . and the annuals are easy. Following is a list of summertime annuals that we like the best:

- **Bedding begonia.** *Begonia semperflorens.* These versatile annuals are most useful in shady gardens (although some types can take more sun). The flowers of bedding begonias come in shades of white, pink, and red. Leaves may be shiny green or bronze-red. Begonias with red flowers seem more sun-tolerant. Most varieties grow about 12 inches (30 cm) high. Bedding begonias are best started from transplants.

- **Madagascar periwinkle.** *Catharanthus roseus* (also known as annual vinca or vinca rosea). These cheery plants are workhorses in the summer garden. Compact with deep green leaves, Madagascar periwinkles produce an abundance of white, pink, red, or lavender blooms that often have a pink or white spot in the center. These plants grow 12–20 inches (30–50 cm) high and perform best in full sun (but can take some shade). You can grow these plants from seed, but they are more easily grown from transplants.

- **Coleus.** *Coleus hybridus.* Grown for its intensely colored foliage, coleus comes in a variety of color combinations and different leaf shapes. This plant grows best in the shade and from transplants. You can also grow coleus as a houseplant. Pinch off the flowers to keep the plant compact.

- **Cosmos.** *Cosmos bipinnatus.* Bright green, airy plants bear brilliant blooms of white, pink, lavender, purple, or bicolored daisylike flowers. *C. sulphureus* has red, yellow, or orange flowers. Most types grow tall (upwards of 5 feet, or 1.5 m, high), but dwarf varieties stay more compact. Cosmos is easy to grow from seed or transplants, and the plants reseed. Plant in full sun.

✔ **Sunflower.** *Helianthus annuus.* Few annuals make a statement the way sunflowers do. Most sunflowers reach 8–10 feet (2.5–3 m) high, topped with huge, sunny, yellow blooms. But sunflowers also come in small-flowered forms in shades of red, orange, and white. Some dwarf varieties, such as 'Sunspot', stay under 2 feet (61 cm) tall. All sunflowers have edible seeds. Plant from seed in full sun.

✔ **Impatiens.** *Impatiens wallerana.* These plants are the stars of the shady garden and one of the most popular annual flowers. The 1- to 2-inch-wide (2.5–5 cm) blooms come in bright shades of white, red, pink, salmon, orange, and lavender. Bicolored varieties of impatiens are also available. Impatiens have dark green or bicolored leaves and grow 12–30 inches (30–75 cm) high. Grow from transplants.

✔ **Lobelia.** *Lobelia erinus.* Deep to light blue blooms cover this low-growing (and often spreading) plant. Few blues are as bright as those of lobelia; white- and pink-flowering forms are also available. All lobelias reach about 4–6 inches (10–15 cm) high. Grow lobelia from seed, but transplants are easier to start. Plant in full sun to light shade.

✔ **Flowering tobacco.** *Nicotiana alata.* Small, tubular, often fragrant blooms come in shades of white, pink, red, lime green, and purple. Flowering tobacco plants grow 12–36 inches (30–91 cm) high, depending on variety. Plant flowering tobacco in full sun or light shade. Grow these from seed or from transplants.

✔ **Petunia.** *Petunia hybrida.* This much-loved annual has single or double, usually trumpet-shaped flowers in a myriad of single and bicolored shades. Petunias are compact plants that range from 10 to 24 inches (25–60 cm) high. Start from transplants and plant in full sun.

✔ **Sage.** *Salvia* species. Tall spikes of bright white, red, blue, or purple flowers top these compact, sun-loving plants. Some types of sage are perennials in mild-winter climates. Sages range in height from 10 to 36 inches (25–1 m). Plant in full sun and use transplants.

✔ **Marigold.** *Tagetes* species. Marigolds are one of the most popular summer annuals, with blooms in the sunniest shades of yellow, orange, and red. Many varieties are available. Blossoms can be big or small, as can the plants. Plant in full sun. Easily grown from seed or transplants.

✔ **Verbena.** *Verbena hybrida.* Brightly colored clusters of white, pink, red, purple, or blue flowers appear on low-growing, spreading plants. Verbenas grow 6–12 inches (15–30 cm) high. Plant in full sun. Start these plants from transplants.

✔ **Zinnia.** *Zinnia elegans.* A cut-flower lover's dream. Zinnias come in a huge range of flower colors (except blue), flower shapes and sizes, and plant heights. Small types, such as 'Thumbelina', stay under 12 inches (30 cm) high. 'State Fair' grows up to 5 feet (1.5 m) high and has long stems for cutting. Plant in full sun. Easy to grow from seed or transplants.

Chapter 5

Perennials

- -

In This Chapter

▶ Getting to know perennials

▶ Using perennials in beds and for borders

▶ Putting perennials in the ground

▶ Digging into some can't-miss perennials

- -

*P*erennials are the phoenixes of garden plants: Every winter they die only to rise from the ashes the following spring, fuller and more beautiful than before. Perennials are essential in cold winter climates because they grow and sometimes begin flowering while annuals are still warming up and getting started.

Perennial plants, grown for their flowers, their foliage, or both, are with us like the seasons — perennials return with their beauty year after year. Compared with annuals (which you need to replant every year), perennials stay in place to grow, to look better, and to bloom more, season after season.

Perennials encompass some of the best-loved flowering plants, such as daisies, chrysanthemums, and carnations. Spectacular foliage plants, such as ornamental grasses, hostas, and lamb's ears, are also perennials.

What's a Perennial?

A *perennial* is a plant that can live for several years, sprouting new growth and making new blooms cyclically year after year. If you start a typical perennial, such as columbine, from seed in May, it spends the summer growing foliage and dies back completely to the ground when winter arrives. The following spring, it starts growing again, blooms that summer, dies back again, and repeats the pattern of blooming and dying back for years.

When we say *perennials,* however, we're talking about a specific type of perennial: *herbaceous flowering perennials.* These perennials have soft, fleshy stems (as opposed to a sturdy, woody trunk like that of an oak tree). Herbaceous perennials bloom with worthwhile flowers or have attractive foliage, and they live for several years under the right conditions.

Some of these perennials are *deciduous,* meaning that they lose their leaves at some point in the year, usually in winter, or they die back completely to the ground. Other perennials are *evergreen,* especially in mild climates. Some stay evergreen in mild climates but die way back — or just plain die — in cold climates, where they are considered annuals.

Perennials generally have one main bloom season, usually in spring or summer. The season can be as brief as a few weeks or last a couple of months. Evergreen perennials in mild climates can be the wild cards — blooming every month of the year, as a marguerite in Monterey will.

Perennials are interesting for a variety of reasons. They're interesting in the range of their flowers — from tiny fragrance-packed lavender to towering blue delphiniums. They're interesting in their sheer numbers and variety — thousands of kinds are available. Perennials are interesting in the challenges they present: how to cut back, how to divide, what to do with them in the winter. You don't just relegate them to the compost pile at the end of the season as you do with annuals.

Beds and Borders

Flower beds come in two basic configurations:

- ✔ **A border** is a flower bed located alongside a wall, fence, hedge, or pavement. Border gardens are usually long and narrow as they follow the contours of the backdrop.
- ✔ **An island bed** is a free standing flower bed surrounded on all sides by lawn, gravel, or pavement. The edges can be straight or curved. Island beds can be any shape or size.

The classic use of perennials is to combine many of them in a large planting bed, known as a *perennial border.* A well-designed perennial border has something in bloom throughout the growing season. This type of border not only has a well-thought-out color scheme, but also relies on plant texture for visual interest. Designing a spectacular planting can take years of experience, but even beginning gardeners can create a workable, pleasing border, adding to it over the years as their knowledge increases.

For most gardeners, a perennial border is constantly evolving, which is part of the fun of creating it. If certain plants don't work, you can replace them with something else. If the border has some downtime when nothing is in bloom, add some flowering annuals to fill in the gap or plant some flowering shrubs, such as floribunda roses, which bloom over a long season. When your border consists of a medley of flowering plants, including small trees, shrubs, bulbs, annuals, herbs, and even vegetables, you have a *mixed border*.

Designing a Perennial Border

Even though individual experience is the best teacher, here are some pointers that we've found useful in designing a perennial border:

- ✔ **Start with a plan and keep records.** Draw your bed on paper, making sure to give plants the room they need to grow. Work with a simple color scheme, such as three of your favorite colors, and use plants that bloom only in those colors.

- ✔ **Plan for a succession of bloom.** Think seasonally, aiming for something always in bloom. Keep records of blooming times so that you'll know which gaps to fill in during the next planting season. And don't forget winter. Even in cold climates, you can use shrubs that have colorful berries or attractive bark.

- ✔ **Prepare the soil carefully.** You won't be remaking this bed every year. Dig deep, add organic material, and most important, eliminate perennial weeds. For details on how to battle weeds, refer to Chapter 16 in this book.

- ✔ **Plant in groups.** One plant, alone, gets lost in the masses. We find that grouping plants in odd numbers (whether it's 3, 9, 15, and so on) looks the most natural. But don't get hung up on such rules. If you have room for only two of something, go right ahead and plant with confidence.

- ✔ **Don't forget the foliage.** Use plants with dramatic foliage to set off the flowers. Ornamental grasses or bold-textured shrubs make excellent focal points.

- ✔ **Use grays and whites.** Gray-foliaged plants (such as lamb's ears) and plants with white flowers highlight other colors and can tie everything together visually. These plants also reflect light and look great on those nights when the moon is bright.

- ✔ **Consider the background.** A dark green background enriches the color of most flowers. Consider planting a hedge (possibly of flowering shrubs or evergreens) at the back of the border.

Beyond borders

Don't feel that you have to limit perennials to beds and borders. Tuck in a few favorites wherever you have room — and perennials are great for cutting gardens.

Perennials in pots

If you live where winters are sufficiently mild (with a few exceptions, zones 9 through 11), perennials are equally at home in permanently planted containers. A container also is the way to provide conditions that a prized perennial may not get in the ground (acid soil or shade, for instance).

For a good-looking arrangement, plant several perennials together in one container varying the color, shape, and size of the flowers. Make sure you use a large container (at least 14 inches, or 36 cm, in diameter), and water it as often as daily or twice daily in hot weather. The following perennials are all good choices for container life.

- African lily, or lily of the Nile *(Agapanthus)*
- Asparagus ferns *(A. setaceus, A. densiflorus)*
- Tickseed *(Coreopsis grandiflora)*
- Ferns
- Coral bells *(Heuchera)*
- Plantain lily *(Hosta)*
- Lavender *(Lavandula)*
- Purple fountain grass *(Pennisetum setaceum* 'Rubrum')

Perennials for cutting

You can grow perennials specifically to cut them for indoor use — usually in rows or beds like a vegetable garden. Or work favorite bouquet-makers into your regular flower beds. Either way, the following perennials are long-lasting and striking as cut flowers:

- Yarrow *(Achillea)*
- Golden marguerite *(Argyranthemum frutescens)*
- Pinks *(Dianthus)*
- Coral bells *(Heuchera)*
- Peonies *(Paeonia)*
- Black-eyed coneflower *(Rudbeckia fulgida* 'Goldsturm'*)*
- Pincushion flower *(Scabiosa)*

> ✔ Goldenrod (*Solidago*)
>
> ✔ Stokes' aster (*Stokesia laevis*)
>
> ✔ Speedwell (*Veronica*)

Planting Perennials . . . and Afterwards

In the United States you can usually buy perennial plants in six-packs, 4-inch pots, quarts, or 1- to 2-gallon containers. Many mail-order suppliers, nurseries, and garden centers sell a wide selection of plants bare-root.

You can plant container-grown perennials any time that you can work the ground. However, the best time to plant such perennials is in the autumn or early spring because the plants have time to get established before hot weather begins. In cold winter regions, plant no later than early fall so that transplants have three or four weeks of good growing weather before harsh temperatures end the growing season.

For more details about transplanting and planting seedlings, see Chapter 13.

Watering and feeding

How often you water perennials depends on the usual factors: your climate, soil type, sun and shade exposure, and such. Most perennials require water only when the top few inches of soil dry out but before the plants start to show symptoms of drought stress. Perennials from arid habitats generally benefit from a longer dry interval between waterings. Plants from wet places prefer never to dry out completely. You can find out a lot more about the whens, whys, and hows of watering in Chapter 14.

Following are a few other special guidelines for perennials to keep in mind:

> ✔ In regions with cold winters, start lengthening the intervals between waterings in late summer to toughen *(harden off)* your plants for winter. You don't want perennials to face the first frost with new growth that's easily damaged.
>
> ✔ Mediterranean flowers and others from similar, dry summer climates often require a summer dormancy period. Keep the soil fairly dry during this "naptime." During summer, deep-soak infrequently — only when the soil is completely dry.
>
> ✔ Where winters are cold and dry, plan on watering perennials once a month if it doesn't rain or snow for a few weeks. Water when temperatures are above freezing and the soil surface thaws out.

Fertilizing perennials is simple. One application of a complete fertilizer (see Chapter 14) to your perennial bed in early spring should be enough. If you think that plants are lagging (weak or pale growth), follow up with another shot or two of the same fertilizer during the growing season.

Pinching and pruning perennials

Many perennials benefit from being cut back at various times during their growth cycles. To stimulate branching on lower stems and to make the plant bushier, for example, pinch out new growth at the top of the plant. (See Figure 5-1.)

Deadheading is the process of pinching or cutting off faded flowers while the plant is in bloom. Deadheading forces the plant to spend its energy on developing more flowers instead of setting seed. The result of deadheading is usually a longer bloom cycle. (See Figure 5-2.)

Figure 5-1:
Pinching out new growth at the top of the plant helps it develop lower branches and become bushier.

Figure 5-2: Deadhead spent flowers to offset seed production and to divert plant energy to producing new blooms.

Some perennials, such as coreopsis, delphinium, and gaillardia, rebloom if cut back by about one-third after the initial bloom cycle.

At the end of the growing season, cut back most perennials (some shrubbier types are an exception) to a height of 6 to 8 inches (15–20 cm). Cutting back growth rejuvenates the plant and results in a better bloom next season. Where the ground freezes in winter, mulch plants with at least 6 inches (15 cm) of organic matter such as straw or loose leaves. If you use leaves, start with an 8- to 12-inch (20–30 cm) layer because over the course of winter the leaves pack down substantially.

Taller perennials, such as delphiniums, and bushy types, such as peonies, may need staking to prevent the flowers from falling over. Figure 5-3 shows two types of staking: thin metal wire loops (for bushy plants) and bamboo stakes ties (for taller perennials).

If older plants become overcrowded or bloom poorly, rejuvenate them by *dividing*. In fact, division is a good way to increase plant numbers. (For more about plant division and other propagating methods, see Chapter 15.)

Figure 5-3:
Support plants as they grow with either metal loops or bamboo stakes and ties.

Our Favorite Perennials

Everyone has a list of favorite perennials, so here is a look at ours. The descriptions of a few others, which gardeners often grow as annuals, appear earlier in this chapter. Some perennials are technically *biennials*, meaning that they grow mostly foliage the first year, bloom the second year, and then die.

- ✔ **Yarrow.** *Achillea* species. Yarrow is a useful group of easy-care, summer-blooming perennials with ferny gray foliage and tight, upright clusters of yellow, red, or white blooms. Yarrows range in height from low-growing ground covers to tall plants — up to 5 feet (1.5 m) high. One favorite is *A. filipendulina* 'Moonshine', with bright yellow flower clusters atop 2-foot (61 cm) stems. Plant in full sun. Most are hardy through zone 3. (See Figure 5-4.)

- ✔ **Artemisia.** *Artemisia* species. This very useful group of mounding, silver-foliaged plants is great for highlighting other plants. One of the best is the hybrid 'Powis Castle' with lacy, silver foliage on a plant about 3 feet (91cm) high. Plant in full sun. Hardy through zone 5.

- ✔ **Columbine.** *Aquilegia* species. These widely adapted perennials have fernlike foliage and beautiful, spurred flowers. Columbine bloom in spring and early summer in a number of single colors and multicolors. Wildflower seed mixes include many native forms of columbine. The plants range in height from about 6 inches to 3 feet (15–91cm). Columbine are easy to grow from seed, and they reseed. Plant in full sun to light shade. Hardy through zone 3.

Yarrow (*Achillea* species)

Figure 5-4:
Yarrow sizes range from ground cover to 5 feet (1.5 m) tall.

✔ **Aster.** *Aster* species. Colorful, late-blooming perennials with daisylike flowers, appear mostly in shades of blue, purple, red, pink, and white with yellow centers. Asters usually bloom in the late summer to autumn. Some begin flowering in early summer or late spring. *A. frikartii* grows to about 2 feet (61 cm) and produces blue flowers almost year-round in mild-winter climates. Asters range from 6 inches to 6 feet (15 cm–1.8 m) high, depending on the species. Plant in full sun and divide every two years. Hardy through zone 4.

✔ **Basket-of-gold.** *Aurinia saxatilis.* Brilliant gold blooms cover the gray foliage in spring. Basket-of-gold grows about 12–15 inches (30–38 cm) high and spreads. The plant also withstands drought. Plant in full sun. Use in foreground. Hardy through zone 3.

✔ **Bellflower.** *Campanula* species. The much-loved family of mostly summer-blooming perennials produce bell-shaped flowers in shades of blue, purple, or white. (See Figure 5-5.) You can choose from many species that vary from low-growing spreading plants to taller types, some of which are 6 feet (1.8 m) high. Flower size and shape also vary.

Bellflower (Campanula)

Figure 5-5:
Bellflowers
get their
name from
their bell-
shaped
flowers.

Favorite species include the Serbian bellflower, *C. poscharskyana* — a low, mounding plant, 4–8 inches (10–20 cm) high, with blue flowers. Another favorite is the peach-leaf bellflower, *C. persicifolia,* which is also spreading, can reach up to 3 feet (91cm) high, and has blue or white blooms.

Campanulas grow best in light shade but can take sun in cool-summer climates. Hardy through zone 3.

✔ **Chrysanthemum.** This very diverse, useful group of perennials includes the familiar garden mums (*Dendranthema grandiflora,* zone 5), so useful for autumn bloom. The group also includes types such as the painted daisy (*Tanacetum coccineum,* zone 5), marguerite daisy (*Argyranthemum frutescens,* zone 9), and the Shasta daisies (*Leucanthemum maximum*; zone 4). All chrysanthemums are wonderful cut flowers. Chrysanthemum plants vary in height, flower color, bloom season, and hardiness. You can find a suitable chrysanthemum for almost every garden and situation. Most grow best in full sun. Except for *C. frutescens,* they are hardy to all zones.

✔ **Coreopsis.** *Coreopsis* species. Sunny yellow, daisylike flowers top these easy-to-grow plants. The flowers appear from spring through summer. *C. grandiflora* is one of the most common. This variety grows to about 3 feet (91cm) high and has single or double flowers. Plant in full sun. Hardy through zone 4.

✔ **Dianthus.** *Dianthus* species. This lovely family of usually fragrant, spring- and summer-flowering plants includes carnations, *D. caryophyllus*. You can grow many varieties of dianthus as annuals. Favorites include Sweet William and cottage pinks. Sweet William (*D. barbatus)* grows 6–18 inches (15–45 cm) high and has tight clusters of white, pink, red, purple, and bicolored flowers. Cottage pinks are hybrids that have very fragrant, frilly, rose, pink, white, or bicolored flowers on stems reaching about 18 inches (45 cm) high above a tight mat of foliage. Plant in full sun or light shade (in hot-summer areas). Hardy through zone 3.

✔ **Purple coneflower.** *Echinacea purpurea.* Tall, purple or white, daisylike flowers top this fine, long-lasting perennial. Purple coneflower reaches 3–5 feet (91 cm–1.5 m) high and blooms in summer. Plant in full sun. Hardy through zone 3.

✔ **Blanket flower.** *Gaillardia grandiflora.* The petals on these sunny-colored, daisylike flowers are a combination of red and yellow or are straight red or yellow. The plant blooms heavily in summer and grows 1–3 feet (30–91 cm) high. Plant in full sun. Hardy through zone 2.

✔ **Blood-red geranium.** *Geranium sanguineum.* This is one of the best of the species *geraniums,* which is a large group of fine perennials. Dainty-looking, purplish-pink, red, and white flowers appear in abundance above good-looking, deeply cut leaves that turn red in the autumn. Blood-red geranium blooms spring to summer and mounds to about 18 inches (45 cm) high. Many varieties are available. Plant in full sun to light shade. Hardy through zone 4.

✔ **Daylily.** *Hemerocallis* species. A dependable group of summer-flowering perennials, daylilies produce stalks of large, trumpet-shaped flowers. (See Figure 5-6.) Blooms appear in single and bicolored shades of yellow, orange, pink, red, and violet. Some daylilies are fragrant. Daylilies have grassy foliage that reach 12–24 inches high. The flower stems of some daylilies are 3 feet (91 cm) tall or more. Plant in full sun. Hardy through zone 3.

✔ **Coral bells.** *Heuchera sanguinea.* Wiry spikes of tiny, bell-shaped, white, pink, or red flowers are held 12–24 inches (30–60 cm) above lovely, lobed leaves. Coral bells bloom in the spring. Plant in light shade, although the plants can take sun in cool-summer climates. Hardy through zone 3.

✔ **Plantain lily.** *Hosta* species. These very useful foliage plants make a nice contrast to shade-loving flowers. Plantain lily leaves are usually heart-shaped and often crinkled or variegated. Flower spikes appear in summer. Plants and leaves range from small to large. One favorite is the blue-leaf plantain lily, *H. sieboldiana,* which has large 10–15-inch (25–38 cm), crinkled, blue-green foliage and pale purple flowers; it grows 3 feet (91 cm) high. Hardy through zone 3.

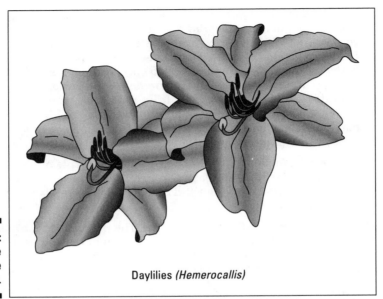

Daylilies *(Hemerocallis)*

Figure 5-6:
Some
daylilies are
fragrant.

✔ **Candytuft.** *Iberis sempervirens.* In early spring, snow-white flowers completely cover this dainty, compact plant. Candytuft grows from 4 to 12 inches (10–30 cm) high and makes a wonderful edging. Plant in full sun. Hardy through zone 4.

✔ **Ornamental grasses.** The term *ornamental grasses* designates a large group of wonderful plants grown for their grassy foliage and feathery, plumelike flowers. Ornamental grasses make stunning focal points among other blooming plants. The dried flowers often look good well into winter. Some favorites include purple fountain grass, *Pennisetum setaceum* 'Rubrum', with purplish-red leaves and plumes that reach over 6 feet (2 m) high; the huge (often more than 8 feet or 2.5 m) variegated eulalia grass, *Miscanthus sinesis* 'Zebrinus', with yellow-striped leaves and broomlike plumes; and blue oat grass, *Helictotrichon sempervirens,* with gray-blue foliage 2 to 3 (60–91 cm) feet high. Growing conditions and hardiness vary.

Beware! Some ornamental grasses get very large and can become invasive.

✔ **African Daisy.** *Osteospermum barberae.* These rugged perennials, shown in Figure 5-7, bloom fall through spring, and on and off throughout the summer in coastal climates. Flowers are lavender with pink and blue shadings. Most have dark blue centers. Several forms are available — including 'Compactum', which is hardy through zone 5. Most are hardy only through zone 9.

Figure 5-7:
African
daisies are
rugged
plants.

African daisy

✔ **Garden penstemon.** *Penstemon gloxinioides.* These spring-blooming, mounding plants grow 2–4 feet (60–120 cm) high. Garden penstemon features spikes of tubular flowers in many single and bicolored shades of white, pink, red, and purple. Plant in full sun. Hardy through zone 8. Check nursery catalogs for other species that are hardier.

✔ **Summer phlox.** *Phlox paniculata.* Large clusters of small white, pink, red, salmon, and purple fragrant flowers bloom in mid- to late summer. The plants grow 2–4 feet (60–120 cm) high. Plant in full sun. Hardy through zone 3.

✔ **Gloriosa daisy; black-eyed Susan.** *Rudbeckia hirta.* This is a free-blooming, easy-to-grow perennial or biennial. These plants have large yellow, orange, maroon, or mahogany daisylike flowers with dark, domelike centers. Some kinds are bicolored. These plants bloom from summer to autumn. The plants grow 2–4 feet (60–120 cm) high, are easily grown from seed, and reseed themselves heavily. The plants can be invasive. Plant in full sun. Hardy through zone 4.

✔ **Salvia.** *Salvia* species. So many excellent perennial salvias are available that we could write a book about them alone. Most are best adapted to dry-summer areas with mild winters. Many are shrublike; others are perennials that are usually grown as annuals. (See Chapter 4.)

Still others are valuable herbs. Favorite flowering types include *S. superba* (zone 4), with violet-blue summer flowers reaching 2–3 feet high, and *S. azurea grandiflora* (zone 5) with 4- to 5-foot-high (1.2–1.5 m), rich gentian-blue flowers in late summer. Plant in full sun. Hardy through zone 6.

✔ **Lamb's ears.** *Stachys byzantina.* This is a lovely, low-growing foliage plant with soft, fuzzy, silver-gray leaves. Lamb's ears grow 6–12 inches (15–30 cm) high and have insignificant purplish-white flowers in summer. This perennial is a fabulous edging plant for flowering perennials. Plant in full sun. Hardy through zone 4.

One of the surest pleasures of gardening is feasting your eyes on brilliantly colored flowers. And in spring, the banquet is served. Annuals, perennials, and bulbs—like these ranunculus—combine to create a season-long feast of color.

Bedding begonias
Begonia semperflorens-cultorum
Warm-season annual, or short-lived perennial in zones 9-11

Cockscomb
Celosia argentea
Warm-season annual

Cosmos
Cosmos bipannatus
Warm-season annual

Floss flower
Ageratum houstonianum
Warm-season annual

Impatiens
Impatiens walleriana
Warm-season annual

Mexican sunflower
Tithonia rotundifolia
Warm-season annual

Love-in-a-mist
Nigella damascena
Cool-season annual

Nasturtium
Tropaeolum majus
Cool-season annual

Pansy
Viola wittrockiana
Cool-season annual

Madagascar periwinkle
Catharanthus roseus
Warm-season annual, or short-lived perennial in zones 9-11

Garden verbena
Verbena hybrida
Warm-season annual, or short-lived perennial in zones 9-11

Petunia
Petunia hybrida
Warm-season annual, or short-lived perennial in zones 9-11

Bleeding heart
Dicentra
Perennial, zones 3-9

Sedum
Sedum 'Autumn Joy'
Perennial, zones 2-9

Gloriosa daisy
Rudbeckia fulgida 'Goldsturm'
Perennial, zones 4-10

Golden Prayers plantain lily
Hosta 'Golden Prayers'
Perennial, zones 3-8

Hardy chrysanthemum
Dendranthema 'Clara Curtis'
Perennial, zones 4-7

West Elkton peony
Paeonia lactiflora 'West Elkton'
Perennial, zones 3-8

Purple coneflower
Echinacea purpurea
Perennial, zones 3-8

Purple foxglove
Digitalis purpurea
Biennial, zones 4-9

Bearded iris
Iris
Perennial, zones 3-10

Bee balm
Monarda didyma
Perennial, zones 4-9

Daylily with purple **yarrow**
(Hemerocallis 'Little Grapette'*)*
(Achillea millefolium 'Rubra'*)*
Perennials, zones 3-9

Yellow coreopsis and gayfeather
(Liatris 'September Glory'*)*
at peak late-summer bloom.

Hybrid tulip
Annual, occasionally perennial bulb, all zones

Daffodil
Narcissus
Perennial bulb, all zones

Fancy-leaved caladium
Caladium bicolor
Annual tuber for warm, humid regions

Asiatic hybrid lily
Lilium 'Apricot Beauty'
Perennial bulb, all zones

Chapter 6

Bulbs

In This Chapter

▶ Understanding bulbs

▶ Caring for bulbs

▶ Dividing and propagating bulbs

▶ Taking stock of our favorite bulbs

*B*ulbs are a dream come true for many people, especially for those who have never had much luck growing any plants. Think of bulbs as flowering powerhouses: plants that pack most of what they need for a season's worth of growth into some type of underground storage device, the bulb. Plant a bulb at the right time of year and at the proper depth, and you're almost guaranteed a spectacular bloom — true, you have to wait a few months, but the wait is worthwhile.

What Are Bulbs?

When you think of plant bulbs, you probably envision daffodil or tulip bulbs — brownish things that look something like an onion. All those bulbs are true bulbs, including the onion. But the term *bulb,* as used in gardening, refers to a great number of different types of plant bulbs. In addition to true bulbs, other forms include corms, rhizomes, tubers, and tuberous roots. Each one of these types looks different. In all cases, common plant parts — roots, stems, or leaves — have evolved over time into underground plant parts that can store the plant's energy over seasons unfavorable to plant growth. Some are underground stems surrounded by modified fleshy leaves, and others are swollen underground stem bases. Some are thickened, branching storage stems, and others are swollen roots.

All bulbs have a growing period and a resting time. But there, the similarity ends. For one thing, bulbs don't all grow and rest simultaneously. Some early spring bulbs — the familiar tulips, daffodils, hyacinths, and such — blossom early in the year when nothing much else is growing and then rest while the majority of other plants are growing. Other bulbs — lilies, ornamental onions, and gladiola for example — bloom later on, when all sorts of plants are busy growing. Some bulbs, colchicum for one, flower in autumn when just about everything else is going dormant. For the full nitty-gritty on plant bulbs, check out *Flowering Bulbs For Dummies*, by Judy Glattstein and the Editors of The National Gardening Association, published by IDG Books Worldwide, Inc.

What You Can Do with Bulbs

Plant bulbs wherever you want to see them bloom: in the smallest little spot by the front door, in pots, in large swaths under trees, or among other flowering plants. Some bulbs, such as the English bluebell, look particularly good in woodland settings, while others, such as tulips, do well in formal gardens.

One of our favorite designs involves planting large beds of tulips or daffodils. We then plant low-growing annuals or perennials (such as sweet alyssum, pansies, violas, or iberis) right on top of these bulb beds. The bulbs come up through the other flowers and create wonderful combinations. After the bulbs are through blooming, the other flowers cover up the leftover foliage of the bulbs.

Plan for a long season of color from bulbs. Even though some of the most familiar bulbs (such as daffodils and tulips) bloom in spring, other bulbs (such as dahlias) bloom in summer and autumn.

In mild winter climates (zones 8–10), bulbs work especially well in containers. With containers, you can really pack bulbs tightly for a spectacular bloom (*but* the tighter you pack the bulbs, the less likely they'll bloom the following year).

If you really want to have fun, try forcing bulbs to bloom indoors. (See "Bulbs in Containers," in this chapter.)

When and How to Buy Bulbs

The best time to buy and plant bulbs depends on whether the bulb blooms in spring or summer.

Spring-blooming bulbs

Hardy, spring-bloomers are the major-league bulbs that most people know: crocus, daffodils, hyacinths, and tulips are most common and what most people picture when the think of bulbs. You plant the bulbs in fall and they bloom in spring. If you live someplace with cold winters, you can plant all spring-blooming bulbs except tulips as soon as you have them in your hands in the autumn. Hold off on planting tulips until the soil begins to cool off. In mild winter regions of the Southwest, that time period can be late November or early December! In areas with mild winters, wait until the soil begins to cool off to plant any of these spring-blooming bulbs.

If you live in a warm-winter climate, you may have to refrigerate bulbs that require winter chilling (such as hyacinth and tulip) before planting. Check the bulb package for such a recommendation or ask at your nursery. To chill bulbs, place them in the refrigerator for six to eight weeks prior to planting. Keep these other chilly tips in mind:

- ✔ Place the bulbs in a bag and close it. Brown paper bags usually work best.

- ✔ Don't store the bulbs near apples, which emit ethylene gas that can stymie blossoms.

- ✔ Storing bulbs in the vegetable crisper, with its higher humidity, is the best spot, but anywhere except the freezer is okay.

- ✔ Don't forget to clearly label your bags of bulbs — you don't want anyone slicing up a hyacinth instead of an onion for a salad!

Nurseries get the bulk of their spring-blooming bulbs around the Labor Day weekend. Here are some tips to getting the pick of the crop:

- ✔ **Buy early, and buy everything you intend to get.** Supplies of a popular, sold-out item may or may not be replenished.

- ✔ **Make reservations.** If some bulbs are in limited supply, an early order reserves them for you. Orders are often shipped in rotation — early order, early shipping; later order, later shipping.

- ✔ **Specify a shipping date for mail-order suppliers.** Most, if not all, mail-order sources promise to ship *at the appropriate time*.

- ✔ **Have your checkbook ready.** On the downside — some (but not all) mail-order sources require you to pay for bulbs at the time you place the order.

Summer-blooming bulbs

Most bulbs that bloom in summer are frost-tender types, such as dahlias and begonias, that you plant in spring. In mild winter regions, you can plant some summer-blooming bulbs once and leave them in the ground year round. Canna lilies are an example. If you live in an area with cold winters, wait until close to tomato-planting time (after last spring frost) if you intend to plant the bulbs directly in the ground. Space permitting, you can pot up dahlias and canna lilies a month or six weeks before the last frost. Then plant outdoors in active growth.

Nurseries, chain stores, and supermarkets often start selling summer-blooming bulbs while it's still winter. Instead of thinking about your snow shovel, dream about your hoe and rake as you seek out your summer bulbs. Just follow these tips:

- **Don't wait.** Buy dormant, summer-blooming bulbs when you see them. If you want to decide later, the bulbs may already be gone. Remember — you can always return what you don't want.

- **Aim for early blooms.** You can pot up your summer-blooming bulbs a month early — before frost-free weather arrives — if you have the appropriate indoor space to grow them. Doing so gives you a jump-start on the season.

- **Cheat a little.** Once the weather is mild and settled, some tender bulbs may be available as potted growing plants — dahlias, canna lilies, and caladiums in particular. You can buy, plant, and enjoy all on the same day — no waiting!

Shopping tips

Always purchase fine-quality bulbs — they give you more bang for your buck. Never forget that with bulbs, bigger is better. Larger bulbs, although more expensive, give you more bloom. Bargain bulbs are often poor performers. Avoid bulbs that are soft and mushy or have obvious signs of decay. Keep the following advice in mind as you shop:

- A good bulb is plump and firm. Reject any that are shriveled up or soft and mushy.

- A good bulb is healthy — no moldy patches growing on it. Judge a flowering bulb just like you would an edible one, like an onion.

- Size is relative — you'll never see a crocus corm as big as that of a gladiolus — but within a category, bigger is better. A large daffodil called *double-nosed* has more flowers than a smaller, single nosed or *round* of the same variety.

If you buy your bulbs through a mail-order catalog, you should rely on a reputable dealer to send you sound bulbs. Mail order is the only way to buy bulbs that are not locally available. (Appendix B lists several companies that offer an assortment of bulbs.) A specialty nursery can offer a wider selection of particular bulbs by mail than local nurseries can afford to stock. Take a look at some pointers for mail-order shopping:

- A good catalog gives lots of information — more than just when a bulb flowers, its color, and size.

- Be cautious about the truth of claims of fabulous displays that grow anywhere and everywhere. If it sounds too good to be true, it probably isn't true.

- If prices in one catalog are significantly lower than in other catalogs or local sources, then smaller bulb sizes can explain the difference. Undersize bulbs are inexpensive, and their flowering display is correspondingly small.

- Because you are buying the bulbs sight unseen, you need to trust the dealer to be reputable and send you quality bulbs.

Planting Bulbs

Planting bulbs is easy, especially if you're using a shallow container. You can break a serious sweat, however, if you're doing mass plantings. Either way, the two most important points that you should know about planting a bulb are

- Set the bulb at the correct depth.
- Make sure you place the bulb right side up in the hole.

The chart in Figure 6-1 shows the recommended planting depths and proper positioning for common bulb types. As a general rule, most bulbs should be planted at a depth equal to three times their diameter. For example, plant a 2-inch (5 cm) bulb 6 inches (15 cm) deep. Remnants of roots on the bottom of the bulb should tell you which side of the bulb points down. If you see no sign of root remnants, plant the bulb so that the most pointed, narrow part points up. If you have any doubts, ask your local nursery.

If you have heavy clay soil, try planting at one-half the recommended depth. The bulb won't have to expend as much energy struggling through the dense clay.

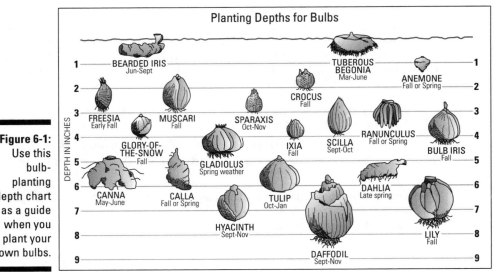

Planting Depths for Bulbs

Figure 6-1:
Use this bulb-planting depth chart as a guide when you plant your own bulbs.

You can plant bulbs individually by using a hand trowel or bulb planter. If you are planting many bulbs, dig one big trench or hole and place the bulbs in the bottom.

Most bulbs require well-drained soil. (Bulbs can rot in soggy, overly wet ground.) Before planting your bulbs, mix a slow-release, complete fertilizer into the soil in the bottom of the hole, then add a little more soil so that the bulb itself doesn't come in contact with the fertilizer granules. You can find appropriate bulb fertilizers in nurseries and garden centers. After planting the bulbs, water them thoroughly.

What's your style?

The planting method and type of bulb you choose can depend on the design style you want to achieve: natural or formal. *Naturalizing* refers to the ability of some bulbs to come back year after year. A synonym is *perennialize*. Some of the species tulips are good naturalizers, as are some crocus and many daffodils (and many other bulbs). In naturalistic design, you do your best to imitate a natural planting for a particular type bulb, and you choose bulbs that go on to naturalize on their own, thereby making the planting look more natural year after year.

In formal design, it's unlikely you'd need or want bulbs that come back every year. Also, you might want to plant in carefully excavated beds to be sure that bloom times are identical.

Beware the creatures

A gardener can be pretty perplexed when the 200 bulbs he or she planted last fall make just a meager showing in the spring. Yes, the reason could be inferior bulb quality or improper planting depth, but a likely culprit could be an animal. Chipmunks, voles, mice, deer, woodchucks, squirrels, and other animals forage for and feast on newly planted bulbs. But don't despair — you can grow beautiful flowering bulbs. Consider the following:

✔ Most critters leave daffodils and snowdrops alone, one big reason so many of these plants naturalize so well.

✔ Use bulb fertilizer or superphosphate instead of bone meal, which can attract some animals.

✔ If burrowing animals are a problem, plant in wire mesh bulb baskets.

✔ Use traps, barriers, or scare tactics.

Caring for Bulbs

With many bulbs (especially those bulbs that bloom in spring), you won't have much else to do. Plant the bulbs and forget them. The bulbs grow, bloom, die back, and come back again the following year. Summer-blooming bulbs, like dahlias and begonias, however, need regular watering and fertilizing during their growth cycle. Most bulbs, in fact, benefit from a once-a-year application of nitrogen fertilizer during their growing season.

Pinch off faded blooms just as you would for most flowers. (See Chapter 15 for the how-to on pinching.) Doing so steers the plant's energy into building food reserves rather than producing seed. After the bloom finishes, don't cut down the bulbs' foliage. The foliage provides the food for the bulb, preparing for next year's bloom. Let the foliage die down naturally and then trim off the withered leaves or just let them dissolve into the soil. In the same vein, don't braid or bundle up the leaves either. Doing so impedes the food-gathering process and results in poor blooms the following year.

Digging and storing bulbs is necessary for tender bulbs such as canna and gladiolus that grow in cold-winter climates. Wait until the foliage is almost dried out or frost-damaged and gently dig the bulbs up. (A spading fork works well.) Brush the dirt off the bulbs and allow them to dry for a week in a cool, dark place. After drying the bulbs for a week, discard any damaged or rotting bulbs and dust the remaining bulbs with sulfur or another fungicide. Finally, pack the dusted bulbs in dry peat moss or perlite and store them in a cool, dark place until replanting time.

If digging and storing tender bulbs is too much work, just treat them like annuals and plant new ones every year. Likewise, in mild-winter climates, you may find that traditional spring-blooming bulbs — tulips especially, but also hyacinths — just don't bloom after that first spring. The best approach is to dig them up and discard them after their first year.

Dividing and Propagating Bulbs

Some bulbs, particularly smaller types of bulbs (such as crocuses and daffodils), can remain undisturbed for years. Such "naturalizers" just get better year after year. But other bulbs multiply so rapidly that they become too crowded and deplete the nutrients in the soil around them. And others, notably tulips, make smaller and smaller flowers over time. If your bulbs are vigorous and crowded, they need dividing. If they produce fewer and fewer blooms, dig them up and discard them.

Dividing occurs just after the foliage turns yellow and begins to die back. Dig up the clump by using a garden fork, being careful not to injure the bulbs. Next, break off the individual bulbs, keeping the roots intact. Replant the bulbs immediately or store them in a dry place until autumn planting time. Water the area well and allow any foliage to mature and die before removing it. The newly planted bulbs should bloom the following spring.

Larger bulbs (for example, lily) or corms (for example, gladiolus) develop small, immature offspring at the base of the bulb. Remove these *offsets* after the plant has bloomed and the leaves have died; then plant the offsets in an inconspicuous area where they can grow until they are big enough to blossom (usually a year or two).

You can use another method to divide and increase true bulbs, such as lilies. Bulbs of most true lilies resemble artichokes, with many swollen, scalelike sections. You can remove the individual *scales* of true bulbs and grow them to form new bulbs for planting the following spring. This process is somewhat involved, however, and best left to the more advanced gardener.

Bulbs in Containers

Forcing bulbs — bringing them indoors and getting them to bloom before their normal season — is easier to do than you probably think. Several spring bulbs — hyacinths, daffodils (especially the ones called *paperwhites*), and some tulips — are good choices for indoor flowering. Generally, the larger grades of bulbs are better for forcing because they produce more and bigger flowers. (Avoid the bargain bulbs.)

In many climates you can also grow bulbs in containers and *not* force them for early, indoor blooms. Plant the bulbs in autumn, about the same time you'd plant bulbs in the open soil. Move the container to an out-of-the-way location for the winter. (In cold winter areas, cover the pot with mulch or store in a heated garage or basement.) Come spring, the bulbs will begin their growth. That's when you move the pot to the "display" location.

Shallow clay or plastic pots called *bulb pans* are the best containers for forcing bulbs because they require less potting mix than ordinary pots and are less likely to tip over. The general rule for forcing bulbs is to have the pot at least twice as deep as the bulb is tall.

Any soilless mixture of peat moss and perlite or vermiculite works well for forcing bulbs. Don't bother buying expensive *bulb bark,* a special mix for forcing bulbs. In the autumn, fill the chosen pot ³/₄ full with the soilless mix and place the bulbs, ¹/₂ inch (1.25 cm) apart, on top of the mix, with the bulb's pointed end facing up. When forcing several kinds of bulbs together in one container, place the largest bulbs in the center and fan out the smaller bulbs around the largest ones. Gently press the bulbs into the mix so that the tips of the bulbs are level with the rim of the pot. Then fill the pot with more of the soilless mix and water the pot until the soil is evenly moistened.

Set the potted bulbs in a cool (40°F–45°F or 4°C–7°C), dark place for 8 to 15 weeks to allow the bulbs to grow roots. Smaller bulbs may need a little less time; larger bulbs may need slightly more time.

You can use your refrigerator for this cool phase, if it has the space. If you use the refrigerator, cover pots with a slightly open plastic bag, and keep apples and other fruits away as the ethylene gas they produce will abort the bulb's flowers.

After the required cooling period, check your pots. You should begin to see evidence of shoots emerging from the soil mix. To gradually reintroduce the pots to light and warmth, place the pot in a cool room with indirect sunlight. By the end of one week, move the pot into direct sun with temperatures to 65°F (18°C). Within a month of being brought into warmth, the bulbs should begin to flower. Forced bulbs won't flower a second time so just add them to your compost pile after the blossoms fade.

Favorite Bulbs

Whether it's stately lilies, fragrant hyacinths, or cheery daffodils, everyone has a favorite bulb. Following is a list of a few of our favorites. For more information, consult some of the bulb catalogs that appear in Appendix B.

✔ **Lily-of-the-Nile.** *Agapanthus orientalis*; summer bloom. This very dependable, summer-blooming bulb produces tall stalks of bright blue flowers that reach from 4 to 5 feet (1.2–1.5 m) high. The plant gets by on little water. Straplike foliage is evergreen in mild climates. Dig and store the bulbs over winter in cold-winter climates. 'Peter Pan' is a compact variety, reaching only 8–12 inches (20–30 cm) high, so it is excellent in containers. Varieties with white flowers are also available. Plant in full sun or light shade. Hardy as a perennial in zones 9–10.

✔ **Begonias.** *Begonia tuberhybrida*; summer bloom. Begonias are one of the most beautiful of all flowering plants. Many varieties are available to choose from. Some varieties have large flowers (up to 8 inches across), wheras other flowers are smaller and borne on "weeping" plants. Few begonias grow more than 12–18 inches (20–45 cm) high. Begonia flowers come in almost all shades except blue and green. Foliage is good-looking and succulent. They make ideal container plants and grow best in light shade. Dig up and store the bulbs over winter in all regions.

✔ **Fancy-leafed caladium.** *Caladium hortulanum*; summer foliage. Brightly colored foliage livens up shady areas. Caladiums feature large, tropical-looking leaves painted with shades of green, white, pink, and red. The plants grow from 12–24 inches (30–60 cm) high and are great in containers. Caladiums are hardy only in zone 10 but can be dug up and stored or grown as an annual anywhere.

✔ **Canna.** *Canna* species; summer bloom. This upright plant produces showy flowers in shades of yellow, orange, salmon, pink, and red. Some have bicolor flowers. The plants have large, tropical-looking leaves that in some cases are multicolored themselves. Some canna lilies grow more than 5 feet (1.5 m) high, but many are shorter. Plant in full sun. South of zone 7, canna lilies can be naturalized with little care. Elsewhere, dig and store them over winter.

✔ **Lily-of-the-valley.** *Convallaria majalis*; spring bloom. Small, dainty clusters of white, very fragrant, bell-shaped pink or white flowers appear in spring. The plants grow from 6 to 8 inches (15–20 cm) high. Growth is fast and dense, so it works well as a ground cover. Plant the root sections (called *rhizomes* or *pips*) in light shade and acid soil and keep the soil moist. The plant is also available with pink blossoms, but supplies can be rare. This plant naturalizes in cold-winter climates and is hardy through zone 4, but does not thrive where winters are warm.

✔ **Dahlia.** *Dahlia* species; summer bloom. This huge, diverse family of hybrids offers an incredible array of flower form and sizes. Some dahlia blossoms are tiny balls; other blossoms are huge, star-shaped blooms more than 8 inches (20 cm) wide. Available in almost every color but blue, dahlia plants range in size from 6 inches (15 cm) high to more than 5 feet (1.5 m) high. Plant in full sun and water regularly. Hardy in zone 9 and warmer, but they grow anywhere as long as tubers are dug and stored over winter. Smaller varieties are often grown as annuals.

✓ **Freesia.** *Freesia* species; spring bloom. These dependable bulbs naturalize freely in mild climates. Freesia's arching clusters of trumpet-like flowers come in almost every color. Some freesias are fragrant. The plants grow to about 18 inches (45 cm) high. Plant in full sun or light shade. Freesias are hardy through zone 9, but the bulbs must be dug or used as an annual elsewhere.

✓ **Snowdrops.** *Galanthus* species; very early spring bloom. Lovely, drooping, bell-shaped white flowers punctuate this plant. Snowdrops naturalize nicely in cold-winter climates. Snowdrops grow from 8 to 12 inches (20–30 cm) high. Plant in full sun or partial shade. (Snowdrops are great under trees.) Hardy through at least zone 4. The giant snow-drop, *G. elwesii*, naturalizes farther south, into zone 9.

✓ **Gladiolus.** *Gladiolus* species; summer bloom. This much-loved cut flower bears tall spikes of trumpetlike flowers. Blossoms come in almost all colors except blue. Most grow to 4–5 feet (1.2–1.5 m) high, but smaller types are available. Plant in full sun. Hardy in zone 9, but dig the bulbs or use the plants as annuals elsewhere. Baby gladiolus, *G. colvillei,* grows lower and is hardier. You can leave baby gladiolus bulbs in the ground, and they can naturalize in all but the northernmost areas.

✓ **Common hyacinth.** *Hyacinthus orientalis*; early spring bloom. Wonder-fully fragrant spikes are composed of white, red, pink, yellow, blue, or purple bell-shaped flowers. Common hyacinth grows to about 12 inches (30 cm) high. Hyacinths look best when planted in masses or containers. Plant in full sun or light shade. Hyacinths do best in cold-winter climates; they need chilling elsewhere. Hardy through zone 4.

✓ **Iris.** *Iris* species; spring to summer bloom. A huge group of elegant plants, you can choose from many different types. Favorites include the bearded iris, which has huge blooms and gracefully arching petals. Irises come in many colors and reach from 6 inches to 4 feet (15 cm–1.2 m) high. The plants spread freely. Plant in full sun or light shade. Most need to have water regularly. Hardiness varies, but most survive into at least zone 5, some through zone 3.

✓ **Snowflake.** *Leucojum* species; early spring bloom. This plant is very similar to snowdrops (see **Snowdrops** in this list) with white, drooping flowers. Snowflake plants naturalize in cold-winter climates. Plant in full sun or light shade. Hardy through zone 5.

✓ **Lilies.** *Lilium* species; mostly summer bloom. Lilies are a large family of beautiful bulbs. Most have large, trumpet-shaped flowers, but a great diversity of lilies exists. Blossoms come in almost every color but blue, and plant heights range from 2 to 6 feet (60 cm–1.8 m). Plant lilies so that the roots are in the shade but the tops can reach for the sun. A mulch or low ground cover will help. You can also plant the bulbs among low shrubs. Water regularly during summer. Most are hardy through zone 4.

- **Grape hyacinth.** *Muscari* species; spring bloom. These wonderful little bulbs form carpets of fragrant, mostly blue, flowers and grassy foliage. Grape hyacinths grow from 6 to 12 inches (15–30 cm) high and naturalize freely. Plant in full sun or light shade. Hardy through zone 3.

- **Daffodils and Narcissus.** *Narcissus* species; spring bloom. Carefree bloomers flower year after year, even in mild climates. If you plant only one type of bulb, this should be it. Narcissus plants generally bear clusters of small, often fragrant, flowers. Daffodils have larger blooms. You can choose from many daffodil and narcissus varieties (mostly in white and yellow shades). 'King Alfred' is an all-time favorite, large-flowered, yellow trumpet type. Plant daffodils and narcissus in full sun to light shade. Hardy through zone 3.

- **Persian buttercup.** *Ranunculus asiaticus*; spring to summer blooms. Bright-colored flowers come in shades of white, yellow, orange, red, and purple. Some Persian buttercups are multicolored. The plants grow from 12 to 24 inches (30–60 cm) high and have deeply cut leaves. Plant in full sun or light shade. Hardy through zone 8, but dig and store the bulbs in autumn.

- **Tulips.** *Tulipa* species; spring bloom. These much-loved bulbs with the familiar cup-shaped flowers come in almost all colors (including multicolors) except blue. Tulips usually grow from 10 to 24 inches (25–60 cm) high and are best planted in full sun. They rebloom only in cold-winter climates; they're hardy through zone 3. Elsewhere, you must dig up the bulbs and chill them before replanting. However, many species of tulips, such as *T. clusiana*, naturalize even in mild-winter areas. Most tulips thrive as far south as zone 8.

- **Calla lily.** *Zantedeschia* species; summer bloom. Spectacular, tropical-looking plants bear large, usually white, cup-shaped flowers and bright green, arrow-shaped leaves. Yellow, pink, and red shades are also available. Calla lily plants generally grow from 2 to 3 feet (60–90 cm) high, but dwarf forms are also available. Best grown in light shade, these plants can also take sun in cool climates. They need regular watering and are hardy through zone 8.

Chapter 7

Roses

- -

In This Chapter

▶ Speaking the language of roses

▶ Choosing varieties for you

▶ Landscaping with roses

▶ Buying and planting

▶ Pruning and other mysteries

▶ Facing up to rose problems and quirks

- -

*F*or a gardener, falling in love with roses is easy. As if their sumptuous petal colors and shapes weren't enough, many roses seduce with an intoxicating scent designed precisely, it seems, to snag a susceptible gardener. But even from the most pragmatic gardener's point of view there's even more to the alluring power of a rose.

Roses are charter members of that club of plants that grow just about anywhere. That's why you see roses and rose gardens in San Diego, Atlanta, Bonn, and Bejing — often the same varieties. While all over the world large-flowered and long-stemmed roses on 4–7-foot (1.2–2.1 meter) plants are favorites, the diversity of roses means there's almost surely one to fit your needs and to suit your taste, no matter where you live or how you define beauty. Do you prefer roses short or tall? Do you like your flowers simple with 5 petals, or complicated with 60? Is strong rose scent more important or less important than color and shape?

Now don't get us wrong. Roses really aren't that complicated. And you can sure find a lot of information about them in books, magazine articles, and advertisements, along with thousands of different rose varieties from which to choose.

We want to guide you through this maze of information. Let us boil things down a bit. If you want to grow roses successfully, pay special attention to the following two points.

> ✔ **Know something about the various types of roses.** Don't buy a rose just because you like the picture — you may find it to be a variety that's difficult to grow in your area or that it blooms only once a year and perhaps briefly.
>
> ✔ **Learn a few of the quirks about rose care.** Pruning is easier than you think but is important. Same thing is true for fertilizing. And it's a fact that roses run into a few more problems than typical, tough landscape plants, so be prepared to deal with common maladies.

And for a lot more information, check out *Roses For Dummies* by Lance Walheim and the Editors of the National Gardening Association, published by IDG Books Worldwide, Inc.

Kinds of Roses

You can choose from literally thousands of kinds of roses, short to tall, big to little flowers, fragrant or not — you name it. But most of the roses found in garden and home centers, and available by mail-order are "modern roses," which means they are one of the following: hybrid tea, floribunda, grandiflora, climber, or miniature. Many more kinds of roses than these are available (see the section "Old garden roses" in this chapter), but this is a good place to start.

The entire Northern Hemisphere came equipped with several hundred species of roses. Over the centuries, growers have selected, crossed, and recrossed those species to form numerous types, or *classes,* of roses. If you aspire to become a rabid rose hobbyist, you need to learn about polyanthas and noisettes and other historical strains; but if you just want to grow some roses, jump right into the following pool of varieties in this section.

Trying out hybrid teas

The blossoms of *hybrid tea roses* look like the roses that come from a florist, yet usually smell much better. The plants are upright and rather angular, and their distinctive flowers and buds on long stems have come to typify what a rose is for most people. The hybrid tea is the latest development in the history of the rose and is by far the most popular rose today. The big plus of hybrid teas is that they're *ever-blooming,* meaning they bloom all summer. (But that's a bit optimistic. Though some varieties come close to being in bloom all season, most bloom in waves every six weeks or so beginning in spring and peaking again in fall.)

You can use hybrid teas as specimen shrubs in mixed flower beds or group them in a special rose bed. Some varieties are relatively hardy. Most varieties, however, require special attention to keep the plants vigorous where winters are severe.

The following hybrid teas have earned consistently superior ratings from the American Rose Society for their lovely flowers and all-around outstanding performance:

- **'Dainty Bess'.** Simple pink flowers, strongly scented
- **'Double Delight'.** White blushed with red and very fragrant
- **'Mister Lincoln'.** Perfect dark red, deeply scented flower
- **'Olympiad'.** Velvety red, perfect but unscented blossoms
- **'Peace'.** Ivory with pink blush, light fragrance
- **'Pristine'.** White tinged with pink, light fragrance
- **'Tiffany'.** Soft pink, strongly scented
- **'Touch of Class'.** Coral pink, slight fragrance

Fun with floribundas

Floribunda roses, which are crosses of *polyantha roses* (cluster-flowering roses) with hybrid teas, were developed in an attempt to bring larger flowers and *repeat bloom* (bloom early in the season, stop, and then bloom again later) to winter-hardy roses. Roses in the floribunda class have blossoms shaped like those of hybrid teas, but the flowers are usually smaller and often are grouped in loose clusters. Yet floribundas are comparatively rugged and make great specimen shrubs or hedges.

All the following are fantastic floribundas. Those with superior fragrance are noted.

- **'Angel Face'.** Lavender, strongly scented
- **'Europeana'.** Deep red
- **'Iceberg'.** Pure white
- **'Red Ribbons'.** Dark red
- **'Sexy Rexy'.** Light pink
- **'Scentimental'.** Burgundy-red with creamy white swirls and strong, spicy scent
- **'Simplicity'.** Medium pink
- **'Trumpeter'.** Brilliant orange-red

Hail to the queen

The class called *grandiflora* was invented to describe stately 'Queen Eliza-beth', which came about as a cross between a pink hybrid tea and a red floribunda. The flowers have the size and form of hybrid teas but are more freely produced, singly or in clusters, on taller, exceptionally vigorous plants. Subsequent breeding efforts to expand the grandiflora class have yet to produce roses as fine as the queen herself, with the possible exception of 'Gold Medal', a colossal yellow rose.

Additional top-rated grandifloras include:

- ✔ **'Caribbean'.** Bright orange-yellow
- ✔ **'Love'.** Petals are bright red on top, silver beneath
- ✔ **'Mt. Hood'.** White
- ✔ **'Prima Donna'.** Fuchsia-pink
- ✔ **'Solitude'.** Brilliant orange
- ✔ **'Tournament of Roses'.** Two-toned pink

Climbing high with roses

Climbing roses are very long-branched roses that you can tie onto (or weave into) a support structure so that the roses look as though they're climbing. Climbing roses can be old-fashioned roses, hybrids, or chance variants of hybrid teas. The supporting structure can be anything from a chain-link fence to a fancy iron archway. Tie climbing roses gently with pieces of stretchy cloth or old pantyhose.

Some great climbers are

- ✔ **'Altissimo'.** Deep red
- ✔ **'America'.** Bright pink
- ✔ **'Fourth of July'.** Red, white, and pink stripes

"Honey, I shrunk the roses!"

Miniature roses have small leaves, short stems, and small flowers; they usually grow less than 2 feet tall (61 cm). Miniatures fit easily into small beds and make great edging plants. You can also grow them in containers.

The following six varieties are remarkably hardy, fragrant, disease-resistant, and long-blooming (height follows flower color):

- 🗸 **'Jingle Bells'.** Bright red (20 inches, 51 cm)

- 🗸 **'Magic Carousel'.** Red edged in white (18–24 inches, 46–61 cm)

- 🗸 **'Party Girl'.** Apricot-yellow and salmon-pink (12–14 inches, 30–56 cm)

- 🗸 **'Rise 'n Shine'.** Yellow (24 inches, 61 cm)

- 🗸 **'Scentsational'.** Pink, nicely scented (18–24 inches, 46–61 cm)

- 🗸 **'Starina'.** Orange-red (12–18 inches, 30–46 cm)

When a rose is a tree

Another fun trick rosarians have played on the hapless rose is turning it into a tree. These trees are called *standards,* and you can buy almost any kind of popular rose this way. Imagine a regular rose, but on stilts. Standards cost more because it takes more time and effort to create one, but they're worth it. The secret? Growers graft desired roses on top of a tall trunk. We like standards because they raise the flowers to nose height. So-called *patio* roses are the same idea, but smaller.

Shrub roses

We can't think of any reason at all to confine roses to the rose garden. While growing roses for their charm alone has many rewards, hundreds of kinds of roses serve as colorful landscape shrubs, ground covers, and vines. *Shrub roses* as a group combine some of the best traits of the toughest roses with the most beautiful. Ideal features of shrub roses are:

- 🗸 Profuse and nearly continuous bloom

- 🗸 Pest and disease resistance

- 🗸 Cold and heat hardiness in most regions

- 🗸 Minimal pruning needed

- 🗸 Attractive plant shape

David Austin or English roses

David Austin (or English) roses, created by rose breeder David Austin, were the first to mix the blossom shapes and scents of almost-forgotten old garden roses with the disease resistance and ever-blooming qualities of newer types. More than 60 varieties are currently available. Most are strongly scented. Varieties differ regarding plant size and hardiness, but most are reliably cold-tolerant through zone 6.

- ✔ **'Emily'**. Pink flowers on tall and spreading shrub
- ✔ **'Gertrude Jekyll'**. Strongly fragrant shell-pink blossoms on a plant that you can prune into a bush or train as a climber
- ✔ **'Glamis Castle'**. White, myrrh scented, 3 feet high (1 m)
- ✔ **'Golden Celebration'**. Pinkish buds open to shockingly fragrant yellow blossoms on a big plant that likes to sprawl; demands elbow room
- ✔ **'Heavenly Rosalind'**. Soft pink, simple flowers with few petals on a 4–5-foot shrub (1.2–1.5 m)
- ✔ **'Heritage'**. Extremely well-behaved pink rose with a citrus scent; perfect as a specimen shrub in a mixed border
- ✔ **'Tradescant'**. Velvety red and strong old-rose scent; tall enough to serve as climber

Generosa roses

Like the Austins, *generosa roses* combine the best traits of modern roses (continuous bloom and disease resistance) with the best of the old (old-fashioned flower shapes, strong scent primarily). Three of the best of these new roses include:

- ✔ **'Claudia Cardinale'**. Bright yellow turning coppery red
- ✔ **'Martine Guillot'**. Soft apricot, gardenia-like fragrance
- ✔ **'Sonyia Rykiel'**. Coral pink, very strongly perfumed

Ground-cover roses

Ground-cover roses produce long, wide spreading canes, but grow no higher than about 2 feet (61 cm). They make good covers for slopes. Plant about 4 or 5 feet (1.2 or 1.5 m) apart. Also use them in containers where they can spill over sides, or plant them wherever you'd like to have a trespass-preventing barrier. All are vigorous, very cold hardy (through zone 4), and produce many flowers; all grow 12–18 inches (30–46 cm) high and 36–48 inches (1–1.2 m) wide.

Here are eight of the best ground-cover roses:

- ✔ **'Flower Carpet'**. Pink (12 x 42 inches, 30 x 107 cm)
- ✔ **'Magic Carpet'**. Blend (18 x 36 inches, 46 x 91 cm)
- ✔ **'Pink Bells'**. Pink (18 x 40 inches, 46 x 102cm)
- ✔ **'Ralph's Creeper'**. Red (12 x 48 inches, 30 x 122 cm)
- ✔ **'Rosey Carpet'**. Rose-red (12 x 36 inches, 30 x 91 cm)
- ✔ **'Sea Foam'**. White (18 x 36 inches, 46 x 91 cm)
- ✔ **'Snow Shower'**. White (12 x 36 inches, 30 x 91 cm)
- ✔ **'White Meidiland'**. White (12 x 36 inches, 30 x 91 cm)

Hardy roses

If you live in zones 3 through 5, consider growing one of the following *hardy roses.* They survive year after year in cold winter regions with no special protections or effort on your part. Most of these roses become 3–5-foot (1–1.5 m) shrubs.

- ✔ **'Applejack'.** Rose with crimson spots, shrub
- ✔ **'Captain Samuel Holland'.** Red, fragrant, climber
- ✔ **'Country Dancer'.** Rose-red, shrub
- ✔ **'David Thompson'.** Red, fragrant, climber
- ✔ **'George Vancouver'.** Red, shrub
- ✔ **'John Cabot'.** Red, climber
- ✔ **'John Franklin'.** Red, shrub
- ✔ **'Morden Amorette'.** Deep pink, shrub
- ✔ **'Morden Blush'.** Light pink, shrub
- ✔ **'Morden Centennial'.** Pink, shrub
- ✔ **'Morden Fireglow'.** Red, shrub
- ✔ **'Prairie Dawn'.** Pink, shrub
- ✔ **'Prairie Princess'.** Pink, shrub
- ✔ **'William Baffin'.** Deep pink, climber

Hybrid musk roses

Hybrid musk roses are large, 6–8-foot (2–2.5 m) nearly ever-blooming shrubs or climbers. They descend in large measure from the musk rose, *Rosa moschata.* Flowers are typically pink, and many produce bright orange hips in the fall. Compared to most roses, hybrid musk roses grow well in light shade.

Some of the best varieties are

- ✔ **'Buff Beauty'.** Light apricot
- ✔ **'Cornelia'.** Light pink
- ✔ **'Felicia'.** Pink
- ✔ **'Kathleen'.** Blush pink
- ✔ **'Penelope'.** Shell pink
- ✔ **'Will Scarlet'.** Red

Old garden roses

When we talk about an *old garden rose,* we usually mean old in the sense that the rose was popular among Victorians. And some types, such as the *centifolias,* have been grown for centuries. The plants you buy are, of course, only a couple of years old, same as any rose you purchase. Here are a few old roses:

- ✔ **Alba.** All descended from *Rosa alba,* the White Rose of York, and made famous during England's fifteenth-century War of the Roses. They make tall, vigorous, and thorny plants; flowers are fragrant and usually pale-colored. Blooms once per season. Varieties include 'Alba Semiplena', 'Great Maiden's Blush', and 'Königin von Dänemark'.

- ✔ **Bourbon.** Tall, vigorous plants. Blooms more than once per season. The first Bourbons in the early 1800s were hybrids of *R. chinensis* and *R. damascena* 'Semperflorens'. Many forms evolved, shrubs to climbers, and most were very fragrant. One of our favorites is the pink-flowered shrub/climber 'Souvenir de la Malmaison'. Also consider the red and fragrant 'Madame Isaac Pereire'.

- ✔ **Centifolia.** Favored by Dutch painters of the 1700s, all are varieties of *Rosa centifolia.* All have flowers with so many thin, overlapping petals that early on they were compared to a head of cabbage (thus the name "cabbage rose"). Centifolias have arching, thorny stems. Fragrant flowers come in spring only. Pink 'Rose des Peintres' is typical.

- ✔ **China.** Descendents of *R. chinensis,* these are the roses that came back to Europe from China via the tea trade in the early 1800s. Their capacity to bloom more than once in spring quickly created a sensation, and the genes of these plants are prominent in most modern roses. The originals are delicate plants with lots of twiggy growth.

- ✔ **Damask.** These roses descend from *R. damascena,* the rose of the perfume industry. Damask roses have thorny, arching stems. Flowers are usually pink and very fragrant. Most bloom only once per season. One variety, *R. d.* 'Semperflorens' (also known as the Rose of Castile) blooms twice.

- ✔ **Gallica.** Many varieties of the French rose *R. gallica* exist. Plants are mostly a compact, 3–4 feet high (90–120 cm)with arching stems. Fragrant roses come in clusters once per season. Varieties include *R. g.* 'Officinalis', the Apothecary Rose.

- ✔ **Hybrid perpetual.** Just prior to the advent of the modern roses in the early twentieth century, these were the garden rose to have. Oversize 8-foot (1.5 m) plants produce huge and often strongly fragrant flowers, some as large as 7 inches (13 cm) in diameter. Cold hardy through zone 4 with minimal winter protection; plant deeply.

- **Moss.** Roses with moss-like fur over their flower stems and buds are called moss roses. Two species of roses produce moss roses: *R. centifolia* (softer moss) and *R. damascena* (stiffer moss). Flowers are white, pink, or red and often very fragrant. Some bloom once per season; some varieties repeat bloom. 'Communis' (pink) is typical. Red 'Henri Martin' blooms more than once a season.

- **Portland.** These small shrubs are also known as Damask perpetuals. They were among the first hybrids to combine the new China roses with the old European types, in this case *R. damascena* 'Semperflorens'. Fragrant flowers are typically pink. The original variety from about 1800, 'Duchess of Portland', had bright scarlet flowers. Also consider bright pink 'Jacques Cartier'.

- **Tea.** These relatively tender but "flowerful" plants are the dominant ancestor of most of the roses common today. Along with their fast repeat bloom, they gave modern roses a range of colors and delicate flower shapes that have become standard. Original tea varieties you can grow include pink 'Duchesse de Brabant', and dark pink to red 'Monsieur Tillier'.

Romantica roses

The intention of the "romantica" roses is right there in the name: They are intended to inspire, if not make you swoon, with their old-fashioned charm and strong fragrance. In this way, Romanticas contend with the David Austins and the Generosas. The newest include

- **'Leonardo da Vinci'.** Pink
- **'Jean Giono'.** Apricot
- **'Johann Strauss'.** Pearl pink
- **'Traviata'.** Red

Rugosa roses

These roses are all descendants of *Rosa rugosa,* a species of roses noted for its hardiness to cold and sea spray. The deeply quilted pattern in their leaves is also distinctive. Though the native species blooms only once, in spring, these hybrids will bloom a second time. Fragrance is light, but at best, spicy. Plants produce large hips that are well suited to jams and jellies.

- **'Buffalo Gal'.** Pink
- **'Linda Campbell'.** Red
- **'Snow Owl'.** White
- **'Topaz Jewel'.** Yellow

Looking for roses without the thorns? Now you can find in most nurseries a type of rose called Smooth Touch. Remarkably, they are absolutely thornless. Flowers are about 3 inches (8 cm) wide and nicely shaped. Various colors are available including red, pink, and white. Hardy through zone 6.

As you jump into the world of roses, be sure to check in with the American Rose Society. (Insiders refer to it as the *ARS*.) If you're searching for a particular rose, or for more information on any rose subject, write to the ARS at P.O. Box 30,000, Shreveport, LA 71130-0030; phone 800-637-6534; Web site `www.ars.org`. Annual membership in the ARS, which includes a one-year subscription to the monthly magazine, *American Rose,* costs $32.

Got a rose question? Get an answer quick via the American Rose Society's Consulting Rosarians Online. Find the one nearest you at `www.ars.org/cronlinr.html` on the Internet.

Landscaping with Roses

Roses in formal rows are a typical sight in public gardens, but the plants are a lot more versatile than that. You can use roses in many more ways in your own garden.

You can put several roses together in a special rose bed, plant a group of the same kind of rose in a line to create a hedge, or work your roses into a mixed bed or border with other flowers. In all three of these situations, you soon discover that roses are not beautiful all the time. Solve this problem by using companion plants that look great while your roses aren't blooming. In most climates, your roses look less than attractive three times during the year — winter, early spring, and midsummer.

- ✔ **For winter allure.** Keep the scene lively with small evergreen shrubs, ground cover junipers, or ornamental grasses.

- ✔ **For spring excitement.** Punctuate your rose planting with small clumps of daffodil, muscari, or crocus bulbs; or incorporate mounds of creeping phlox (or perennial candytuft) or an edging of pansies.

- ✔ **For midsummer color and contrast.** Choose one or more of these as possible partners: perennials such as geraniums, blue salvias, dwarf daylilies, and moss rose *(Portulaca);* and foliage herbs, like rosemary, thymes, artemisias, and lamb's ears *(Stachys).*

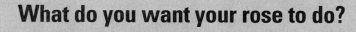

What do you want your rose to do?

✔ **Formal beds and borders:** Floribundas; hybrid teas

✔ **Hedges:** Shrub roses; old roses; grandifloras

✔ **Perennial and shrub borders:** All classes, but especially floribundas or shrubs

✔ **Edging and low borders:** Miniatures; small shrub roses

✔ **Formal rose garden:** Hybrid teas, floribundas, grandifloras, and others

✔ **Cutting:** All roses

✔ **In arrangements:** All classes, but especially hybrid teas for long stems

✔ **Fragrance:** Many new and old roses

✔ **Walls or trellises:** Tall climbers, hybrid musks

✔ **Low fences:** Short climbers

✔ **Low-care gardens:** Modern shrub roses

✔ **Long-flowering:** Hybrid teas; floribundas; grandifloras; shrub roses; most miniatures

Buying Roses

The best selection of roses hits the garden centers in mid to late winter, when plants are sold bare-root (see Figure 7-1) out of beds of sawdust or shavings, or with their roots tightly wrapped in plastic. Such roses look dead, but they're merely dormant, or sleeping. At other times of year, roses are available in containers; treat and plant them like you would any other shrub you bring home from the nursery. (See Chapter 13 for details on how to plant landscape plants.)

If you want your roses to hit the ground running, spend the little extra money for #1 grade plants, which have more stems and roots than less-expensive #2 grade plants. Whether bare root or in a container, a #1 grade hybrid tea or grandiflora has three fresh, moist (green, not shriveled) canes that are at least 18 inches (46 cm) long. Most roses are really two plants — the first plant is the hardy, vigorous root, and the second plant is the fancy rose grafted onto that root. The graft or bud union should look like a solid bulge just above the roots, and the plant should have at least three main canes reaching for the sky.

Other tips for choosing healthy and strong rose plants:

✔ Check to see that roots are firm and moist.

✔ Look for plants with canes that are ¹/₂–³/₄-inch (3–4 cm) thick.

✔ If buying roses in containers, choose a plant that has deep green, leaves that are free of pests, and stems that show many flowers or flower buds.

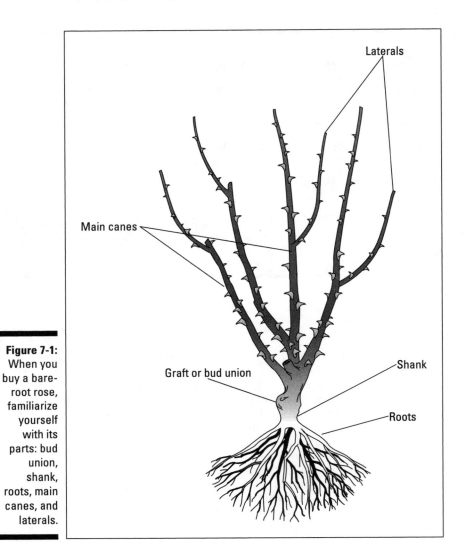

Laterals

Main canes

Graft or bud union

Shank

Roots

Figure 7-1:
When you buy a bare-root rose, familiarize yourself with its parts: bud union, shank, roots, main canes, and laterals.

The latest and greatest roses are usually patented. Having patents is fair because if the rose is successful, a royalty from the patent rewards the hybridizer who invested years of cross-breeding into its development. By the same token, you can look for nonpatented roses. The plants are just as healthy and vigorous, and you save a few dollars.

If you pay any attention to roses at all, sooner or later you'll come across the acronym *AARS,* which stands for All-America Rose Selections. While the AARS serves primarily as a public relations arm of the rose industry, rose varieties that win the AARS designation are generally among the best.

Planting Roses

Roses are sun-loving plants, so place your roses where they can get at least six hours of sun each day. In cool, cloudy climates, roses grow best with all-day sun; in really hot regions, afternoon shade gives them a much-needed break. Only one type of rose, the hybrid musks, are notable for shade tolerance and even these prefer full sun.

Roses need sufficient air circulation to help their leaves dry quickly whenever they get wet — don't crowd the plants in close quarters. Also, make sure that you can reach your roses easily when the time comes to cut flowers, trim, and prune them.

Like most other plants, roses need very good soil drainage. They prefer a near-neutral soil pH of 6.5 to 7.0 (see Chapter 11 for details on testing and adjusting your soil pH) but beyond that, they are not picky about the kind of soil in which you plant them.

To plant a bare-root rose in good, rich topsoil, dig a hole wide enough to extend the roots without bending them. If the roots are damaged, trim them as needed. Adjust the depth of the hole and the height of the soil cone until the graft union is just at or slightly above the soil level. In cold climates (zones 6 and 7) set the graft slight below the soil level, and in harsh winter climates (zones 4 and 5) plant so the graft is 4–6 inches (10–15 cm) below soil level. Spread the roots over a low cone of soil in the center of the planting hole. (See Figure 7-2.) Backfill with the soil removed from the hole, firming the soil in place with your hands. Finally, water thoroughly to settle soil and eliminate air pockets.

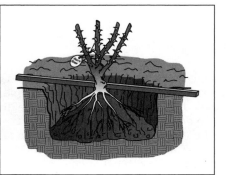

Figure 7-2:
Spread the
bare roots
over a cone
of soil.

To plant a rose in tight clay or porous sand, dig a roomy planting hole about 18 x 24 inches (46 x 61 cm) square, put the excavated soil in a wheelbarrow. Mix the excavated soil with 25 percent composted fir bark and 25 percent bagged compost, and a couple of handfuls of an organic fertilizer such as composted manure. Partially refill the hole, spread out the roots of your rose, add some more soil, and water well. Then finish dumping in your enriched soil.

Non-grafted or *own-root roses* are a better bet if you live in zones 3–5. When the part of the rose above the graft of a grafted rose dies, you've lost the rose you purchased. But when the top of an own-root rose dies, it can regrow from its roots the following spring. Many of the shrub and hardy roses (see "Hardy roses" in this chapter) are normally own-root roses.

Planting modern roses deep gives extra protection from cold winters. Most modern roses are only reliably hardy through zone 6 when planted with grafts at ground level. But you can extend the hardiness of grafted roses by planting them extra deep. Set the plant's height so that the bud union is 4–6 inches (10–15 cm) below the soil surface. This way, many otherwise tender, zone 6 roses will survive year after year in zone 4.

When transplanting a potted rose to the garden, dig a hole that is twice the width and about the same depth as the container. If planting in very heavy clay soils, make the hole slightly shallower, just as for planting any shrub (see Chapter 13). Use a utility knife to carefully cut the pot away so that the roots are disturbed as little as possible.

Roses planted in early spring can suffer some damage if the graft union freezes hard. Cover the graft union with a mound of extra soil when you plant; then remove the extra soil after all danger of frost has passed.

Fertilizing and Watering

Most roses need frequent applications of fertilizer to keep them growing vigorously and blooming repeatedly. To keep the process simple, go to the nursery and buy fertilizer labeled "Rose Food," and follow the directions on the package. Or if you prefer to do it yourself, one of our favorite formulas is a 50-50 mix of alfalfa meal and cottonseed meal. (Both are available at nurseries or animal feed stores.) Cultivate 10 cups (2.5 liters) of the mix into the soil around each bush and cover it with two inches of compost or organic mulch. Do this in early spring before roses are really growing, and repeat every eight to ten weeks.

GARDENING TIP

High-powered rose fertilizer

If you want to grow prize-winning roses, take some advice from a rose guru friend of ours:

1. **A week after plants leaf out, use a 20-20-20 soluble fertilizer at the rate of 1 table-spoon (15 mL) per gallon (3.8 liters) and 2 gallons (7.5 liters) per rose plant.**

2. **One week later, scatter ½ cup (125 mL) of Epsom salts around each plant and water it in.**

3. **The third week, apply fish emulsion, also at the rate of 1 tablespoon (15 mL) per gallon (3.8 liters) and 2 gallons (7.5 liters) per plant.**

4. **Week four, apply a liquid fertilizer with an approximate 16-4-2 ratio and which also includes a soil penetrant and chelated micronutrients, again at 1 tablespoon (15 mL) per gallon (3.8 liters), 2 (7.5 liters) gallons per plant.**

5. **Week five, start all over again.**

We can't guarantee this regimen to work for every rose gardener, but our friend has won hundreds of awards for his perfect roses.

Make your first application about four to six weeks before growth begins in spring, or, in cold-winter climates, about when you remove your winter protection. Continue feeding through summer until about six weeks before the average date of your first frost. In cold-winter climates, that means you should stop fertilizing in mid-August. In mild-winter areas, feed as late as October, but then stop — otherwise, the plant may continue growing through winter and become more difficult to prune.

Watering is the other key to productive roses. Of course, all kinds of variables (your climate, soil, and much more) can affect how you water. Consider a few major guidelines:

- Roses need more water more often in hot weather than in cool weather.
- Even if it rains often where you live, rainfall alone may not provide enough moisture for your roses.
- When you water, do it deeply enough to wet the entire root zone — to a depth of at least 18 inches (46 cm).
- If you want to be sure that the root zone is wet enough, dig into the soil. If the top 2 to 4 inches (5 to 10 cm) are dry, you probably need to water.
- To reduce disease problems, water the soil, not the leaves by using soaker hoses or drip irrigation.
- Mulch to conserve moisture in the soil.

For more tips and ideas about watering see Chapter 14.

The Mystery of Pruning

The following sounds hokey, but when it comes to knowing exactly how to prune a rose, you must discuss the matter with your plant. The first year with any rose is like a blind date — you don't know what the rose thinks of you; you don't know what you think of it. Here are some things to look for when you think that your rose is subliminally telling you that it wants to be pruned:

- **Long, skinny canes with a tuft of leaves at the end:** Carefully examine the canes for tiny, pinkish, pointed bumps called *leaf buds*. Find a good leaf bud that faces away from the center of the plant and is no more than halfway down the cane. Prune about $1/4$ inch (1 cm) above that bud.

- **Branches that come up out of the ground below the graft union:** Gently dig down to where these guys begin and cut them off with a sharp knife. These branches are shoots from the rootstock, usually an ultravigorous but unattractive type of rose. If you don't cut them out, they can take over the rose plant. (If your rose is not grafted, then there is no graft union and you might want to keep canes from below ground.)

- **Sickly looking branches where most of the leaves show black, circular freckles:** This combination of symptoms indicates a common disease called black spot (see Chapter 16). Prune off badly affected branches to keep black spot from spreading out of control.

- **Dead canes:** Prune them out.

Hybrid teas require somewhat more pruning to bring out their best performance. The rule is cut back farther (leaving canes 12–18 inches, or 46 cm, long) for fewer but larger flowers; cut back less (leave canes 2–3 feet, or 60–91 cm) for more but perhaps smaller flowers.

In early spring, cut back vigorous hybrid tea canes to the height of the other canes on the plant. Make cuts at a 45° angle, about $1/4$ inch (1 cm) above a bud. If you see brown tissue in the center of the cane, cut back farther, until the cane is clear and healthy all the way through. (Daub some white glue on the cut tips to prevent cane borers.) Remove suckers and any dead or crowded branches. All this effort keeps the center of the plant *open,* meaning free of twiggy growth, and allows sunshine to reach all parts of the plant. See Figure 7-3.

You also need to prune off dead blossoms. If your rose blooms very heavily and then looks as if it's ready to die, prune the whole plant back by one-third, fertilize the plant lightly, and water it well. Within two weeks you should see lots of new branches budding all over the plant, and within a month you should once again be smelling like a rose.

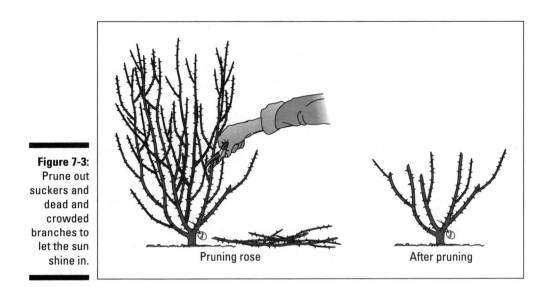

Figure 7-3:
Prune out
suckers and
dead and
crowded
branches to
let the sun
shine in.

Pruning rose   After pruning

Other Rose Quirks

How perfect do you want your roses to be? That determines the extent of
your pest and disease control program. We recommend a commonsense
approach. Live with a few bugs. But if they begin to wipe out your plants,
you can take some steps to control problems. However, use only products
that have the least impact on the environment. See Chapter 16 for details on
insecticides.

You can do a number of things to keep potential pest and disease problems
to a minimum:

- **Grow healthy plants.** Feed, water, and prune on a regular basis.

- **Plant problem-free varieties.** As you shop, pay attention to the descriptions that cite resistance to diseases, especially black spot.

- **Encourage beneficial insects.** The good guys include lady beetles,
  green lacewings, and parasitic nematodes.

- **Keep your garden clean.** Doing so reduces the number of hiding places
  for pests and diseases.

- **Apply a dormant spray.** A combination spray (horticultural oil and
  fungicide) smothers insect eggs and kills disease organisms. The best
  time to apply is right after you prune in late fall or winter.

Be prepared for the inevitable. No rose is totally immune to insects that typically prey them: aphids, cucumber beetles, Japanese beetles, June beetles, caterpillars, rose midges, rose chafers, rose stem borers, spider mites, and thrips. Typical diseases are black spot, mildew, and rust. For descriptions and controls about these pests and diseases, see Chapter 16.

Helping Roses Survive Winter

In zones 6–8, mulch the base of every plant to keep the base from freezing, thawing, and refreezing over and over. Don't cut back too early. In early winter, when the plant seems to be nodding into dormancy, cut the canes back halfway. Dump a cone of soil, sawdust, compost, or other insulating material, 6–10 inches deep (15–25 cm), over the base of the plant. Then, encircle the base of the plant with a wire cage or cardboard box and stuff it with shredded leaves. The goal is to preserve the leaf buds on the bottom 8 inches of each cane. Remove whatever insulation you use in spring so that sunlight can reach the soil and warm it. If you live in zones 3–6, see the section, "Hardy roses" in this chapter. Also note information under "Planting Roses" about planting tender roses more deeply to aid their winter survival.

You know that you have chosen good roses for your climate and are giving them suitable care if the plants get bigger and stronger with each passing year. But a certain amount of trial and error exists in growing roses. If at first any rose does not succeed, you can always try again.

Part III
Sculpting with Plants

The 5th Wave   By Rich Tennant

IT WAS A MOMENT FROZEN IN TIME WHEN A LONE MOLE TOOK A STAND FOR ALL OF MOLEDOM THAT SUNNY AFTERNOON ON TIANANMEN'S LAWN.

In this part . . .

We live in a three-dimensional world, so naturally you want your garden to be interesting and functional in all dimensions. For example, give your garden a sense of perspective — and a feeling of privacy — by using trees, shrubs, and hedges. Or go horizontal with lawn and ground covers, which also are the best way to protect and enhance your garden's soil. And get out of the rut of looking at eye-level: Use vines to put your garden up over your head!

This part brings your garden into fine perspective while also dealing with such pragmatic matters as afternoon shade and erosion control. You'll find our favorite trees, flowering shrubs, grasses, ground covers, and vines here, so you can do a little sculpting of your own.

Chapter 8

Trees and Shrubs

· ·

In This Chapter

▶ Seeing what a tree can do

▶ Choosing the right tree for you

▶ Looking at our favorite trees

▶ Getting close to shrubs

▶ Digging into our favorite shrubs

· ·

*T*rees and shrubs are the most fundamental types of plants. They may not be the most exciting or colorful in your garden (although they can well be), but they're the ones you typically count on the most — for shade, scale, background planting, property dividing, screening, and all sorts of other landscape functions (not to mention tree houses). Think of trees and shrubs as the skeleton of the landscape — the bones that you build beauty around by using other plants like flowering annuals and perennials.

But don't limit trees and shrubs to workhorse-duty only. As you discover in this chapter, these plants can add beauty and interest to any garden.

What Trees Can Do for You

No home or neighborhood should be without trees. Trees bring a home into scale with the surrounding landscape and give a neighborhood a sense of place. Deciduous or evergreen, trees provide protection from the elements by buffering strong winds and blocking hot summer sun. In our crowded world, trees can also provide privacy by screening you from neighbors or unpleasant views. And planting trees can increase your property value — studies have shown that homes with large trees usually sell for more money than similar properties without trees.

However, more than anything else, trees offer beauty: Beauty in flowers held high among the branches, or simply beauty in their leafy green canopy. Beauty in colorful berries and seed pods dangling among the limbs. Beauty in dazzling hues created by autumn leaves. Even beauty in winter, when the texture of their bark and the structure of their branches add strength and permanence to the landscape. Beauty in diversity, too — after all, without trees, where can the birds perch or the squirrels dash?

In our fast-paced world of concrete, asphalt, and hazy sky, trees are the great equalizers. They shade our streets and cool our cities and neighborhoods, they absorb dust and air pollution, and their roots hold the soil in place and prevent erosion.

Lower heating and cooling expenses

Providing cooling shade is one of a tree's greatest assets, especially in regions where summers are long, hot, and dry. If you plant *deciduous* trees (trees that drop all their leaves and are leafless for a period of time) on the warmest side of your house (usually the southwest or west side, but the east side can also be warm), the shade that they provide keeps your house cooler in summer and reduces your air-conditioning expenses. The best shade trees spread wide and tall enough to shade a one- or two-story home.

Of course, you don't have to worry about deciduous trees cooling your home in winter: Trees lose their leaves (right when you need them to) so that the warm sun can shine through, thus reducing heating costs.

You can save energy by planting trees as windbreaks. Planted close together and at right angles to prevailing wind, upright, dense-growing trees can reduce the chilling effects of winter winds and lower heating bills. (Energy conservation aside, planting trees is just a good way to create a comfortable and inviting place in the garden.)

Make you look marvelous

After you decide on the kind of tree you need in terms of size, shape, and adaptation, you have a wealth of ornamental characteristics to choose from. Consider the following points.

> ✔ **Seasonal color.** Many trees, including flowering fruit trees, bloom on bare branches in early spring. Others bloom later in spring, and some, like crape myrtles, in midsummer. And you can choose almost any color.
>
> With trees such as sweet gum *(Liquidambar)* stunning autumn color is possible even in warm-winter climates. These trees offer a whole palette of colors to choose from.

✔ **Colorful fruit.** Trees such as crab apples and hawthorns follow their blooms with colorful fruit, which can (if the birds don't eat it) hang on the tree into winter after the leaves have fallen.

Don't overlook trees that produce edible fruit when you're making your choices. Many fruit and nut trees are exceptional ornamentals and have the added bonus of bringing food to the table.

✔ **Attractive bark.** The white bark of birch trees is familiar to most people, but many other trees have handsome peeling or colorful bark.

Choosing the Right Tree

People who know trees like to say that there is no perfect tree, and they're right. You have so many trees to choose from that many of them can probably do the job for you. But as with people, every tree's personality has its good and bad aspects. Before you plant one, you need to learn everything you can about the tree, both the good and the bad. Most trees get big and live a long time (possibly longer than you), so if you make a mistake and plant the wrong one in the wrong place, it may be very costly to remove or replace. Removing it may even be dangerous to people and property. Figure 8-1 shows the general shapes that trees come in.

Get to know a tree before you commit to it.

✔ How fast does it grow?

✔ How tall and wide will it get?

✔ Is it adapted to your climate and the sun, soil, and water conditions at the proposed planting site?

✔ Does it have any common problems — invasive roots, weak limbs, insects, diseases?

✔ Does it need any special maintenance, such as pruning?

✔ How does the shape of the tree fit into your overall landscape?

✔ How messy is it? Does it drop excessive amounts of flowers, fruits, or leaves?

A local nursery is a good place to find out how a tree performs in your area; so are city or county parks departments. Extension offices can help you with information about trees; and parks and university campuses often have fine plantings to study. Botanical gardens and arboretums are especially good places to observe a wide variety of trees.

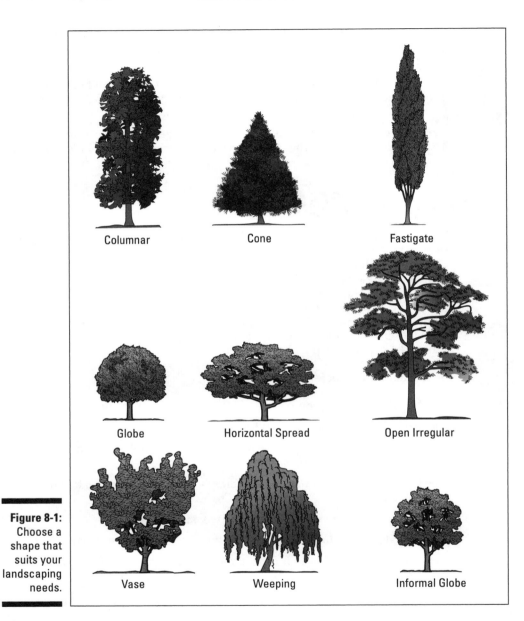

Columnar

Cone

Fastigate

Globe

Horizontal Spread

Open Irregular

Figure 8-1:
Choose a
shape that
suits your
landscaping
needs.

Vase

Weeping

Informal Globe

Contact your city or county planning or parks department before planting trees along streets. The officials there may have a list of suitable street trees — if they let you plant them at all. If you plant something not on their list, they may make you remove it.

To help get trees planted in the public areas of your community or in forests damaged by fire or abuse, contact Global ReLeaf, a campaign of *American Forests*. For $10, this organization will plant ten trees in your name and return a personalized certificate; call 800-873-5323 to order. For more information, write P.O. Box 2000, Washington, DC 20013; or call 202-667-3300, or visit their Web site at www.amfor.org/ on the Internet.

Don't Try This at Home

The following sections point out some things that you should *not* do when planting a tree, for practical and aesthetic reasons. (See Chapter 13 for more about planting trees.)

- ✔ **Planting too close to buildings.** Even smaller trees should be planted at least 10 feet away from the side of a house or building. Larger trees should be even farther away. Otherwise, the trees don't have room to spread and develop their natural shape. Also, aggressive roots can damage the foundation; falling limbs can damage the house.

- ✔ **Planting a tree that's too big at maturity.** Some trees can get huge — more than 100 feet tall and almost as wide. These trees belong in parks and open spaces where they can spread out. But even smaller trees can be too big for a planting site, eventually crowding houses or shading an entire yard. For example, horse chestnut and weeping willow can overwhelm a small garden in only a few years. Choose a tree that, when mature, will be in scale with your house and won't crowd out the rest of your garden. See Figure 8-2 for an illustration of how large some trees get at maturity.

Figure 8-2: Be sure to consider the mature height of the tree you plant.

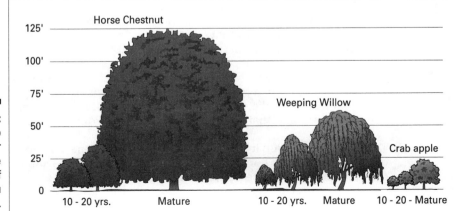

✔ **Don't plant trees where they will grow into power lines or utilities.** Pruning such trees is dangerous and costly and results in misshapen trees; and fallen limbs can cause power outages. Also, don't plant a big tree in a small yard. Not only will it look cramped, but branches overhanging the house and walkways can be hazardous.

✔ **Planting too close to paving.** Some trees are notorious for having shallow roots that, as they grow, buckle sidewalks and raise patios. Actually, almost any tree, especially larger species, will cause problems if planted too close to paving. Leave at least 3 or 4 feet (1–1.2 m) between the trunk and the paving. If you live where trees require watering to supplement rainfall, apply water slowly and for long periods so that it can soak deeply into the soil. This practice encourages roots to grow deep and not near the surface.

✔ **Planting a messy tree in the wrong place.** All trees shed some leaves at one time or another, but certain species are messier than others. Don't plant trees that drop wet fruit or excessive flowers near patios or sidewalks. They not only make a mess (and more work for you) but can also make the surface slippery, causing a passerby to fall.

✔ **Planting too many fast-growing trees.** Fast-growing trees are valuable for providing quick shade, but they are often also weak-wooded and short-lived. Consider planting a mixture of slow- and fast-growing types and then removing the less desirable trees when the slower ones reach functional size.

Our Favorite Trees

We divided the following lists of trees into two main groups: *deciduous* and *evergreen*. Evergreen trees include both conifers, such as pine and fir, and broadleaf evergreens, such as the Southern magnolia. To make your final choice, you need more information than we can provide here — see Appendix A for gardening books that discuss trees; or consult the experts at nurseries that specialize in trees (see Appendix B.)

Unlike *deciduous* trees, *evergreen* trees retain their leaves for more than one growing season. Which type of tree is the first decision you need to make. Then you have to make sure the tree you plant will survive year to year where you live, and that raises the question of hardiness zones.

To see what zone you live in refer to the USDA Hardiness Zone maps in the color section of this book. To learn more about your zone and how to best use zone information, see Chapter 2.

GOOD ADVICE

Choosing a healthy tree at the nursery

The easiest way to have tree problems down the road is to purchase and plant one that's unhealthy to begin with. Here are some tips for buying a healthy tree:

✔ Avoid trees that have been in a nursery container for too long or are unhealthy and growing poorly — they'll probably be disappointing once in the ground.

Examine the top of the root ball. Avoid specimens that have large, circling roots near the surface, a sign the tree has been in the container too long.

✔ Avoid trees that are the smallest or largest of a group. Select ones that are well proportioned from top to bottom.

✔ Select trees that can stand on their own without being tightly tied to a stake. (Tightly tied stakes can be like crutches, preventing a tree from developing a strong trunk).

✔ Ideally, pick a tree that has an evenly tapered trunk from bottom to top.

✔ Look for healthy, even-colored foliage.

✔ Pick a tree that's free of insects and disease. (See Chapter 16 for more about common pests and diseases.)

Crisp air, squirrels hunting for acorns, and the crunch of leaves underfoot . . . that's autumn! Here's our list of favorite deciduous trees.

✔ **Maple.** *Acer* species. Maples are a large group that includes many trees known primarily for their wonderful autumn color. Most are hardy through at least zone 5. Three of the most popular maples are the sugar maple (*A. saccharum,* zones 4–8), silver maple (*A. saccharinum,* zones 3–7), and Norway maple (*A. platanoides,* zones 4–7).

Most maples perform poorly in areas with very mild winters or hot, dry summers, including large, upright species like the red maple, *A. rubrum* (zones 3–9) which can reach up to 50 feet (15 m) high, and some very useful smaller types, like the spreading Japanese maple, *A. palmatum* (zones vary, usually 5–8).

The Japanese maple is one of the most popular small trees (ranging from 5 to 25 feet (1.5–7.5 m) high, depending on the variety). It comes in dramatic weeping forms with finely cut leaves and bright autumn color, mostly in shades of red, orange, and yellow. Some varieties, like 'Bloodgood', have purplish leaves the entire growing season. In hot, dry-summer areas, Japanese maples are best planted in partial shade.

✔ **European white birch.** *Betula pendula.* Loved for its papery white bark, the European white birch has multiple trunks and yellow autumn color. The tree is hardy in zones 2–7, but is often grown in zones 8 and 9 as well. Avoid planting were summers are hot and dry, or where birch borers are prevalent. Call your extension office or local nursery to find out about birch borers.

✔ **Redbud.** *Cercis canadensis,* the eastern redbud, is the most popular type. It reaches 20–30 feet (6–9 m) high and spreads almost as wide. Hardy from zones 5 to 9. 'Alba' has white flowers; 'Forest Pansy' has maroon foliage. (For hardy zone 4 trees check with your nursery to be sure plants are northern-grown from northern seeds.)

✔ **Flowering dogwood.** *Cornus florida.* The key attributes are deep-red autumn color and large white or pink midspring flowers followed by bright-red fruit. This is a fine small (20–30 feet) tree. Hardy in zones 6–9, (zone 5 if grown from northern seeds). Flowering dogwood is not well adapted to hot, dry climates but often can grow successfully in partial shade. Anthracnose and borers can be serious problems. Hybrids 'Aurora', 'Galaxy', 'Constellation', and 'Stellar Pink' are less prone to anthracnose disease.

✔ **Hawthorn.** *Crataegus* species. These small trees (most are 20–25 feet, or 6–7.5 meters high) offer a long season of color: white, pink, or red flowers in midspring, bright-orange-to-red fruit in autumn and winter, and usually orange-to-red autumn leaf color. Hardiness varies by species, but many are hardy in zones 4–8. Fireblight and rust can be a serious problem.

✔ **Russian olive.** *Elaeagnus angustifolia.* This tough, single- or multitrunked tree has narrow, silvery leaves. Spring flowers are fragrant but not showy and develop into small, yellow fruit. Russian olives form an excellent hedge or screen in difficult, dry situations but can be weedy where summers are wet. Grows 30–35 feet (9–10.6 m). Hardy through zone 2.

✔ **Ash.** *Fraxinus* species. These are mostly large, spreading-to-upright trees, with many reaching well over 50 feet (15 m) high. They're good, fast-growing, tough shade trees that can thrive under a variety of conditions. Most grow throughout zones 4 through 9. Many have excellent autumn color. Though ash trees have many virtues, a variety of pests and problems, such as anthracnose disease and borers, plague them. The best advice is to only plant named varieties, which in most every case are an improvement over unnamed, seedling trees.

Our favorite ash tree for home gardeners is the smaller size Raywood ash, *Fraxinus oxycarpa* 'Raywood'. It is a full-size (30–40 feet, or 9–12 m) but not huge tree, and its leaves turn a striking purple color in autumn. It's hardy in zones 5 through 9.

✔ **Crape myrtle.** *Lagerstroemia indica.* Crape myrtles are beautiful, summer-blooming, small trees (usually 10–20 feet, or 3–6 m, high but can also be grown as a multitrunked shrub, especially in cold winter areas where often dies back to the ground). Hardy in zones 7–9. (Gardeners in zone 6 sometimes grow crape myrtle as a shrub that dies to the ground each winter.) The flowers are huge, crinkly, and crepelike, in shades of white, pink, red, and purple. Crape myrtles also have shiny, peeling brown bark and orange-red autumn color. The tree grows best in areas with hot, dry summers. Elsewhere, plant mildew-resistant varieties, which usually have Native American names, such as 'Cherokee' and 'Catawba'.

✔ **Sweet Gum.** *Liquidambar styraciflua.* Tall (40–50 feet, or 12–15 m, and higher), narrowly upright trees put on bright autumn colors, in shades of yellow, orange, red, or purple. Some are multicolored. Named varieties, such as 'Cherokee', 'Gold Dust', and 'Palo Alto' differ in autumn colors. Sweet gums also have interesting seedpods, which can be messy. Hardy in zones 5–9.

✔ **Magnolia.** *Magnolia* species. The deciduous magnolias bloom stunningly on bare branches in early spring. Flowers are huge, often more than 10 inches (25 cm) across, and come in shades of white, pink, and purple. Some are bicolored. The leaves are large and leathery. Magnolia trees usually grow 15–25 feet (4.5–7.5 m) high, and are often multitrunked. They are hardy and grow well throughout zone 5 (sometimes zone 4) up to zone 9. One of the best types is the saucer magnolia, *M. soulangiana*, which bears large, cup-shaped flowers, usually white on the inside, purplish on the outside. 'Big Pink', 'Lennei', and 'Rustica Rubra' are good named varieties.

✔ **Flowering crab apples.** *Malus* species. Crab apples differ from apples in that the fruit measures less than 2 inches (5 cm) in diameter. You have many species and varieties to choose from, ranging in tree size and shape. Spring flowers come in white, pink, or red. Colorful red, orange, or yellow edible fruit often hang on the bare branches into winter. Most are hardy through at least zone 4 (some varieties can be grown into zone 3 and further north) and grow best where winters are cold. Subject to severe diseases, including fireblight, powdery mildew, and scab (see Chapter 16). Ask for disease-resistant varieties such as 'David', 'Dolgo', 'Donald Wyman', Sargent crab apple *(M. sargentii)*, *M. sieboldii zumi* 'Calocarpa', 'Prairiefire', and 'Professor Sprenger'.

✔ **Chinese pistache.** *Pistacia chinensis.* This wonderful, spreading shade tree develops stunning yellow, orange, or red autumn color. The tree grows 30–35 feet (9–10.6 m) high, has divided leaves, and is hardy in zones 7–9. It is drought tolerant.

- ✔ **Flowering fruit.** *Prunus* species. The large family of early spring-blooming trees includes flowering cherries and plums. Flowers are usually fragrant and come in shades of white, pink, or red. Most are hardy in zones 5–9 and range in height from 15 to 20 feet (4.5–6 m). Favorite fruitless types include Kwanzan flowering cherry, and *P. serrulata* 'Kwanzan', with drooping clusters of double pink flowers. Another favorite is Newport purple-leaf plum, *P. cerasifera* 'Newport', which has pink flowers and reddish-purple leaves. All the purple-leafed plums are subject to a variety of pests and are best considered short-lived trees.

- ✔ **Ornamental pear.** *Pyrus calleryana.* The best known and most widely planted of this group is 'Bradford', followed perhaps by 'Aristocrat'. These and all varieties have white flowers in early spring. Shiny green leaves turn bright orange, red to purple in cold-winter climates. Height is 35–45 feet (9–13.7 m). 'Bradford' is a good tree but has been overplanted and tends to split catastrophically. Other good varieties include 'Aristocrat', 'Capital' (very narrow and upright), 'Earlyred', and 'Redspire'. All are hardy in zones 5–9.

- ✔ **Oaks.** *Quercus.* This is an extensive family of varied trees, many of them very large and suitable for open areas only. Some have good autumn color. Natives — such as the red oak, *Q. rubra* (zones 3–8) in the eastern United States, and the English oak, *Q. robur* (zones 4–8), throughout western Europe. However, many species are widely adapted. (See also "Oaks" in the following list of evergreen trees.)

And here are our favorite evergreen trees. First on the list are conifers (needlelike leaves). The rest are all broad-leafed evergreens.

- ✔ **Conifers.** The pines, junipers, spruces, firs, hemlocks, and cedars are a diverse group of evergreens, most with needlelike leaves. They are widely grown throughout the world and are especially valuable for year-round greenery and as windbreaks and screens. Most are large trees and need room to grow, but many dwarf forms are available. The overall pyramidal appearance of these varieties is often similar, but foliage density, color, and texture varies. Adaptation also varies. Check with a local nursery for species adapted to your climate.

- ✔ **Camphor.** *Cinnamomum camphora.* Light green, aromatic leaves form dense foliage on this tree. Camphors grow 40–50 feet (12–15 m) high with a round head. Hardy in zones 8–11. The tree withstands drought, and has aggressive surface roots.

- ✔ **Eucalyptus.** *Eucalyptus* species. This large group of fast-growing, mostly drought-tolerant plants are native to Australia. Most are valued in dry-summer and mild-winter climates; few can be grown north of zone 8. Some are too large for home landscapes. All have heavily aromatic leaves. Many have very colorful flowers and interesting seed capsules.

Home landscape scale eucalyptus include Nichol's willow-leaf pepper-mint, *E. nicholii* (zones 8–10). It grows to about 40 feet (12 meters) high, but with languid branchlets that droop like those of a willow tree. Interestingly, its leaves are peppermint-scented. Another is the coolibah, *E. microtheca* (zones 8–10), also reaching about 40 feet (12 m) high, with one trunk or several and "willowy" blue foliage.

✔ **Southern magnolia.** *Magnolia grandiflora.* Huge (up to 12 inches, or 30.5 cm, across), fragrant, white summer flowers held among bold, deep green leaves make this tree one of the all-time favorite evergreen trees for mild-winter climates. The trees get large, upwards of 80 feet (24 m) high. Dwarf varieties, such as 'Saint Mary', grow a quarter to a third as high. 'Bracken's Brown Beauty' grows to about 40 feet (12 m) and is slightly more cold tolerant than the typical zones 6–10.

✔ **Evergreen pear.** *Pyrus kawakamii.* By virtue of both size and habit, this tree adapts well to most home gardens. Its mature height of 15–25 feet (4.5–7.5 m) is convenient, and its root system permits many other plants to grow nearby. Leaves are shiny and bright green. White flowers come in spring. It is hardy in zones 8–10, but will drop its leaves (which often turn a beautiful red before falling) in the coldest areas. Grows 15–25 feet (4.5–7.5 m) high with a wide-spreading canopy.

✔ **Oaks.** *Quercus* species. As for the deciduous oaks, there are many evergreen kinds, most of which get quite large and spreading. Widely adapted species include the southern live oak, *Q. virginiana* (zones 8–10), which grows 40–60 feet (12–18 m) high, is wide spreading. Another one is the holly oak, *Q. ilex* (zones 8–9), which reaches 20–35 feet (6–10.6 m) high. In mild-winter regions, the cork oak, *Q. suber* (zones 8–10), may be a good choice. In California, the coast live oak, *Q. agrifolia* (zones 9 and 10), is widely planted.

Rub-a-Dub-Dub, What's a Shrub?

Both versatile and hardworking, shrubs are the backbone of the landscape. They tie the garden together, bringing unity to all the different elements, from tall trees to low-growing ground covers.

The term *shrub* covers a wide variety of plants. They can be deciduous or evergreen, and they provide a variety of ornamental qualities, from seasonal flowers to colorful fruit to dazzling autumn foliage color. But equally impor-tant, shrubs offer diversity of foliage texture and color, from bold and dramatic to soft and diminutive. As the backbone of the landscape, shrubs are always visible, whether or not they're in bloom. So you should always consider the foliage and form of the plant when selecting shrubs and deciding how to use them.

Technically, a *shrub* is a woody plant that branches from its base. But that's actually too simple a definition. Shrubs can range from very low-growing, spreading plants that are ideal ground covers (see Chapter 9) to tall, billowy plants that you can prune into multitrunked trees. In general, shrubs cover themselves with foliage from top to bottom. Try to pigeonhole all shrubs into an absolute size range, and you run into many exceptions. For our purposes, most shrubs range from 1–15 feet (30.5 cm–4.5 m).

What Shrubs Can Do for You

Like trees, shrubs are large and long-lived plants, so it is essential to select ones that can thrive in your region and at your specific site. Consider the advice offered in Chapter 2 regarding climate and hardiness and also be mindful of soil types and quantity of light or shade.

So many shrubs are available that you are sure to find several that can thrive no matter what the condition of the soil is in your garden. However, if you make even modest improvements in your soil, such as improving the drainage of heavy soils or the moisture retention of sandy soils, adjusting pH, or increasing the fertility of poor soils, the number of shrubs that can grow well dramatically increases. You can read more about improving your soil in Chapter 11.

You can buy shrubs in containers, bare-root, or balled-and-burlapped. The majority of shrubs sold in the United States are in containers. Examine the container-grown shrub carefully to be sure it is not damaged. Slide out the root ball — this is easy to do if the shrub is in a plastic pot. Look for young, white roots — these are essential for efficient uptake of water and nutrients. Older, darker roots function primarily to stabilize the plant. See the section on choosing container-grown trees and shrubs in Chapter 13 for more information.

Design considerations

Shrubs serve so many functions in gardens that categorizing them is useful. As you consider your garden design, use these following categories to understand how to best use shrubs.

   ✔ **Foundation plantings.** Traditionally, one of the most common uses of evergreen shrubs is to plant them around the base of a house to conceal the foundation and to soften the transition between the lawn and the building. This use of shrubs also gives the landscape winter appeal.

However, using too many of one species of plant leads to monotony and an unnatural look. Try mixing groups of plants with different sizes and textures. And don't plant too closely to the house. Bring the plantings out some distance to gain a smoother transition and to give the shrubs more growing room.

✔ **Unity.** Repeating small groupings of plants in different parts of a landscape ties everything together and gives the yard a feeling of order and purpose. Similarly, shrubs serve well when planted among shorter-lived perennials in border plantings. Because shrubs are usually larger and more substantial, they provide a foundation for the more extravagant perennials and a structure for the garden when the perennials are dormant. For more about perennials, see Chapter 5.

✔ **Accent.** Some shrubs, such as azaleas and rhododendrons, are spectacular bloomers. Others have stunning berries or autumn color. Just a plant or two in a special place can light up a whole yard. And don't forget the foliage — a bold hydrangea with large leaves can make a stunning statement among plants with smaller leaves, like azaleas.

As you select shrubs for your garden, be sure to note the season of the shrub's peak interest. For example, many shrubs produce flowers in early spring, but others — such as several of the hollies — are showy in winter, particularly against a backdrop of snow. By mixing shrubs with different seasons of peak interest, you can be sure to have plants worth admiring in your garden any time of the year.

✔ **Hedges, screens, and ground covers.** Many types of shrubs can form hedges or screens when you plant them close together and maintain them as such. For example, you can clip some shrubs, including boxwoods and euonymus, into the rigid shape of a formal hedge to give a garden a very organized look. Let other types grow naturally to create screens for privacy. Many prostrate (low-growing) shrubs make excellent ground covers. For more information about ground covers, see Chapter 9.

✔ **Background and barriers.** Shrubs can be the perfect backdrop for flower beds. A consistent, deep green background is one of the best ways to highlight blooming plants. If you want to keep pets (or people) out of a certain area, plant a line of thorny pyracantha or barberry. These interlopers will get the "point."

Organizing shrubs by height

When planting a mixture of different shrubs or when planting shrubs with other plants (such as flowering perennials), consider the mature height of the shrub. You can follow the old gardening axiom: Place low growers in front, medium-sized plants in the middle, and tall plants in back. With that approach, nothing gets blocked out and you can see all the plants.

Height also determines which shrubs you use for hedges and screens. The following chart lists shrubs according to common name and size — small (1–5 feet high), medium (6–10 feet high), and large (over 10 feet high). Many names appear in two or more categories because many types of shrubs include species or varieties of varying heights. Use this list to get you to the right type of shrub and then read on to find the one that grows to an appropriate height. You should also know that mature heights of plants are, at best, only generalizations. Plants often grow taller in areas with long, warm growing seasons than they do in areas with short summers.

Small	Medium	Large
Glossy abelia	Glossy abelia	Cotoneaster
Barberry	Barberry	Euonymus
Boxwood	Butterfly bush	Holly
Camellia	Camellia	Juniper
Rockrose	Flowering quince	Oleander
Gardenia	Cotoneaster	Photinia
Holly	Euonymus	Indian hawthorn
Juniper	Forsythia	Rhododendron
Heavenly bamboo	Hydrangea	Flowering fruit
Bush cinquefoil	Holly	Lilac
Hydrangea	Juniper	Viburnum
Indian hawthorn	Oleander	
Azalea	Photinia	
Rose	Tobira	
Mugho pine	Flowering fruit	
Spiraea	Firethorn	
	Indian hawthorn	
	Rhododendron	
	Rose	
	Spiraea	
	Lilac	
	Viburnum	

Our Favorite Shrubs

The following shrubs are just about foolproof. All are widely available, and most are broadly adapted. Regarding specific soil needs, please refer to Chapter 11 to see how to adjust soil as needed for certain plants. Likewise, see Chapter 16 to read more about the pests to which some shrubs are prone. For more about hardiness zones, see Chapter 2 and the color maps that show USDA Hardiness Zones.

We organize our favorite shrubs by botanical name; however, we list the common name first.

- **Glossy abelia.** *Abelia grandiflora.* Evergreen. This handsome, arching plant has bright green, glossy foliage. New growth is bronzy red. Leaves turn reddish purple in winter. Small, fragrant, white flowers appear in summer. The glossy abelia loses its leaves in colder areas and can be grown as a hedge. Plant in full sun or light shade. Hardy in zones 6–9.

- **Barberries.** *Berberis* species. Evergreen and deciduous. These shrubs are known for their thorny stems, red berries, and tough constitution. Some have showy yellow flowers and colorful foliage. Upright-growing barberries make excellent hedges and barriers. The deciduous Japanese barberry, *B. thunbergii,* is generally 4–6 feet (1.2–1.8 m) high with arching stems. However, you have many varieties from which to choose, varying in height and foliage color. Most have good autumn color. 'Atropurpurea' has reddish-purple foliage during the growing season. It is hardy in zones 4 –9 (zone 8 in the eastern United States). Evergreen barberries include *B. mentorensis,* a compact, dense plant growing 6–7 feet (1.8–2.1 m) high. It is hardy in zones 5–8. Most barberries can grow in sun or partial shade and thrive under a variety of growing conditions.

- **Butterfly bush.** *Buddleia davidii.* Deciduous. The much loved, summer flowering shrub has long, arching clusters of lightly fragrant flowers that attract butterflies. Most varieties bloom in shades of purple, but you can often find selections with pink or white flowers. Buddleias grow very fast, reaching up to 10 feet (3 m) high in areas with long summers. Cut back severely in winter to keep the plant compact and attractive. Plant in full sun. Hardy in zones 5–9.

- **Boxwoods.** *Buxus* species. Evergreen. The boxwood is one of the finest plants for a tightly clipped, formal hedge. Small, dark green leaves densely cover the branches. The Japanese boxwood, *B. microphylla japonica* (zones 6–9), is one of the most popular types. Unpruned, it grows to about 4–6 feet (1.2–1.8 m) high. 'Winter Gem' and 'Green Beauty' are two varieties that stay bright green all winter. Others pick up a brownish tinge. Grow in full sun to partial shade. The English boxwood, *B. sempervirens* (zones 5–8) is the classic boxwood of the mid-South. Many named varieties are available.

✔ **Camellias.** *Camellia* species. Evergreen. With its glossy, deep green leaves and perfectly formed flowers, camellias are one of the finest shrubs for shady conditions. Flowers come in shades of red, pink, and white, with some bicolors. Most types bloom in winter and early spring.

The Japanese camellia, *C. japonica* (zones 8–10), is most commonly grown, usually reaching 6–12 feet (1.8–3.6 m) high. Many hundreds of varieties are available, varying by color and flower form. A few of our favorites include 'Alba Plena' (white), 'Bernice Boddy' (light pink), 'Debutante' (light pink), and 'Nuccio's Pearl' (white with pink).

Sasanqua camellias, *C. sasanqua* (zones 8–10), has smaller leaves and earlier flowers (often in autumn). They range from small shrubs to more spreading, vinelike plants. 'Mine-No-Yuki' (white), 'Setsugekka' (pink), and 'Yuletide' (red) are favorites.

Most cold hardy types, through zone 6, are *C. oleifera* hybrids. Named varieties include 'Winter's Beauty', 'Winter's Interlude', 'Winter's Star', and 'Winter's Waterlily'.

✔ **Flowering quince.** *Chaenomeles.* Deciduous. Among the first shrubs to bloom in early spring, flowering quince are tough, reliable plants that never let you down. The flowers are borne on bare stems in shades of mostly red and pink, but also white. Plants range in size and shape depending on variety, but generally grow 5–10 feet high, are upright and have thorny branches. You can clip flowering quince as a hedge, and they usually look best with regular pruning. Bring cut branches indoors in late winter to force into early bloom. Many named varieties are available, differing mostly in flower color. Plant in full sun. Hardy in zones 5–9.

✔ **Rockroses.** *Cistus* species. Evergreen. Particularly well-adapted to dry summer climates, such as in the western United States, rockroses are tough, colorful plants that can get by on little water. Several species and hybrids are available. Most grow between 3 and 6 feet (1–1.8 m) high and bloom in late spring to early summer. The round, silky blooms are 1–2 inches (2.5–5 cm) wide, come in shades of white, red, and pink, and are often spotted or marked. Foliage is gray-green. Plant in full sun. Hardy in zones 8–10.

✔ **Cotoneaster.** *Cotoneaster* species. Evergreen and deciduous. You can choose from many types, which range from low-growing ground covers to tall, upright shrubs. Most share a profusion of white spring flowers followed by red berries and are tough, widely adapted plants. Deciduous kinds often have good autumn color. Taller types include the evergreen Parney cotoneaster, *C. lacteus* (zones 6–9), which reaches about 8 feet (2.4 m) high and equally as wide. Deciduous *C. divaricatus* (zones 4–7) has stiff, arching branches to 6 feet (1.8 m) high and bears a heavy crop of berries.

Plant in full sun. Fireblight disease can be a problem. Ground-cover types of cotoneaster are described in Chapter 9.

✔ **Euonymus.** *Euonymus* species. Evergreen and deciduous. Euonymus are workhorse foliage plants. Deciduous kinds, such as winged euonymus, *E. alata,* are hardy in zones 4–8 and often have stunning red autumn color. The European spindle tree, *E. europaea* (zones 4–7) grows to about 20 feet (6 m) high and produces attractive red berries in autumn.

Evergreen euonymus, such as *E. japonica* (zones 7–9) and *E. fortunei* (zones 5–9) come in numerous named varieties: 'Silver King' (white with green) and 'Aureo-variegata' (yellow with green), are very popular. They range in height from 6 to 20 feet and make fine hedges. Plant euonymus in sun or light shade. *E. japonica* is susceptible to powdery mildew and scale.

✔ **Gardenia.** *Gardenia jasminoides.* Evergreen. Intensely fragrant, pure-white summer flowers and beautiful deep green leaves make gardenias a favorite shrub wherever they can grow. Plants usually grow 3–6 feet high and must have acid soil and consistent moisture. Plant in full sun in cool climates, partial shade in warmer areas. 'Mystery' is a popular, large-flowered variety. Hardy in zones 8–10.

✔ **Hydrangea.** *Hydrangea* species. Deciduous. The big, bold leaves and huge summer flowers of these unique plants put on a great show in shady gardens. The bigleaf hydrangea, *H. macrophylla,* is most commonly grown. Flower clusters are up to a foot across and are white or light to deep blue in acid soil, pink to red in alkaline soil. Plants usually grow 4–8 feet high and must be pruned heavily to encourage compactness and heavy bloom. Hardy in zones 6–9.

Smooth hydrangea *(H. arborescens)* 'Annabelle', hardy in zones 4–9, has large, 1-foot wide (30.5 cm), white flowers.

The most cold hardy is the peegee hydrangea, *H. paniculata.* Hardy in zones 3–8, it grows 10–20 feet (3–6 m) high and produces large flower clusters in the fall. Compared to the species, *H. p.* 'Tardiva' blooms as late as September.

The oakleaf hydrangea, *H. quercifolia,* grows in zones 5–9 and is notable for fall color. Several varieties, such as 'Snowflake' and 'Snow Queen' are available.

✔ **Hollies.** *Ilex* species. There are many kinds of hollies and all are notable for the red berries they produce in fall. Because holly plants are either male or female, both types must be present in order for female plants to produce berries.

Hollies are deciduous or evergreen. Grow deciduous kinds, such as common winterberry *(I. verticillata)* if you live in zones 3–8. A good, compact hedge variety is the 3–5-foot (1–1.5 m) 'Red Sprite'; pollinate it with 'Jim Dandy'. Other good dedicuous hollies are hybrids 'Sparkleberry' and 'Harvest Red' (pollinate either with 'Apollo'). These become 10-foot (3 m) or taller plants and are hardy only through zone 5.

Evergreen hollies are notable for their bright-red berries and clean-looking, spiny, often multicolored leaves. Many make excellent hedges. Most familiar is the English holly, *Ilex aquifolium.* It generally grows 15–25 feet (4.5–6 m) high but can get larger; hardy in zones 7–10. Varieties such as 'Argenteo-marginata', with leaves of diverse shades of white, make excellent accents. Other popular types include the compact 'Burfordii' and 'Dazzler', varieties of *I. cornuta;* hardy in zones 7–9. They grow 8–10 feet (2.4–3 m) high.

'Nellie Stevens' is a hybrid that grows at least 15 feet (4.5 m) high. Hardy in zones 6–9, it's a good choice for the southern tier of the United States.

The Meserve hybrid hollies *(I. meserveae)* include some the hardiest evergreen types. Examples are 'Blue Girl' and 'China Girl' (use male-named counterparts as pollinators). They're hardy in zones 5–8.

✔ **Junipers.** *Juniperus* species. Evergreen. The low- and wide-spreading growth pattern of most junipers makes them most useful as ground covers and are hardy through zone 3 or 4. (See Chapter 9.) However, many more upright, shrubby types exist, including forms of the Chinese juniper, *J. chinensis,* such as 'Pfitzerana' and 'Torulosa'. Very columnar varieties are also available, such as 'Wintergreen' and 'Spartan'. Plant in full sun. Hardiness varies; most are reliable in zones 4–9.

✔ **Heavenly bamboo.** *Nandina domestica.* Evergreen. Light and airy in appearance, heavenly bamboo has divided leaves and straight, erect stems of a small bamboo. However, it is much more ornamental. New growth is bronzy red when the plant is grown in full sun. The entire plant turns red in winter. White spring flowers turn into bright red berries. Grows 6–8 feet high, but many dwarf forms are available. Hardy in zones 7–10.

✔ **Oleander.** *Nerium oleander.* Evergreen. Oleander is a tough plant that puts on an incredibly long show of color throughout summer and into autumn. The flowers are borne in large clusters in shades of white, pink, and red. The plants are low maintenance and thrive in hot summers. Oleanders are densely foliaged and generally grow 10–20 feet (3–6 m) high but can be kept lower with annual pruning. You can also choose dwarf varieties. Plant in full sun. Hardy in zones 8–10.

Oleander is one of the few common (in zones 8 through 10 especially) shrubs that is genuinely toxic. The toxin is contained in all parts — leaves, stems, flowers, and seeds. Wear gloves and goggles when pruning them, and don't burn prunings because the smoke is toxic as well.

✔ **Photinia.** *Photinia* species. Mostly evergreen. Photinia encompasses several species of useful shrubs that show bronzy-red new growth in spring followed shortly by clusters of small, white flowers and often black or red berries. *P. fraseri,* which reaches 10–15 feet (3–4.5 m) high, is popular because of its resistance to powdery mildew, but it does not have berries. Japanese photinia, *P. glabra*, is slightly lower growing and has red berries that gradually turn black. Plant photinias in full sun. They are hardy in zones 7–10.

✔ **Mugho pine.** *Pinus mugo.* Evergreen. This neat, compact pine rarely exceeds 4–8 feet (1.2–2.4 m) in height. Mugho pines are easy to care for as a specimen or in group plantings. Plant in full sun. Hardy in zones 3–7.

✔ **Tobira.** *Pittosporum tobira.* Evergreen. Tobira is a handsome, well-behaved shrub with glossy deep-green leaves and clusters of white, fragrant spring flowers. The species is rounded and can reach over 10 feet (3 m) high but easily can be kept lower with pruning. The variety 'Wheeler's Dwarf' grows into a neat, mound-shaped plant only 2 feet (61 cm) high. 'Variegata' has light gray-green leaves edged with white; it grows 5–10 feet (1.5–3 m) high. Plant in full sun to light shade. Hardy in zones 8–10.

✔ **Bush cinquefoil.** *Potentilla fruticosa.* Deciduous. Particularly valuable in cold-winter climates, bush cinquefoil is a handsome little shrub with bright green, fine-textured foliage and colorful, wild-roselike blossoms. Plants bloom from late spring into autumn in shades of red, yellow, orange, and white. Yellow varieties, such as 'Katherine Dykes', are most popular. Heights range from just under 2 feet (61 cm) up to 5 feet (1.5 m). Plant in full sun. Hardy in zones 2–6.

✔ **Flowering fruit.** *Prunus* species. Evergreen or deciduous. Many valuable shrubs belong to this large family of plants, which includes some of our most popular fruit, such as peaches and plums. Carolina cherry laurel, *(P. caroliniana)*, English laurel *(P. laurocerasus)*, and Portugal laurel *(P. lusitanica)* are evergreen with white spring flowers, handsome foliage, and tall stature (20 feet, or 6 meters, high or more). They are useful as tall screens, but their smaller varieties are more appropriate for most landscapes. For example, 'Bright 'n' Tight' is the dwarf form of Carolina cherry laurel that reaches about 10 feet (3 m) high. 'Zabeliana' is a fine-leafed form only 6 feet (1.8 m) high. 'Otto Luyken' is a small version of English laurel that grows to only 6 feet (1.8 m) high. Evergreen flowering fruit plants are generally hardy in zones 8–9 and grow best in full sun.

The purple-leafed sand cherry, *P. cistena*, is a very hardy deciduous flowering fruit tree. It makes white spring flowers, purple leaves, and produces small edible plums. The sand cherry grows to about 10 feet (3 m) high and is hardy in zones 3–7.

The Nanking cherry, *P. tomentosa*, grows about 10 feet (3 m) high and spreads to about 15 feet (4.5 m). White flowers appear very early in spring and are followed in fall by scarlet fruits. Hardy in zones 3–7.

Dwarf flowering almond, *P. gladulosa*, is a small flowering shrub that grows 4–6 feet (1.2–1.8 m) high and is hardy in zones 4–8. Plant it in full sun.

✔ **Firethorn.** *Pyracantha* species. Evergreen. Colorful and dependable, firethorn comes in a wide range of forms, from low-growing ground covers (see Chapter 9) to upright, spreading shrubs. All cover themselves with clusters of small, white flowers in spring followed by showy, orange-to-red berries that last into autumn and winter. Branches are sharply thorned. Popular types include the very hardy *P. coccinea* 'Lalandei', which grows 8–10 feet (2.4–3 m) high and has orange berries. Fireblight can be a serious problem; hybrids 'Mojave' and 'Teton' are fireblight-resistant. They grow to about 12 feet (3.6 m) high, with orange-red and yellow-orange berries, respectively. Plant firethorn in full sun. Most are hardy in zones 6–9; a few are cold hardy through zone 5 or 6.

✔ **Indian hawthorn.** *Rhaphiolepis indica.* Evergreen. It's hard to go wrong with Indian hawthorn. Compact and carefree, the plants bloom profusely from late winter into spring. The pink-to-white flowers develop into blackish-blue berries. New growth is tinged bronze. Plants generally grow to 3–6 feet (1–1.8 m) high. *R.* hybrid 'Majestic Beauty' is taller than the species, growing up to 15 feet (4.5 m) high, and has large leaves. Plant Indian hawthorn in full sun. Hardy in zones 7–10.

✔ **Azaleas and rhododendrons.** *Rhododendron* species. Evergreen and deciduous. This is a huge family of much-loved flowering shrubs. You can choose from many types, but all grow best in acid soil. Most prefer moist, shady conditions and soil rich in organic matter. Some can take full sun. Hardiness varies.

Azaleas are generally lower-growing, compact plants that cover themselves with brightly colored spring flowers in shades of pink, red, orange, yellow, purple, and white. Some are bicolored. Favorite evergreen types include Belgian Indicas, Kurumes, and Southern Indicas. Deciduous kinds include Knapp Hill-Exbury Hybrids, Mollis Hybrids, and the very hardy Northern Lights Hybrids.

Rhododendrons are usually taller with larger flower clusters. They come in basically the same color range but are not as well adapted to hot-summer climates as are azaleas.

Rhododendrons include some of the most cold-hardy evergreen shrubs, a few of which tolerate zone 4 winters. Deciduous azaleas share the rhododendron's cold tolerance. The Northern Lights series is also hardy through zone 4. Evergreen azaleas are much less tolerant of cold. Belgian Indicas are hardy through zone 9 and Kurumes through zone 8.

✔ **Roses.** *Rosa* species. Deciduous. Many roses are outstanding landscape shrubs. Among the best are the hardy rugosa roses, which are notable for the "quilted" look of their leaves. They flower in spring and produce large, edible rose hips in autumn. There are so many roses for so many garden situations, we've set aside an entire chapter for them (the one just before this one), Chapter 7.

Shrubs for multi-season color

If it's color you're after, certain shrubs provide it in abundance through a combination of flowers, fruit, and fall color. In other words, these are shrubs that provide more than one season of color. Here are some of our favorites:

- **Azalea.** Flowers, fall color

- **Barberry.** Flowers, fruit, fall color, colorful foliage

- **Cotoneaster.** Flowers, fruit, fall color

- **Euonymus.** Fruit, fall color, colorful foliage

- **Firethorn.** Flowers, fruit

- **Flowering fruit.** Flowers, colorful foliage

- **Heavenly bamboo.** Flowers, fruit, colorful foliage

- **Holly.** Berries, colorful foliage

- **Hydrangea.** Flowers, colorful foliage

- **Photinia.** Flowers, colorful foliage

- **Roses.** Flowers, fruit

- **Spirea.** Flowers, fall color

- **Tobira.** Flowers, colorful foliage

- **Viburnum.** Flowers, fall color, fruit, colorful foliage

- **Spiraea.** *Spiraea* species. Deciduous. You have many types of spiraeas to choose from. Many are mounding, fountainlike shrubs with an abundance of tiny, white flowers in mid-spring to late spring. Included among these is the bridal wreath spiraea, *S. vanhouttei,* which grows to about 6 feet (1.8 m) high and at least 8 feet (2.4 m) wide. Its small, dark green leaves turn red in autumn. Other spiraeas, like *S. bumalda* 'Anthony Waterer', have clusters of pink-to-red blooms later in summer. Plant spiraeas in full sun. Hardiness varies, but most grow in zones 3–8.

- **Common lilac.** *Syringa vulgaris.* Deciduous. Wonderfully fragrant clusters of spring flowers make lilacs a favorite wherever they grow. Most bloom in spring in shades of lavender and purple, but some are white or rosy pink. Plants usually grow 8–15 feet (2.4–4.5 m) high and have dark green leaves. Plant in full sun. Powdery mildew can be a problem. Lilacs grow best where winters are cold; they're hardy in zones 3–7.

- **Viburnum.** *Viburnum* species. The viburnums represent a large family of evergreen and deciduous shrubs that are wonderful additions to the landscape. They offer great variety of form and function, and their ornamental characteristics include colorful flowers, brightly colored berries, and, often, autumn color. Favorite evergreen types include the neat-growing *V. tinus,* which grows 10–12 feet (3–3.6 m) high and has pink-to-white spring flowers followed by metallic-blue berries. The variety 'Variegatum' has leaves colored with white and creamy yellow. 'Compactum' is lower growing than is typical for the species. All make good unpruned hedges and are hardy through zone 7.

Choices among deciduous types include the Korean spice viburnum, *V. carlesii,* which has very fragrant clusters of white flowers in spring followed by blue-black berries. Leaves turn red in autumn. Plants grow about 8 feet (2.4 m) high, spreading just about as wide. The horizontal-branching *V. plicatum* is also distinctive, with rows of white spring flowers and red autumn color. It grows about 15 feet (4.5 m) high.

Plant viburnums in full sun or partial shade. Hardiness varies. Some deciduous kinds are reliably cold hardy through zone 3; most grow in zones 5–9.

Drought-tolerant shrubs

Many of the shrubs listed in this chapter — such as junipers, cotoneaster, oleander, rock-rose, and Indian hawthorn — can withstand periods of drought, which are common in dry summer areas like parts of the southwestern United States. However, many other plants are also well-adapted to such conditions and are particularly well suited for dry climates. Following are a few popular drought-resistant plants.

✔ **Manzanita, or bearberry.** *Arctostaphylos* species. This varied group of plants, native to western states, includes trees, shrubs, and ground covers. Handsome shiny bark, small pink-to-white flowers.

✔ **Cassia.** *Cassia* species. These Australian natives are particularly well-adapted to desert climates. Attractive foliage and yellow flowers.

✔ **Wild lilac.** *Ceanothus* species. The evergreen shrubs and ground covers have dark green foliage and mostly blue spring flowers. Native to western states.

✔ **Hop bush.** *Dodonea viscosa.* The tough, fast growing, evergreen shrub has narrow leaves. With growth up to 12–15 feet (3.6–4.5 m) high, it makes a good screen. 'Purpurea' has brownish-green leaves.

✔ **Toyon.** *Heteromeles arbutifolia.* Native to California, this evergreen has shiny, dark green leaves, white flowers, and bright red berries. Grows 15–25 feet (4.5–7.5 m) high.

✔ **Lavender.** *Lavandula* species. This attractive, tough family of evergreen herbs has fragrant blue flowers and gray-green leaves.

✔ **Mahonia.** *Mahonia* species. Mahonia is an evergreen with spiny leaves and yellow flowers. It performs well in the shade. Grows 5–12 feet (1.5–3.6 m) high.

✔ **Rosemary.** *Rosmarinus* species. This upright to spreading, evergreen herb has blue, white, or pink flowers and aromatic foliage. Some varieties are excellent ground covers.

✔ **Germander.** *Teucrium* species. Germander is an evergreen shrub with colorful flowers and attractive, dense foliage.

Chapter 9

Lawns and Ground Covers

. . . .

In This Chapter

▶ Deciding on size and grass variety

▶ Planting seeds

▶ Planting sod

▶ Taking care of your lawn

▶ Considering the virtues of ground covers

▶ Choosing the right ground cover

. . . .

*F*or most people, a landscape isn't complete without at least some lawn. The lush color and smooth, uniform look are a practical and attractive way to complement your homes, trees, shrubs, and other plantings. It's tough to beat a grassy area as a place for family and pets to relax and play. Many grasses can handle heavy foot traffic, and some even thrive in moderately shady areas; so lawns solve certain landscaping problems.

The utility of a well-kept lawn is undeniable. That's why for decades, putting in a lawn was the first thing that people did when they bought a new home. But recently, many people have started to question the amount of time, money, and resources that lawns demand. You should do the same as you decide on the type and size of lawn you want — or if you even want a lawn.

If foot traffic is not an issue, you may decide to plant ground covers instead of a traditional lawn. Ground covers can offer your landscape a natural look and are relatively low maintenance. The selection of good ground cover plants is so broad that you can find several to fit any landscape situation and climate.

Lawn Decisions

Putting in a lawn is a lot of work. There's soil preparation, perhaps installing a permanent, underground irrigation system, and the actual planting. But the sweating doesn't stop there — you must maintain it year after year. A lawn also uses resources — water, fertilizer, and pesticides — that may be in short supply in some areas or can be sources of pollution if not used correctly.

Do a little homework before you run down to the local garden center and purchase 50 pounds (23 kilograms) of seed. First, figure out how much space you need for a lawn. Then determine which type of grass does best in your area. After this research, you're ready to plant and you have more choices — mainly whether to plant from seed or sod.

How big?

If you have a newly built home and you're starting from scratch with the landscaping, think seriously about how much weekend time you want to spend pushing the lawn mower (or sitting on the riding mower) and the appropriate water use for your part of the country. You also want to think about the costs of water, irrigation system, fertilizer, and things like paying someone to mow and maintain your grass.

The one easiest way to save money in the long run is to plan for and plant a smaller lawn. For instance if you have about 1,000 square feet (93 square meters) where you can plant a lawn, you can reduce long-term costs by 40 percent by planting only 600 square feet (56 square meters).

In dry-summer regions, such as the western United States, conserving water, a limited resource in many areas, is another factor to consider when deciding on the size of your lawn. In areas where water conservation is an issue, water agencies say that homes need only 600–800 square feet (56–74 square meters) of grass — enough for a small play area or lounging space.

Where summer rainfall is common and water conservation isn't a factor, an average lawn runs about 7,000–10,000 square feet (650–929 square meters). If your plans include lawn games like badminton or croquet, you need a rectangle measuring 45 x 80 feet (14 x 24 meters), or 3,600 square feet (334 square meters).

Which grass is for you?

Growing the appropriate variety of grass for your area is critical. Your decision makes all the difference between a thriving lawn and one that doesn't survive the winter or languishes in the heat of your climate.

Turfgrasses (grasses specially bred for use as a lawn) fall into two broad groups: cool-season and warm-season grasses. *Cool-season grasses* grow best between 60°F and 75°F (16°C and 24°C) and can withstand cold winters. Warm-season grasses grow vigorously in temperatures above 80°F (27°C); plant these grasses in mild-winter regions. In general terms, cool-season grasses are grown in zones 6 and colder; warm-season grasses are grown in zones 7 and warmer. (See the USDA Hardiness Zone maps in the color section of this book to determine which zone you live in.)

Each type of grass has its named varieties, many of which have been bred for improvements like tolerance of drought, shade, or sheer ruggedness. Your local extension office or garden center can recommend varieties for your area.

For much more detail about lawns and kinds of grasses, check out *Lawn Care For Dummies* by Lance Walheim and the Editors of The National Gardening Association (IDG Books Worldwide, Inc.).

You can start a new lawn several different ways: from seed, sod, plugs, or sprigs. Some types of grass are available only as sod, or as *plugs* (chunks of turf) or *sprigs* (single plants or stems) that are set into little holes in the soil. It can take a couple of years before grass plugs or sprigs completely fill the area and look like a real lawn. Keeping weeds out of the bare soil until the lawn fills in is critical.

Turfgrass short list

The following sections describe cool-season and warm-season turfgrasses. Use these descriptions to help you decide which type of grass is best for you.

Cool-season grasses

When most North Americans and Europeans picture a perfect lawn, they're seeing a cool-season lawn grass, particularly one that is predominantly Kentucky bluegrass. It stands to reason that Kentucky bluegrass and other cool-season grasses are the appearance standard, as these are the grasses that grow best in most of Europe and in the eastern and northern United States.

The peak growth seasons for cool-season grasses are spring and fall. The four kinds of cool-season turfgrass you should know are:

- **Fine fescue.** The *fine* in their name refers to their needlelike blades, so narrow and pointed that, if they were stiff enough, they'd serve as a sewing needle. There are various kinds of fine fescue: chewings, red, and hard fescue. All are quick to germinate and become established, and all grasses do well in less than ideal growing conditions. Fine fescues are the most shade-tolerant of the northern grasses, and they grow better than other cool-season grasses in the presence of many tree roots. Compared to other cool season grasses, they are drought-tolerant and require little fertilizer. Newer varieties offer insect resistance.

  Hard fescue makes a nearly ideal low maintenance lawn in northern, humid regions (such as the northeastern United States). Varieties like 'Biljart', 'Discover', 'Reliant II', and 'SR 3100' need mowing only twice a season. Their fertilizer needs are similarly minimal.

- **Kentucky bluegrass.** The most common lawn grass for cold-winter regions, this grass is relatively slow to form a turf, but once established, it spreads and fills in nicely. Its soft, fine texture and rich green color is the look most gardeners prefer. Kentucky bluegrass is very hardy and comes in many disease-resistant varieties, but it requires somewhat more fertilizer than many other grasses. A few of the current top-rated varieties of Kentucky bluegrass include 'America', 'Midnight', 'Nuglade', 'Odyssey', and 'Rugby II'.

  Varieties that combine natural Kentucky bluegrass good looks with more Spartan maintenance needs include: 'Bartitia', 'Belmont', 'Caliber', Colbalt', 'Challenger', 'Midnight', 'Monopoly', 'Ram-1', and 'Unique'.

- **Perennial ryegrass.** This is a fine-textured, fast-growing grass. It can produce a walkable, mowable turf in as little as one week. Compared to Kentucky bluegrass, it is not as cold hardy and it doesn't mow as cleanly. It is somewhat shade tolerant, but not as much as fine fescue. Newer varieties, such as 'Regal' and 'SR 4200', offer insect and disease resistance. 'Yorktown II', 'Manhattan II', 'Palmer II', and 'Fiesta II' have superior heat, shade, and cold tolerance.

- **Turf-type tall fescue.** Casual observers may have a hard time distinguishing this grass from rye or Kentucky bluegrass, but compared to both of these grasses, leaf blades of turf-type tall fescue are wider and its color is not quite as dark green. Because it can take more heat, this grass makes an attractive and practical lawn grass for zones 7 and 8 where Kentucky blue and fine fescues suffer in summer's heat. New varieties are resistant to everything: heat, drought, diseases, and insects. Look for 'Bonsai', 'Crewcut', 'Crossfire', 'Pixie', and 'Rebel Jr.'. 'Titan', 'Shenandoah', and 'Tribute' contain high levels of a natural pest repellent called *endophyte*.

Warm-season grasses

Warm-season grasses are pretty much the only grasses that grow in zones 10 and 11, and a few are common in zones 8 and 9. Most have wider, stiffer leaf blades. Aptly named, they love heat. In tropical, zone 11 climates, they grow pretty much year-round. In subtropical zones 9 and 10, their growth slows in fall and winter, picking up again in late spring. The seven warm-season grasses you're most likely to encounter are:

- ✔ **Bahia grass.** This low-growing, coarse-textured grass is not as attractive as some of the other warm-season grasses, but it requires little maintenance and grows in partial shade. Named varieties to look for include 'Argentine', 'Pensacolo', and 'Paraguay'.

- ✔ **Bermuda grass.** The most common lawn grass in mild-winter climates, Bermuda grass textures range from coarse to fine, depending on the variety. This rugged, drought-resistant grass spreads quickly and can crowd out weeds, but it needs frequent, close mowing. Some varieties offer disease and insect resistance. Grow common Bermuda grass from seed; varieties include 'Sundevil' and 'Yuma'. Start improved hybrids as sod or plugs (sections of sod). Golf green-perfect hybrids like 'Tifgreen' look great but are high maintenance. The most home-practical hybrid is 'Santa Ana'.

- ✔ **Buffalo grass.** A fine texture and curled, gray-green blades identify this grass. A heat- and drought-resistant Great Plains native, buffalo grass requires little mowing and little or no fertilization. Some varieties are available as seed; others come as sod only. 'Top Gun', 'Tatanka', and 'Plains' are top-rated seed varieties. 'Prairie' and '609' are sod only but are preferred for their superior appearance.

- ✔ **Centipede grass.** The original "lazy man's grass" of the southeastern United States, centipede grows slowly and needs little fertilizer. The texture of this grass is coarse to medium texture and it has flat, blunt blades. This low-maintenance, shade-tolerant grass does well in soils that are acidic or low in fertility. Centipede grass is somewhat resistant to disease. You can sow seeds of the preferred 'Centiseed' variety; or sprigs of 'Oaklawn'.

- ✔ **St. Augustine grass.** This coarse-textured grass tolerates partial shade. It's generally susceptible to insect and disease problems, but some improved varieties — notably 'Seville' and 'Floritam' — have come to market in the past few years. You can plant it from sod or sprigs.

- ✔ **Zoysia grass.** Stiff, narrow blades mark this coarsely textured grass. It grows slowly but is very tough once established. Zoysia is drought-resistant and shade-tolerant. The best varieties, such as 'De Anza', 'Diamond', 'El Toro', 'Emerald', and 'Victoria', are planted from sod only.

For the very latest information about top-performing grasses, check the Web site of the National Turfgrass Evaluation Program at hort.unl.edu/ntep/contents.htm. Two good Web sites for more information about lawns are the Turf Information Center at Michigan State University, www.lib.msu.edu/tgif/, and "Lawn Talk" from the Illinois Cooperative Extension Service at www.urbanext.uiuc.edu/lawntalk/.

Putting in a New Lawn

The most common and economical way to plant grass is by spreading seed. Proper soil preparation and follow-up care are the keys to success here.

The fastest way to put in a new lawn is by _laying sod_ — setting large sections of fully grown turf in place on the soil. The idea of an instant lawn certainly has its appeal; however, sod is an expensive option, and you still have to prepare the soil as thoroughly and maintain the newly planted area as carefully as you would for a lawn from seed.

The first step in preparing the area to be sown is to test your soil to see whether it's fertile and has the proper pH to grow grass. Turfgrasses prefer a nearly neutral soil pH of 6.5 to 7.5. If your soil is acidic, you may need to raise the pH by applying ground dolomitic limestone. To lower the pH of alkaline soil, you apply elemental sulfur. See Chapter 11 for more on testing soil and adjusting the pH. The results of your soil test will indicate how much of these soil amendments to use.

If you don't have reasonably fertile soil that can be worked to a depth of 6 to 8 inches (15 to 20 cm), you'll need to purchase a load of topsoil — rich soil that's high in organic matter.

Spread the topsoil smoothly over the area to be seeded, mixing some of it in with the native soil below to prevent a water barrier. Make the topsoil layer 1 inch (2.5 cm) below the final level of the lawn if installing sod or ¹/₂ inch (1 cm) below if sowing seed, and have it slope slightly away from the house for proper drainage.

Planting Lawn from Seed

The best time to seed a new lawn is just prior to the grass's season of most vigorous growth. For cool-season grasses, that means late summer to early fall. Early spring is the second-best time. The best time to start warm-season grasses is late spring.

Shopping for seed

Your lawn is a landscape feature that you'll have for years to come, so skip the cheap stuff. How do you recognize fine-quality seed? Look for the following on the label:

- A variety name, such as 'Nuglade' Kentucky bluegrass instead of generic Kentucky bluegrass

- Weed and other crop seed content of 0.5 percent or less; the highest-quality seed is free of weed and other undesirable crop seed

- *Germination percentage* (percentage of seeds in your bag that will sprout and begin to grow) of 85 percent or greater for Kentucky bluegrass and above 90 percent for all other grasses

How much seed to buy

To determine how much seed you need to purchase, start with a pretty close estimate of the size of the area you aim to plant. For example, a rectangular lawn that is 20 x 50 feet (6 x 15 m) is 1,000 square feet (93 square meters) in area. Most lawns aren't so convenient to measure, and if yours is one of these, don't worry. For one thing, your measurement needn't be precise. You can also measure the area by dividing it into separate, discrete shapes and then add them all together at the end.

Measure with your stride: An adult stride is usually around 3 feet (1 m). Measure yours with a yard stick until you know what a 3-foot (1 m) stride feels like before heading out onto your lawn. If your lawn measures in acres rather than feet, consider renting one of the distance-measuring tools available at local rental yards.

If you buy a seed mix for home lawns, the package label will most likely specify how much area the seed in the package will cover. If you aren't buying packaged seed, use the size of your area and Table 9-1 to figure out how much seed to buy.

Table 9-1	How Much Seed to Sow	
Grass Name	*Pounds of Seed/1,000 sq. ft.*	*Kilograms of seed/ 93 sq. m.*
Bahia	8 to 10	3$\frac{1}{2}$ to 4$\frac{1}{2}$ kg
Bermuda grass	2 to 3	1 to 1$\frac{1}{2}$ kg
Buffalo grass	2 to 3	1 to 1$\frac{1}{2}$ kg
Centipede	1 to 2	$\frac{1}{2}$ to 1 kg
Fine fescue	4 to 5	2 to 2$\frac{1}{4}$ kg

(continued)

Table 9-1 *(continued)*		
Grass Name	*Pounds of Seed/1,000 sq. ft.*	*Kilograms of Seed/ 93 sq. m.*
Kentucky bluegrass	1 to 2	$\frac{1}{2}$ to 1 kg
Perennial ryegrass	4 to 5	2 to $2\frac{1}{4}$ kg
Turf-type Tall fescue	6 to 10	$2\frac{1}{2}$ to $4\frac{1}{2}$ kg

Planting day

When you're ready to plant, assemble all the tools, materials, and equipment that you need, including:

- **Soil amendments.** These include the lime or sulfur that a soil test indicates is needed; also fertilizers and most significantly 2 to 3 inches (5 to 8 cm) of organic material (composted fir bark or similar) that is needed to improve soil structure.

- **Rototiller.** You need one of these to mix the amendments into the soil. Various machine sizes are available to rent.

- **Grass seed.** Refer to Table 9-1 to find out how much to sow.

- **Lawn spreader.** This tool scatters seed evenly as you roll it over the soil — also called a mechanical spreader.

- **Board scraper.** A board that you drag over the soil surface.

- **Rake.** You need a stiff-tined rake to level soil after tilling.

- **Lawn roller.** A large, heavy drum with a handle that you roll over the scattered seed to press it into the soil. You can fill the drum one-third to one-half full with water to increase the weight.

- **Mulching material.** Use straw or other organic material to lightly cover the seed and protect it from birds and to keep it moist.

If you don't own large tools, you can rent them for the day. When you have all your materials together, follow these steps:

1. **Spread any amendments required to correct the pH over the soil and apply a complete fertilizer recommended for new lawns. Follow the directions given on the fertilizer bag.**

   Chapter 11 has more information about soil and pH levels.

2. **Rotary-till the soil a few inches deep to loosen it.**

   Don't overcultivate — leave small lumps and cracks to catch seed so that it sprouts quickly. Remove stones and sticks.

3. Level the soil with a board scraper or rake.

Leveling the soil eliminates high spots where the mower would cut the grass too short, as well as depressions where it may miss spots or where water may collect.

4. Roll the seedbed with the empty roller to firm the soil as shown in Figure 9-1.

Make sure that the soil is dry before you roll; otherwise, it compacts, preventing seeds from sprouting.

5. Sow the seed as shown in Figure 9-2.

Don't be tempted to oversow; if you do, the plants won't develop properly. Although a mechanical spreader helps spread the seed uniformly, spreading seeds by hand is also practical, especially with larger seeds, such as ryes and fescues. Whichever way you spread the seed, coverage will be more even if you apply half the seed moving one direction across the lawn area, and the other half moving the opposite direction.

Figure 9-1:
Roll over tilled and raked soil to firm the planting surface before seeding.

Figure 9-2:
Spread
seed with
a drop
spreader or
with a
hand-held
broadcast
spreader.

6. **Rake the surface lightly, barely covering about half the seed and leaving the rest exposed.**

7. **Roll once more with the empty roller to press seeds in contact with the soil. (Refer to Figure 9-1.)**

8. **Lightly mulch the seedbed to cover and protect seeds and to keep the soil moist until the seeds germinate. (See Figure 9-3.)**

   The mulch keeps rain from washing the seeds away, provides protection from the drying sun, and prevents birds from getting a free meal.

9. **Give the newly seeded area a thorough initial soaking, shown in Figure 9-4, and then keep it well watered until the grass is established.**

   Water more deeply but less frequently as the grass becomes more established.

   Each watering should penetrate the soil to a depth of several inches to promote good root growth.

Figure 9-3:
Spread mulch to keep the soil moist.

Figure 9-4:
Give the newly seeded ground a good soaking.

Planting Lawn from Sod

Sod has two important advantages over seed: Climate permitting, you can plant a sod lawn almost any time of year, and the layer of sod covers and buries existing weeds in soil, which means you start out with a perfectly weed-free lawn.

In most areas you can plant sod just about any time of year, but your results are better if you plant at the ideal season: early fall or early spring for cool-season grasses, mid to late spring for warm-season types. But if you can water enough to keep a newly sodded lawn healthy through a summer drought or heat spell, you can plant anytime. In zones 9 through 11, you can also plant a sod lawn in the middle of winter.

Buying sod

Sod is expensive, so buy from a quality supplier. Look for sections that are about 1 inch (2–3 cm) thick , with no brown patches or dried-out edges. Have the sod delivered on planting day so that it doesn't sit in a pile and heat up (a stack of fresh sod will literally cook itself to death, just like a compost pile). And to help prevent drying out, keep the sod in a shady location until you plant it.

Laying sod

When you're ready to lay the sod, assemble all the tools and equipment that you need: soil amendments, rotary-tiller, board scraper or rake, and a lawn roller. Prepare the planting area as you would for a lawn from seed. (Check out Steps 1 through 3 in the "Planting day" section of this chapter.)

Next, follow these instructions for laying sod:

1. **Roll out a piece of sod and press it into position. Fit the next section against it tightly but don't overlap, as shown in Figure 9-5.**

2. **Continue laying sections, staggering them slightly like bricks.**

   Lay a board across the sod so that your feet don't break through the sod, as shown in Figure 9-6. Trim odd-shaped sections with a heavy utility knife, as shown in Figure 9-7, and fill gaps with small cut sections, as shown in Figure 9-8.

Figure 9-5:
Roll out sod so that pieces don't overlap.

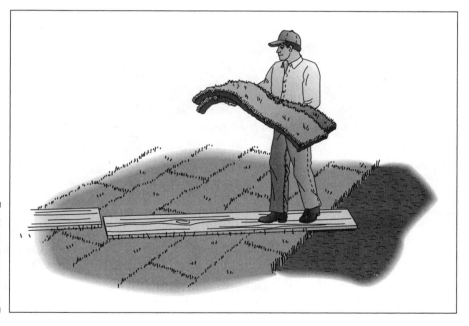

Figure 9-6:
Use walking boards to avoid damaging sod.

Figure 9-7:
Trim sod
with a
heavy knife
until it fits
curves, odd
shapes, and
around
obstacles.

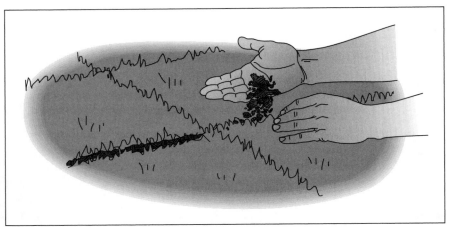

Figure 9-8:
Filling gaps
in sod.

3. Use a roller over the newly laid turf, as shown in Figure 9-9, going back over it a second time at right angles to the first pass.

4. Rake the new lawn lightly to lift up the flattened grass, and keep the soil moist until the sod is well established.

Figure 9-9:
Rolling the
sod with a
roller.

Planting Plugs and Sprigs

Prepare the planting area as you would for a lawn from seed. (See Steps 1 through 3 in the section "Planting day".) Then follow these instructions for planting plugs and sprigs:

1. **Dig holes 2 to 3 inches (5 to 7 cm) deep and 6 inches (15 cm) apart for zoysia grass or 12 inches (30 cm) apart for Bermuda grass.**

   Set the plugs or sprigs in place. Water well.

2. **Keep the bare soil weed free until the lawn is established.**

Care and Feeding of Lawns

It's no secret that your lawn requires some regular maintenance to keep it looking its best. Basic lawn care consists of weeding, mowing, and fertilizing. Take care of those things and you may avoid more complex chores like pest and disease control. The following sections give you some tips on performing the basic chores. For more advanced lawn maintenance techniques, check out *Lawn Care For Dummies* by Lance Walheim and the Editors of the National Gardening Association (IDG Books Worldwide).

Weeding

The best technique for keeping weeds under control in your lawn is to grow the right kind of grass and take good care of it. Weeds can't get established in a thick patch of healthy turf.

If you want to yank out the prime offenders, you can find tools for this purpose at most garden centers. But you don't need to be obsessive — a few weeds won't spoil the overall look or purpose of the lawn.

Garden centers offer an array of herbicides, sometimes mixed with fertilizers, that you can spray or spread over your lawn. We are not thrilled by most of these herbicides simply because they tend to wash off the lawn and make their way to streams, rivers, and lakes where they can cause harm. Our favorite is *corn gluten meal*. It may sound crazy, but this agricultural by-product is both an organic fertilizer and weed preventative. It won't kill existing weeds, but it will go a long way toward reducing the amount of crabgrass and other weeds in your lawn. See Chapter 16 for more about weeds and herbicides.

Mowing

The mowers available today make the inevitable task of mowing the lawn easier and more enjoyable. If you're in the market for a new mower, read about some of your options in Chapter 17.

Here are some tips to keep your grass healthy and well manicured:

✔ Keep cool-season grasses at a height of 2½ to 3 inches (6 to 7 cm). During the summer and for warm-season grasses, keep a height of 1 inch (2–3 cm). Cutting too short affects the roots in their search for nutrients in the soil and reduces the nutrients manufactured by the leaves.

✔ Mow when the grass is ⅓ higher than its recommended height. Letting the lawn grow long and then shortening it by half its height all at once weakens it.

✔ Mow when the grass is dry.

✔ Mow in a different direction each time — north-south one week, east-west the next. You can even mow at a diagonal. Changing the mowing pattern prevents soil compaction and helps the grass grow upright.

✔ Leave clippings in place as long as they aren't too long or piled up in small mounds — they add nitrogen to the soil as they break down.

Fertilizing

Fertilizing lawns has grown into a whole science, and you really don't need to know about it unless you're the head greenskeeper at Augusta — in which case, we're surprised and flattered that you're reading this book.

Remember that a well-fertilized lawn is healthier, denser, and more weed-free than a poorly managed one. Most grass varieties need regular fertilizing (except for the native grasses like buffalo grass, which require very little to no fertilizing).

When to fertilize depends on your type of grass. Grasses need nitrogen and other nutrients during their seasons of active growth; fertilizing grass when it's dormant is useless. The most important time to feed cool-season grasses is in the fall and sometimes in the winter (in milder climates). In mild-winter regions, fall fertilizing keeps a lawn greener into winter and also encourages stronger growth in the spring. In cold-winter regions, fall fertilizing promotes deeper rooting and greater tolerance of winter stress. Generally, the best time to fertilize warm-season grasses is from late spring to early fall.

For most lawns, choose a slow-release fertilizer with approximately a 3:1:2 or 4:1:2 ratio of N-P-K (the three prominent numbers on any bag of fertilizer). (See Chapter 14 for more information on fertilizer labels.) Good lawn fertilizers with 4:1:2 ratio include 16-4-8 and 32-8-16.

To know how much to apply, read the label directions. Most lawn fertilizer products specify exactly how much to apply, even how to adjust various commercial spreaders to apply the right amount.

Organic fertilizers and manures have advantages and disadvantages compared to commercial lawn fertilizers. Organics contain less nitrogen per pound, meaning that you need to apply more for your lawn to gain an equivalent benefit. You usually end up paying much more (per unit of nitrogen) and doing more muscle work to fertilize your lawn. On the other hand, organic fertilizers deliver a host of nutrients and benefits to soil that commercial fertilizers can't.

Most lawns need between 2 and 6 pounds (1–3 kg) of actual nitrogen per year for good growth.

For more detail about fertilizers, see Chapter 14.

Keep an eye on your soil pH and adjust it if necessary. (See the section on adjusting pH under "Before you plant" in this chapter.) The plants can't make use of fertilizer when they're growing in soils that are too acidic or too alkaline.

Tune-ups and face-lifts

You've got too many thin spots, weeds have gotten the upper hand, or the wrong type of grass is struggling to survive: What do you do? Relax — you probably don't have to tear out the whole thing and start over. As long as your lawn is at least 50 percent grass (as opposed to weeds), you can give it a face-lift by seeding an improved grass variety right on top. (The process is called *overseeding*.)

Overseed cool-season grasses in autumn and warm-season grasses in spring. Here's how:

1. **Mow your lawn closely and thoroughly rake out the mat of dead grass and stems called *thatch*.**

   Loosen compacted soil with a *coring machine*, a piece of power equipment that cuts out small plugs of soil to improve air and water circulation around the grass roots and also gets rid of some of the thatch.

2. **Adjust the soil pH if necessary and fertilize.**

3. **Sow seed at the rate recommended on the package, or see the table in this chapter "How much seed to sow."**

4. **Sprinkle a light layer of mulch over the lawn (called *topdressing*) and water thoroughly.**

Winter overseeding

If you live in zones 9 to 11 — the region turf experts call the "transition" zone — you likely have a warm-season grass lawn that goes dormant in winter. Yet there's no snow to cover it up. The grass just sits there, brown, for the four or five months until spring unless you "overseed" it, and that's exactly the common practice for many gardeners in mild-winter regions.

Most often, you overseed Bermuda grass in winter when it would otherwise turn brown. You can have a green lawn by overseeding with a cool-season grass, such as annual or perennial ryegrass, that grows during the winter. The following summer, this cool-season grass will be the one to go dormant.

In the autumn, before the permanent lawn goes dormant, mow it about $1/2$- to 1- inch (1.2–2.5 cm) high and rake it thoroughly. Your lawn may be so thick with *thatch* (the mat of clippings, roots, and stems that accumulates on top of the soil) that your mower won't cut into it. If so, rent a machine called a *power rake* — like a lawn mower with vertical blades that comb out heavy thatch as they slice into the soil. Overseed with $1^1/2$ times the amount recommended on the package. After the Bermuda grass goes dormant, mow at a height of 3 (7.5 cm) inches through the winter.

Ground Covers instead of Lawns

Perhaps you don't want a lawn, maybe you have an area too shady for grass, or maybe you want something in addition to lawn: You may be considering a lawn alternative for one of many reasons. That's where ground covers come in. *Ground covers* (low-growing, spreading plants) come in hundreds, maybe thousands, of varieties, and they fill in enough to give solid coverage when planted close together. Some ground covers are less demanding than lawns, but others aren't as tough or as forgiving as a lawn. And rarely can you walk or play on a ground cover like you can a lawn.

Ground covers range from very low-growing plants that are just a few inches high to more shrubby types that are several feet high. Some of the lowest-growing ground covers, such as chamomile and creeping thyme, can take a little foot traffic; you can plant these types between stepping-stones or in other areas where people occasionally walk.

Ground covers have an artistic side, too. You can create a nearly infinite variety of contrasts with ground covers, and you can mix in other shrubs, vines, annuals, and perennials for a variety of effects. Foliage textures can range from grassy to tropically bold, and colors can range from subtle shades of gray to vibrant seasonal colors. Ground covers provide a naturalistic appearance, so look to the local wild areas for ideas. Choose plants that mimic what you see in wooded areas, in unmown fields, in meadows, or on steep slopes.

Planting Ground Covers

Plants sold as ground covers usually come in small nursery containers or in nursery flats, depending on their growth habits. Those ground-cover plants that are grown in flats are cut into individual sections before planting.

The spacing between ground covers is very important. If you space the ground-cover plants too far apart, they take a long time to fill in, which gives weeds more time to gain a foothold. If you plant them too close together, the plants may quickly become overcrowded. Recommended plant spacings are included in the plant descriptions given later in this chapter. For best results, plant ground covers in rows, as shown in Figure 9-10. Staggering the rows gives even more complete coverage.

If you're planting your ground covers from containers, you can place the plants into individual holes. To plant small plants from pots or packs, dig a hole just deep enough for the root ball. For larger, container-grown plants, taper the hole outward at the base and create a mound for the root ball.

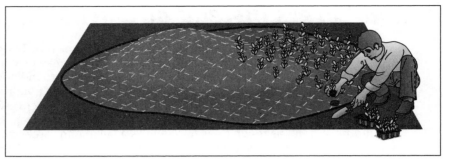

Figure 9-10:
Plant rows
of ground-
cover
seedlings
to achieve
maximum
coverage.

If starting from flats, prepare the whole planting area as if you were planting a lawn (see "Planting day" earlier in this chapter). As with all plantings, you need to attend to soil needs (see Chapter 11) before introducing your plants to your landscape. Newly set out plants need adequate watering to help get them established; after the plants are growing well, many types need only minimum maintenance.

If you're planting a ground-cover plant on a steep slope, set the plant on its own terrace (with the top of the root ball slightly above the soil level) and provide a watering basin behind the plant.

Control weeds between plants until the ground cover is established. We like to use an organic mulch or, for shrubby ground covers, landscape fabric (see Chapter 16) to control weeds. One advantage of organic mulches is that they also protect the plants in winter.

An occasional shearing can rejuvenate or freshen up many spreading, nonwoody ground covers such as English ivy, St. John's-wort, and vinca. (Shearing also prompts various suburban critters like roof rats and voles that have set up housekeeping in your ground cover to promptly relocate!) Cut the plants back to just several inches above the ground in spring and then fertilize them. Within a few weeks, the plants will regrow and look full, clean, and healthy.

If you have a lawn or weed mower that you can set to cut high enough, use it to shear and rejuvenate your ground cover.

Top Ground-Cover Choices

Although the number of possible candidates is nearly infinite, the following common ground-cover plants have proven themselves in a multitude of situations and environments.

- ✔ **Woolly yarrow.** *Achillea tomentosa.* This tough, spreading, evergreen ground cover reaches 6–9 inches (15–23 cm) high. Small yellow flower clusters top its ferny, gray-green leaves in summer. Woolly yarrow can take some foot traffic but also can be invasive. Plant 6–9 inches (15–23 cm) apart in full sun. Hardy in zones 4–10.

- ✔ **African daisies.** The group of fairly similar, spreading, evergreen plants produces daisylike flowers. Widely grown as ground covers in mild-winter climates, they are generally hardy in zones 9–11. Favorite choices include the trailing African daisy *(Osteospermum),* with white-to-purple spring flowers on 1- to 3-foot-high (30–90 cm) plants (depending on the species) and gazanias *(Gazania)* with sunny summer flowers in single and multicolored shades of white, red, pink, yellow, and orange borne on 6- to 12-inch-high (15–30 cm) clumping or trailing plants. Plant 1–2 feet (30–60 cm) apart in full sun.

- ✔ **Carpet bugle.** *Ajuga reptans.* Evergreen. This plant forms a low-growing, spreading ground cover with attractive dark green or purplish-green foliage reaching 2–6 inches (5–15 cm) high. Carpet bugle has blue flowers in summer. Plant in partial to full shade (some types with colored foliage can take more sun), 6–12 inches (15–30 cm) apart. Hardy in zones 4–9.

- ✔ **Kinnikinnick.** *Arctostaphylos uva-ursi.* Several selections of this hardy, evergreen shrubby plant make excellent ground covers. It features shiny green foliage. The plants' small, urn-shaped, white spring flowers produce red berries. 'Point Reyes' and 'Radiant' are two fine choices and generally stay below 12 inches (30 cm) high. Plant in full sun about 3 feet (90 cm) apart. Hardy in zones 2–6 (in some regions, through zone 8).

- ✔ **Barberries.** *Berberis.* Several types of barberries make excellent ground covers. One of the most popular is the deciduous *B. thunbergii* 'Crimson Pygmy'. This variety grows to about 18 inches (46 cm) high, has purplish-red foliage (when grown in full sun), bright-red autumn color, and red berries. As a ground cover, plant 'Crimson Pygmy' 15 to 18 inches (38–46 cm) apart. Hardy in zones 4–8.

- ✔ **Chamomile.** *Chamaemelum nobile.* Chamomile's fine-textured, aromatic evergreen foliage can take some foot traffic. The plant has small yellow flowers in summer. Chamomile stays low and compact in full sun, rarely getting over 6 inches (15 cm) high; plants grow taller in partial shade. You can mow chamomile or plant it between stepping-stones. Plant in full sun, spacing plants about 6 to 12 inches (15–30 cm) apart. Hardy zones 4–9.

- ✔ **Cotoneasters.** *Cotoneaster.* Deciduous or evergreen. Cotoneasters are a large family of shrubs that includes many dependable ground covers known for their bright-green foliage, small flowers, and red berries. Favorites include the evergreen bearberry cotoneaster, *C. dammeri* (which grows only 8 inches, or 20 cm, high and spreads up to 10 feet, or 3 m; zones 5–8), the deciduous rock cotoneaster, *C. horizontalis* (which grows 2–3 feet, or 60–90 cm, high and has orange-to-red autumn color, zones 5–7), and the evergreen rockspray cotoneaster, *C. microphyllus* (which rarely exceeds 2–3 feet, or 60–90 cm, in height, zones 5–7). Hardiness is a good guide, but most of these will grow in zones 8 and 9 in the less humid regions. Check with your local nursery. Plant at least 3 feet (90 cm) apart in full sun. (Some of the widest-spreading types should be spaced 5 feet, or 1.5 m, apart.)

✔ **Winter creeper.** *Euonymus fortunei.* This very hardy, evergreen plant comes in many fine ground-cover varieties. 'Colorata', the purpleleaf winter creeper, has bright green foliage that turns purple in autumn and winter. 'Colorata' grows about 2 feet (61 cm) high . 'Ivory Jade' has green leaves edged with white and also grows about 2 feet (60 cm) high. 'Kewensis' grows only 2 inches (5 cm) high and makes a very dense ground cover. Plant winter creeper in full sun, spacing the plants from 1 to 3 feet (30–90 cm) apart. Most grow well throughout zones 5–9, and in zone 4 with a good snow cover.

✔ **Blue fescue.** *Festuca glauca.* Silver-blue foliage highlights this mounding, grassy ground cover. It grows 4 to 10 inches (10–25 cm) high and gets by on little water. Plant in full sun, spacing the plants 6 to 12 (15–30 cm) inches apart. Grow in zones 4–9.

✔ **English ivy.** *Hedera helix.* With its dark green, lobed leaves, English ivy is one of the most popular ground covers. This evergreen grows well under many conditions, including sun or shade. Many varieties (differing in leaf size, texture, and color) are available. English ivy can be invasive, climbing into trees and over structures if not kept under control. Space plants 12 to 18 inches (30–45 cm) apart. Hardy in zones 6–10, occasionally through zone 5.

✔ **Aaron's-beard; Creeping St. John's-wort.** *Hypericum calycinum.* These adaptable, evergreen ground covers thrive under a variety of conditions. They grow 12 inches (30 cm) high and have bright-yellow flowers in summer. The plants spread rapidly and can be invasive. They prefer full sun but will take partial shade. Space the plants 12 to 18 inches (30–45 cm) apart. Hardy in zones 5–9.

✔ **Ice plants.** Many different, trailing, succulent ice plants are useful ground covers in mild-winter climates, especially in arid areas. Two popular blooming types are rosea ice plant, *Drosanthemum floribundum,* which grows to about 6 inches (15 cm) high and has pink flowers in spring and summer; and trailing ice plant, *Lampranthus spectabilis,* which grows 12–15 inches (30–38 cm) high, covering itself with pink, red, or purple flowers in spring. Plant these evergreens in full sun, spacing them 12–18 inches (30–46 cm) apart. Most are hardy in zones 9–10.

✔ **Junipers.** *Juniperus.* Many prostrate junipers (differing in height and foliage color) are available. Junipers are tough, evergreen plants that get by with little care but must have well-drained soil. *J. chinensis* 'San Jose' has grayish-green leaves and grows 2 feet (60 cm) high. *J. horizontalis* 'Bar Harbor' grows about 1 foot (30 cm) high and spreads up to 10 feet (3 m); the gray-green leaves turn bluish in winter. *J. h.* 'Wiltonii' is only 6 inches (15 cm) high and has silver-blue foliage. Plant junipers in full sun. Most should be spaced 2 to 5 feet (60–1.5 m) apart, depending on the variety. Hardy in zones 3–9.

✔ **Mondo grass or lily turf.** *Liriope* or *Ophiopogon.* Mondo grass and lily turf are two similar, grasslike plants that make attractive evergreen ground covers in shady situations. *Liriope spicata,* creeping lily turf, is one of the most adaptable, growing 6 to 10 inches (15–25 cm) high. *L. muscari* grows up to 2 feet (60 cm) high and has blue summer flowers that are partially hidden by the foliage. Some varieties have variegated leaves. *Ophiopogon japonicus* is a common mondo grass with dark green leaves; the plants grow 8 to 10 inches (20–25 cm) high. Space these plants 6 to 18 inches (15–45 cm) apart, depending on height. The hardiness of both species varies, but most can be grown in zones 5–10.

✔ **Japanese spurge.** *Pachysandra terminalis.* Japanese spurge is an attractive spreading, foliage plant for shady, moist conditions. This evergreen features rich green leaves on upright 10-inch (25 cm) stems, with fragrant white flowers in summer. Plant in partial to full shade and space them 6 to 12 inches (15–30 cm) apart. Hardy in zones 4–9.

✔ **Spring cinquefoil.** *Potentilla neumanniana* (alternatively *P. tabernaemontanii* or *P. verna*). This evergreen plant's dark green, divided leaves form a soft-textured cover 3 to 6 inches (8–15 cm) high. It has small clusters of yellow flowers in spring and summer and can take some foot traffic. Plant in full sun to partial shade and space the plants 10 to 12 inches (25–30 cm) apart. Hardy in zones 4–9.

✔ **Creeping thyme.** *Thymus praecox arcticus.* This low-growing, creeping evergreen herb is especially useful between stepping-stones. It can take foot traffic and can even be grown as a lawn alternative. Creeping thyme grows 3 to 6 inches (8–15 cm) high and has white-to-pink flowers in summer. Plant in full sun and space the plants 6 to 10 inches (15–25 cm) apart. Hardy in zones 4–10.

✔ **Star jasmine.** *Trachelospermum jasminoides.* The evergreen, spreading, vining plant has shiny green foliage and fragrant white flowers in spring. It grows to about 18 inches (45 cm) high when left to sprawl. Confederate vine, *T. asiaticum,* is similar but grows slightly lower, has dull green leaves, and bears yellowish-white flowers. Plant in full sun and space the plants 2 to 3 feet (60–90 cm) apart. Hardy in zones 8–10.

✔ **Dwarf periwinkle.** *Vinca minor*. This spreading, deep green ground cover is good for shady conditions. The evergreen grows from 6 to 12 inches (15–30 cm) high and has violet-blue flowers in spring and summer. It can be invasive. Space the plants 6 to 8 inches (15–20 cm) apart. Hardy in zones 4–9.

Over in the Meadow

One trend in lawn alternatives is the new interest in using native grasses and other low-growing, prairie-type plants. These plants create meadowlike landscapes that can be beautiful year-round.

Native grasses are superbly adapted to their native ranges and are often well adapted to other areas, too. Native grasses can survive on less water than traditional lawn grasses and can be left unmown (or mown infrequently) and therefore are low maintenance. Common types of native grasses include wheat grass (a very drought-tolerant native grass of the Rocky Mountains), blue grama grass, and buffalo grass, both native to the Great Plains. Certain wildflower mixes composed of low-growing plants can also be used for meadowlike lawns. Meadow lawns are less formal-looking than most grass lawns but can be walked or played on and have a wild beauty all their own.

Chapter 10

Vines

● ●

In This Chapter

▶ Understanding how vines work . . . and work for you

▶ Getting to know some vine do's and don'ts

▶ Providing necessary support

▶ Looking at our favorite vines

▶ Exploring a few annual vines

● ●

*V*ines can be a garden's beautiful prima donnas — think morning glory in full bloom — or a gardener's nightmare — think of that same morning glory smothering your backyard shed.

Vines can do some amazing things: cool a blazing hot patio, beautify a blank wall, or create privacy with a wall of foliage. You should become acquainted with them — for their beauty and for their usefulness.

In this chapter, we help you understand how vines work and how to put them to work for, not against, you. Then, we share some of our favorite vines — permanent types as well as fast-growing annuals.

Let's Play Twister

Vines need to grow on something, either another plant or a trellis that you provide. Before deciding what kind of support to provide for your favorite climbers, you need to know exactly how the climbers hold on. Vines fall into several groups, according to the way they climb, as shown in Figure 10-1.

   ✔ **Clinging vines.** Examples are English ivy and Boston ivy. These vines have specialized growths — like little suction cups or claws — along their stems that can hook onto any surface they touch.

✔ **Sprawling vines.** An example is a climbing rose. These vines are often just very vigorous, spreading plants. In order for them to climb, you need to tie them to a trellis or support.

✔ **Twining vines.** These vines come in two types. Some, like star jasmine, wrap around anything that falls in their way. Others, like grapes, have small, twining *tendrils* at the bases of their leaves. The tendrils grab and wrap around anything they can reach.

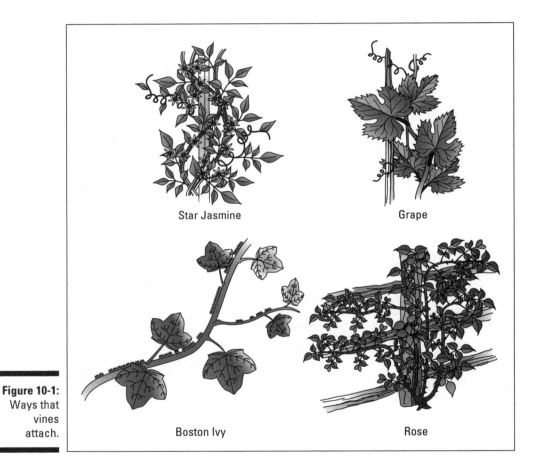

Star Jasmine

Grape

Figure 10-1:
Ways that
vines
attach.

Boston Ivy

Rose

Using Vines Effectively

Like other plant groups, vines offer a variety of ornamental characteristics, including seasonal flower color, bright berries, and autumn color. Because most grow vertically, you can use them in tight spots where few other plants would fit. And they are versatile — vines can create privacy, provide shade, and conceal unattractive landscape features.

Because of their hasty growth rate and the way they attach to structures, some vines can cause problems as they mature. The following sections give you tips on avoiding problems with vines.

Don't let vines grow where they shouldn't

Clinging vines, such as English ivy and Virginia creeper, can attach so firmly to walls and fences that getting them off without damaging the structure becomes almost impossible. And sometimes the attaching parts of the plant work their way into cracks and crevices. As the vines enlarge and grow, they can lift shingles and damage even the sturdiest materials, such as concrete and brick.

Letting a vine attach directly to the walls of your house usually isn't a good idea, unless the house is made of brick, or stone — and the type of vine also makes a difference. And even then you can have problems. Instead, build a trellis a few feet away from the side of the house and let the trellis support the vine. That way, you can also paint the wall if you need to.

Don't let vines climb into the tops of trees. The vigorous vine almost always compromises the health of the tree, covering its canopy and shading its foliage. You can allow some deciduous vines, such as clematis, to grow into trees. Their delicate, open habit seldom harms the other plant.

Provide sturdy support

As vines grow, the branches enlarge, and the plant gets heavier. If the supports aren't strong enough, they can buckle under the weight. Build supports that are sturdy and long-lasting. Two-inch galvanized pipe and pressure-treated 4 x 4 (90 x 90 mm) lumber are both good choices. (See the section "Choosing a Vine Support" later in this chapter for more information.)

Prune for healthy vines

Pruning prevents vines from getting out of control, becoming too heavy, or growing into places where they're not wanted. Prune with vigor to keep the vine healthy and attractive. (For more information on pruning, see Chapter 15.)

Winter is a traditional time for pruning, but you can prune in any season to keep a rampant vine in check. Prune flowering vines, such as wisteria, immediately after the plants drop their blooms. The best time to do your major pruning of vigorous-growing fruiting plants, such as grapes and kiwi, is during their dormant season (winter). But you can nip back plants of any kind whenever they begin to grow out of the bounds that you set for them.

Lean on Me

You have many ways to support a vine, from arbors to lath trellises to wires strung between secure anchors. The important thing is to plan the supporting device in advance, make it strong, and design it to fit the growth habit of the vine.

Heavy fences or the walls of outbuildings are another place to plant climbers, and these supports require little work from you. And then there is the whole world of trellises, arbors, and other special supports for vines.

Although the chief purpose of supports is to hold up climbing plants, trellises and their kin also add height to the garden and maximize ground space. These structures can be decorative, as well as practical, when they turn a plain wall into a vertical garden, frame a view, or create a privacy screen.

The most important guideline for choosing a structure is that it be large and sturdy enough to support the plant when fully grown. Choose a simple garden structure that harmonizes with your home and existing garden features. And remember that some climbing plants naturally cling to their supports, but others must be trained and tied.

Recycled nylon hosiery, cut into strips, is one of the very best materials for tying plants to their supports. Nylons are strong, yet stretchy, so they don't bind and cut plant stems.

Choosing a Vine Support

You can grow most types of vines on one or more of the supports described here. (The exception is vines with adhesive disks, which grow best on stone or brick walls.) When choosing a structure for your garden, first consider the type of plant that you are growing and how it will fit and look on the structure. After that, your choice is a matter of personal taste, maintenance considerations, and budget. (See Figure 10-2.)

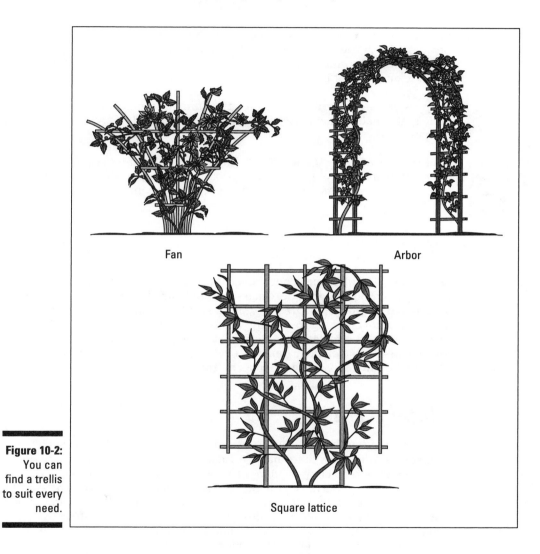

Fan

Arbor

Square lattice

Figure 10-2:
You can find a trellis to suit every need.

Bamboo teepees

Perhaps you remember bamboo teepees from your childhood. Bamboo teepees have long been popular in vegetable gardens for supporting climbing green beans. Teepees are quick and easy to make, and you can reuse the bamboo stakes for many garden seasons.

To make a teepee, arrange three or four 12-foot (3.7 m) bamboo stakes around a 3–4 foot (1–1.2 m) circle. Space the stakes at least 18 inches (46 cm) apart. Push each stake into the ground at least 12 inches (30 cm) deep. Lash the top of the stakes together with twine.

Plant beans (or other annual climbers) at the base of each stake. As the beans start to grow, direct them up the stakes; once started, the plants don't need additional training or tying. At the end of the season, clean off the bamboo and store it indoors.

Teepees can serve double-duty when they provide support for climbers and create shade beneath for plants, such as lettuce, that prefer cooler temperatures.

Mini-teepees of $\frac{1}{4}$- or $\frac{1}{2}$-inch (0.5–1 cm) diameter bamboo canes (often dyed green and sold at garden centers) are useful supports for annual climbers in containers. Try planting sweet peas or climbing nasturtiums at the teepee's base.

Chain-link fences

Okay, so chain-link fence is not the most attractive plant support, but such fencing is strong and durable. Chain-link's industrial appearance practically screams to be cloaked in greenery. For an attractive barrier or privacy screen, plant a climbing rose at the base of a chain-link fence. (The links provide both air circulation and spaces for tying branches.) Or cover the fence with a dense climber (such as evergreen *Hardenbergia* in warm climates) or an annual vine (such as morning glory).

Metal trellises

Chic, freestanding metal trellises come in many shapes and sizes. Such trellises are whimsical to formal in design and are made from a variety of materials, including copper tubing, epoxy-coated wrought iron, and galvanized steel (with a hardened oil finish). Metal trellises are sturdy and easy to install (simply push their feet into the soil), but they're not very wide (most are less than 2 feet, or 60 cm, wide). Metal trellises look most attractive when placed in front of simple walls, and then draped with a single vine. Expect to pay $50 to $100 (or more!) for each trellis.

For an impressive selection of decorative metal trellises, check the catalogs in Appendix B.

Latticework trellises

Premade lattice trellises are usually constructed of wood, although trellises made of plastic are also available. Lattice is designed for mounting on walls or fences; or attach it to fence posts to make inexpensive screens. Look for lattice at lumberyards and home-building centers.

When securing lattice directly to a solid surface, extend connecting supports several inches beyond the solid surface so that the trellis does not lie directly upon the surface. This extra space improves air circulation around the plant, which helps reduce pest and disease problems.

To make house painting or other maintenance easier, fasten the latticework to hinges at the bottom so that you can lay the trellis back for easy access to the wall. Use metal hooks and eyes to attach the lattice to the wall at the top. Many vines, including star jasmine *(Trachelospermum jasminoides)* and winter jasmine *(Jasminum nudiflorum)* are flexible enough to bend as you raise and lower the lattice.

Sturdy lattice is also suitable for attachment to the top of a wooden fence; such lattice adds height to the fence and extends the growing area. Two vines useful for topping fences are clematis, and Spanish jasmine *(Jasminum grandiflorum)*. The latter plant gives an open, airy effect.

Fan trellises

Made from wood or plastic, store-bought fan trellises come in many sizes. Each fan trellis generally supports a single climber. You can use fan trellises in much the same way as you would use lattice. A fan trellis also can support a climber in a container. Try to secure the fan trellis to the inside of the container before planting in the container. (This task is easiest to accomplish if you use a wooden trellis and a wooden container.) Grow annual vines, such as sweet peas or black-eyed Susan vine.

Plastic netting

Lightweight plastic netting (often in an unobtrusive green) is a quick fix for vining vegetables like pole beans, peas, and cucumbers. Plastic netting is easy to install: Just suspend it between vertical posts. Although some types of plastic netting are resistant to ultraviolet radiation and can last for years, you need some patience to remove old vines and tendrils without cutting or ripping the mesh.

Pillars

Simply put, a pillar is a sturdy, rot-resistant wood or metal post set in the ground. (Perhaps you have a lamp post just waiting for a vine.) Pillar dimensions can vary, but the pillar's base should be buried at least 2 feet (61 cm) deep. Climbing roses are a traditional pillar plant. Examples of good pillar roses are 'Dortmund' (cherry red with white eye), 'Climbing Iceberg' (white), and 'Sombreuil' (white). You need to use ties to train roses up a pillar.

Wall-mounted supports

If you have masonry walls, you can create a sturdy support system with galvanized wire. Attach eye bolts to the wall with expanding anchors and then thread and tie 14- or 16-gauge wire through the eye bolts. Arrange the wires horizontally, vertically, or in a fan shape, depending on the space and the plant to be grown. This system is sturdy and supports heavy climbers like roses and honeysuckles.

As an alternative, simply attach *plant ties* (any flexible material used for tying plants — your nursery sells several types) through the eye screws and eliminate the wires. Either way, extend the eye screws a couple of inches beyond the wall to provide air circulation.

Arbors

Decked with wisteria, bougainvillea, climbing roses, or clematis, an arbor raises the garden to new heights. Arbors may be works of art in their own right, or they may have simple designs that highlight plants without competing with them. A heavy-duty arbor anchors the landscape, creating a feeling of permanence as well as a feeling of comfort. Placed over a path at the garden's entrance, an arbor becomes a welcoming doorway.

Arbors may be homemade or prefabricated. Above all else, they must be sturdy. To avoid damaging the growing plant while working, put the trellis or support in place before planting.

Vines We Love

You can choose from dozens of vines to adorn the sides of buildings or fences as well as ramble through your shrubs and trees. If your space is limited, look for kinds of vines that offer more than one benefit, such as those with handsome foliage as well as beautiful flowers or delectable fruit. Some vines provide handsome bark in winter, and others offer superb autumn color.

Following are a few of our favorite vines. The temperatures given indicate the average winter minimum temperature that the plant can tolerate:

- **Bougainvillea.** *Bougainvillea* species. Evergreen or partially deciduous, bougainvillea is one of the most spectacular flowering vines. Stunning flowers in electric shades of purple, red, pink, orange, yellow, and white cover the plant all summer and beyond. Leaves are an attractive bright green. Plants are shrubby and must be tied to a sturdy support and given room to grow. Plant in full sun or, in the hottest climates, partial shade. Plant carefully, being sure not to disturb the roots. Bougainvillea needs little water once established and can grow in mild-winter areas with only light frosts (zones 10 and 11) or protected areas in zone 9.

- **Clematis.** *Clematis* species. This diverse, mostly deciduous family of eye-catching flowering vines is available in hundreds of selections. Large-flowered hybrids, with summer blooms up to 10 inches (25 cm) across in shades of white, pink, red, blue, and purple, are most popular. Delicate plants can twine more than 10–15 feet (3–4.5 m) high. Plant where the roots are cool and shaded but where the top can grow into full sun. For example, set the plant at the base of a large shrub and let it ramble through to the sunny top. Or plant clematis anywhere and cover the roots with a thick mulch. Many are hardy from zones 4–10.

- **Evergreen clematis.** *C. aramandi.* Masses of fragrant white flowers appear in early spring. The leaves are handsome, shiny, and dark green. It grows under similar conditions as other clematis but quickly reaches 20 feet (6 m) high and is hardy in zones 8–10.

- **Creeping fig.** *Ficus pumila.* This very compact, evergreen foliage vine tightly adheres to any surface it touches. Creeping fig has good-looking, small, heart-shaped leaves. Best grown on stone or masonry. Plant in sun or shade. Hardy in zones 8–11.

- **English ivy.** *Hedera helix.* Evergreen, fast-growing, tenacious, and adaptable, English ivy comes in many varieties differing in foliage size, shape, and color. The species has deep green, heart-shaped leaves and is very vigorous. It clings with small aerial rootlets and takes over open areas in a minute — you have to keep your eyes on this one! English ivy can damage all but the hardest surfaces. 'Hahn's Self-Branching' is a small-leafed type with more restrained growth. 'Baltica', whose leaves are a mixture of white and green, is one of many varieties with colorful, variegated leaves. Plant in sun or shade. Generally hardy throughout zones 5–10.

- **Chinese jasmine.** *Jasminum polyanthum.* The wonderfully fragrant flowers of Chinese jasmine perfume the air for months in spring. The small blooms are borne in clusters, white on the face, pink on the back. The twining stems hold bright green, divided leaves and are very fast growing to 20 feet high. This evergreen is a good choice to cover a fence, trellis, or arbor. It prefers partial shade. Hardy in zones 8–11.

✔ **Virginia creeper** and **Boston ivy**. *Parthenocissus* species. These two deciduous vines are known for their dramatic red and gold autumn color. Virginia creeper, *P. quinquefolia,* has leaves divided into five leaflets. Boston ivy, *P. tricuspidata,* has glossy, three-lobed leaves. Both climb vigorously, clinging to surfaces with their small adhesive discs. Plant in sun or shade. Boston ivy is hardy in zones 4–9; Virginia creeper is hardy in zones 3–8.

✔ **Climbing roses.** *Rosa* species. You can use many types of vigorous-growing roses the same way as vines. (See Chapter 7 for more details on roses.)

✔ **Star jasmine.** *Trachelospermum jasminoides.* The evergreen star jasmine is one of the most attractive and well-behaved vines for mild climates. Showy clusters of fragrant white flowers almost obscure the shiny, dark green foliage in late spring to summer. Twining stems reach up to 20 feet high (6 m); they're not invasive but need support. This plant is great for climbing through lattice or on fences. Plant in full sun or light shade. Hardy in zones 8–10.

✔ **Grape.** *Vitis* species. The sprawling grapevine is one of the best choices for covering an arbor or trellis. In addition to interesting gnarled trunks, good-looking leaves, and autumn color, you also get edible fruit. This deciduous plant is hardy from zones 3 or 4–9, depending on the type of grape.

✔ **Chinese wisteria.** *Wisteria sinensis.* Purely elegant — that's about the best way to describe one of the finest deciduous vines you can grow. Beautiful, large (often over 12 inches, or 30 cm, long), dangling clusters of fragrant purple blooms hang among bright green, divided leaves in spring. The twisting, twining shoots keep growing almost indefinitely. As the shoots mature, they take on the classic "muscular" appearance. Casting just the right shade, wisteria is the perfect cover for a sturdy arbor or trellis. It also looks great on fences. This vine requires annual pruning to look its best and to bloom prolifically. Plant in full sun. Hardy in zones 5–10.

Annual Vines

Want a really fast — but temporary — vine? Consider an annual vine. Like a petunia or other annual flower, an annual vine grows quickly and blooms in one growing season, which may be just fine for screening off a summer eyesore. (We're not talking about your neighbor's mowing his lawn with his shirt off). An annual vine can also provide glorious summer flowers.

Here are five favorite annual vines that are easy to grow:

- ✔ **Canary creeper.** *Tropaeolum peregrinum.* This fast-growing vine can reach 15 feet (4.5 m) in one season. The name comes from the 1-inch (2.5 cm), bright yellow flowers that look like they have wings. Plant near a fence or trellis, or provide stakes for support.

  Sow seeds directly in the ground in full sun or part shade after all danger of frost has passed. Thin seedlings to stand 12 inches (30 cm) apart. Canary creeper does best in cool-summer climates. Keep roots cool with an insulating mulch of organic matter.

- ✔ **Morning glory.** *Ipomoea imperialis.* This is the standard for fast-growing, big-leafed, free-flowering summer vines. Varieties can climb as much as 15 feet (4.5 m) in one season. Trumpet flowers up to 4 or 5 inches wide (10 or 13 cm) come in a rich range of blues, pinks, and purples. Newer varieties stay open for longer, not just the "morning" suggested by the name. Plant near a trellis, fence, or arbor, and let vines climb.

  Sow seeds directly in the ground in full sun in spring after all danger of frost has passed. Space 12 inches (30 cm) apart. The seeds have a hard coat and don't sprout easily. Help them germinate by notching seeds with a knife or file, or soaking for a couple of hours in warm water before planting.

- ✔ **Nasturtium.** *Tropaeolum majus.* Nasturtiums make themselves right at home in a casual garden. Edible, bright flowers in orange, yellow, cream, red, or pink bloom abundantly through the summer (or winter and spring in mild climates). The bright green, round leaves can make a thick low carpet that's attractive in its own right. Climbing varieties, which trail up to 6 feet (2 m), can be trained on a trellis or as a ground cover.

  Sow seeds directly in the ground in full sun or part shade in spring after all danger of frost has passed, in fall in mild-winter climates. Thin seedlings to stand 12 inches (30 cm) apart. Nasturtiums are easy to grow in well-drained soil, and are quick about it. Best in cool-summer climates, they live through winter in mild climates and can reseed themselves — the nicest sort of "weed" if you like a wild look.

- ✔ **Thunbergia, or black-eyed Susan vine.** *Thunbergia alata.* Tubular flowers, from 1 to 2 inches (2.5–5 cm) across, bloom all summer until frost, in orange, white, or yellow with a dark eye in the center. Plant near a fence or trellis and the vine will twine up to 10 feet (3 m).

  If transplants are available, set them out in full sun or part shade in spring after all danger of frost has passed and warm weather has arrived. Space plants 12 inches (30 cm) apart. Seeds can be sown directly in the ground at the same time and spacing. Make sure plants get plenty of water through their whole season. Blooming is best in cool weather, before and after summer heat.

✔ **Sweet peas.** *Lathyrus.* If you appreciate old-fashioned charm and heady fragrance, find a sunny spot for sweet peas.

Tall climbers are the most familiar sweet peas, vining to 5 feet (1.5 m) or so, and the best for cut flowers. Colors include blue, orange, pink, purple, red, and white. You need to provide something for sweet peas to climb on. 'Royal', with abundant $1^1/_2$-inch flowers (4 cm), in mixed colors, on 12 inch-stems (30 cm), has been a favorite for years and still ranks high among the many varieties sold.

Sweet peas can't stand heat and do best in cool climates. If you live in a typical cold-winter, hot-summer climate, plant early in spring as soon as the soil can be dug so blooming can take place while weather is still cool. In hot climates, make sure you choose varieties labeled as heat-resistant; in the hottest climates, even these varieties won't work.

In mild-winter climates such as California, plant sweet peas in the fall for blooms in winter and early spring. Choose varieties labeled early-flowering or spring-flowering.

Sweet peas perform best if seeds are planted directly where they are to grow. Choose a spot in full sun with a climbing surface — a trellis, net, wire fence, or other kind of support. To hasten seed germination, soften the seed coat by soaking seeds in water for at least a few hours up to 24 hours before planting.

Part IV
At Ground Level

In this part . . .

This is the part where you get your hands dirty. (If you have an aversion to getting a bit of soil on your hands, now is your chance to take up stamp collecting.) Even though it's the stuff that happens above ground that draws all the ooohs and aaahs, most of the important action that determines whether your plants will flourish takes place below ground.

Here you find out how to improve your soil so that your garden has its best chance to succeed, how to plant seeds, and how to transplant seedlings and saplings.

Chapter 11

Understanding and Improving Soil

- -

In This Chapter

▶ Clearing a site

▶ Understanding and testing your soil

▶ Improving your soil

▶ Digging and tilling

▶ Making raised beds

- -

*P*reparing your soil is probably the most important step toward bringing your garden to life. The reason? *Roots.* This underground lifeline makes up half of every plant — sometimes more. You may often forget about roots, however, because you don't see them — except for the occasional maple root that the lawn mower keeps hitting. But the roots are there, spreading, digging, and questing for nutrients and moisture.

Before you plant, take some time to get acquainted with your soil. (It's more interesting than you think!) Chances are, you'll find out that you need to make some improvements — typically by adding organic matter (a process called *amending the soil)* and a perhaps a few other goodies, as well. Your goal, as you discover in this chapter, is to create an airy soil, rich in oxygen and nutrients that enable your plants to thrive.

Clearing the Site

The perfect spot for your garden may already be occupied. Whether it's a beautiful sweep of lawn or a patch full of weeds and brush, you need to clear your site of existing vegetation before testing and improving the soil. Follow these steps for clearing a site where you intend to place your garden:

1. **Outline the area where you'll go to work.**

   If you're developing a square or rectangular area, you can establish straightedge lines by stretching a string between two sticks. Leave the string in place or mark the line with a trickle of white ground limestone, spray paint, or flour. For curved portions of the garden, use a garden hose or rope to lay out the line. Adjust the hose position until the curve looks smooth.

2. **Use a flat spade to dig a small trench that establishes the outline of the garden plot.**

3. **Clear the surface by removing plants, sod, brush, and rocks.**

4. **Mow the site to clear the rough ground.**

5. **Cut down woody plants and dig out the roots.**

6. **When the vegetation is down to a manageable level, you can remove the sod and other low vegetation.**

You can use several techniques for clearing the site. If the garden is currently lawn, you can strip off the turf, roots and all, by using a flat spade or sod cutter. This method is hard work but does a thorough job.

Stripping sod

Your site-clearing process may very well involve getting rid of natural sod. Here's how:

1. **A couple of days prior to digging, water the area that you want to clear.**

   Stripping sod is easier when the soil is lightly moist.

2. **If you haven't done so already, mark the edges of the plot.**

3. **Starting at one side of the plot, slip your spade under the grass and slide it under the sod.**

   Don't dig too deep; you want to remove merely the sod and an inch or two of roots.

   Another system is to precut the sod into square or rectangular sections and then loosen each section with the spade.

4. **Pivot the tool up, letting the sod flip up over the spade.**

5. **Slice off the sod section and toss it into a wheelbarrow to take to the compost pile.**

6. **Gradually continue in this manner until the garden is free of sod.**

Many garden experts get rid of grass sod by spraying it with a nonselective herbicide, such as Roundup or Finale. When the grass is completely dead, they till it into the soil, adding organic matter to the soil in the process!

However, our feeling is that most gardeners are better off avoiding herbicides, even considering the promise of saving time and energy. To use herbicides or not is a decision you have to make for yourself.

If you have a large area of sod to clear, consider renting a sod cutter. These machines are the size and weight of full-size rototillers, so you need a pick-up truck or trailer to get one home. (Some rental yards deliver and pick up heavy equipment, but of course charge extra.) After stripping the sod, stack the strips like bricks into a 3- or 4-foot (1 or 1.2 m) pile and let it become compost.

Other soil-clearing methods

You can use other ways to clear a garden: Cover it with black plastic or layers of newspapers, or simply use repeat cultivation.

- **Black plastic.** After a month under black plastic, existing plants die from lack of sunlight. Spread the plastic over the entire garden area, securing the edges with spare rocks, bricks, or boards. Overlap neighboring pieces of plastic by several inches so that no light can penetrate. Come back in a month, remove the plastic, and rototill the dead plant matter into the soil. Wait about ten days for errant weeds to sprout. (Because you haven't removed weed seeds, you're sure to get some growth.) Cut down or pull out any weeds that emerge.

- **Newspapers.** To use newspapers, spread a layer of newspapers, five to six sheets thick, over the entire area in the fall. Overlap the sheets about 5 inches (12.5 cm). Use black and white newsprint only — color ink may contain lead or other heavy metals. Cover the newspaper with straw or other mulch and leave it alone for one season. After a few months, the sod, newspaper, and other material will have decomposed enough to till under. You've recycled the newspapers; and the decomposed sod adds nutrients.

- **Repeat cultivation.** If you have plenty of time or if your garden is too large for the other site-clearing methods to be practical, then consider the *repeated tilling method*. This process adds good organic matter to the soil and kills existing weeds but takes much of the growing season to complete.

  1. **In spring, rototill the garden area and broadcast seeds of a cover crop such as buckwheat, Sudan grass, or black-eyed peas.**

  2. **After the cover crop gets to be about 6 inches (15 cm) high, till again to work it into the soil.**

  3. **Let the cover crop decay, which takes a couple of weeks during warm weather. Then till again and prepare to plant.**

Meeting Your Soil

Taking time to create a healthy underground environment before you plant goes a long way toward ensuring a healthy, productive garden. You need to know only a few basics and perform some easy tests to determine the characteristics of your soil, and you're ready to start improving your soil like an expert!

To understand your soil, keep in mind what plants need from soil: moisture, air, and nutrients.

Soil texture

Soil comprises air spaces, organic matter, and, mostly, mineral particles. Soil minerals come in three types: sand, silt, and clay. Sand is the largest particle in most garden soils. Silt particles are smaller than fine sand and larger than clay. Clay is the smallest particle. The relative proportions of these particles in the soil determine its texture.

The ideal soil texture is *loam*, which is composed of sand, silt, and clay. Loam soils have the properties of all three mineral types in roughly equal proportions — enough sand to allow good water drainage and air circulation, but enough clay to retain moisture and nutrients. (See Figure 11-1.)

Most garden soils are best understood as either sandy, clay, or loam. (Silty soils occur but are not common.)

- **Sandy.** Water drains through sandy soils fast, so it dries quickly. Nutrients also pass through sandy soils quickly. Plants in sandy soils often need lighter, more frequent applications of water and fertilizer.

- **Clay.** Soils dominated by clay particles are heavy and tend to pack tightly. Clay soil sticks to your shoes and shovel when it's wet, and cracks when dry. Water enters and drains slowly from clay soils, which can make them difficult to manage. On the other hand, clay soil's ability to retain moisture and nutrients makes them very fertile.

- **Loam.** Loam soils come in many types, but all combine the properties of sand, silt, and clay. A "perfect" loam soil contains 40 percent sand, 40 percent silt, and 20 percent clay. Loam soils have such a good reputation because they are ideal for most plants. But many plants grow well in non-loam soils.

Seasonal and day-to-day changes make every walk through your garden an adventure. Here, brilliant azaleas, rhododendrons, and other spring-blooming shrubs signal the beginning of a new gardening season in USDA Zone 8. See the climate zone maps at the end of this section to see which zone you live in.

Sweet alyssum softens
the edges of a walkway.

Wide borders for perennials and
shrubs flank a lawn-paved entry.

A cutting garden that includes both annuals
and perennials mirrors the sweeping curve
of a lawn.

Grow a cottage garden like this one
by planting foxglove (tall spikes),
campanula (blue and white), and pink roses.

Each daylily flower lasts only one day, but they are produced in such abundance that you'll have plenty for cutting.

Gardeners in zones 3 to 10 can grow the brilliant blue perennial in the foreground: catmint. Yellow spears of lupine accentuate it.

For a cacophony of color, plant all-star perennials like shasta daisies and yellow coreopsis.

In a zone 9 or 10 "subtropical" garden, planting possibilities abound with exotic potential.

Japanese painted fern
(*Athyrium nipponicum*)
Perennial, zones 3-9

Early spring-blooming Dutch crocus (*Crocus vernus*)
are naturalized in this southern Oregon lawn.

Bishop's hat
Epimedium rubrum
Perennial, zones 4-8

Autumn Fern
Dryopteris erythrosora
Perennial, zones 5-8

Daylilies and bee balm, among other perennials, make a colorful lawn alternative.

A healthy lawn surrounded by flower beds adds value to your house.

Colorful annuals and perennials border an entryway.

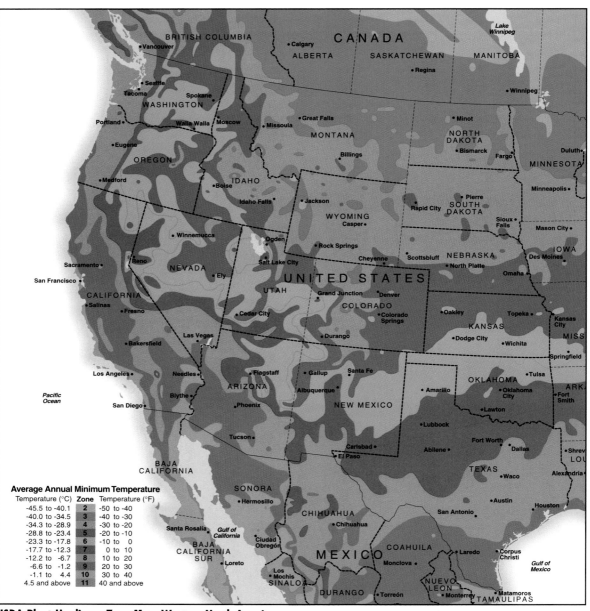

Average Annual Minimum Temperature

Temperature (°C)	Zone	Temperature (°F)
-45.5 to -40.1	2	-50 to -40
-40.0 to -34.5	3	-40 to -30
-34.3 to -28.9	4	-30 to -20
-28.8 to -23.4	5	-20 to -10
-23.3 to -17.8	6	-10 to 0
-17.7 to -12.3	7	0 to 10
-12.2 to -6.7	8	10 to 20
-6.6 to -1.2	9	20 to 30
-1.1 to 4.4	10	30 to 40
4.5 and above	11	40 and above

USDA Plant Hardiness Zone Map, Western North America

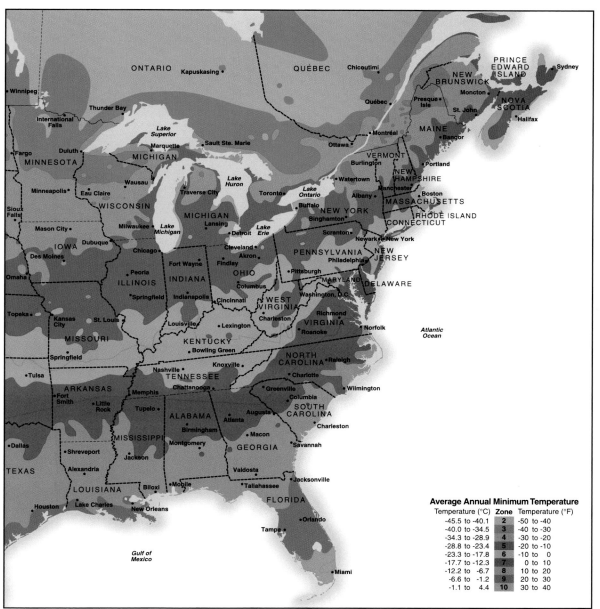

Average Annual Minimum Temperature

Temperature (°C)	Zone	Temperature (°F)
-45.5 to -40.1	2	-50 to -40
-40.0 to -34.5	3	-40 to -30
-34.3 to -28.9	4	-30 to -20
-28.8 to -23.4	5	-20 to -10
-23.3 to -17.8	6	-10 to 0
-17.7 to -12.3	7	0 to 10
-12.2 to -6.7	8	10 to 20
-6.6 to -1.2	9	20 to 30
-1.1 to 4.4	10	30 to 40

USDA Hardiness Zone Map, Eastern North America

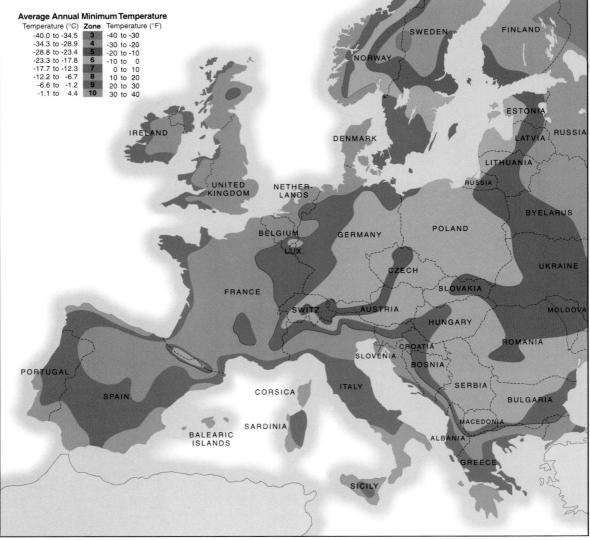

Average Annual Minimum Temperature

Temperature (°C)	Zone	Temperature (°F)
-40.0 to -34.5	3	-40 to -30
-34.3 to -28.9	4	-30 to -20
-28.8 to -23.4	5	-20 to -10
-23.3 to -17.8	6	-10 to 0
-17.7 to -12.3	7	0 to 10
-12.2 to -6.7	8	10 to 20
-6.6 to -1.2	9	20 to 30
-1.1 to 4.4	10	30 to 40

USDA Hardiness Zone Map, Europe

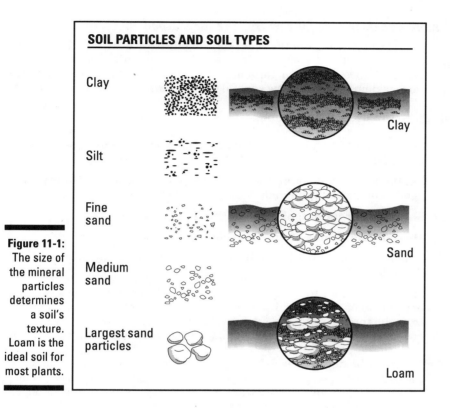

SOIL PARTICLES AND SOIL TYPES

Clay

Silt

Fine
sand

Medium
sand

Largest sand
particles

Clay

Sand

Loam

Figure 11-1:
The size of
the mineral
particles
determines
a soil's
texture.
Loam is the
ideal soil for
most plants.

A quick test for texture: Ribbons and bows

You can use two methods to identify your soil's texture: the *ribbons-and-bows method* and the *jar method*.

Get a general idea of your soil's texture by taking a handful of moist soil, squeezing it into a ball, and working it out in a ribbon between your thumb and your forefinger. Stand the ribbon straight up in the air.

- ✔ If you can't form a ribbon, the soil is at least 50 percent sand and has very little clay.

- ✔ If the ribbon is less than 2 inches (5 cm) long before breaking, your soil has roughly 25 percent clay in it.

- ✔ If the ribbon is 2–3¹/₂ inches (5–9 cm) long, it has about 40 percent clay.

- ✔ If the ribbon is greater than 3¹/₂ inches (9 cm) long and doesn't break when held up, it is at least 50 percent clay.

A more accurate test for texture: The jar method

For most gardeners most of the time, knowing the exact texture of your soil is not so important. But once you do know, that information can help explain much of what goes on in your garden. You can then tailor your soil management for maximum effect. Allow several days to carry out the following test.

Here's how to use the jar method:

1. **Put 1 inch (2.54 cm) of dry, crushed garden soil in a tall quart (liter) jar.**

2. **Fill the jar $2/3$ with water and add 1 teaspoon (5 mL) of a dispersing agent, such as a liquid dish detergent or table salt.**

3. **Shake the jar thoroughly and let the contents settle.**

4. **Measure the depths of the different layers of soil.**

   When the sand settles to the bottom (in about a minute), measure the depth of that layer.

   Silt settles in four to five hours. You should see a color and size difference between the silt and sand layers; if not, subtract the sand depth from the total to determine the silt depth. The clay takes days to settle, and some of the smallest particles may remain permanently in suspension.

By measuring the depth of each layer, you can figure out the approximate percentages of sand, silt, and clay in your soil. For example, you have loam soil if the 2 inches (5 cm) of soil settles down like this: The sand and silt layers are about $3/4$-inch (1.9 cm) each, and the clay layer is less than $1/2$ inch (1.25 cm).

Soil structure

The way in which sand, silt, and clay particles combine or cluster is called the *soil structure.* Structure modifies the influence of texture. Most often, gardeners use additions of organic matter — compost, peat moss, mulch, and so on — to improve soil structure.

No matter what kind of soil you have, adding organic matter improves the soil structure. Organic matter helps form *humus,* which enables small clay or silt particles to stick together to form larger aggregates; in sandy soils, humus acts like a sponge to catch and hold moisture and nutrients. For more details about humus, see this chapter's section, "Exactly what do you add?"

Two methods of determining your soil structure are the *percolation method* and the *metal-rod method,* which we explain in the following sections.

A quick test for structure: Percolation

The percolation do-it-yourself test evaluates *water drainage* — the ability of water to move through the soil, which is called the *percolation rate*. To evaluate drainage:

1. **Dig several holes 1 foot deep × 2 feet wide (30 × 60 cm) in various places in your garden.**

2. **Cover the holes with sheets of plastic to let the soil dry out.**

3. **When the soil is dry, fill each hole to the top with water and record the time it takes for the water to completely drain.**

   The ideal time is between 10 and 30 minutes.

   - If the water drains in less than 10 minutes, the soil will tend to dry out too quickly in the summer. Amend the soil with moisture-retaining matter such as peat moss and humus.

   - If it takes 30 minutes to 4 hours to drain, you can still grow most plants but you have to water it slowly to avoid runoff and to allow the water to soak in deeply.

   - If your soil takes longer than 4 hours to drain, you may have a drainage problem. In sandy soil, dig a foot or two (30–60 cm) deep to see whether a hard layer is blocking water movement. If so, break it up in the area you want plants to grow. You may have to dig down with a post-hole digger, though in some cases, the impermeable layer is too deep even for that. You can also use a nozzle on the end of a pipe to make a water jet bore through an impermeable layer.

   If your soil is clay, create a raised bed and use purchased soil or a homemade soil mix for planting. The goal is to get plant roots up out of the soggy soil and into well-drained, elevated soil rich with organic matter.

Another test for structure: The metal-rod method

In some regions, particularly ones that receive little rainfall, a concretelike layer lies just under the soil. This layer, which is known as *caliche*, prevents normal water movement and root growth.

In addition to caliche, some soils suffer from a layer of dense, clay soil called *hardpan*. Though not as hard as caliche, this dense layer also prevents good plant growth. (See the section "Improving Your Soil," in this chapter.) The simplest way to see whether your soil has a hardpan or compaction layer below the surface is to take a metal rod and walk around your property sticking it into the ground. If you can't easily push the rod into the soil at least 6 to 8 inches (15–20 cm) deep, you need to improve the structure of your soil. If you push it down and consistently meet resistance at a certain depth, you may be hitting a hardpan layer.

One more big thing: Soil pH

Just to intimidate the rest of us, chemists use a chemical symbol to represent the relative alkalinity (sweetness) or acidity (sourness) of the soil. This symbol, *pH*, represents the "negative logarithm of hydrogen ion concentration." (Better make a note. You'll be tested on this later.)

Soil pH is rated numerically on a logarithmic scale of 1 to 14, but you'll almost never see a soil with a pH of 2 or 13. In practice, soil with a pH of 4.5 is strongly acidic and a pH of 9.5 is strongly alkaline. Most soils in the world range between a pH of 5 and 9. An absolutely neutral pH is 7.0.

The correct pH for your plants is important because certain nutrients are available only to plants within a specific pH range. The ideal pH for most plants is from 6.0 to 7.0. A few plants (such as acid-loving rhododendrons and blueberries) prefer more extreme conditions. Usually, areas of high rainfall have a low pH, and areas of low rainfall have a high pH.

Kits for testing pH are available in many garden centers. You can also figure out your soil's pH by using a professional soil test. For a quick check of your soil's pH, try the following fizz tests. These tests are not very accurate, but can be fun to watch!

✔ To check whether your soil is severely alkaline, take a tablespoon (15 mL) of dried garden soil and add a few drops of vinegar. If the soil fizzes, the pH is above 7.5. (The "free carbonates" in the soil react with the acid at a pH of 7.5 and above.)

✔ To check for acidity in the soil, take a tablespoon (15 mL) of wet soil and add a pinch of baking soda. If the soil fizzes, the soil is probably very acidic (pH less than 5.0).

Your soil, in detail

For the definitive word on your soil's chemistry and makeup, a professional test is the next step. Your local extension office may be able to test your soil or recommend a private lab. The results of these tests can tell you about soil nutrient levels, soil structure, and pH. You also get suggestions on how to make your soil even better.

Keep in mind that the reliability of any soil test depends on the accuracy of the soil sample. Avoid contaminating soil samples with residue from tools, containers, or cigarette ash, for example. The small sample that you send to a lab must also be representative of your garden. Gather soil from several places and mix it together to form a composite picture of the plot. However, don't mix soil from different garden areas where you'll be growing plants with different needs or with soil near foundations or walls where construction residues may remain. Follow the directions from the soil lab or extension office for best results.

Improving Your Soil

If your soil is a nice, fertile blend — one that grows good grass — you may not need to do anything special to it to grow most garden plants. But beefing up the organic content never hurts, because organic matter is constantly being broken down. *Organic matter* — such as decaying leaves, hay, grass clippings, compost, and decomposed cow or horse manure — releases nutrients and other chemicals that make soil fertile and productive. Organic matter is especially valuable for adding richness to sand and lightness to clay. The organic material makes good gardens great and poor gardens better by making any soil more like the ideal loamy soil. Be careful not to use cat or dog droppings, because this waste can contain parasites.

Before planting in reasonably good soil, dig in 1 or 2 inches (2.5 or 5 cm) of organic matter, such as compost, peat moss, decayed livestock manure, shredded leaves, or decayed lawn clippings. Then, each year, mulch planted areas with an inch or more of compost or organic mulch.

Amending your soil before planting is not always necessary, especially if you're planting long-lived trees and shrubs and if your soil is reasonably good, if not perfect. On the other hand, if you find that your soil is not what it needs to be for the kinds of plants you want to grow, try to correct the problem before you plant. Be prepared to amend the entire planting area so that plant roots can grow freely without encountering a bewildering range of different soil blends. Dramatically different soil types can stop root growth cold. Apply a layer of organic matter, at least 2–4 inches (5–10 cm), and till it into the soil.

Plan to maintain your improved soil by adding several inches of organic material each year — even more in warm climates or particularly difficult soils. Here are some tips to improve tough soils:

- Add a 1- to 2-inch (5–10 cm) deep topdressing of compost to compacted soils in perennial beds annually. No need to rake it into the soil.

- Break up a compacted layer and build extra-deep top soil in annual gardens by double digging (see the section "Double digging" in this chapter) or by deeply tilling the soil below the hardpan layer and mixing in generous amounts of organic matter.

✔ Build a raised bed if the thickness of the hardpan layer doesn't allow for planting. (See "Simple raised beds" in this chapter.) Build the bed about 8 inches (20 cm) high — or even higher if you install a retaining wall. Cover the existing soil with commercial topsoil that's preblended with about 20 percent compost.

Exactly what do you add?

Organic matter that you can add to your soil comes in so many forms and varieties that this book couldn't possibly list them all. Nursery and garden centers offer many kinds, often in 20- or 40-pound (10 or 20 kilogram) bags. But if you have really big plans, consider buying your organic amendment by the truckload. By the bag or by the truckload, here are some of the tempting tidbits that you'll find can do wonders to improve the texture of garden soil:

✔ **Compost.** When different kinds of dead plant material get piled together, dampened, and stirred or turned every week or so to keep air in the mixture, they become compost after a month (or two or three). Products labeled as compost can originate from all sorts of stuff, but enterprising people who have tapped into the yard-waste stream usually create them. Fallen leaves, shredded Christmas trees, and wood chips left from tree-trimming crews often find their way to compost-manufacturing facilities. Compost ingredients can also include sawdust from lumber mills, peanut hulls from peanut processing plants, and hundreds of other agricultural by-products.

One place to get lots of compost cheap is from your own city. Many municipalities offer free compost and mulch. Some charge a modest fee for it. The only caveat is quality. Some cities compost industrial by-products that you might not want to have in your garden. Check with your local Department of Public Works.

Expect to find little bits of sticks and other recognizable things in a bag of compost, but mostly judge quality by the texture of the material, which should be soft and springy. If you plan to buy a large quantity of compost, compare products packaged by different companies to find the best texture. A 3-inch (7.5 cm) layer of packaged compost, worked into the soil, is a liberal helping that should give instant results. To estimate how much you need, figure that a 40-pound bag (18 kg) (that may actually weigh more or less, depending on how it's been stored) covers a square yard (0.84 m²) of bed space.

✔ **Composted manure.** In addition to its soil-improving properties, composted or "aged" manure also contains respectable amounts of nitrogen and other important plant nutrients. Nutrient content varies with the type of manure. Composted chicken manure is very potent, whereas steer manure is comparatively lightweight. Packaged sheep manure is quite popular among gardeners, and you may eventually encounter some truly exotic renditions based on the waste from zoo animals, bats, and even crickets.

The amount of manure you should use depends on your soil type. With bulky manure from large animals (cow, horse, goat, sheep, elephant), start with a 1-inch (2.5 cm) layer, or about 40 pounds (18 kg), per 3 square yards (2.5 m²). Follow package application rates when using stronger manure from rabbits, chickens, and other birds.

✔ **Humus.** Bags labeled as *humus* are the wild cards of the soil-amendment world. Anything that qualifies as organic matter for soil, or any soil-organic matter mixture, can be considered humus. Unlike compost, which is supposed to be "cultured" under controlled conditions, humus can come from more humble beginnings. For example, humus may be 2-year-old sawdust and wood chips from a lumber mill mixed with rotten leaves and dark topsoil. Or, it could be rotten hay mixed with soil and sand. You just don't know what to expect until you buy a bag and open it up. If the humus has a loose, spongy texture and dark color, and you like the way it feels and smells, go for it. A 2–3 inch (5–7.5 cm) layer (40 pounds per 2 square yards, or 18 kg per 1.7 m²) is a good estimate.

✔ **Topsoil.** Breaking into bags of topsoil to see what's inside is always interesting. Sometimes the soil is exactly what you might find in bags of humus or compost, and other times it may look more like unbelievably black soil. Whatever the bag contents include, topsoil is almost always cheap. You can use bagged topsoil as a soil amendment, or use so much of it that your flower bed is filled with mostly imported topsoil and only a little of the native stuff.

✔ **Peat moss.** Peat moss is a very spongy acidic, brown material harvested from peat bogs in Canada, Michigan, and a few other places. On the plus side, peat moss absorbs and holds huge amounts of water and nutrients while frustrating soil-borne fungi that can cause plant diseases. Peat moss is more beneficial in sandy soil as opposed to clay soils. In sandy soils, the water-holding power of peat is put to good use. Clay soil retains water, so adding peat moss is overkill.

On the negative side, some gardeners are concerned about the sustainability of peat moss harvesting. Peat bogs that are damaged by overharvesting may require a thousand years to regenerate. Because of this, you might want to limit your use of peat moss to situations where it most valuable, such as creating special soil mixtures for container-grown plants, or for planting shrubs that really like it a lot, like azaleas and rhododendrons. We think most, but not all, of the peat moss in nurseries and garden centers is harvested responsibly and sustainably. Gardeners in some areas use shredded coconut husks as a substitute.

Changing pH

If you're growing pH-sensitive plants, or if you're dealing with very acidic or very alkaline soils, you can adjust pH with specific soil amendments. To make soil less acidic, add ground limestone. To increase alkalinity, add soil sulfur. But rather than commit to the ongoing need to adjust pH, consider choosing landscape plants that grow well in your native soil with its existing pH. Amending soil with many kinds of organic matter gradually lowers pH. (Some animal manures tend to have an alkaline effect so should not be used to acidify.) Likewise, most nitrogen-containing fertilizers, natural or manufactured, acidify soils — some a great deal, others only slightly. But if your soil pH is significantly too low or too high for the kinds of plants you want to grow, you need to add ground limestone or soil sulfur. To increase or decrease your soil pH, do the following:

- ✔ **Add limestone to raise your soil pH from 5.0 to 6.5.** To each 1,000 square feet (93 m^2) of sand, add 41 pounds (18.6 kg); to each 1,000 square feet of loam, add 78 pounds (35.4 kg); and to each 1,000 square feet of clay, add 152 pounds (69 kg).

- ✔ **Add sulfur to lower your soil pH from 8.5 to 6.5.** To each 1,000 square feet (93 m^2) of sand, add 46 pounds (20.8 kg); to each 1,000 square feet of loam, add 57 pounds (25.8 kg); and to each 1,000 square feet of clay, add 69 pounds (31.3 kg).

Adding nutrients

If your soil is low in nutrients, which you can determine by having the soil tested or by seeing that plants grow poorly, add extra nutrients. If your soil has been tested, add amendments and fertilizers according to the lab's recommendations. If you haven't tested the soil, add a complete fertilizer according to package directions. A *complete fertilizer* is one that contains nitrogen, phosphorus, and potassium, the major nutrients that all plants need.

Green manure crops and cover crops

One easy way for gardeners to add organic matter and nutrients to the soil is to grow *green manure crops.* These are plants grown to be chopped and tilled or spaded into the soil when they are still green (before they blossom and produce seeds). The succulent plant material breaks down quickly, adding nutrients and improving soil texture. These crops are usually grown during the main gardening season — between crops or just after harvesting a crop. In many climates, green manure crops remain standing over the winter and get plowed into the soil before spring planting.

Cover crops are often the same plants that are used for green manure crops. However, the primary purposes of a cover crop are to prevent soil erosion and to choke out weeds, usually when the soil is bare of crops before and after the harvest.

The plants used as green manure and cover crops can be divided into two broad categories: *legumes* and *nonlegumes*. Legumes have special nodules on their roots that house nitrogen-fixing bacteria of the genus *Rhizobium*. Examples of legumes are soybeans, vetches, cowpeas, and clovers. If you till the legumes back into the soil, succeeding crops benefit from the nitrogen that the legumes and its *Rhizobium* absorbed from the air.

Although nonlegumes don't add as much nitrogen to the soil as legumes do, many nonlegumes are very useful as green manure and cover crops simply for the organic matter that they add to the soil.

Loosening the Soil

The depth and techniques that you use to loosen the soil depend on which plants you intend to grow and the condition of your soil. For your average garden of annual flowers and vegetables, for example, you can use a process called *single digging* to break up the top 8 inches (20 cm) of soil by using a spade or rototiller.

In existing gardens with light, fluffy soil, you may be able to turn the bed with a spade without too much difficulty and minimize organic matter loss. If you prepare the soil in autumn, let frost help break up the soil clumps. Then spade again in spring and finish up with a rake.

When to work the soil

Have you ever grown your own mouth-watering melon, checking it daily to see whether it's perfectly ripe? Preparing the soil is similar. You need to wait until the soil is in the right condition — lightly moist, but not wet. If too wet, clays can dry into brick. If too dry, soil can turn into dust and blow away, leaving beneficial soil life to perish. If your soil tends to be wet and clammy in spring when you're ready to plant annual flowers, you can avoid this frustration by preparing your beds in the fall, when dry conditions often prevail.

Fortunately, the right soil condition is easy to evaluate. Take a handful of soil and squeeze it in your fist. Tap the resulting ball with your finger. If it breaks up easily, the soil is ready. If it stays in a sodden clump, the soil needs to dry out more. If it doesn't cling at all, the soil is dry: Water the area, wait a day, and try again.

Begin digging by removing a section of soil the width of the bed and the depth of your spade. Place excavated soil in a garden cart or wheelbarrow, or simply pile the soil to the side temporarily. Soon, you'll have what looks like a shallow grave. Next, slice down into the adjacent portion of soil with the spade and roll that soil into the trench you just made. Continue this process until you have covered the garden width (or length). Finally, haul the soil excavated from the first trench and place it into the last space.

After your first pass with the shovel, break up the clods and add the soil amendments and fertilizer. Then dig through the bed again, rake vigorously to break up clods and to mix in the amendments. Use a garden rake to comb through the soil and remove rocks, clods, and any chunks of vegetation or plant roots that you missed previously. Smooth the soil over the entire bed by raking, and you're ready to plant.

Time for a tiller

Digging a small flower bed is a good exercise program, but preparing a large one by hand in one day is almost impossible without the help of a tiller. If you need to cultivate more than 1,000 square feet (93m^2), consider renting, borrowing, or buying a tiller. (Of course, exactly how much is too much to do by hand depends on your strength and ambition.) Lightweight minitillers are sufficient for many tilling chores. For larger jobs, look to either front- or rear-tined tillers. Professional growers usually favor the latter.

Another option is to have someone else till your garden. No matter where you live, you can usually find someone in your community who does this for a living in the spring. Look in the classified ads in the newspaper or call local garden centers to find this most valuable resource person. Before the person arrives to churn up your soil, have all the soil amendments on hand that you intend to use. After you or your hired person has tilled the area and raked out the weeds, spread out your soil amendments and fertilizer, and till it again.

Rototillers are a handy tool for occasional use. Beware, however, that repeated use of tillers can create a hardpan layer (known as *plow pan* or *pressure pan*). Tillers promote faster breakdown of soil organic matter because of how they stir and mix the soil; and tillers cultivate soil to only one depth, so the soil beneath the tilled layer becomes compacted from repeated pressure from the tiller.

Double digging

Double digging works the soil more deeply than single digging and is useful for deep-rooted plants or areas where drainage needs improvement. This process takes a lot of work, but the effects last for years.

1. **Mark out a bed 3 or 4 feet (1 or 1.2 m) wide and up to 25 feet (7.6 m long).**

2. **Across the width of the bed, remove a layer of the topsoil to create a trench 6–8 inches (15–20 cm) deep and 1-to-2 feet (30–60 cm) wide. Place the soil in your wheelbarrow.**

3. **With a digging fork, break up the subsoil at the bottom of the trench to the full depth of the tines — about 6–8 inches (15–20 cm). Mix in plenty of soil amendments.**

4. **Step down into the bed and dig the topsoil from the adjacent strip, moving it onto the exposed, loose subsoil of the first trench.**

5. **Break up the newly exposed subsoil with the garden fork, and add amendments.**

6. **Continue in this fashion until you break up upper and lower layers across the entire bed. The soil from the first trench, held in the wheelbarrow, goes into the last trench.**

7. **Spread soil amendments over the entire bed and rake it into the top 6–8 inches (15–20 cm) of soil.**

After you finish, the earth is mounded up high in the bed. Walk on the adjacent ground rather than on the raised bed. When you go to prepare the bed in subsequent planting seasons, you'll be amazed at how little work it takes to loosen the ground.

Simple raised beds

Raised beds are an ideal way to loosen the soil of the garden and define planting areas. To make a raised-bed garden, outline the beds with string. For vegetable gardens, a 3-foot (1m) wide bed is best; for ornamental plantings, choose a size that best fits your design. After you define the beds, loosen the soil in the bed by using a shovel or a garden fork. Then shovel soil from an adjacent path onto the bed. Figure 11-2 shows a basic raised bed and one edged with wood.

Roses, carrots, parsnips, and other deep-rooted plants grow best when you loosen the soil 12 inches (30 cm) deep or deeper. This requirement calls for building a raised bed over the existing garden or for double digging.

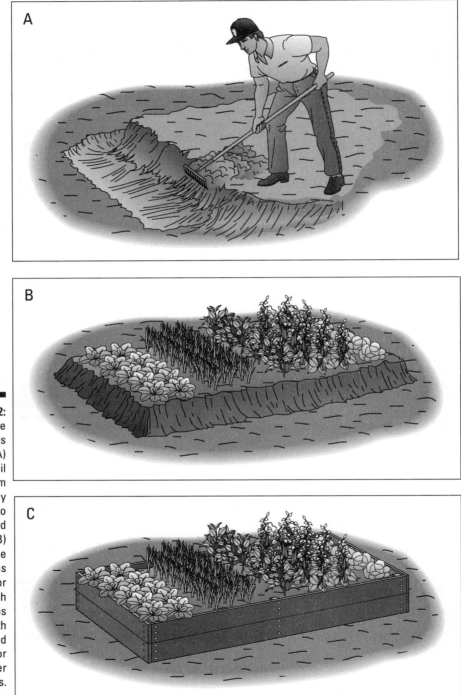

Figure 11-2:
Create raised beds by first (A) drawing soil from walkway areas onto loosened soil. (B) Leave the edges as they are, or (C) finish the edges with untreated wood or other materials.

Chapter 12

Raising Plants from Seeds

● ●

In This Chapter

▶ Shopping smart

▶ Sowing right in the ground

▶ Top choices for direct sowing

▶ Starting seeds indoors

▶ Top choices for indoor sowing

● ●

*S*tarting some plants from seeds can't be simpler. On a warm June day, say, you poke a big fat sunflower seed into moist ground, stand back, and — almost before you know it — a towering 10-foot (3 m) plant is looking down on you. But, as you may expect, some plants are not so easygoing — like that Australian wildflower seed whose first step calls for something like "Scorch rock-hard seed shell with a blowtorch."

Naturally, we're going to stay closer to the sunflower camp. The plants that are easiest and most rewarding to start from seeds are annuals (marigolds, zinnias, and many more) and vegetables (squash, corn, and many more).

Why start flowers and vegetables from seeds when so many different kinds of seedlings are available at the nursery?

✔ With seeds, you have a greater variety of choices than you'd find with small plants in a garden center. One seed catalog may offer dozens of different marigolds, whereas a garden center could have just six or eight.

✔ Seeds can save you money. One pack of seeds, which can produce hundreds of plants, can cost less than a six-pack of the same variety of small plants.

✔ Some plants do better or just as well when started as seeds in the spot where you want them to grow to maturity.

✔ Sowing seeds is satisfying and fun. Do we need to explain why?

What Those Needy Seeds Need

Flower seeds come in all shapes and sizes, from begonia seeds the size of dust grains to nasturtium seeds the size of peas. Larger seeds are the easiest to handle, and they often grow into comparatively large seedlings. Be forewarned that tiny seeds usually take longer to grow into big plants.

Growing flowers from seeds is pretty straightforward. You plant them in soft soil, add water, and keep them constantly moist until they sprout. Here are the basic necessities for growing seeds:

- **Moisture** triggers the germination process and softens the hard outer covering of the seed, called the *seed coat,* so the sprout can emerge.

- **Soil temperature** affects the speed of the process. For most seeds, the warm side of 70°F (21°C) is just about right.

- **Light** is critical for seedlings from the moment the sprout breaks through the soil. If you want to grow healthy seedlings indoors, you need a greenhouse or some sort of supplemental light; tabletop fluorescent fixtures are perfect for this.

Seedlings grow roots as rapidly as they grow leaves, and some annual flowers put a huge amount of energy into roots right off the bat. Flowers that spend their infancy developing long, brittle taproots often are difficult or impossible to transplant, so they are best sown in their designated garden spot. This is the reason you hardly ever see larkspur or Shirley poppies, for example, sold as bedding plants.

Smart Shopping

Every garden center and home supply store puts big seed racks where you can't help but see them. Those packets usually contain good quality seeds. Just to be sure, though, look beyond the beautiful picture on the front of the packet to find other information that reveals much more important data:

- Species and/or variety name

- Mature height

- Packing date (Don't purchase if the seeds are more than 1 year old.)

- Special planting instructions

Some seed companies also put the expected germination rate on their seed packets, which should always be above 65 percent. This number indicates the percentage of seeds in the packet that you can realistically expect to sprout. If no germination rate is available, you can usually assume that the seeds meet or exceed the germination standards for that species. All reputable seed companies discard bad seeds rather than sell them.

Mail-order seed companies can maintain huge selections, and they tend to be meticulous about storage conditions. However, because mail-order companies display and guarantee their seeds in their catalogs, the actual packets often give little information beyond variety name and the approximate number of seeds inside. As soon as your seeds arrive, read over the packet labels and write the year on the packets if the date isn't stamped on there somewhere. Doing so reminds you just how long ago it was that you bought that packet, and you can get a fresh supply when you need it. For a list of mail-order seed suppliers, see Appendix B.

Sowing Seeds Right in the Ground

Direct sowing means planting seeds outdoors in the soil in the place where they are to sprout and mature. This method is the best way to grow many flowers and vegetables that don't transplant well (for example, larkspur, Shirley poppies, sweet peas, beans, beets, carrots, peas, and radishes) and a very good way to grow many other plants.

Follow these guidelines for successful seed sowing in open soil:

- ✔ **Use the recognition factor.** Plant seeds of plants you will recognize or that have a distinctive appearance. Otherwise, you can easily mistake a bean or pea seedling for a weed.

- ✔ **Give seeds a head start.** Moisten large seeds by leaving them overnight in a tray or bowl with moist vermiculite or perlite, or between layers of a moist towel. But once the seeds are moist, be sure they don't dry out prior to planting. This moistening process really speeds things along when you are sowing hard-coated seeds like sweet peas.

- ✔ **Sow seeds at the right season.** Some direct-seeded annuals are best planted in fall or first thing in the spring; others do best planted in warmer soil in early summer. Plant seeds in soil that's warm enough for the particular plants you're working with. For example, peas germinate nicely when the soil is about 60°F (16°C), but basil needs soil that is 70°F (21°C) to sprout well.

- ✔ **Prepare the planting bed thoroughly.** (See Chapter 11.) Take extra care to rake smoothly — lumpy soil and clods interfere with germination.

- ✔ **Sow seeds in a definite pattern.** Some seeds are best sown in rows, while you can scatter others. (Mix seeds with sand to help you broadcast them more evenly if you like.) When you see a pattern of little sprouts in your soil that look the same and germinated at the same time, you will know those baby plants are flowers or vegetables and not weeds.

✔ **Read the label.** Pay attention to directions for best planting depth. If you plant deeper than indicated on the packet, the seeds may not contain enough energy for seedlings to reach the surface. A light layer of sifted compost may be sufficient coverage; or just press seeds into the soil with the back of a hoe.

✔ **Water carefully and gently.** Keep soil damp until seeds sprout. The best way to water is with a *soaker hose* or *drip irrigation.* Soaker hoses and drip irrigation systems are ground-hugging tubes that let moisture trickle out without splashing or compacting the soil. (See Chapter 14 for more information about watering systems.) You can water from overhead as long as you do it gently with a fine spray from a hose or sprinkler.

✔ **Weed early and often.** If you have trouble weeding around small seedlings, use a table fork to gently pull out awkward little weeds. For more about dealing with weeds, see Chapter 16.

✔ **Create some elbow room.** When the seedlings have developed two sets of *true leaves,* thin out seedlings that stand too close together. (The first leaves a seedling produces are called *seed leaves* or *cotyledon,* which are followed by the true leaves.) To *thin out* seedlings, gently pull extra seedlings without disturbing the ones you want to keep; or snip them off with scissors just above the soil line.

You have a choice of planting patterns to use. Here are some tips on arranging your garden:

✔ Plant small vegetables — carrots or lettuce, for example, or flowers that you want to transplant later — in wide beds that are a couple of feet wide. Many gardeners find that beds 3 feet (1 m) wide are an ideal size for vegetable gardens because beds that size adapt well to trellises and "season extenders" (such as row coverings) and allow easy access to plants from either side of the bed.

✔ If you like a neat, exact garden, use a wire grid of hardware cloth to calculate your spacing. With carrots, for example, use wire mesh with inch-square openings. Lay the wire mesh across the bed and press a few seeds down into the soil through each opening. *Thin* (remove excess seedlings) when the seedlings arise so that each carrot has at least 3 square inches (19 cm²) of space. For larger plants, such as lettuce, you can plant a seed every four or five squares to eliminate overcrowding.

You can also plant carrots the way most gardeners do: Scatter the seeds as evenly as possible over the planting area, as shown in Figure 12-1a. Sometimes this method means having to do a bit more thinning than otherwise might be necessary, but some gardeners like the insurance of sowing the extra seeds.

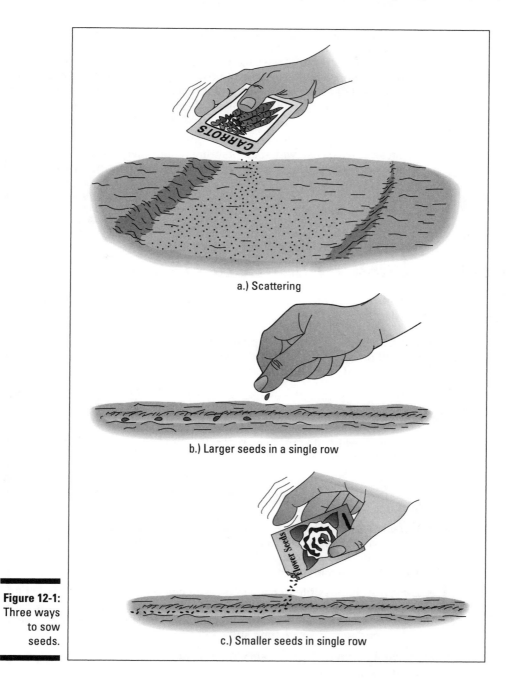

a.) Scattering

b.) Larger seeds in a single row

c.) Smaller seeds in single row

Figure 12-1:
Three ways
to sow
seeds.

✔ Larger plants need more space. You can plant them in wide beds, alternating two or three plants across the bed in a diamond or triangle. Another method is to place seeds of larger plants in single rows, as shown in Figure 12-1b. To make the rows straight, tie a string between two stakes. Following the string line, run a hoe through the soil to dig a trench of the proper depth for the seeds you're planting. Set the seeds in the trench at the proper spacing. Then cover the seeds with soil.

✔ In a decorative annual-flower garden, you can plant in rows, as shown in Figure 12-1c or use wide-bed planting techniques to create clusters or drifts of flowers. Use a trickle of ground limestone (or gypsum if your soil pH is alkaline) to mark the place where you want a mass of seed-grown flowers, such as zinnias or nasturtiums. Set the seeds within that space as you would for a wide bed.

A Dozen Easy Annuals to Direct-Sow

These plants are easy to grow from seeds sown directly in carefully pre-pared beds:

✔ **Basil.** Seeds love warm soil, so don't hurry planting. Wait a week or so until all danger of frost is past, and sow in moist soil. Try sowing a few seeds around your tomato plants.

✔ **Black-eyed Susan vine.** Seeds of this pretty but rampant summer vine germinate best in warm, moist soil. Soak the seeds overnight before planting and sow in a group at the base of a fence.

✔ **Cleome.** Sow in late spring after the last frost has passed. Cover the soil after planting to keep seeds moist.

✔ **Cosmos.** Sow plenty of seeds in early spring to be sure of getting a good stand. The yellow or orange flowered species often does best in hot summer areas.

✔ **Hyacinth bean.** This big purple bean looks like an ornamental pole lima. Soak the big seeds before planting them. When the plants are a few inches tall, add mulch around them to keep down weeds; train the vines up the nearest fence or arbor.

✔ **Larkspur.** Impossible to transplant, you can plant superhardy larkspur in fall in all but the coldest climates. The seedlings stand as feathery green mounds through winter and grow tall first thing in spring. In very cold areas, sow over melting snow in early spring.

✔ **Marigold.** You can grow a very nice border of little French marigolds from one packet of direct-sown seeds.

- **Melampodium.** This low-maintenance flower is best sown in late spring. Plants grow into big mounds 2 feet (61 cm) tall, covered with small yellow flowers.

- **Morning glory.** In long-season climates, common morning glories produce so many seeds that they can become weedy in the garden. Grow them near mowed areas where they are less likely to get out of control. In short-season climates, their ability to "self-sow" is less a problem and more welcomed.

- **Nasturtium.** Carefree and easy to grow, nasturtium leaves look like little green flat umbrellas. Both the flowers and leaves are edible.

- **Pole beans.** Normally these are counted in the "vegetable" category, but they're also a good looking vine and an annual. Sow seeds in warm soil in mid- to late spring. Try growing them up an arbor or fence post — they're not choosy.

- **Poppies.** Sow delicate Shirley poppies in fall by scattering the tiny seeds atop cultivated soil. Never try to move the plants. Sow California poppies in fall or spring. Both types of poppy produce pods filled with seeds that are easy to gather for the next year's sowing.

- **Sunflower.** Sunflowers are now available in a rainbow of hot colors. The large leaves shade out weeds, and the plants often reseed themselves. Some new truly dwarf varieties grow to less than 2 feet (61 cm) tall.

- **Sweet pea.** Sweet pea seeds benefit from soaking for a full day before planting. Sow in late winter or early spring while the soil is still quite cool. In mild-winter areas, sow in fall for winter and early spring bloom. Sweet pea seedlings easily survive spring frosts.

Starting Seeds Indoors

Annual vegetables and flowers tend to be the quickest and easiest to grow from seed. When you sow seeds for these plants in winter or early spring, they can be ready for the garden at the earliest possible planting dates for your region. In addition, many plants get off to a better start when they are sown indoors in containers and later transplanted into the garden.

Here's one basic seed-sowing method that works for us:

1. **Choose a container to hold the soil. The container should have drainage holes.**

   You can plant in flats or pots. The container can be store-bought or homemade from recycled aluminum foil pans, fast food containers, plastic cups, yogurt containers, or whatever.

2. **Buy a commercial planting mixture specifically formulated for starting seeds.**

   Garden centers offer several kinds of these; they usually say "seed starting mix" on the bag. Pour some in a bucket and thoroughly moisten it.

3. **Fill the container to ¹/₂ inch (1.25 cm) from the top with the mixture and level it, as shown in Figure 12-2.**

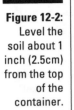

Figure 12-2:
Level the soil about 1 inch (2.5cm) from the top of the container.

4. **Plant the seeds.**

   - **Small seeds.** Broadcast over the soil surface and cover with a fine layer of the moistened planting mix.

   - **Large seeds.** Plant in shallow furrows (trenches) scratched or pressed into the soil surface or poke each one into the soil individually, as shown in Figure 12-3. Cover these seeds as recommended on the seed packet, usually to a depth equal to twice the seed diameter. Press the mixture gently yet firmly.

Figure 12-3:
Poking holes to contain larger seeds.

5. **Water the seeds gently.** Use a gentle mist from a watering can, or use a poultry baster to carefully moisten the soil without washing the seeds. Another watering method is to place the planters in a larger tray. Add 1 to 2 inches (2.5–5 cm) of water to the larger tray, as shown in Figure 12-4. The plant container uptakes as much water as needed through the drainage holes.

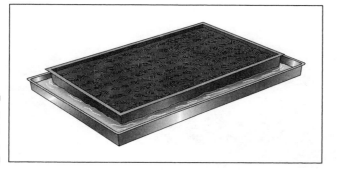

Figure 12-4: Water the seeds.

6. **Cover the container with a plastic bag, as shown in Figure 12-5, to conserve moisture and keep light out. (Check the seed packet — a few types of seeds need light to germinate.)**

   Place the container in a warm spot (ideally 75°–85°F or 24°–30°C), such as the top of a refrigerator or near another heat source.

7. **Start checking for growth in about three days.**

   As soon as plants emerge, remove the plastic and move the container to bright light. Water as needed to keep the planting mix moist.

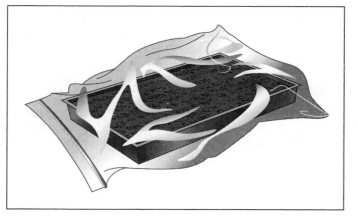

Figure 12-5: Cover the container with a plastic bag.

You can find fluorescent bulbs that are specifically designed to provide plants with ideal light for growth, as shown in Figure 12-6. Adjust the height of the lights so that they're nearly touching the seedlings (raise the lights as the seedlings grow) and leave the lights on for 16 hours per day.

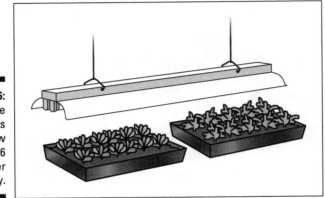

Figure 12-6:
Leave plants under grow lights for 16 hours per day.

8. **When the seedlings have a second pair of true leaves, it's time to transplant them to small, individual pots filled with moist planting mix.**

   Use a narrow spatula or similar tool to help scoop the plants from their original container. If necessary, gently pull the seedlings apart — hold the plants by the leaves rather than by their fragile stems, and plant them. Space them 2 or 3 inches (5 or 7.5 cm) apart in larger containers if you have too many for individual pots.

9. **Place the container in bright, indirect light and keep the planting mix moist.**

   In most homes, the seedlings should receive the brightest light available as soon as they emerge. Seedlings thrive under fluorescent lights. If you have a fluorescent fixture, set seedlings 1 or 2 inches (2.5 or 5 cm) below the tubes. Begin feeding seedlings with liquid fertilizer. Follow label directions or, to be safe, begin feeding at half the recommended rate.

10. **One or two months after transplanting, you can harden off most plants and plant them in the garden.** (See this chapter's sidebar entitled "Hardening off seedlings to their new environment.")

LEARNING THE LINGO

Hardening off seedlings to their new environment

Seedlings and cuttings raised in comfortable indoor conditions need gradual adjustment to the more strenuous outdoor environment. This process of acclimating plants to the wind, strong light, and cooler temperatures outdoors is called *hardening off*.

1. One week before you begin hardening off your plants outdoors, cut back the amount of water you give them, stop fertilizing them, and, if possible, keep temperatures slightly cooler by lowering the thermostat.

2. Starting about ten days before transplanting into the garden, place plants outdoors in bright, indirect light for a couple of hours.

Protect the plants from strong winds and be sure to keep them watered, because the plants dry out more quickly outside.

3. Each day, increase the time that the plants are left outdoors and gradually expose them to more intense light and wind and a range of temperatures.

4. The last few days before transplanting, you can leave them outdoors overnight if weather permits.

A cloudy, windless, warm day is the best time for easing the plants into their new home outdoors.

A Dozen Easy Annuals to Start Indoors

Here are a dozen easy annuals well worth the trouble of planting early indoors.

- ✔ **Bells of Ireland.** *Moluccella laevis.* The plants develop tall spires studded with little green seashell-like structures. The seeds are large and easy to grow.

- ✔ **Calendula.** *Calendula officinalis.* These bright yellow and orange flowers love cool weather and make great companions for poppies and bachelor buttons.

- ✔ **Celosia.** *Celosia cristata, C. plumosa.* Wait until spring warms up before you start the seeds. The plume types are lovely additions to any garden, but some people really like the cockscomb types, with rippled flower heads that look like brains.

- ✔ **Globe amaranth.** *Gomphrena.* Flower arrangers covet gomphrena for both fresh and dried uses. Set out seedlings late in spring, after the last frost is long gone.

✔ **Marigolds.** *Tagetes.* Incredibly easy to grow, marigold seeds are easy to handle, quick to germinate, and hardy.

✔ **Nicotiana.** *Nicotiana alata.* This old-fashioned strain of flowering tobacco produces fragrant white flowers on tall spikes that open at night. You may have to grow it yourself — nurseries rarely sell seedlings.

✔ **Salvia.** *Salvia.* Experiment with unique colors by growing more unusual varieties from seeds.

✔ **Statice.** *Limonium.* Strains are available in several soft single colors, including purple, rose, and yellow. The seeds are easy to handle.

✔ **Strawflower.** *Helichrysum.* Harvested and dried, the flowers last forever. Be sure to thin seedlings to one plant per 2-inch (5 cm) seedling pot.

✔ **Sweet alyssum.** *Lobularia maritima.* This dainty little flower is often used to edge beds, or as a companion plant in containers and window boxes. Plant the seeds in pans or trays, and thin seedlings to only 1 inch (2.54 cm) apart.

✔ **Mexican sunflower.** *Tithonia rotundifolia.* Tall, heat-loving tithonia lights up the background of a sunny garden. Start seeds in late spring and use the plants as replacements for others that wear out in hot weather.

✔ **Tomatoes.** *Lycopersicum esculentum.* Here is the one "annual" that's most often planted indoors. Sow seeds in moist soil six to eight weeks before the last spring frost in your area.

Chapter 13

Choosing and Planting Seedlings, Trees, and Shrubs

● ●

In This Chapter

▶ Planting seedlings

▶ Working with container-grown trees and shrubs

▶ Knowing what to do with bare-root plants

▶ Getting balled-and-burlapped trees and shrubs into the ground

● ●

*N*urseries in the same geographic location tend to sell certain types of plants during certain seasons and in certain ways. (Think of fruits and vegetables in a grocery store: Some are available only during specific seasons, and different types may be packaged very differently, each requiring a specific type of cleaning and preparation prior to eating.) Understanding when to shop for your plants and how to plant different plant types is a useful and important gardening skill.

Most annuals and vegetables are available as *seedlings* or *transplants* — the little guys that come in packs or small pots.

Larger, permanent plants — shrubs, trees, and vines, for example — come typically in containers of gallon size to 15 gallons (3.8–57 l) and larger. You can find container-grown plants year-round in mild climates and throughout the growing season in colder regions.

Plants are also available in two other, more seasonal forms: *bare-root* and *balled-and-burlapped.* Each has its own reasons for being and its own special planting techniques.

Of course, you can use other ways to get plants started — like bulbs (see Chapter 6). And roses are so popular that we give special planting directions for them in Chapter 7.

Buying and Planting Seedlings

In this section we talk mostly about annuals and vegetables sold in plastic cell-packs of various sizes and in small pots (usually 3 or 4 inches, 7.5 or 10 cm) wide). Of course, the same planting advice also applies to seedlings you have grown yourself, as described in Chapter 12.

Exactly when plants are available locally depends on your climate. Early in spring and again in fall, expect to find seedlings that grow best in cool conditions. Plants that require warmer weather arrive later on and keep coming as long as customers keep buying.

As you shop, look for seedlings that are a vibrant green color and are relatively short and stocky. Also look around at the display. Has the retailer simply lined everything up in the blazing sun or gone to the trouble of placing shade lovers like coleus and impatiens under benches or shade-cloth? Most bedding plants, including those that grow best in full sun, hold better in small containers when kept in partial shade.

Plants grown in small containers cost less than those in larger ones. Larger plants with more extensive root systems have a head start over smaller plants; however, larger, more developed bedding plants may have one disadvantage. In any container, a plant's roots tend to grow into a thick spiral. If the root system is extremely crowded, the roots may refuse to spread outward after transplanting.

At the nursery, don't be shy about tipping the plant out of its pot or pack and inspecting its roots. Avoid plants with thick tangles of root searching for a place to grow — like out the bottom of the container's drainage hole.

If you buy plants already in flower, pinch off the blossom when you set out the plants. This preemptive pinching encourages the plants to grow more buds and branches.

Figuring Out Spacing for Transplants

Flowering annuals vary in how much space they need to grow. Plant spacing tends to be very tight in window boxes and containers, but in open beds your best strategy is to space plants so that they will barely touch each other when they reach full maturity. Space very small annuals like sweet alyssum and lobelia only 4 to 6 inches apart (10–15 cm), whereas big coleus and celosia may do better 18 inches (46 cm) apart. Most other annuals grow best planted 10 to 12 inches (25–30.5 cm) apart, more or less. The plant tags stuck into the containers of purchased bedding plants often suggest the best spacing.

Instead of setting your annuals in straight lines, you get better results by staggering them in a concentrated zigzag pattern so that you have two or more offset rows of plants. Better yet, plant different annuals in natural-looking teardrop-shaped clumps (called *drifts*). The clump approach also makes many flowers easier to care for. A closely spaced group of plants that need special care is much simpler than a long row when you need to pinch, prune, or water and feed.

You can estimate spacing with just your eyes if you like, and simply go over the prepared bed, making little holes where you intend to set the plants. Or, you can mark the planting spots with craft sticks or lightly dust each spot with plain, all-purpose flour. If you purchased plants in individual containers, simply place each one where you intend to plant it, and move them around as needed until you are happy with the arrangement.

Planting Seedlings, Step by Step

Whether you buy your seedlings at the nursery or grow your own from seeds, follow these steps to ensure a seamless transition from nursery to garden.

1. **A day or two before transplanting, water the planting bed so that it will be lightly moist when you set out your plants.**

2. **At least one hour before transplanting, water your seedlings thoroughly. Doing so makes seedlings much easier to remove from their containers.**

   Ideal transplant time is anytime temperatures are moderate, neither too hot nor cold or too windy. If weather is particularly hot when seedlings are ready, wait for morning or afternoon. If it's midsummer and you're in a hot climate, try waiting for a cloudy day. Transplanting under the hot sun causes unnecessary stress to the little plants.

3. **Check to see if small roots are knotted around the outside of the drainage holes.**

   If you find roots knotted in such a manner, break them off and discard them before trying to remove the plants.

4. **Remove the plant from the container by pushing and squeezing on the container bottom so that the entire root ball slips out intact, as shown in Figure 13-1.**

   If the root ball doesn't come out easily, use a table knife to gently pry it out, the same way you might remove a sticky cake from a pan. For stubborn trees and shrubs, carefully use a strong utility knife to slice through the container. Pull on the top of the plant only as a last resort.

5. **Use your fingers or a table fork to loosen the tangle of roots at the bottom of the root ball.**

   Loosening the roots is important! Otherwise, the roots may make little effort to spread out into the soil.

6. **Make final spacing decisions, and then dig small planting holes slightly wider than the root balls of the plants.**

7. **Set the plants into the holes at about the same depth they grew in their containers.**

   You may need to place a few handfuls of soil back in the hole and then set the plant in place to check the height.

8. **Lightly tamp down the soil around the roots with your hands so that native soil comes in contact with the root ball, as shown in Figure 13-2.**

   Tamping down the soil helps remove some pockets of air, which can dry out roots. Keep a watering can handy to help settle soil around roots.

Figure 13-2:
Firming the soil removes pockets of air around the roots.

9. **Mix a batch of balanced or high-phosphorous water-soluble fertilizer and give each plant a good shot (high-phosphorous fertilizers have a large middle number, such as 5-10-5).**

   If you mixed in fertilizer while preparing the planting bed, you shouldn't have to fertilize more now. Generally not essential, high-phosphorus fertilizers promote strong flowering. For more about fertilizers see Chapter 14.

10. **Water the entire bed until it is evenly moist.**

11. **After a few days, check to make sure soil has not washed away from the top of the plants' roots.**

    If the root ball is exposed, use a rake or small trowel to add more soil, making sure the root ball is covered.

12. **As soon as new growth shows, mulch around plants with an attractive organic material such as shredded bark, pine needles, or shredded leaves.**

    A 2- to 3-inch (5–7.5 cm) layer of mulch greatly discourages weeds and radically reduces moisture loss from the soil due to evaporation. It also prevents the soil from forming a crust by cushioning the impact of water drops from rain and sprinklers.

Container-Grown Trees and Shrubs

Most shrubs and trees that you buy these days are in containers — often called *cans* although they're probably made of plastic not metal. This system has several advantages: The plants are easy to move around, and you don't have to plant them right away. (Be sure to continue their watering routine until you are ready to plant.)

Planting your own trees and shrubs saves costs, but planting larger plants requires stamina. Start with smaller, container-grown shrubs that are not too heavy and that can be planted any time the weather is mild. Large balled-and-burlapped trees are heavy and may require a crew of several strong people. Select your plants carefully and calculate placement and hole width and depth in advance so that you don't have to attempt last-minute corrections.

Choosing container-grown trees and shrubs

You want plants that have healthy appearance — with sturdy branches, dense foliage, and other signs of vigorous growth depending on the type of plant. Inspect the root system as well as you can. You don't want a plant that has spent too little or too much time in the container. If recently planted, the root system may not have developed enough to hold the soil ball together; soil can just fall off the roots as you plant. If the plant has been in the can too long, it may become *root-bound* — when roots are so tangled and constricted, the roots have a tough time spreading out into the soil and growing normally.

Look for these classic root-bound symptoms:

- ✔ Roots stick out the container's drain holes.

- ✔ Roots bulge out above the soil line.

- ✔ Plants are spindly (tall but with few leaves), poorly proportioned in relation to the container, or have a lot of dead growth.

Avoid root-bound plants; or, failing this, at least gently loosen and untangle the roots without shattering the ball of soil at planting time.

If a plant is extremely root-bound, slice right through the bottom of the root-bound ball, going up a little more than halfway. Spread open the two flaps over a mound of soil and plant as usual. Or using a sharp knife, slice through the outer roots is several places. This causes the roots to branch out and form new growth.

Transplanting trees and shrubs from containers

Follow these steps for planting container-grown trees and shrubs:

1. **Dig a hole as deep as the original root ball (use a stick to determine depth) and three times as wide as the root ball.**

   Slant the walls of the hole outward and loosen them with a shovel or garden fork to allow easy root penetration. In heavy clay soil, ensure good drainage around the plant by digging the hole 1 or 2 inches (2.5–5 cm) shallower than the depth of the original root ball.

   If you have average or better soil, don't bother to amend the soil that you use to refill the hole; roots may not grow beyond the amended area if you do. If your soil is especially poor, work compost or organic matter such as composted fir bark into the soil that goes back into the hole.

   Locate any underground wires, cables, or pipelines before you begin digging and proceed around them carefully. You can easily cut through a wire with a sharp spade or fork.

2. **Remove the plant from its container.**

   Most plant containers are plastic and plants slip right out. If they don't, trim away any roots protruding from drainage holes and water the plant thoroughly. Tap the bottom or knock the rim of the can on a hard surface, and then tip the can upside down (or onto its side, for large plants) and slide out the root ball.

   Most nurseries are happy to take back empty plastic containers, either for recycling or reuse. Some even charge a deposit.

3. **Place the plant into the hole, at the right depth, and fill around the root ball with soil, as shown in Figure 13-3.**

   Stand back and check the plant's position to be sure it's oriented the way you'd like, and then begin backfilling. Once you've replaced about half the backfill, tamp down with your hands or the end of a shovel. Water and let the water drain before continuing to fill to the soil level (which is usually the same as the root-ball level).

4. **Water the plant well by letting a hose trickle into the planting area until the area is soaked.**

   To help direct irrigation and rainwater to the new roots, shape loose surface soil with your hands into a water-holding basin. Make it 3 to 4 inches (7.5–10 cm) high just outside the root ball.

Figure 13-3:
A cutaway
view of a
container-
planted
tree.

Continue to water any time the soil begins to dry out for the next six months to a year. Don't count exclusively on sprinklers or rain to water new plants. To see if soil is dry, dig down 4 to 6 inches (10–15 cm) with a trowel. If it's hard to dig, and if the soil is very dry, the root ball needs water.

5. **Mulch the plant.**

   Cover the excavated soil and several inches beyond (the larger the plant, the wider the circle) with 2 to 3 inches (5–7.5 cm) of mulch. After spreading the mulch, pull it an inch or two away from the main stem of the plant. (Sometimes mulch there will promote disease problems.)

6. **Stake, if necessary.**

   Some trees in some situations need support for a year or two until they can support their own weight. Two situations when stakes are needed are if the trunk is very narrow or if you've planted in a very windy situation. Otherwise, most trees are better off without stakes.

To stake a tree, drive a stake or two into the soil beyond the roots. Attach ties to the tree at the lowest point at which the top remains upright. Tie loosely so that the tree can move in the wind and gain trunk strength. Figure 13-4 shows how to stake a tree with a single stake and with two stakes.

If using guy wires, establish the lowest point on the trunk where the tree needs support. Use cable or heavy twine to connect the tree from that point to stakes in the soil, as shown in Figure 13-5.

Whatever kind of staking you use, be sure to check once or twice a year to see if it is still necessary. Remove the stakes as soon as practical. Stakes left in place beyond their usefulness are a common cause of tree problems.

A tree with a strong trunk stands on its own without staking. However, if the tree was staked in the nursery or if you are planting in a windy location, proper staking supports the tree during its first year in the ground.

Figure 13-4:
Staking a tree with one stake or two stakes.

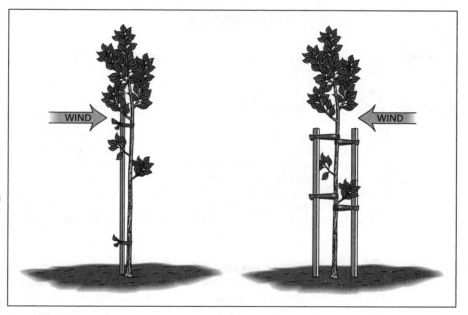

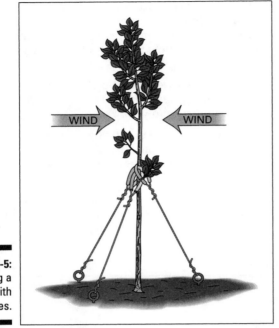

Figure 13-5:
Staking a
tree with
guy wires.

WIND

WIND

Bare-Root Planting

The tried-and-true method of bare-root planting offers benefits to the plant and to the gardener. During the dormant, leafless season, nursery workers dig up *deciduous* (leaf-shedding) plants and remove the soil around the roots. Bare-root plants are easy to transport and handle — which allows for a lower price than the same plants sold in containers. Bare-root is also a good way for plants to get off to a good strong start; roots can follow their natural direction better than they can in the confines of a container.

Choosing bare-root plants

The most important factor to look for in bare-root plants is roots that are fresh and moist, not dried out and stringy. Check for damaged, soft, broken, mushy, or circling roots and prune them back as necessary to healthy, firm growth. Inspect the top growth for broken branches and damaged buds. Ask a nurseryperson about proper preplanting pruning for the specific plant. Don't let the roots dry out; soak them in a bucket of water before planting, if necessary.

Planting bare-root plants

Plant bare-root plants by using the same procedure for container-grown plants described in the section "Transplanting trees and shrubs from containers." The only difference between the two procedures is in the shape and depth of the hole you dig.

For bare-root planting, set the base of the roots on a cone of soil in the middle of the hole, as shown in Figure 13-6, adjusting the cone height so that the first horizontal root is just below the soil surface. Spread the roots in different directions and then refill the hole gradually, tamping down soil around roots.

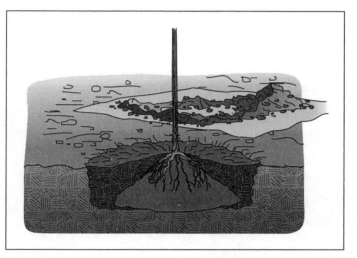

Figure 13-6: Spread the roots of a bare-root plant around a central cone of soil.

Burlap-Wrapped Root Balls

Another time-honored method for distributing plants, particularly evergreen shrubs and trees such as spruce, pine, and fir, is the wrapped root-ball method. During fall and winter, nurseries dig these plants from growing fields and wrap the root balls in burlap (sometimes also wrapping both burlap and root ball in a wire cage for the extra support).

Choosing balled-and-burlapped plants

When looking at balled-and-burlapped plants, be sure to check for major cracks or breaks in the root ball. Make sure that the trunk doesn't rock in the soil ball or move. Keep the root ball moist if you can't plant right away; cover it with organic matter such as ground bark, and moisten thoroughly. Keep the plant in a shady spot until you plant it.

Planting balled-and-burlapped plants

Dig a hole with a circumference twice as large and a depth equal to the root ball. The root ball should sit on firm soil to avoid settling. Set the root ball into the hole; check the position of the plant, and then remove all burlap, nails, and any twine or wire to prevent interference with the plant's future growth. If you can't remove all the burlap, use a sharp knife to cut off everything except for what is directly underneath the ball. (See Figure 13-7.)

To get balled-and-burlapped planting height just right, open the root ball and remove some soil from the top until you find the first *root flare* or horizontal root. That root should be positioned just below the soil surface. Many trees are planted too deeply because they have too much soil over the roots in the root ball.

Like many things, burlap isn't quite what it used to be. Don't assume that it will decay in a season or two, where it would be fine to leave in the soil around the root ball. Nowadays, "burlap" is often a coarsely woven synthetic that can take years to dissolve in the soil, if ever.

Figure 13-7:
Remove any metal, burlap, and twine to avoid inhibiting growth.

Part V
Caring for Your Plants

In this part . . .

Yippee! You made a garden! Or maybe you just inherited one.

Do you need water? How much? What about fertilizer? And what about weeds . . . and pruning or feeding? Oh yeah, and what about pests? What tools do you use to care for your garden?

We answer all these questions in this part. Garden care may sound like a lot of work, but it's really not. And anyway, it's fun. Garden maintenance is a misnomer of sorts — there's nothing janitorial about it.

Caring for your garden is, in fact, the essence of gardening.

Chapter 14

Feed Me, Seymour! Watering, Feeding, and Composting

In This Chapter

▶ Looking at the whys of watering

▶ Figuring out the hows of watering

▶ Understanding plant nutrients

▶ Fertilizing your plants

▶ Mulching around

▶ Dabbling in the art and science of composting

*W*hat's the most important thing you can do in your garden? The answer you get depends on whom you talk to and where that gardener lives. An Arizona gardener may say nothing is more important than watering (unless it's keeping roadrunners out of the barrel cactus collection). Someone with a lot of container plants will put fertilizing first. If you have horrid soil, nothing, we mean nothing, is more essential than composting.

So, what do we say? Our answer, of course, is . . . all of the above. But the amount of watering, feeding, and composting (the Big Three of your support system for healthy plant growth) you do depends on where you live, what you grow, and all sorts of other local conditions. But take our word for it — each of the three is extremely important.

Watering Basics

How much water your plants need to stay healthy depends on a number of factors:

✔ **Climate.** If you live in an area like Seattle, Washington, or Biloxi, Mississippi, where rainfall is regular and reliable, watering isn't a constant chore — except in prolonged dry spells or periods of drought. In drier areas like Los Angeles, watering is something that gardeners need to squeeze into their schedules almost on a daily basis.

✔ **Weather.** The average weather where you live on a season-to-season, year-to-year basis determines climate. Weather is what's happening outside right now. Out-of-the ordinary weather can wreak havoc on your plants. Hot, dry winds can fry plants even when the soil is moist.

✔ **Soil types.** Different soil types also affect how often a garden needs water.

- **Sandy soil** holds water about as effectively as a sieve. Water penetrates sandy soils readily and deeply but tends to filter right on through. Adding organic matter, like compost, leaf mold, peat moss, or ground bark helps sandy soils retain moisture.

- **Heavy clay soil** is the exact opposite of sand — the dense particles in clay cause the soil to crust over and deflect water drops. Water applied slowly and in stages soaks in deeply; water applied quickly just runs off. Saturated clay holds water very well — sometimes so well that the plants rot. Adding plenty of organic matter helps break up the soil and improves drainage.

✔ **Location.** In general, shady gardens need less water than those receiving direct sun. However, in places where trees cast the shadows, their roots may greedily hog all the water, leaving little for the flowers. In such cases, applying enough water to satisfy both the trees and the flowers without causing disease or other problems may be almost impossible.

✔ **Genetic disposition.** Most plants need a consistent supply of moisture to remain healthy and free-blooming. Some types, however, can get by on less water than others.

Getting water to your garden

The best watering method for you may depend on how large a space you have. For example, with just a small bed of marigolds, you may find that watering with a hand-held watering can or hose is not only effective but rewarding. If, however, you have a 200-square-foot (19 square meter) mixed flower bed, watering effectively by hand is not only impractical, it is impossible.

In some areas, certain watering techniques become a matter of necessity instead of practicality. Where droughts are common or water supplies are unpredictable, conservation is the order of the day. You need to water in ways that hold every drop precious. Where foliage diseases like powdery mildew are common, you want to keep water off the plant leaves and apply the water only to the roots.

The following sections describe many fundamental watering methods.

Hand watering

If you want to stand among your heliotrope with a hose and water the plants by hand, that's fine. Hose-end attachments soften the force of the spray and help apply the water over a larger area. You can control the amount of water each plant gets and even do some pest control at the same time — blast that blanket flower to wash away aphids! Hand watering, however, takes time, especially in large gardens — and most of us aren't patient enough to stand and water the entire time it takes to supply enough water.

Sprinklers

Hose-end sprinklers come in a wide range of styles and sprinkler patterns. You've probably used a few of them. The problem with watering with sprinklers is that you have to drag the hose all around and move the sprinkler every so often. Also, most hose-end sprinklers don't apply water very evenly. If you forget to turn off the sprinkler, you waste a lot of water.

If you need help remembering to turn off the sprinklers, check out the various timers that are available. Some fit conveniently between the faucet and hose and so help prevent wasting water when watering the lawn.

One other possible problem with sprinkler watering is the wet foliage that results. In humid climates, overhead watering can spread disease and turn flowers into a moldy mess. On the other hand, in hot dry climates, wetting the foliage rinses dust off the leaves, cools the plants, and helps prevent spider mite infestations.

Furrow irrigation

Furrows are shallow trenches that run parallel to your rows. Usually you dig the furrows with a hoe at planting time and then plant a row of flowers or vegetables on either side of the furrow. Ideally, the bed should slope just the tiniest bit so that water runs naturally from one end of the furrow to the other. (See Figure 14-1.) When you want to water, you just put a slowly running hose at the end of the furrow and wait for the water to reach the other end.

Figure 14-1:
Furrow
irrigation
uses gravity
to carry
water from
one end of
the furrow
to the other.

Furrow irrigation, unlike sprinkler watering, keeps the foliage dry and doesn't promote disease. However, you do have to move the hose around frequently, and furrow watering doesn't work well on fast-draining, sandy soil. (The water soaks in too quickly and never reaches the other end of the furrow.)

Drip irrigation

Drip irrigation is a very effective and efficient way to water plants. Water slowly drips through tiny holes, or *emitters*, in black plastic pipe. The pipe connects to a water supply, filter, and, often, a pressure regulator. The pipes weave among and around the plants, applying water directly to the base of the plants. You can either lay the pipe right on top of the soil and cover it with a mulch, or bury it a few inches deep. Most people like to keep the pipe close to the surface so that they can check it for clogs or fix breaks.

Drip emitters can wet an entire planting bed from one end to the other at each watering. (You can either snap the emitters into the pipe or buy the pipes with the emitters already installed.) Space the emitters 12 inches (30.5 cm) apart along the length of the pipe. Arrange the pipes so that you have no more than 18 inches (45 cm) between lengths or loops, as shown in Figure 14-2. The moisture radiates sideways and underground, and wets the soil between emitters.

Drip systems usually have to run for at least several hours to wet a large area. Watch the soil carefully the first few times you water. Dig around to see how far the water has traveled over a given time and then make adjustments in how long you water in the future.

Most nurseries sell drip irrigation systems. You can also purchase them through the mail (see Appendix B). Emitters are available with different application rates, varying by the number of gallons applied per hour. Pressure-compensating emitters apply water consistently from one end of the line to the other regardless of pressure changes due to uneven ground. Leaky pipe hoses, which are made of recycled tires, leak water along their entire length, but they apply water unevenly if the ground is not perfectly level.

Figure 14-2:
Drip
irrigation is
an efficient
watering
solution.

If you live in an area where the soil freezes, don't leave your drip system outside in winter to prevent bursting. Instead, drain the water, roll up the tubing, and store it in the garage.

Automated watering systems

Automated watering systems can be real time-savers and can give you the freedom to safely take a vacation in the middle of summer. You can find an interesting mixture of timers at your local irrigation supplier or in mail-order catalogs. (See Appendix B.) Some timers hook between hose bib and hose; others connect to valves and underground pipes that supply sprinklers. You can even build a moisture sensor into an automated system so that the water comes on only when the soil is dry. You can automate both drip and sprinkler systems.

Grass lawns have their own special water requirements as well as a world of irrigation methods. See Chapter 9 for specifics.

Determining the amount and frequency of watering

A plant's water needs vary with the weather and the seasons. Even an automated system needs adjusting to water less in spring than in summer. You need to learn to be a pretty good observer and make adjustments accordingly.

Irrigation hardware is useless if you don't have a clue as to how much water your plants need. The answer is to water just enough, but not too much.

The best way to water is to replace the moisture the plants use up by watering daily, three times per week, or weekly. Plants lose moisture through their foliage because of transpiration. The soil also gives up water by evaporation. The combination of evaporation and transpiration is evapotranspiration.

Evapotranspiration, the combined loss of water from soil due to evaporation and transpiration through a plant's leaves, is one way to figure how much water you need to apply. Hot, dry, and windy weather causes plants to use much more moisture than they do on a cool, overcast day. The *evapotranspiration rate,* measured as the total number of inches of water per week or month, tells how much water you can add to replace what the soil lost and what the plants used. Using the evapotranspiration rate is a more accurate way to judge how much to water than the old-fashioned, and often inaccurate, "one inch (2.5 cm) per week" general rule.

If you live in regions where irrigation is a fact of life, the local newspaper (usually on the page with the weather report) gives the recommended watering rate for lawns based on the evapotranspiration rate. If your local newspaper doesn't include such information, check with your local cooperative extension service.

To figure out how long you need to run the sprinklers to deliver a particular amount of water (usually expressed as inches of water), place containers in important locations throughout your sprinkler's spray pattern. Be sure the containers have straight, vertical sides — juice cans work well. Run the sprinkler for a specific length of time, such as one hour. With a metal ruler, measure the depth of water in each can. Use the can with the least amount of water as the standard (hopefully it's not too different than the others), because even the area that receives the least must get enough.

Now you can water by the newspaper's guideline. If, for example, the sprinkler test shows that your sprinkler puts out $3/4$ inch (2 cm) per hour and the paper says to apply $1^1/2$ inches (about 4 cm) of water this week, run your sprinkler for two hours. This same rate is a good starting point for trees, shrubs, annual flowers, and vegetables.

However, you can use other ways to tell when your plants need water:

> ✔ **Note the condition of your plants.** When plants start to dry out, the leaves get droopy and wilt. The plant may also lose its bright green color and start to look a little drab. Now, your goal is to water before a plant gets to that point, but the plant will show you when it needs water more often.

✔ **Dig in the ground.** Most plants need water when the top two to three inches (5–7.5 cm) of soil is dry. So take a small trowel or shovel and dig around a bit. If top of the soil is dry, you need to water.

Eventually, through observation and digging, you start to develop a watering schedule, and a lot of the guesswork disappears.

Conserving water

Water shortages are a reality in almost any climate or region. Following are a few things you can do when water is scarce or limited, when you want to reduce your water bill, or when you just want to conserve the precious resource of fresh water.

✔ **Use a timer.** Don't tell us you've never forgotten to turn the water off and flooded half the neighborhood. Just set an egg timer or an alarm clock to let you know when it's time to shut off the water. Or get even more high-tech and use one of the automated timers mentioned in this chapter.

✔ **Install drip irrigation.** This watering method applies water slowly without runoff. Drip is definitely the most frugal watering system you can use.

✔ **Mulch, mulch, and mulch some more.** Several inches of compost, shredded fir bark, leaf mold, or other material cools the soil and reduces evaporation, thus saving water. And as the mulch breaks down, it improves the soil. For more on mulches, see this chapter's section "A-Mulching We Will Go . . ." and Chapter 11.

✔ **Pull weeds.** Weeds steal water meant for your plants. Pull out weeds regularly. For more on weeds, see Chapter 16.

✔ **Water deeply and infrequently.** Shallow sprinkling does very little good. Water to a depth of 8 to 10 inches (20–25 cm), then let the soil dry out partially before you water again. This method encourages plants to develop deep roots, which can endure longer periods between waterings.

✔ **Water early.** Water early in the day when temps are cooler and it's less windy. That way, less water evaporates into the air and more reaches the roots.

✔ **Use rainwater.** Put a barrel or other collector where the drain pipes from your roof empty out. Then use that water on your garden.

✔ **Measure rainfall.** Keep track of how much rain you get. An inch is usually enough to let you skip a watering.

✔ **Plant at the right time.** Plant when your plants have the best chance of getting fully established before the onset of very hot or very cold weather.

Providing a Balanced Diet for Your Plants

Before you head for the nursery to pick up a bag of fertilizer, remember that understanding the nutrients that plants need and how plants use them is helpful.

Sixteen elements are known to be essential for healthy plant growth. Plants particularly need carbon, hydrogen, and oxygen in large quantities. Plants also need energy from sunlight for *photosynthesis,* the process by which green plants take carbon dioxide from the air and water from the soil to produce sugars to fuel their growth. Apart from watering plants, gardeners can trust nature to supply these big basic requirements.

Plants also need nitrogen, phosphorus, and potassium in relatively large quantities. These three elements are often called *macronutrients,* or *primary nutrients.* Plants take up these three nutrients from the soil. If they are not present in the soil, you can supply them by adding fertilizers. The percentages of these nutrients are the three prominent numbers on any bag or box of fertilizer, and the nutrients always appear in the same order. For more on fertilizer, see this chapter's section "Don't Compromise, Fertilize!"

✔ **Nitrogen (N).** This nutrient, represented by the chemical symbol N, is responsible for the healthy green color of your plants. It is a key part of proteins and *chlorophyll,* the plant pigment that plays a vital role in photosynthesis. Plants with a nitrogen deficiency show a yellowing of older leaves first, along with a general slowdown in growth.

✔ **Phosphorus (P).** Phosphorus is associated with good root growth, increased disease resistance, and fruit and seed formation. Plants lacking in phosphorus are stunted, have dark green foliage, followed by reddening of the stems and leaves. As with nitrogen, the symptoms appear on the older leaves first.

✔ **Potassium (K).** This nutrient promotes vigorous growth and disease resistance. The first sign of a deficiency shows up as browning of the edges of leaves. Older leaves become affected first.

✔ **Calcium, magnesium, and sulfur.** Plants need these three *secondary nutrients* in substantial quantities but not to the same extent as nitrogen, phosphorus, and potassium. Where the soil is acid (areas of high rainfall), calcium and magnesium are important to add to acidify the soil. Doing so maintains a soil pH beneficial to plants and supplies the nutrient that the plants need. Where the soil is alkaline (areas of low rainfall), adding sulfur to the soil is similarly beneficial. For more about pH, see Chapter 11.

✔ **Iron, manganese, copper, boron, molybdenum, chlorine, and zinc.** These seven elements are the *micronutrients,* meaning plants need only minute quantities for good health. These nutrients are often not lacking in the soil, but they may be unavailable to plant roots. The cause of this problem is usually a soil pH that is too acid or too alkaline. In this case, rather than adding the nutrient, adjusting soil pH is the remedy. Too much of any of these nutrients can be harmful.

Don't Compromise, Fertilize!

After you decide to feed your plants, you'll face a myriad of fertilizers at the nursery. How do you know which kinds to buy?

When you buy a commercial fertilizer, its analysis appears on the label with three numbers. These three numbers are helpful because they let you know the amounts of nutrients (N-P-K) that are in a particular fertilizer.

- ✔ The first number indicates the percentage of nitrogen (N).
- ✔ The second number, the percentage of phosphorus (P_2O_5).
- ✔ The third, the percentage of potassium (K_2O).

A 100-pound (43 kg) bag of 5-10-10 fertilizer consists of 5 percent nitrogen (5 pounds, or 2.3 kg); 10 percent phosphate (10 pounds, or 4.6 kg); and 10 percent potash (10 pounds, or 4.6 kg). Altogether, the bag has 25 pounds of plant-usable nutrients. The remaining 75 pounds (34 kg) usually consists of only *carrier,* or filler; a small amount of the filler may contain some plant-usable nutrients.

Any fertilizer that contains all three of the primary nutrients — N-P-K — is a *complete fertilizer.* The garden term *complete* has its basis in laws and regulations that apply to the fertilizer industry: It does not mean that the fertilizer literally contains everything a plant may need.

Common fertilizer terms

You don't need a degree in botany to have a lovely garden. But when looking for the right fertilizers, you do need to understand some of the terminology.

Take a look at some of the fertilizing terms you may encounter:

- ✔ **Chelated micronutrients.** The word *chelate* comes from the Latin word for *claw,* and that's a useful way to understand how these micronutrients function. These compounds bind to certain plant nutrients and essentially deliver them to the plant roots. Nutrients that plants require in minute quantities — such as iron, zinc, and manganese — are often available in chelated form. The chelated fertilizer you buy may be a powder or liquid.

✔ **Foliar.** As the name implies, foliar fertilizers are liquids that you apply on a plant's leaves. These fertilizers contain nutrients that plant leaves can absorb directly. Although a plant's roots also can absorb the nutrients in most foliar fertilizers, those absorbed via leaves have a quick effect. Don't apply foliar fertilizers in hot weather because leaves can become damaged.

✔ **Granular.** These fertilizers are the most common and most often sold in boxes or bags. Most granular fertilizers are partially soluble. For example, a 10-10-10 granular fertilizer is best applied to the soil about a month prior to planting in order for the nutrients to be available at planting time. You also can get special formulations, such as rose food or azalea food. These specialized fertilizers supply nutrients over a longer period of time than liquid or soluble fertilizers but not as long as slow-release kinds. (See Figure 14-3.)

Figure 14-3:
Use a spreader to apply granular fertilizer.

✔ **Liquid.** Most kinds of fertilizers are dry, but some come as liquid in bottles and jugs. On a per-nutrient basis, liquid fertilizers are more expensive than most dry fertilizers. Most liquid fertilizers need further dilution in water, but a few are ready-to-use. Liquid fertilizers are easy to inject into irrigation systems, which is the reason many professional growers prefer them. (See Figure 14-4.)

Figure 14-4:
Applying a liquid fertilizer with a hose-end sprayer.

✔ **Organic.** These fertilizers are often made from dead or composted plants and animals. Examples are blood meal, fish emulsion, and manure. Usually, organic fertilizers contain significant amounts of only one of the major nutrients; for example, bone meal contains only phosphorus. Nutrients in organic fertilizers are made available to plant roots after soil microorganisms break down the nutrients. Activity of these microorganisms is fastest in summer when soils are warm. As a general rule, half the nutrients in organic fertilizers are available to plants the first season.

✔ **Slow-release.** These fertilizers release the nutrients they contain at specific rates in specific conditions over an extended period. For example, Osmocote fertilizers release nutrients in response to soil moisture. The nutrients inside the tiny beads "osmose" through a resin membrane. Soil microorganisms slowly act on another type, sulfur-coated urea, until the nutrients release. Some fertilizers can release their nutrients for as long as eight months. Slow-release fertilizers are very useful for container plants that otherwise need frequent fertilizing.

Kinds of fertilizers for various plants

Different kinds of plants need different kinds of fertilizers, and Table 14-1 lists our recommendations. Of course the best advice before using any fertilizer is to have your soil tested. For more about soil testing, see Chapter 11.

Table 14-1	Fertilizing at a Glance	
Plant	*Fertilizer*	*Comments*
Annuals	Granular	Apply before planting, supplemented by liquid soluble applications after planting.
Bulbs	Granular 8-8-8 or similar	Apply at planting time.
Fruit trees	Granular and/or organic	Apply as necessary in spring only.
Hanging baskets	Slow-release or liquid soluble	Apply every two weeks.

(continued)

Table 14-1 *(continued)*

Plant	Fertilizer	Comments
House plants	Slow-release or liquid soluble	
Lawns	Granular and/or organic 28-7-14 or similar, preferably slow-release; or an organic, high-nitrogen fertilizer	
Perennials	Granular and/or organic	Apply in autumn; supplement with liquid soluble.
Roses	Granular and/or organic	Apply in spring and autumn for good growth.
Trees and shrubs	Granular and/or organic	Apply in autumn; supplement with complete granular (10-10-10 or similar) if spring growth is poor.
Vegetables	Organic	Applied in autumn or at least one month prior to planting. Continually enrich soil with organic fertilizers; supplement with granular 5-10-10 first two gardening seasons.

Organic fertilizers

Organic or natural fertilizers such as manure and composts are more cumbersome and possibly more expensive than synthetic fertilizers, but nothing quite takes their place. These fertilizers provide some nutrient value and, when you incorporate them into the soil, improve soil structure, which increases the soil's ability to hold air, nutrients, and water.

Plants take up nutrients in specific forms, regardless of whether the source is organic or synthetic. You can supply all the nutrients that plants need by using only organic materials, but you need to use some care and effort to ensure that sufficient amounts of nitrogen, phosphorus, and potash are available to the plants throughout the season.

Because the nutrients in organic materials are tied up in more complex molecules, these nutrients often take longer to become available to the plants, which can result in temporary nutrient deficiencies, especially in the spring.

Fresh manure can "burn" plants (damaging leaves and growth from excess application) just as surely as any chemical fertilizer, whereas woody materials (wood chips, sawdust, leaf piles, and so on) can cause a temporary nitrogen deficiency until they are sufficiently decomposed. The microorganisms that help the decay process may use up all the available nitrogen to break down the woody material. You can counteract this effect somewhat by applying a little extra nitrogen in the spring. A rule of green thumb is that when the material starts to resemble soil, it is ready for the garden.

Piling Onto the Compost Bandwagon

As we visit the gardens of friends and neighbors around the country, a stop at the compost pile is a must in almost every garden tour. Meeting a gardener who shows off a rich, dark, earthy compost as eagerly as towering dahlias is not at all unusual.

Not so long ago, we gardeners hid our compost piles. In privacy, we would witness the magic of composting, the transformation of garden and yard waste into sweet-smelling black gold. We feared that others (especially neighbors) would judge our passion as a waste of time and space.

Attitudes have changed. Landfills are filling up, and some states even ban yard waste from landfills. Composting is now widely recognized as an easy, effective way to reduce solid waste at home.

More to the heart of gardeners is the fact that compost is a valuable, natural soil amendment. Adding compost to garden beds and planting holes enhances nutrients and improves soil texture. Compost helps loosen heavy clay soils, and it increases the water-holding capacity of sandy soils. (See Chapter 11 for more about soils.)

A *compost pile* is a collection of plant (and sometimes animal) materials, combined in a way to encourage quick decomposition. Soil microorganisms (bacteria and fungi) do the work of breaking down this organic material into a soil-like consistency.

These organisms need oxygen and water to survive. Turning the pile over provides oxygen, and an occasional watering helps keep it moist. If the pile is well made and the organisms are thriving, it heats up quickly and doesn't emit any unpleasant odors. Finished compost that looks and feels like dark, crumbly soil can thus take as little as a month to produce.

From refuse to riches

Whether you make your compost in an elaborate store-bought bin (one that closes tightly) or simply in a freestanding pile, the essentials of good composting are the same. To get fast results, follow these steps:

1. **Collect equal parts, by volume, of dried, brown, carbon-rich material (like old leaves or straw) and fresh, green, nitrogen-rich material (fresh-cut grass, green vegetation, and vegetable kitchen wastes).**

   A few materials should *not* be used in an open compost pile. Although farm animal manures are a safe source of nitrogen for the pile, dog and cat waste can spread unhealthy organisms. Meat, fats, bones, and cooked foods decompose slowly, may be smelly, and may attract animal pests — add these only to compost bins that close tightly. Avoid chemically treated lawn clippings and diseased plant material. Finally, keep out tenacious weeds that spread by runners and roots, such as Bermuda grass.

2. **Chop or shred the organic materials into small pieces, if possible.**

   Pieces that are ³/₄ inch (2 cm) or smaller are ideal because they break down quickly.

3. **Build the pile at least 3 feet x 3 feet x 3 feet (1 *cubic yard or 1 cubic meter*), alternating layers of the carbon-rich material with the green material.**

   Layer a thin covering of soil for every 18 inches of depth. The soil carries more microorganisms that aid in decomposition.

4. **Wet the pile as you build it.**

   Keep the material moist, not soaked. (It should be about as moist as a wrung-out sponge.)

5. **After the temperature begins to decrease, turn the pile, wetting it as necessary to keep it moist.**

   A well-built pile heats up in approximately a week, peaking between 120°F and 160°F (49°C to 71°C). If you don't have a compost thermometer, use a garden fork to turn the pile every week or so the first month.

Bin there, done that!

A compost pile cares not whether it's caged or freestanding. An enclosure, called a *compost bin,* mostly keeps the pile neat and can help retain moisture and heat. Depending on its design, a compost bin also keeps out animal pests. For these reasons, especially in urban settings, a bin is a good idea. (See Figure 14-5.)

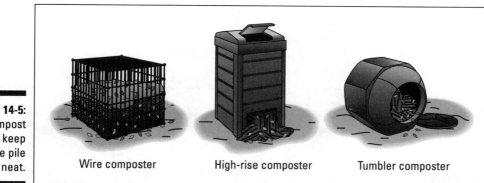

Figure 14-5:
Compost
bins keep
the pile
neat.

Wire composter   High-rise composter   Tumbler composter

To build or to buy?

Bins are available by mail order and, increasingly, through nurseries, garden centers, and even discount stores. You can spend up to $400 or more for a commercial compost bin, or you can make your own with scrap materials.

A *wire bin* is perhaps the easiest type to make. You need an 11-foot (3.5 m) length of 36-inch-wide (1 m), welded reinforcing wire with a grid of about 2 x 4 inches (5 x 10 cm). Simply bend the wire to form a hoop and tie the ends together with strong wire. Lining the wire mesh with landscape fabric helps prevent the pile from drying out excessively. This bin holds about a cubic yard when full.

To use the bin, fill it with the appropriate balance of organic material. When the pile is ready to turn, lift off the wire mesh and set it next to the pile; then, turn the material and fork it back into the enclosure.

Another option is a *wooden compost bin,* made with wooden pallets, wooden scrap boards, and wire or — for the more elaborate model — 2 x 4 (5 x 10 cm) and 2 x 6 (5 x 15 cm) lumber. The Cadillac of the wooden compost bins uses three bins arranged side by side, as shown in Figure 14-6. Though this bin can be time-consuming to construct, some gardeners prefer the convenience of a three-box bin. Each bin is for compost at a different stage of maturity. For example, fresh material is added to the far-left bin, turned into the middle one after a few weeks, and then turned into the bin at the far right to finish.

Commercial bins come in four basic flavors:

> ✔ **Containers for hot compost.** Usually made out of recycled plastic, these bottomless boxes or cylinders are designed to be used in much the same way as the wire bin. You completely fill the bin with the right blend of materials and let the pile heat up. To turn the compost, when

the bin is full, you lift off the top section of compost and place it on the ground (the section on top now becomes the section on the bottom). Then you reach in with a fork and lift some of the lower compost, making it the top section of compost, and so on.

Figure 14-6:
A wooden
compost bin
with three
bins allows
for easy
turning.

Some of these containers are stackable, which makes removing them and turning the compost easier. With sufficient turning, this type of bin delivers fast results.

✔ **Bins for a static pile.** With these plastic units (which usually have air vents along the sides), you make a compost pile by putting a balance of waste materials in the top of the bin and letting the mixture sit. As the waste decomposes, you remove the finished compost from the bottom of the bin and add more waste to the top.

This type of bin is the most commonly available bin, although not necessarily the best. You don't need to do any turning, and you can add waste at any time; however, decomposition is slow, and you get only small amounts of compost at a time. Because the pile does not get very hot, weeds, seeds, and plant diseases may survive.

✔ **Tumblers.** With a tumbler, you place your compost inside the container and then turn the entire bin to toss the compost inside. Some tumblers have crank handles for turning. One tumbler system is designed to roll on the ground, tumbling the compost inside as it goes.

With these units, you make a hot compost by balancing the waste materials and turning the bin frequently. Tumblers are generally the most expensive type of bin, but the ease of turning and the fast results may be worth the money. Choose one with at least a 1-cubic-yard (1 m³) capacity and test it for ease of loading and turning before you buy.

✔ **Anaerobic containers.** These sealed, closed-to-air compost bins require no turning or aerating. You simply fill the container with organic material, close the lid, and wait, sometimes up to six months.

Although no maintenance is required, this type of bin often has insect and odor problems. The decomposed product is slimy and requires drying before use, and shoveling the compost out of the bin is difficult. We give this product low marks for home gardeners.

Composting aids . . . who needs them?

You don't need to have any store-bought gadgets to make compost. With or without accessories, you can create a perfect pile. A few supplies, however, do make composting faster, more exacting, and perhaps easier. Here's a rundown of these handy items for your consideration. All are available through mail-order garden supply catalogs. (See Appendix B.)

✔ **Compost starters.** Manufacturers say these products, sometimes called *inoculants* or *activators,* accelerate the composting process and improve the quality of the finished compost. We say you don't really need them, and that adding a little garden soil for every 12- to 18-inch (30–46 cm) layer of yard waste will accomplish the same thing. At most you might want to add a little cotton- or soybean meal, but only then if the materials are mostly brown (high in carbon).

As an alternative to buying a commercial starter, make a thin layer of rich garden soil when you first build your pile.

✔ **Compost thermometer.** This thermometer consists of a face dial and a steel probe (about 20 inches, or 50 cm, long). You use this tool to accurately monitor the temperature of compost. The instrument measures temperatures from 0°F to 220°F (–18°C to 104°C and enables you to know when your pile is cooking and when it is cooling down and ready to turn. After you insert the steel probe into the pile, you can see the temperature reading on the face dial. If the compost gets hot, meaning up to 140°F to 160°F (60°C to 71°C), most of the bad players — weeds, diseases, and insect eggs — get killed.

✔ **Compost aerating too.** You push a galvanized steel tool, which is about 36 inches (1 m) long, into the compost pile. As you pull the tool out, two paddles open, creating a churning action that enables oxygen to enter the pile.

✔ **Compost sifter.** Because different materials decompose at different rates, you may end up with some large chunks of not-yet-decomposed material in compost that is otherwise ready for the garden. The sifter separates out the large pieces, which you can then toss back into a new compost pile to further decompose.

You can save a few bucks by making your own sifter. To do so, use ¹/₄-inch (0.5 cm) window screen stapled or nailed to a wooden frame made of lumber. Make the frame large enough so that you can position it over a wheelbarrow and sift compost through it.

✔ **Pitchfork.** This long-handled tool, with tines about 10 to 12 inches (25 to 30 cm) long, is the best instrument to use for turning compost.

Heapin' it on

So what else can you put in your compost pile besides the obvious? The following list describes several other materials found around the home and garden that make good additions to any compost pile:

✔ Ashes from the wood stove (sprinkle them lightly between layers; *don't* add them by the bucketful)

✔ Chicken or rabbit manure

✔ Coffee grounds and tea leaves

✔ Eggshells (crush them before adding)

✔ Flowers

✔ Fruit and vegetable peels, stalks, and foliage (everything from salad leftovers to old pea vines)

✔ Fruit pulp from a juicer

✔ Grass clippings (mix them thoroughly to prevent clumping)

✔ Hedge clippings

✔ Shredded leaves (whole leaves tend to mat down and block air)

✔ Pine needles (use sparingly; they break down slowly)

✔ Sawdust

✔ Sod and soil

✔ Wood chips (chipped very small for faster decomposition)

A-Mulching We Will Go . . .

Mulch is any material, organic or not, placed over the surface of soil to conserve moisture, kill weed seedlings, modify soil temperatures, or make the garden look more attractive — or all four at once. Mulch was traditionally thought to mean natural, organic materials such as leaves, wood chips, and sand. Now a multitude of plastic-based films or woven materials are available.

A common goal of mulching is to reduce weeding, so it makes little sense to use mulch that is chock-full of weed seeds. Instead, use seed-free organic mulches or inorganic mulches such as the following:

- ✔ Grass clippings (from a weed- and pesticide-free lawn)
- ✔ Leaves (shredded or composted)
- ✔ Newspaper (shredded or flat)
- ✔ Pine needles (for acid-loving crops)
- ✔ Salt hay (a generally weed-free plant from oceanside meadows)
- ✔ Shredded bark
- ✔ Wood chips. Use fresh chips from a local arborist, or better, composted wood chips from a soil or amendment supplier.

Inorganic mulches

Inorganic mulch holds in moisture and stops weeds but doesn't add fertility to the soil. Use this mulch around perennials, shrubs, or trees that are naturally adjusted to your soil and don't require additional fertilizer. Examples of infertile mulch include gravel, landscape fabric, sand, and stone.

Fertile mulches

Double your gardening pleasure by using fertile mulch, which controls weeds *and* provides small amounts of nutrients. All organic mulches made of plant material fit this group. Some organic mulches quickly rot (decompose) and dissolve nutrients into the soil; these are green, fresh, and not too woody. The mulches that quickly decompose are useful in annual flower and vegetable beds. When sprinkled with water, or in rainy-summer areas, organic mulch that decomposes fairly quickly also leaches some nutrients while sitting on top of the soil.

Other organic mulches are slow to decompose and release few nutrients; these are usually dry, woody, and very low in nitrogen. Bark mulches are slowest to decompose because bark is naturally rot-resistant. Use these for pathways, or around trees and shrubs. Chips of tree sapwood may be fresh or composted. The latter is preferable, if available. Fresh wood chips can make an excellent mulch, but you should apply a little extra nitrogen fertilizer over the mulch so that it doesn't take all the nitrogen at your plants' expense.

Fertile mulches that quickly decompose but have weed seeds include cow, rabbit, goat, sheep, and horse manure; hay; some poultry bedding; sewage sludge; and straw. Fertile mulches that also quickly decompose but have no weed seeds include clean grass clippings, leaves, and salt hay.

Newspaper, shredded bark, and wood chips add little fertility to the soil and decompose slowly because they are high in carbon; they have no weed seeds.

All the mulches we mention are just part of a nearly infinite selection of local specialties. Rice hulls, cocoa shells, sugar cane refuse, ground corncobs, peanut shells, and grape pomace are a few you may encounter, depending where you live.

GARDENING TIP

Woven plastic materials (called *landscape fabric*) act as a seedling barrier as well, but these effective materials are not attractive enough for some situations. Also, sunlight deteriorates these mulches, so covering these mulches with a weed-free organic mulch to block the sun's ultraviolet rays is a good idea. The fabric lasts longer and your garden looks better.

ECO-SMART

A well-read mulch

Newspapers provide the ultimate organic "herbicide," a simple and cost-effective way to mulch out weeds. A thin layer of five to ten sheets of newspaper suppresses all sprouting weed seeds, stops some resprouting taproots, and makes life difficult for runner roots. Use newsprint that is plain black and white or that has colored pictures. (We used to recommend not using glossy, color paper for the chemicals, such as cadmium and lead, in the inks. This is less a problem now that most printers have switched to less toxic inks.) The newspapers are best used around woody perennials, shrubs, and trees, but once you're familiar with the process, you can use them around flowers or vegetables.

To apply the newspaper, moisten the sheets so that they don't blow around as you lay them out among the plants. Cover the papers with a thin layer of a weed-free, attractive mulch. The mulch helps the newspaper last for 6 to 18 months, depending on whether you have wet or dry summers, respectively.

Cardboard works even better than newspaper for the really tough weeds.

Chapter 15

A Snip Here, a Snip There: Pruning and Propagating

In This Chapter
▶ Pruning smart
▶ Mastering the basics
▶ Gearing up for pruning
▶ Taking stem cuttings

*O*ne of the images that often comes to mind when you think about gardening is of a wise gardener with a pair of snips in her hand carefully clipping and snipping in a knowing way. What are gardeners doing when they snip and clip? Well, they're probably doing one of two things: pruning or propagating.

You use both pruning and propagating to promote plant growth, but you use them for different purposes. *Pruning* refers to cutting plants to redirect the plant's growth to where you want it. *Propagating* (or taking cuttings) refers to cutting off a part of a plant and using the cutting to start a new plant.

In this chapter, you find out how to make the cut as a pruner and propagator. Okay, you won't leave this chapter as Edward Scissorhands, but we do give you the fundamentals that will have you happily snipping and cutting in no time.

Practical Pruning

Pruning is one of the most misunderstood, and therefore neglected, gardening techniques. Pruning may be a big job, like removing a heavy, damaged limb, or it may involve the simple removal of a spent flower. Pruning is part maintenance, part preventative medicine, and part landscaping. Because plants grow, they change all the time: A branch that was just right last year, is now too long. Or perhaps the plant is overgrown and needs rejuvenation. Pruning is nothing more than snipping or cutting or pinching away some part of a plant for some good reason.

Here are some common reasons for pruning plants:

✔ **Sculpting for decorative reasons.** This is your chance to be fanciful. There are no rules, but be aware that once you embark on pruning a plant to a specific shape, it's hard to go back.

✔ **Shaping a tree or shrub for strength and resistance to wind, snow, and ice damage (or to bear a bountiful crop).** Some fruit trees need annual or semiannual pruning in order to continue bearing crops.

✔ **Keeping the plant healthy.** By removing dead branches, you make it easier for the tree to seal the remaining wound.

As a general rule, don't prune unless you must. Always consider whether the plant really needs to be pruned. Many native or naturalized trees grow perfectly fine without pruning. But roses and fruit trees, among others, need thoughtful pruning for maximum production of flowers and fruit.

When to prune

Type of plant	When
Shrubs that bloom in spring	Just after flowers fade
Shrubs that bloom in summer or fall	Early spring
Rhododendrons and azaleas	Just after flowers fade
Pine trees	Late spring
Formal hedges	Late spring and, if necessary, fall
Most trees, shrubs, and vines	Late winter or early spring

How pruning affects plant growth

To understand how and when to prune, you need to know a bit about a plant's biology (and its inner struggles). Like a fast-growing teenager, a mixture of hormones and food controls a tree's growth. A tree's food consists of carbohydrates that are generated in the leaves by photosynthesis. Some of the tree's important hormones — growth stimulators or regulators — come from the bud at the tip of each leafy shoot or branch. Biologists refer to this bud as the *apical, leading,* or *tip* bud. The tip bud stimulates new, lengthy, vertical growth and stifles the growth of lower potential shoots — called *dormant buds*.

When you clip out any tip bud, you take away the stifling tip hormones and their dominance. The dormant buds below the cut burst into growth and begin to produce the tip hormones themselves.

When a branch is positioned at a 45–60 degree angle, the flow of carbohydrates, hormones, and nutrients naturally favors the formation of flower buds. With many deciduous fruit trees, like apple, almond, and pear trees, the flower buds become long-term fruiting places, called *spurs*, in the following years.

The kindest cuts

All pruning cuts, whether made with a chain saw or finger tips, fall into one of two categories: *thinning* cut or *heading* cut. Both kinds are important, but it helps to know the difference and when to use them.

You prune plants using the following techniques:

- ✔ **Thinning cuts.** Thinning cuts remove an entire branch or limb all the way to its origin. You do this with your fingertips when pinching a coleus or tomato seedling; with hand pruners for larger plants or shrubs; or pruning shears (even a saw) for trees. Regardless of scale, the principle is the same. When thinning, you remove a branch or stem completely to create better air circulation or to reduce crowded conditions. Always make thinning cuts to just above a dormant bud. Cut at a slight angle and leave about $1/4$ (0.6 cm) inch of the shoot above the bud — not a long stub.

- ✔ **Heading cuts.** These cuts shorten a branch or stem. As opposed to thinning, this type of pruning cut shortens a branch and doesn't remove it entirely.

- ✔ **Pinching.** This action can be either a heading or thinning cut. Usually, you pinch soft growth between your thumb and forefinger. Pinching is handy with soft annuals and perennials, but also good for larger plants too, if you do it early enough when their shoots are still young and soft. Any pruning done at this early stage is ideal because the plant suffers minimal harm and recovery is quick.

- ✔ **Shearing.** For this cut, use scissorlike pruning "shears" to keep hedge lines straight and neat. Boxwood and yews are commonly sheared.

Check out Figure 15-1 to see examples of these pruning cuts.

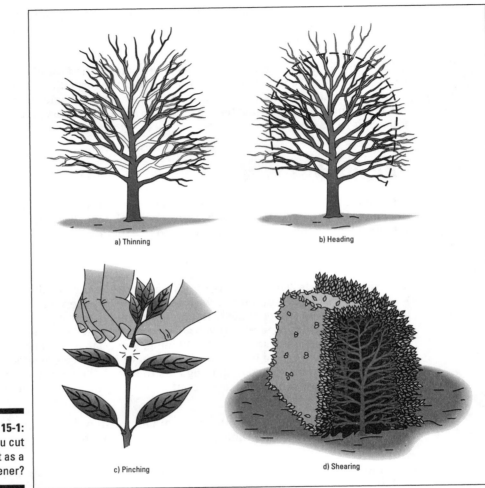

a) Thinning

b) Heading

Figure 15-1:
Can you cut
it as a
gardener?

c) Pinching

d) Shearing

Pruning trees

Usually when pruning trees, you should use thinning cuts, but don't cut absolutely flush to the remaining limb or branch. Leave the *branch collar* intact. The branch collar is slightly wider than the shoot you're removing, is marked with many compact wrinkles, and is usually a slightly different tone or texture than the shoot. Natural chemicals within the branch collar encourage rapid healing and help prevent rot from entering the heart of the tree. Flush cuts allow the rot to slip past the collar and invade the very core of the tree or plant.

Consider these pruning tips before you take out your saw:

- **Sawing a medium-sized limb.** If the limb is small enough to hold so that it doesn't fall while cutting, you can use only one cut with a pruning handsaw. Leave the larger and more noticeable branch collar intact. Don't let the limb drop as you cut through it, or the bark will tear or rip.

- **Sawing a large limb.** You use three cuts to remove large, heavy limbs, as shown in Figure 15-2. First, a few inches (about 8 cm) outside of the branch collar, cut halfway through the limb from the underneath side. Then, a few inches outside of the first cut, make a second cut (from the top), this time going all the way through the limb. If any bark begins to tear, it will stop at the cut underneath. Trim off the remaining stub with a final cut just outside the branch collar.

- **Treating your tree's wounds.** Covering pruning wound with tar or asphalt doesn't really help the tree much. The toxins in the tar might even slow wound healing. If you want to cover the wound for appearance sake, use a diluted water-based paint. Some of the newest kinds of lanolin-based wound sealers might actually be beneficial.

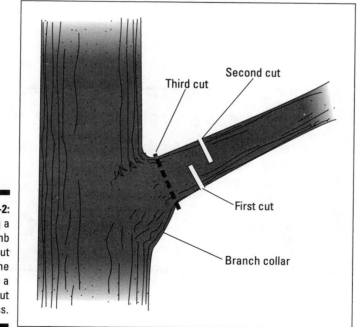

Figure 15-2:
Removing a large limb without ripping the bark is a three-cut process.

Third cut

Second cut

First cut

Branch collar

Pruning in winter

The traditional season for pruning *deciduous* (leaf shedding) plants is while all the buds are dormant — in late winter or very early spring before flowers or leaves open. Such pruning stimulates new vegetative shoots — which are less fruitful with fruit trees. Cutting back a dormant branch causes two or more side shoots to emerge below the cut as a result of lost tip dominance. (See this section "How pruning affects plant growth" in this chapter for more about tip dominance.) Winter pruning is especially helpful when you want to force new shoots to fill air space around the trunk with branches.

When you have many long, vertical shoots — called *suckers* or *watersprouts* — winter pruning only makes the problem worse. Thinning each vertical limb, even if cut to its base, usually multiplies the problem by causing two or more shoots to arise with the spring sap flow. You remedy this situation only with summer pruning.

Pruning in summer

Summer pruning can become the most valuable technique in a gardener's repertoire. Careful summer pruning has the effect of mildly stunting or dwarfing trees. The partial removal of the foliage in summer means fewer leaves to convert sunlight into stored carbohydrates.

Pruning trees and shrubs

A few "rules of limb" apply when pruning all trees and shrubs:

- ✔ Remove dead or diseased wood as soon as possible. (Be sure not to spread certain diseases, like fireblight, with the pruning tools: Clean the blade with a 10 percent dilution of bleach after *every* cut.)

- ✔ Cut out one or two branches or shoots if they rub against each other.

- ✔ Prune in the winter to encourage new shoots and leafy growth.

- ✔ To remove unwanted shoots or limbs without stimulating too many new shoots, prune in the summer.

Because summer pruning is so appropriate for removing unwanted branches, it is the preferred way to begin a program of restoration with neglected and overgrown trees.

Summer pruning is also the best time for thinning cuts. The active photosynthesis allows the trees to begin forming a *callus* over the cut. The well-knit callus tissue that forms a ring around the cut resists the sprouting of new shoots the coming spring.

Pruning too early in the season, during spring's burst of vegetative growth, has a stimulating effect more like dormant pruning. Summer-prune after the initial flurry of spring growth, as the weekly growth rate slows down.

In cold-winter climates, summer-prune by the middle of summer because late summer pruning sometimes forces new, succulent shoots. These tender shoots don't harden off before freezing weather arrives and can die off.

Pruning tools

Poorly constructed tools can cripple or maim a gardener, so select a set of well-made, sturdy pruning tools. Here's a brief list of the essentials.

- ✔ **Hand pruner.** Hand pruners are usually reserved for cuts up to $1/2$–1 inch (1.3–2.5 cm) in diameter. Our favorite hand pruner is the Felco #8 — in our opinion, the most comfortable and easily used bypass pruner on the market.

- ✔ **Lopper.** Loppers can cut limbs up to several inches in diameter. You never need a lopping shear if your trees are well trained from the start. If you're restoring an abandoned tree or shrub, you need a lopper to remove older wood. We suggest choosing a 16–24-inch (41–61 cm) or 30-inch (76 cm) lopper. Aluminum- or fiberglass-handled loppers are lighter than wood and, thus, easier to handle.

- ✔ **Hand saw.** The one hand saw required is probably a 12-inch (30 cm) bladed, folding saw. Make sure that you get one with a locking mechanism for the open position.

  If you're working on a disheveled or abandoned tree with large limbs slated for removal, you may want a large, 24–36-inch long (61–91 cm) curved pruning saw with large 1–2-inch (2.5–5 cm) saw teeth. The bigger the saw's teeth and the wider the space between the teeth, the faster the saw cuts.

- ✔ **Ladder and pole pruner.** If you're caring for really large shade or fruit trees, you need a pruning ladder and/or a pole pruner.

First, buy a three-legged, aluminum (not wooden) orchard pruning and picking ladder. These ladders come in heights of 6–16 feet (2–5 meters) and cost from $75 to $200. The ladders are not cheap, but they are the most comfortable way to prune a large tree with hand pruners and a lopper.

If standing on a ladder makes you nervous, an extending pole pruner is your next best option. Buy one with fiberglass poles (which are light-weight and won't conduct electricity if you happen to touch a wire) that telescope from 6–12 feet (about 2–4 meters). The only variety worth buying has a cast-metal head and a chain-and-gear-driven mechanism. A good pole pruner can set you back $125 to $180.

Appendix B lists several mail-order companies that sell these tools.

Down-to-Earth Propagating

When people speak of propagating, mostly they mean *taking cuttings* — using pieces of stems, roots, and leaves to start new plants. (See Figure 15-3.) The best technique for most gardeners to know is how to take stem cuttings, which you can use to propagate perennials and shrubs.

Figure 15-3: Taking a stem cutting.

Softwood stem cuttings, taken from spring until midsummer, root the quickest. During this time, plants are actively growing, and the stems are succulent and flexible. Here's how to take a softwood stem cutting:

1. **Use a sharp knife to cut a 4–5-inch-long (10–12 cm) stem (or side shoot) just below a leaf, and remove all but two or three leaves at the top.**

2. **Dip the cut end into *rooting hormone*.**

Rooting hormone is a powder or liquid containing growth hormones that stimulate root growth on cuttings. Some also contain a fungicide to control root rot. Check local nurseries or garden centers for the product. If you can't find it locally, you can order it from A. M. Leonard, Inc. (See Appendix B for the address.)

3. **Insert the cutting into a box or container (with drainage holes), filled with about 3 inches (8 cm) of moistened pure builder's sand, vermiculite, or perlite.**

4. **Slip the container into a self-sealing plastic bag.**

   Prop up the bag with something like toothpicks or short twigs so that the plastic doesn't touch the leaves. Seal the bag to minimize water loss, but open it occasionally to let in fresh air.

5. **Place the covered container in indirect light.**

6. **When the cuttings are well-rooted (starting in four to eight weeks, for most plants) and are putting on new growth, transplant them into individual containers of potting soil. As they continue to grow, gradually expose them to more light.**

7. **When the plants are well established in the pots and continue to put on top growth, *harden them off* and plant them in their permanent garden location.**

Here are some easy-to-root plants to grow from stem cuttings.

✔ **Perennials:** Begonia, candytuft, chrysanthemum, carnations or pinks *(Dianthus)*, geraniums *(Pelargonium)*, penstemon, phlox, sage, sedum

✔ **Woody plants:** Bougainvillea, fuchsia, gardenia, heather, honeysuckle, ivy, pyracantha, star jasmine, willow

Getting Plants for Free

Sometimes the best source for plant material for propagating is neighbors and friends. If your neighbor has a plant you'd like to grow (maybe a splendid fuchsia or a geranium that you can't find at the nursery), just ask to take cuttings. (Gardeners love to share.)

Another great way to get new plants is through *division,* the process of pulling apart clumps of plants to create new clumps. (See Figure 15-4.) As plants (like daylilies and peonies) become established in a garden, most develop into larger and larger clumps made up of small plants. Dividing these clumps and replanting is the easiest means of spreading and increasing them. Dividing works great with all but "tap-rooted" plants, namely plants with a main root that grows straight down, such as a carrot. For a list of plants that you can't divide, please check out *Perennials For Dummies* by Marcie Tatroe and the Editors of the National Gardening Association (IDG Books Worldwide, Inc.).

Figure 15-4:
Divide by pulling apart the root ball or by using a spade.

You can divide plants by using the following techniques:

- ✔ Use a spade or digging fork to lift out a mature clump (usually 3–5 years old).

- ✔ Divide fine-rooted types, such as lamb's ears, by hand, gently teasing apart the clump into separate plants.

- ✔ Divide tough or fleshy-rooted types with a spade by cutting down through the roots, or use two garden forks back-to-back to pry the clumps apart.

Each new section for replanting should include several buds. Discard the older central section and replant the divisions as soon as possible.

Knowing the best season to divide plants is important — and it varies by plant and climate. As a general guideline, divide spring-flowering plants in very late summer or early autumn so that the new divisions can become established before winter. Divide summer- and autumn-flowering plants in early spring, while new top growth is just 2 or 3 inches (5 to 8 cm) high.

Chapter 16

Fighting Pests, Diseases, and Weeds

· ·

In This Chapter

▶ Adding an ounce of prevention

▶ Dealing with pesky insects

▶ Controlling 25 common garden pests

▶ Keeping beneficial insects happy

▶ Curing 12 plant diseases

▶ Outwitting greedy animals

▶ Keeping weeds from muscling out your plants

· ·

*W*hen you begin creating that little piece of paradise that is your garden, you may envision picture-perfect plants with no weeds at their feet or holes in their leaves or half-eaten flowers. The reality can be startling, prompting some discouraged gardeners to run to the store for the most potent insect-disease-weed killer they can find. As we explain in this chapter, bringing out the big guns early on can be a big mistake yet completely understandable from an emotional point of view.

The key to a healthy garden may sound a bit strange to some of you, but here it is: Don't sweat the small stuff. The more you try for a perfect, pest-free garden, the more likely you are to invite problems. Accepting a certain amount of damage is not only realistic, it also makes gardening more fun and less frustrating. Don't try to vanquish all enemies and leave them decimated, but do try to outsmart them, perhaps losing a battle but winning the war. In addition, when you learn more about insect and animal pests, diseases, and weeds — and the conditions that invite them — you arm yourself with new techniques to reduce damage while promoting a healthier garden. This chapter gives you a start in that direction.

Preventing Bad Things from Happening

Research suggests that plants emit a chemical signal when they are under stress, and insects home in on this chemical signal like a landing pattern from air-traffic control. Diseases are similarly opportunistic, causing the most problems when plants are already weakened. So, what can you do to give your plants the best possible chance at a good life? Here are some suggestions:

- ✔ **Choose the proper site and soil.** Azaleas planted in full sun, for example, are apt to be more ravaged by azalea lace bugs than those planted in their natural woodland. Planting blueberries in alkaline soil — instead of the acid soil they require — guarantees poor performance. (See Chapter 11.)

- ✔ **Avoid planting the same vegetables or flowers in the same location year after year.** Crop rotation prevents pests and diseases that are specific to certain crops from accumulating in the soil.

- ✔ **Plant several small patches of the same type of vegetable rather than one large patch.** This approach makes it more difficult for insects to home in on and decimate their favorite crop.

- ✔ **Keep your garden clean and tidy.** During the growing season, remove damaged leaves. At season's end, remove crop residue and add it to the compost pile. Place diseased plants in the trash, not the compost pile to avoid spreading. As you prune, sanitize pruning shears between cuts by spraying with Lysol or a bleach solution. Some insect pests — such as aphids, cucumber beetles, and tarnished plant bugs — can spread diseases. Keep them under control, and you'll help prevent disease.

- ✔ **Choose resistant plants when possible.** Many plants (or varieties of plants) are less attractive to plant pests and less susceptible to certain diseases. To reduce corn earworm damage, for example, choose varieties that form a tight husk that extends over the tip of the ear, where the worm normally finds its entry. Look for this information in plant and seed catalogs.

- ✔ **Take steps to encourage beneficial insects into your garden.** (See this chapter's section, "Encouraging 'good' insects.")

- ✔ **Cultivate the vegetable garden soil in the fall and early spring.** Loosening the soil exposes insect eggs, larvae, and pupae that will provide a tasty treat for birds.

- ✔ **Mulch to reduce insects, weeds, and disease.** Keep mulch several inches away from trunks and stems to discourage collar rot. Lightly rake the mulch once or twice a season to expose and kill pests' eggs. Though mulch may provide safe haven for slugs, you can use baits and traps to reduce their numbers.

✔ **Provide for good soil drainage to discourage root rot.**

✔ **Space plants to provide good air circulation.** Leaves dry quickly, preventing spores of some fungus diseases from growing.

✔ **Water the soil, not the plants.** Early morning watering is best because the sun will evaporate any water on the leaves. Avoid evening watering.

✔ **Don't walk amid plants when the foliage is wet because you can spread disease spores from plant to plant.** Avoid handling cucumbers or tomatoes after handling tobacco, including flowering tobacco (*Nicotiana*) to reduce spread of tobacco mosaic virus.

An insect or disease problem is often a symptom of something else being out of whack. Table 16-1 lists conditions and the pests they promote. Treating the causes, not just the symptoms, helps to prevent problems.

Table 16-1	Conditions That Promote Pests and Problems	
Condition	*Pest/Problem*	*Preventative Measure*
High or excessive organic matter in soil	Cutworms	Reduce additions of organic matter, rototill to speed decomposition
Partially decomposed crop debris	Damping-off disease, cutworms	Clean and cultivate garden in fall after harvest
Poorly decomposed manure	Root maggots, weeds	Use only composted manure
Dry and dusty weather	Spider mites	Wash leaves of plants with water
Sandy soils	Root-knot nematode	Plant resistant plants
Acid soils	Clubroot of cabbage, broccoli, and related crops	Raise pH by using ground dolomitic limestone
Too much water	Damping-off and other root rots, weeds	Reduce irrigation or improve drainage
Too much nitrogen	Weeds, aphids	Reduce fertilizer applications

Identifying Damage

When a problem does occur, correctly identifying the cause is essential. Finding out what's wrong can require some sleuthing unless you happen to witness the damage in the making. You can make more-reliable guesses about what's going on in your garden if you visit it often. Taking a stroll just before sunset or in the early morning can reveal insects that hide during the heat of the day. Slugs, for example, feed at night, so an investigative tour with a flashlight (and gloves) after dark can yield a containerful that the birds will appreciate the next day. Japanese beetles are sluggish in the cool hours of the evening and early morning, so you can easily knock them into a can of water.

One of the most frustrating experiences is to care for seeds and seedlings and then have them die or fail to appear at all. Table 16-2 offers a listing of common problems and causes.

Table 16-2	Common Pests of Vegetable Seedlings
What the Problem Looks Like	*Probable Cause*
Seeds fail to germinate or seedlings fail to appear	Seedcorn maggots, damping-off, birds
Seedling collapses	Damping-off, heat, planted too early, planted in soil that is too cold or wet
Stems eaten at soil line	Cutworms
Leaves and stems chewed, torn	Snails, slugs, caterpillars, rabbits
Severely wilted plant (roots eaten)	Wireworms, root maggots, gophers
Small, round pits in leaves	Flea beetles
Threadlike, twisting lines in leaves	Leaf miners
Clusters of small, pear-shaped insects	Aphids
Plants completely removed	Animal pests such as birds or gophers

Homemade compost tea

Compost tea is a genetic cocktail teeming with microorganisms that appear to boost a plant's natural defenses and suppress the growth of some fungi. It can help reduce the spread of botrytis molds, tomato early and late blights, downy mildew, and powdery mildew by 50 to 90 percent. Make the tea by mixing one part mature compost that contains some manure with five parts water in a bucket. Let the mixture sit in the shade for about 10 days. Then filter the solution through cheesecloth, dilute the tea to half strength if you wish, and spray it or dribble it on the leaves. Try to coat both sides. Reapply after two to three weeks. You can also spread the leftover residue on the ground around your plants. Avoid spraying *any* products containing manures directly on leafy vegetables such as lettuce and spinach that you'll soon be harvesting.

Warning: When you use any disease-control remedies on food crops, be sure to wash your harvest well before eating it.

Insect Pests You're Most Likely to Encounter

Do borers drive you buggy? Don't know the difference between a cutworm and a caterpillar? In this section, we describe common North American pests and give you some tips on how to deal with them.

🗸 **Aphids.** These tiny, soft-bodied, pear-shaped pests (shown in Figure 16-1) suck plant sap with their needlelike noses. Colors vary: They may be black, green, red, or even translucent. Aphids leave behind sticky sap droppings that may turn black if covered with sooty mold. Aphids can proliferate quickly on weakened plants. Blast them off with a hose, control with beneficial insects or sticky yellow traps, or spray with insecticidal soap. The beneficial insects green lacewings and ladybird beetles are also excellent controls.

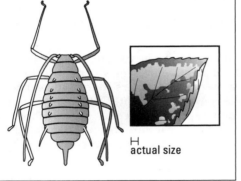

Figure 16-1: Aphids proliferate quickly on weakened plants.

actual size

🗸 **Apple maggot.** Slightly smaller than houseflies, these pests overwinter in soil, then appear beginning in June or July to begin laying eggs in apples, crabapples, plums, and other fruits. Mostly a problem for northern gardeners. Always dispose of infested fruit before maggots emerge and establish in the soil. Trap adult flies by hanging red, apple-shaped spheres coated with sticky goo. Begin trapping by early July and continue through August, cleaning and refreshing the sticky stuff every two weeks. Bait traps with butyl hexanoate pheromone.

Instead of coating the red trap itself with the sticky stuff, enclose the trap in a small plastic bag and cover the bag with the trapping material. To renew the trap, dispose of the old plastic bag and replace with a new one.

An improvement on the red sphere trap is the Ladd trap, a red sphere bisected with a yellow sheet.

- **Bean leaf beetle.** These small, orange-red beetles have a black head and black spots and are about the size of a ladybird beetle. The beetles feed on leaves, creating a lacy pattern. Cover seedlings with lightweight row covers to exclude exploring beetles. To reduce damage caused by an existing infestation, spray with neem or insecticidal soap.

- **Black vine weevil.** This dark, crawling, 1- to 2-inch-long (2.5–5 cm) beetle chews on the foliage of evergreen trees and shrubs such as rhododendrons and yews, while the larvae attack from the other end, eating the roots. Black vine weevils also attack potted plants. Control adults and larvae with beneficial nematodes.

- **Borers.** Several kinds of beetle and caterpillar larvae (they look like small worms and are usually less than 1 inch, or 2.5 cm, long) tunnel into the wood or stems of fruit trees, white birches, dogwoods, shade trees, rhododendrons, German irises, and squash vines. The boring weakens the plant and makes it more susceptible to diseases. The holes can also cut off nutrient flow to the affected limb or vine. Choose species that are less susceptible to borers. For example, try Siberian irises instead of German bearded irises. Keep susceptible plants growing vigorously and watch for signs of borer damage — dead bark, sawdust piles, and poor performance. When you find borers, cut off and destroy severely infested limbs. Inject parasitic nematodes into the remaining borer holes.

- **Caterpillars.** Moth and butterfly larvae are avid eaters that can cause damage to a variety of plants. However, you may decide to overlook the activities of some butterfly caterpillars so that you can enjoy the handsome butterflies later. (See Chapter 20 for more about gardening for butterflies.) Eliminate caterpillars such as the cabbage looper, tomato hornworm, and corn earworm before they do too much damage. If beneficial insects don't keep them in check, spray with Bt.

- **Chinch bug.** These $1/4$-inch-long (0.6 cm), brown or black insects suck grass sap, releasing toxins that make grass discolor and wilt. They can turn entire patches of lawn brown, especially in dry and hot areas. They are especially a problem on St. Augustine grass in southern areas. Dethatch the lawn and let it grow a little longer than usual to discourage chinch bugs. For control, treat with a neem insecticide.

- **Codling moth.** This 1-inch-long (2.5 cm), pinkish-white caterpillar emerges from eggs laid on apples, peaches, pears, and other fruits. The adult moth is about $1/2$-inch long (1.2 cm) and brown. The caterpillars tunnel inside the fruit, usually ruining it. In early spring while the tree is still dormant and leafless, spray dormant oil to kill overwintering eggs. Right after flowering, use pheromone traps to trap egg-laying females. Spray with Bt when apples are about $1/2$-inch (1.2 cm) in diameter, or spray with neem as needed to prevent egg-laying through the growing season. Eliminate wild or unsprayed trees nearby that shelter codling moth populations.

Pheromones are the perfumes of the insect world. Undetectable to us, female butterflies and moths release tiny amounts of these chemicals, which are a siren song to a wandering male of the right type. Professionals use synthetic pheromones to monitor pest populations; you can use them to trap and disorient codling moth. (You can buy pheromone lures from several of the companies listed in Appendix B.)

Hang traps at eye level and spray Bt or neem oil three or four times beginning a week to 10 days after beginning of petal fall, or after the first codling moth is trapped.

✔ **Colorado potato beetle.** This yellow-and-black-striped beetle — ¹/₃ inch (0.8 cm) long, and nearly round — is notorious for obliterating potato plantings, but it also eats tomatoes, eggplant, petunias, and flowering tobacco. Discourage Colorado potato beetles by rotating planting sites. Cover potato plants with floating row covers to keep the beetles off. Spray with Bt formulated for Colorado potato beetles, or use neem. Beneficial nematodes also destroy larvae in soil.

✔ **Corn earworm.** This annoying caterpillar feeds right at the tips of ears of corn. They'll chew right through silk to get to kernels, and sometimes eat leaves. A daub of mineral oil on the developing silk prevents most damage. You can also spray Bt and rely on the help of beneficial trichogramma wasps that parasitize the worms. See this chapter's section, "Encouraging 'good' insects" for more about trichogramma wasps.

✔ **Cucumber beetle.** These ¹/₃-inch-long (0.8 cm) beetles with yellow and black stripes (or spots) swarm on cucumber, squash, and melon plants. You're likely to spot them first crawling around inside flowers. The main threat they pose is a bacterial wilt disease they carry that will kill your plants. That disease is reason enough to keep the beetles away entirely. Cover young vines with floating row covers. Uncover when several flowers open, and spray as needed with pyrethrin or dust with *diatomaceous earth*. (See the later section "Safe and effective pest chemicals.") Till the soil in autumn to eliminate overwintering hideouts.

✔ **Curculio.** These ¹/₄-inch-long (0.6 cm) beetles are easy to identify by the crescent-shaped, egg-laying cut they make in fruit. Unfortunately, after the beetles lay the eggs, the fruit may be ruined. Spread out a tarp or old sheet underneath the tree, shake apple and pear tree branches to knock the beetles off and then step on them. Also destroy prematurely fallen fruit, which may contain larvae. If the problem is severe, consider spraying the insecticide *imidan*. Experts recommend the insecticide as the safest and most effective of available sprays.

✔ **Cutworms.** These ¹/₂-inch-long (1.2 cm), grayish caterpillars emerge on spring and early summer nights to eat the base of young seedling stems, cutting the tops off from the roots, as shown in Figure 16-2. To control, surround seedlings with a barrier that prevents the cutworms from crawling close and feeding. These devices can be as simple as an empty cardboard toilet paper roll or a collar made from aluminum foil — just make sure that the collar encircles the stem completely and set 1 inch (2.5 cm) deep in the soil.

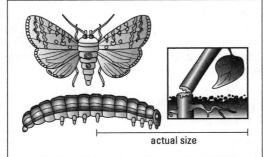

Figure 16-2:
Cutworms can do a great deal of damage before sprouting wings and flying off.

actual size

✔ **Flea beetles.** These tiny black beetles feed on vegetable plants such as eggplant, radish, and broccoli, sometimes riddling the entire leafy area of seedlings with tiny holes. Cover susceptible plants with floating row covers as soon as you plant them. Keep them covered until the plants get fairly large and can withstand a few beetle bites. You also can spray with neem.

✔ **Gypsy moths.** These 2-inch-long (5 cm), gray (with brown hairs), foliage-eating caterpillars or their egg clusters hitchhike across the country on cars, campers, and trains. They eat foliage on a number of shade trees, including oaks, and can defoliate trees when their population gets large enough. Monitor population sizes with pheromone traps. Catch caterpillars as they attempt to crawl up tree trunks by using duct tape treated with a sticky barrier. Spray with Bt or neem.

Sticky pest barriers are just that — bands of goop that a crawling insect cannot navigate. Buy this stuff at garden centers or from one of the mail-order suppliers listed in Appendix B.

✔ **Japanese beetles.** These beetles (pictured in Figure 16-3) are $1/2$ inch (1.2 cm) long, and are metallic blue-green with coppery wing covers. They eat almost any plant with gusto. They're fat, white, C-shaped, $3/4$-inch-long (2 cm) larvae consume turf roots. To control, treat your lawn with milky spore disease, which takes several years to spread through the lawn, or with parasitic nematodes, a quicker-acting helper. Inspect your garden in the evening or after dark for the beetles, knocking them off plants into a can or bucket of soapy water. You can also spray with neem.

Avoid using the Japanese beetle traps that you can hang. The pheromones in these traps attract beetles not only from your yard, but from your neighbors' yards as well. You'll end up with more beetles than you would have had without the traps.

Aliens invade!

The speed and convenience of modern travel and mail has been a boon to insects and diseases too. That's how pests — such as the Asian longhorn beetle, gypsy moth, Japanese beetle, Mediterranean fruit fly, and silverleaf whitefly — got to North America. Historically, the spread of pests has been blocked by geography. Not so anymore. In the United States, the 1,800 inspectors and 62 canine teams (the "beagle brigade" of international airport fame) of the Plant Health Inspection Service (APHIS)

lead the defense. Do farmers and fellow gardeners a favor and don't mail fruits home from foreign locations, and follow U.S. Customs and APHIS regulations when traveling overseas. If you intend to bring plants home, call APHIS first: 301-734-8645. To learn more about APHIS and U.S. Customs regulations, see the Web Sites at www.aphis.usda.gov/oa/new/pe.html and www.customs.ustreas.gov/travel/kbygo.htm#Food/Plants.

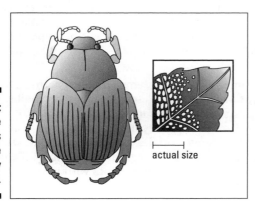

Figure 16-3: Japanese beetles consume almost any plant.

actual size

- ✔ **Leaf miners.** The larval form of tiny flies, these maggots tunnel randomly through leaves of plants such as columbine, peppers, beans, and lilacs. They disfigure plants and are hard to eliminate because they are protected inside the leaf. Prevent infestation by covering predisposed seedlings with floating row covers and removing and destroying infested leaves. Spray with neem in spring when adults begin to lay eggs.

- ✔ **Mealybugs.** These small sucking insects cover their bodies with a white, cottony substance that makes them easy to identify. Plus, they usually feed in groups. Mealybugs are common on houseplants. You can wash off small numbers with cotton dipped in rubbing alcohol. Spray indoor plants with an oil-based "leaf shine" product, and use horticultural oil for landscape plants. Insecticidal soap and neem are also effective remedies.

✔ **Mexican bean beetles.** These ¹/₄-inch (0.6 cm), round beetles are yellowish with black spots. They resemble ladybugs but are avid plant eaters. They can destroy an entire bean planting, enjoying snap beans most but also lima beans, soybeans, and other legumes. The spiny, yellow larvae that appear on the bean plants soon after the adults arrive are just as bad as the adults. Pull up and destroy infested plants, beetles and all, immediately after harvesting. Till the ground to kill beetles hiding there. If necessary, spray with soap, pyrethrin, horticultural oil, or neem.

✔ **Oriental fruit moths.** These small moths produce ¹/₂-inch-long (1.2 cm), white-to- pink larvae that tunnel into the young wood or fruit of fruit and ornamental trees. In spring, work the soil shallowly around infested trees to kill overwintering larvae. Catch adult males in pheromone traps or use pheromones to confuse males and prevent breeding. You can kill moth eggs with horticultural oil.

✔ **Root maggots.** A variety of fly larvae — most are white and less than ¹/₄ inch long (0.6 cm) — that attack the roots of carrots, the cabbage family, and onions. They can disfigure or destroy these plants. Look for resistant plants. Cover new plantings of susceptible types of cabbage, turnips, rutabagas, radishes, kohlrabi, carrots, parsnips, and onions with floating row covers.

✔ **Scale.** Looking like bumps on plant stems and leaves, these tiny sucking insects cling to plant branches, hiding under an outer shell that serves as a shield. These pests suck plant sap and can kill plants if present in large numbers. Look for sticky, honeylike sap droppings, one clue that scale may be present. Remove and destroy badly infested stems. Indoors or on small plants, clean off light infestations with a cotton ball soaked in rubbing alcohol. Spray larger plants with horticultural oil in early spring or summer.

✔ **Snails and slugs.** These soft-bodied mollusks (see Figure 16-4) feed on tender leaves during the cool of night or in rainy weather. Sometimes they're hard to spot: All you see is the slime trail they leave behind. They proliferate in damp areas, hiding and breeding under rocks, mulch, and other garden debris. Clean up dark, damp hiding spots to relocate slugs elsewhere. Catch the ones that remain by setting a saucer with the rim at ground level. Fill the saucer with beer. Slugs crawl in and can't get out. Refill regularly. Or surround plants with copper barriers — metal strips that seem to shock slugs if they attempt to crawl across. Set out traps, commercial or homemade. Look for new, nontoxic baits that contain iron phosphate.

Make your own slug trap by placing a few boards or rolled-up newspaper in the garden. In the early morning, lift the board and destroy the slugs. Toss out the newspaper if it has slugs.

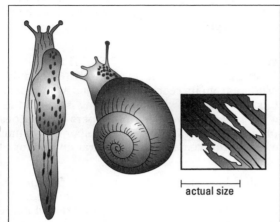

Figure 16-4:
Slugs and
snails like
to live in
cool, damp
areas.

actual size

✔ **Spider mites.** These tiny arachnoids (shown greatly enlarged in
   Figure 16-5) are almost microscopic, but when they appear in large
   numbers, you can begin to see the fine webs that they weave. They
   suck plant sap, causing leaves to discolor and plants to lose vigor. They
   are especially active in arid conditions. You find spider mites on fruit
   trees, miniature roses, potted begonias, and many houseplants. Indoors, wash houseplants often and spray with insecticidal soap.
   Outdoors, wash plants with a strong blast of water, or use dormant oil
   in early spring or light horticultural oil in summer.

✔ **Tarnished plant bugs (lygus bugs).** These ¹/₄-inch-long (0.6 cm), yellow-
   to-brown plant eaters attack many kinds of plants — more than 400,
   including some of our most important economic crops — leaving
   behind dark, sunken leaf spots and wilting or dead shoots. They
   especially like the growing points of apples and strawberries. Catch
   them with white sticky traps. Prevent problems by covering susceptible
   plants with a floating row cover.

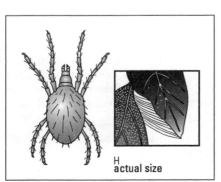

Figure 16-5:
Spider
mites are
easier to
identify by
the damage
they do
than by
sight.

actual size

✔ **Tent caterpillars.** These caterpillars form tentlike webs full of teeming caterpillars on trees and shrubs. In large numbers, they can defoliate an entire tree. Knock caterpillars off severely infested branches with a broom or pole.

✔ **Tomato hornworm.** This large, 3–5-inch (7.5–12.5 cm) long, green caterpillar is notable particularly for its white stripes and the threatening "horn" protruding from its rear. As dangerous as it appears, the horn can do no harm, which is why handpicking is one of the preferred controls. If you have lots of tomatoes (or peppers or potatoes), you may want to spray or dust with Bt in late spring or early summer. Bt is effective as long as worms remain small. Several tiny wasps also parasitize this caterpillar.

✔ **Whiteflies.** Whiteflies look like small, white gnats, but they suck plant sap and can proliferate in warm climates or greenhouses. They can also spread diseases with their sucking mouthparts. Trap whiteflies with yellow sticky traps. Cure infestations with regular sprays of hot (150°F, 66°C) water (directly from your water heater to your infested plants), insecticidal soap, light horticultural oil, or pyrethrin. Be sure to treat leaf undersides where whiteflies and their larvae reside.

Managing Pests

Think of pest management as a staircase. On the first step you can find the least disruptive, innocuous actions, and on the top step are the most toxic and the most potentially harmful measures. The best way to control pests is to start at the bottom and move up the stairs only when absolutely necessary. This strategy is called *integrated pest management,* or IPM. This approach takes advantage of the complex interrelationships between insects and plants to find the least toxic ways to reduce damage to crops.

The following list outlines the actions you can take in your garden to keep a pest from getting the upper hand. The measures move from the least aggressive and potentially harmful to the most aggressive.

✔ **Strong blast from a hose** that knocks small pests such as aphids and spider mites off your plants. Spraying daily can provide good control.

✔ **Barriers** such as floating row covers (translucent, lightweight fabrics that cover plants) that keep flying insects from reaching plants; cutworm collars placed around seedlings; and copper strips that encircle plants and give slugs an electric shock. Make cutworm collars with 4-inch-high (10 cm) rings pushed 2 inches (5 cm) into the soil; use toilet tissue rolls or rolled newspaper.

✔ **Insect traps** that use chemical attractants and colors to lure pests, such as sticky, red balls for apple maggots.

✔ **Bacterial insecticides,** such as *Bacillus thuringiensis* (Bt) for caterpillars, and milky spore disease for soil-dwelling grubs.

✔ **Least toxic controls,** such as insecticidal soaps, horticultural oils, and rotenone insecticides, which kill pests but cause minimal impact on the environment.

✔ **Botanical insecticides,** such as neem.

Encouraging "good" insects

The average square yard of garden contains more than a thousand insects. Some are plant pollinators, some help break down organic matter, and some prey on other more damaging ones. Only a small proportion of the insects cause much damage to your plants.

Beneficial insects prey upon or parasitize garden pests. In nature, beneficial insects keep plant-eating pests under control.

Here are some beneficial bugs and insects that you'll want to keep around your yard:

✔ **Lady beetles.** You're probably aware of the ladybug's voracious appetite for aphids. Both larva and adult stages prey on pests. One ladybug can dine on 40 to 50 aphids a day. Ladybugs also prey on mites and other soft-bodied insects.

✔ **Green lacewing.** Larval stage lacewings feed on aphids, thrips, mites, and various other insect eggs; overall, the most useful insect in home gardens. Both larva and adult stages are beneficial, but the larva much more so.

✔ **Trichogramma wasps.** These tiny wasps parasitize many kinds of caterpillars by laying eggs in them. The wasps are effective against corn earworm, loopers, and tomato hornworm. They cannot attack people in any way.

✔ **Parasitic nematodes.** The tiny worms parasitize many soil-dwelling and burrowing insects, such as grubs, cutworms, and weevils. These are different from the pest nematodes that feed on plant roots.

✔ **Chinese praying mantis.** This general predator is interesting to watch but doesn't provide reliable control of pests.

All these beneficial insects are available from mail-order gardening companies. (You can find several listed in Appendix B.) They each have special requirements about the best time to release them into the garden. Whether you choose to buy beneficials or rely on the ones already present in your yard, you can take steps to encourage them to stick around:

✔ Avoid indiscriminate pesticide spraying, which kills beneficials as well as pests. If you must spray, choose a product that specifically targets the pests you want to eliminate, and use it when it will be least harmful. For example, sprays that are harmful to bees can be used in the evening after bees have returned to the hive.

✔ Make sure that the beneficials have plenty to eat by allowing small numbers of pests to reside in your garden. If you release ladybugs before you've even spotted aphids, they may move elsewhere to find food.

✔ Provide beneficials with shelter. Grow a variety of plants — tall, short, spreading, and upright — to give the insects many potential homes.

✔ Many beneficials also feed on nectar and pollen, so grow flowers such as Queen Anne's lace and evening primrose. Lacewings love fennel, caraway, and dill. Goldenrod has been found to attract more than 75 different species of beneficial insects.

Safe and effective pest chemicals

Gardeners today have at their disposal a handful of effective and safe pesticides. All the following are approved for use by certified organic farmers.

Bacillus thuringiensis (Bt)

Bt exists naturally in most soils. Different strains of Bt occur that produce protein crystals that are toxic to certain insects. The strain for most caterpillars is *B. t. kurstaki*. Commercially prepared Bt spray or powder has no effect on adult butterflies or moths. Remember, however, that not all caterpillars are pests. Strains of Bt have been developed for a few other pests. Some leaf-feeding beetles (including Colorado potato beetle) are susceptible to *B. t. tenebrionis*, for example.

Advantages: One advantage is safety — Bt is essentially nontoxic to humans, other mammals, and birds. The label specifies no waiting period between application and harvest. Bt is also highly selective and easily incorporated with existing natural controls.

Disadvantages: A limitation of Bt is its slow action. After pests consume it, their feeding slows down. But their deaths may not occur for two to five days. Bt also breaks down quickly — if the caterpillars don't eat some while it's fresh, it probably won't work.

 Because Bt is a near-perfect insecticide, there is danger of overuse. Any overused insecticide gradually becomes less effective as insects evolve defenses to it. Some insect pests, such as the diamondback moth and Indian meal moth, were once susceptible and are now at least partially immune to Bt.

How to use: Use Bt against cabbageworms, cutworms, and other caterpillars. *Use B. t. tenebrionis* against Colorado potato beetles. The bacterial toxin causes caterpillar death two to five days after it is eaten; the toxin dissipates in two days or less. It is available as liquid spray or dust. Apply in late afternoon and reapply after rain. Repeat applications as needed. Mix with insecticidal soap for greater effectiveness.

Diatomaceous earth (DE)

Diatomaceous earth, or DE, is a powderlike dust made of the silicate skeletons of tiny water creatures called diatoms. Millions of years ago, as the diatoms died, their skeletons gradually accumulated into deep layers that are mined today from deposits where oceans or large lakes once covered the land. DE acts like ground glass, cutting into the waxy coat of many kinds of insects and causing them to dry out and die. DE is often combined with the botanical insecticide, pyrethrin (described in this section). The addition of pyrethrin makes DE more lethal for many insects.

Advantages: Easy to handle and apply. DE is not toxic and leaves no residue.

Disadvantages: DE is not selective and kills spiders and beneficial insects as well as pests. DE is available in two forms. One, which is used primarily in swimming pool filters, is not an effective insecticide and is dangerous to inhale (can cause a lung disease called silicosis). In your garden, use only the natural grade of DE. Always wear goggles and a dust mask during application.

How to use: Dust DE onto leaves and stems to control pests such as aphids, immature Colorado potato beetles, immature forms of squash bug, immature Mexican bean beetles, and whiteflies. Sometimes a band of DE makes an effective slug and snail barrier. It works best in dry situations; reapply after rain.

One of the most convenient applicators of small amounts of DE is the Spritzer tube duster. This applicator holds a small amount of dust and dispenses it with a pump action. It's available from Perma-Guard Inc., 115 Rio Bravo SE, Albuquerque, New Mexico 87105, phone (505) 505-3061. The Cadillac of dust applicators is the Dustin-Mizer. It holds a pound of dust in a canister and dispenses with a hand crank.

Horticultural oils

Horticultural oils are most often highly refined extracts of crude oil. (Some vegetable oils, such as cottonseed and soybean oil, are also sometimes used.) They kill insects by plugging the pores through which the insects breathe.

Advantages: These oils are increasingly recommended for vegetable garden pest control because they present few risks to either gardeners or desirable species and integrate well with natural biological controls. Also, oils dissipate quickly through evaporation, leaving little residue. Disadvantages: Oils can damage plants if applied at excessive rates or on particularly hot (above 100°F, or 38°C) or cold (below 40°F, or 5°C) days.

How to use: Spray oils in vegetable gardens to kill aphids, leafhoppers, spider mites, and whiteflies. A few drops of oil in the ear tips of corn control corn earworm.

Use highly refined horticultural oils and dilute according to label directions. Do not apply oils to drought-stressed plants, or on hot, cold, or very humid days. Don't apply horticultural oils to green plants at rates recommended for leafless, dormant plants.

Insecticidal soaps

Insecticidal soaps are specific fatty acids that have been found by experiment to be toxic to pests, primarily soft-bodied insects like aphids, mealybugs, spider mites, and whiteflies. Surprisingly, adult Japanese beetles are also susceptible.

Advantages: Insecticidal soap is one of the safest insecticides. Most nontarget insects are unaffected, and the soaps are not toxic to animals. Soap insecticides act fast and leave no residue. You can use them on vegetables up to the moment of harvest.

Disadvantages: Soaps readily burn some plants such as peas, and the effectiveness of the soap diminishes greatly when mixed with hard water (water high in dissolved minerals). Soaps kill pests only when they make direct contact.

How to use: Use against aphids, earwigs, grasshoppers, Japanese beetles (adults), leafhoppers, spider mites, and whiteflies. Apply diluted concentrate or ready-to-use liquid when the air is still. To improve effectiveness, mix with warm, soft water and be sure to cover both sides of leaves. Reapply after rain. Can burn leaves of certain plants during hot weather.

Neem

Neem is an extract derived from the crushed seeds of the tropical neem tree (*Azadirachta indica*). Though intensely studied for many years now, it is still a new botanical insecticide. The primary active ingredient is the compound azadirachtin. Two forms are commonly available. One is a 3 percent solution of azadirachtin, the most insecticidal component, and the other is "clarified hydrophobic extracts of neem seeds," essentially a syrupy oil (make sure the oil is warm before mixing with water).

Both forms of neem work as both an insecticide and as an agent that prevents insects from feeding. They also kill insects in the juvenile stage by thwarting their development and are most effective against aphids, thrips, and whiteflies. Neem oil is also fungicidal and can control black spot of roses, powdery mildew, and rust diseases.

Advantages: Neem has no measurable toxicity to mammals. (In some countries, neem extract is considered healthful to people and is added to various food and personal products.) The Environmental Protection Agency stipulated that neem was exempt from food crop tolerances because it is considered nontoxic.

Disadvantages: Neem doesn't have a quick "knock-down" effect, but a week or so after application, you'll notice a steady decline in the number of pests. It is not effective against adult insects (though it may interfere with egg production) and has little impact on beneficial insects. Once beetle numbers build up on the plant, neem no longer discourages them.

How to use: Neem sprays degrade very quickly in water. Mix only the amount you need and apply all of it immediately. Reapply after rainfall. On the plant, neem retains its activity against juvenile insect pests for about one week. Use neem to kill juvenile aphids, Colorado potato beetles, and thrips and to repel whiteflies, Japanese beetles, and adult Colorado potato beetles. Apply liquid spray morning or evening when humidity is highest. Repeat weekly; spray lasts on plants about one week. As a toxin, apply when pests are young. As an antifeedant, neem is effective against Japanese beetles; apply before the pests appear.

To mix neem oil with water, the oil needs to be a least room temperature. But neem mixes still better if you warm it first in water on the stove, or even in the microwave for about 30 seconds. If you try the latter, be sure to remove the aluminum seal under the cap first.

Pyrethrins

Derived from the painted daisy, *Tanacetum cinerariifolium,* pyrethrins are considered one of the most important natural insecticides. When you must either use a broad-spectrum insecticide in the vegetable garden or lose the crop, pyrethrins are among your best choices.

Broad-spectrum insecticides are products that kill a diversity of insects, pest and beneficial alike. If you need to use an insecticide to control a particular pest, use a product that targets that particular kind of pest without harming beneficial insects. The terminology can be confusing, however. *Pyrethrum* is the ground-up flowers of the daisy. *Pyrethrins* (most always plural) are the insecticidal components of the flowers. *Pyrethroids,* such as cypermethrin, permethrin, and resmethrin, are synthetic compounds that resemble pyrethrins but are more toxic and persistent.

Advantages: Pyrethrins are of low toxicity to mammals and kill insects quickly. In sunlight, they break down and are nontoxic within a day or less.

Disadvantages: Often, pure pyrethrins only stun insects, which is why they often get combined with a synergist (a chemical that enhances the effectiveness of the active ingredients) such as piperonyl butoxide or with another botanical insecticide, such as rotenone. Also, pyrethrin is toxic to honeybees — apply it in the evening after bees are in their hives.

How to use: Use against most vegetable garden pests, such as flea, potato, and bean beetles, including the hard-to-kill pests, such as beetles, squash bugs, and tarnished plant bugs. For best results, apply in the late afternoon or evening. Pyrethrins degrade within one day.

Rotenone

Rotenone is often recommended for organic gardeners because of its botanical origin (derived from the roots of tropical legumes).

Advantages: It is approved for use in organic gardens and breaks down quickly in sunlight.

Disadvantages: Rotenone is toxic to pests and beneficials alike.

How to use: Use this broad-spectrum insecticide as a last resort against cabbageworms, Colorado potato beetles, flea beetles, fruit worms, Japanese beetles, loopers, Mexican bean beetles, thrips, and weevils. Apply in early evening when bees are inactive. It remains toxic up to one week.

Several other types of pesticides are available at nurseries and home centers, but we regard some of them with suspicion and a few with scorn. Our advice: If a pest problem is so resistant to any of these materials and so bothersome, call a professional. Check with your cooperative extension agent first. Consider hiring a professional pest control applicator to spray.

Preventing Plant Diseases

Many plant diseases are difficult — in some cases impossible — to cure. If you suspect that a certain disease is going to show up on your prized plant, such as black spot on roses, you can take steps to prevent infection. Find out when that disease is most likely to strike. Then identify the best product to use and apply it according to recommendations on the label.

When you spot a disease on your plants, try to identify it with the help of reference books or personnel at a local nursery, garden center, botanical garden, or extension service office. Occasionally, you can get products to eradicate or prevent further spread of the disease. At the very least, adapt the following cultural techniques to make your garden less susceptible to disease damage.

Solarization

You can cook the disease right out of your soil by a process called *solarization*. To do this, first cultivate the soil and get it ready for planting. Then moisten the soil to a depth of 2 feet (61 cm). Cover the area with a sheet of 2- to 4-mils-thick, clear, UV-stabilized plastic and secure the edges so that air can't leak. The heat of the sun will raise the temperature underneath high enough to kill many disease organisms (and weeds) that are contained in the upper several inches of soil. Leave the plastic on for one or two months, then remove it and plant. Don't cultivate again before planting or you run the risk of bringing pathogens up to the surface again.

Solarization is most effective if done during the hottest part of the year. Southern gardeners will reap the most benefit from this process, but northerners can increase the heat by using double layers of plastic or by spreading chicken manure or another hot manure on the soil before laying down the plastic.

A dozen dirty diseases: What to do

Here are some tips on how to prevent, identify, and — if possible — treat some common plant diseases:

- ✔ **Anthracnose.** This fungus can attack many trees, including dogwoods and sycamores, as well as tomatoes and melons. It begins by producing small, discolored leaf spots or dead twigs, which can spread to become serious. Avoid by choosing resistant plants. Destroy fallen diseased leaves and dead branches and twigs. Hire an arborist to spray trees that have had the disease three consecutive years. Consider removing susceptible trees and replanting with resistant varieties.

- ✔ **Apple scab.** This fungus attacks apple and crab apple trees, producing discolored leaf spots and woody-brown fruit lesions. Avoid by planting scab-resistant varieties. (See the sidebar, "Scab-free apples and crab apples.") Rake up and destroy leaves in fall to reduce the number of overwintering spores. Susceptible varieties need a preventive spray program during wet spring weather to prevent reinfection.

  Spray sulfur, copper, or *Bordeaux mixture* (a mixture of copper sulfate, lime, and water) as a protective spray at the beginning of scab season (once flower buds in spring), then two or three more times at approximately weekly intervals.

Scab-free apples and crab apples

The best way to beat the most common apple disease, scab, is to plant only varieties of apples that are resistant to it. Here are the best scab-free apples and crab apples.

Variety	Fruit Color	Edible/Ornamental
'David'	Cerise	Ornamental
'Dayton'	Deep red	Edible
'Dolgo'	Red	Edible and ornamental
'Donald Wyman'	Red	Ornamental
'Enterprise'	Yellow with deep red	Edible
'Freedom'	Red	Edible
'Gold Rush'	Yellow	Edible
'Jewelberry'	Bright red	Ornamental
'Jonafree'	Red	Edible
'Liberty'	Dark red	Edible
'Macfree'	Red over green	Edible
'Makamik'	Red	Ornamental
Malus baccata 'Walters'	Yellow-orange	Ornamental
M. sargentii	Dark red	Ornamental
M. sieboldii zumi 'Calocarpa'	Red	Ornamental
'McShay'	Red over green	Edible
'Nova Easygro'	Green-yellow, washed with red	Edible
'Novamac'	Red over green	Edible
'Ormiston Roy'	Yellow-orange	Ornamental
'Prairiefire'	Dark red	Ornamental
'Prima'	Yellow green	Edible
'Priscilla'	Green-yellow and stripped with red	Edible
'Pristine'	Yellow with slight blush	Edible
'Professor Sprenger'	Orange	Ornamental
'Redfree'	Bright red over pale yellow	Edible
'Sir Prize'	Yellow with red blush	Edible
'William's Pride'	Bright red	Edible

✔ **Black spot.** This rose disease causes black spots on foliage and can spread, causing complete defoliation. Avoid problems by growing disease-resistant roses and cleaning up and destroying any diseased leaves that fall to the ground. To prevent black spot on susceptible roses, use a preventive fungicide spray during damp weather. Sprays of captan, copper, or lime-sulfur are most effective. Also try potassium bicarbonate (or baking soda — sodium bicarbonate) at the rate of 1 tablespoon each per gallon of water, weekly or after rain. Apply in morning and not during periods of hottest weather. Neem oil is also effective.

✔ **Botrytis blight.** This fungus attacks a wide variety of plants, including peonies, tulips, geraniums, and strawberries. It causes discolored patches on foliage, browning and droopy stalks on flowers, and premature rotting of fruits. Discourage botrytis by allowing air to circulate freely around susceptible plants. Remove and destroy any infected plant parts. Spray emerging peony shoots in early spring with copper sulfate.

✔ **Brown rot.** This fungus disease is common on peaches, nectarines, and other stone fruits. Brown rot can attack flowers and fruit, ultimately coating the infected parts with brown spores. The fruit rots and shrivels. To avoid, select disease-resistant plants or at least less-susceptible types. Remove and destroy infected plant parts. You'll probably also need a preventive spray program.

✔ **Cytospora canker.** This bacterial disease attacks woody stems on susceptible plants, such as fruit trees, spruces, and maples, forming cankers that can kill infected branches. To avoid, plant resistant or less-susceptible plants. If possible, remove and destroy infected branches.

✔ **Damping-off.** This fungus disease attacks the base of seedling stems, cutting the stem off from the roots. Avoid damping-off by sowing seeds in sterile seed-sowing mix and spacing the seeds so that they don't come up in a crowded mass. Cover the seeds thinly with finely shredded sphagnum moss, which has natural antibiotic action that helps prevent disease. Keep the soil moist but not soggy.

✔ **Mildew** (downy and powdery). These two fungi produce similar symptoms: white, powdery coating on leaves. A variety of plants are susceptible, including roses, grapes, bee balms, zinnias, and lilacs, but a different kind of mildew attacks each kind of plant. A mildew that attacks lilacs won't harm roses. The fungi disfigure plants but may not kill them outright. Instead, they weaken plants, making them unattractive and susceptible to other problems. Downy mildew attacks during cool, wet weather; powdery mildew (shown in Figure 16-6) comes later in the season during warm, humid weather and cool nights. Avoid downy mildew by planting resistant plants and by not getting the leaves wet. Use drip irrigation. Avoid powdery mildew by planting resistant plants.

Figure 16-6:
Powdery
mildew
thrives
during
warm,
humid days
and cool
nights.

✔ **Peach leaf curl.** This fungal disease overwinters on peach tree twigs and migrates to the emerging leaves in humid, wet weather when temperatures are between 50°F and 60°F (10°C and 16°C). The leaves curl, turn red, and eventually die. Typically, the disease develops early the first year, and the tree may grow through it and appear fine. But when the disease becomes established, the leaf curl returns and gets progressively worse each year. Eventually, the tree becomes debilitated. When you see the symptoms, it's too late to stop the organism that season.

You can control peach leaf curl with one or, at most, two applications. First, spray a fungicide such as lime-sulfur or Bordeaux mix in fall when the trees are dormant (leafless). For extra insurance, spray again in early spring before leaves emerge.

✔ **Phytophthora blight.** This bacterial disease attacks a variety of plants, including rhododendrons. It causes leaves to discolor and stems to die, often killing the entire plant. Another form can cause root rot and rapid plant death. Start with healthy plants and provide them with well-drained soil. Work bark into the soil; it seems to discourage the fungus. Try not to wet the foliage in the afternoon or evening.

✔ **Rust.** This fungus disease is easy to identify: It forms a rusty coating on the foliage of susceptible plants, like roses, snapdragons, hollyhocks, and blackberry. (See Figure 16-7.) Avoid susceptible plants or look for disease-resistant varieties. Provide good air circulation. Remove and destroy infected parts.

✔ **Sooty mold.** Insect pests that release sticky drops of honeydew, such as aphids, encourage this harmless but unattractive fungus disease. The black-colored mold grows on the honeydew, a sure sign that sucking insects are at work. Rinse off the mold and sap with soapy water and then control the insect pests.

✔ **Wilt** — *fusarium* and *verticillium*. These soil-borne fungus diseases cause susceptible plants such as tomatoes, peppers, melons, cabbages, and strawberries to suffer leaf yellowing, wilting, and often death. The fungus survives many years in the soil without a host. Grow wilt-resistant or wilt-tolerant varieties. Resistant tomato varieties have the letters VF as part of their name.

Least-toxic disease remedies

Use the following fungicides to make a protective coating on susceptible plants. Most are certified by organic gardening groups and are widely available at nurseries and garden centers.

✔ **Sulfur.** This naturally occurring mineral is nontoxic but is a potential skin and eye irritant. You can buy sulfur in powder or liquid form. Powders can be applied with a dust applicator, or mixed with water according to label directions.

✔ **Lime sulfur.** Powerful and caustic but highly effective for some problems, lime sulfur can burn the leaves of some plants.

✔ **Copper.** This strong, broad-spectrum spray can be toxic to some plants, especially when overused. Use only as a last resort.

✔ **Bordeaux mixture.** A mix of copper and sulfur, this old-time fungicide is less toxic than pure copper but has the same limitations.

✔ **Remedy fungicide.** Harmless as baking soda, the key ingredient, this spray controls a range of fungal diseases on ornamental plants and fruit trees.

Outwitting animals

If you've ever had a newly planted garden decimated by a groundhog, then you know just how long it takes to drive to the store, buy fencing, rush home, and install it. Whether it be greedy groundhogs, nibbling rabbits, browsing deer, or gophers and moles tunneling throughout your yard, animals can be a nemesis to gardeners.

The irony is that the nearby woods or fields or open space that attracted you to living in your home in the first place also provides habitat for many of the animals that plague you. You may, in fact, have moved into their territory.

When trying to coexist with wild animals, the first priority is to keep your sense of humor. Beyond that, you can use a few techniques to protect some of that garden produce for you to enjoy. If you don't succeed with one method, try another:

✔ **Deer.** Deer are creatures of habit. They often travel along the same routes day after day, moving between two locations. Build a deer-excluding fence about 8 feet (2.5 m) high (deer have been known to jump 10-foot, or 3m, fences). Before you invest in a fence, you may want to try surrounding your garden with a heavy fishing line attached to posts at about 3 feet (1 m) high. This can startle deer because they don't see the fishing line, and they may retreat. This wouldn't be a method to try with young children around who could injure themselves on the line.

Deer avoid some plants, although they are notorious for changing their minds about what they want for dinner. In general, pungent or fuzzy-leafed plants are safe.

✔ **Gophers.** These are burrowing, antisocial rodents that can carve out 700 square yards (585 m²) of elaborate underground tunnels. While they tunnel, they work up quite an appetite and any plant roots that happen to be in the way turn into lunch.

Underground barriers made of hardware cloth are effective. Install barriers at least 2 feet (60 cm) deep to block their borrowing.

Various traps are available to catch gophers dead or alive, and traps are the only method used by orchardists and others who are serious about limiting gopher damage. Traps work best when set inside the tunnels.

✔ **Groundhogs (Woodchucks).** The easiest way to eliminate groundhogs is a fence, one that extends 3 to 4 feet (1–1.2 m) above ground and 18 (46 cm) inches below ground. Traps are next best. Groundhogs are one of the easier garden raiders to trap alive with a Havahart trap. Check with local and state ordinances about any restrictions on live trapping, and take care when releasing any wild animal so that it doesn't turn on you.

If you're at wit's end dealing with marauding deer or gophers, or woodchucks, consult your local animal control officer. Normally, you'll find these folks listed under the city, county, or state listings in the telephone book. Another resource is the book *Outwitting Critters: A Humane Guide for Confronting Devious Animals and Winning*, by Bill Adler, Jr., published by Lyons & Burford.

Controlling Weeds

The challenge of combating insects and disease and animal pests is fraught with unknowns: What works today might not work tomorrow. As soon as you let down your guard, your plants get chewed to nubs. Weeds, however, have an element that is much more predictable and comforting: Weeds don't change their minds. You can always count on weeds to behave in a certain way, and there is one strategy that always works: pulling.

Of course, we're not talking here about fields full of wild brambles that you're trying to eliminate. We're talking about common weeds that you are likely to find in your lawn and garden. You can use some general techniques that can make your yard less attractive to weeds.

Weed-control basics

The principle is pretty simple: Stop the weeds before they start. Okay, prevention isn't so simple in many situations. But if you can take sometimes very minor steps before the weeds take hold, you can avoid the really big jobs once they do.

- **Mulch.** No matter what kind of mulch you use, it cuts down on weed growth. A thick mulch for garden pathways and between beds can be made quite easily from layers of newspapers topped with straw or hay. At season's end, you can till the mulch into the garden to provide organic matter.

- **Cultivation.** Prior to planting, cultivate (loosen the soil) to expose weed seeds to sunlight and start them growing. After a couple of weeks, you can pull the weeds or till them under and thus eliminate some major competition for your plants.

- **Cover crops.** Being patient when preparing a garden bed can pay off big time later on. You can dramatically reduce weeds in your newly dug garden by sowing a cover crop such as buckwheat the summer before you plant the garden. The buckwheat grows so densely that it outcompetes the weeds. When you till the buckwheat under, it also enriches the soil with organic matter. Then you can plant another cover crop such as annual rye in the fall, which you can till under the following spring. Your garden will then be practically weed-free and ready to plant. Alternatively, you can plant a late garden after you till under the buckwheat.

- **Landscape fabrics.** Place these barriers on the soil after planting trees and shrubs, and then top with mulch. Annual weeds are successfully impeded, woody perennials less so. Fabric brands include Typar, Weed Block, Weed-X, and Mulch Plus.

✔ **Hand hoeing and pulling.** Not glamorous but still one of the most effective means for most small home gardens, the key is to yank the weeds while they're young.

✔ **Solarization.** Follow the directions given in the section "Solarization" earlier in this chapter.

The most critical time to control weeds is during the first few weeks after transplanting or sowing seed. As long as you help your plants get off to a good start, they will have a fighting chance of producing a crop of food or flowers in spite of future competing weeds.

Nontoxic herbicides

With several effective alternatives to toxic pesticides on the market, you can avoid their risks and, in some cases, even fertilize your garden at the same time. Here are some choices:

✔ **Corn gluten weed killer** is available under several brand names, such as A-maizing Lawn, WOW (With-out-weeds), and WeedzSTOP. This product is a highly concentrated protein extract of cornmeal. Applied in early spring and again in early August, it will prevent seed growth for up to 6 weeks. Since it will also kill other seeds, avoid using it in vegetable gardens and new lawns. As an added bonus, the cornmeal provides nitrogen fertilizer.

✔ **Weed Eraser** is made from pelargonic acid, a fatty acid found in crops such as apples, carrots, and grapes. It lowers the pH enough to kill broadleaf weeds, such as pigweed and dandelions, in two hours.

Ten common weeds

If you remember nothing else about controlling weeds, keep this strategy in mind at all times: Remove perennial weeds as soon as you spot them, and pull annual weeds before they flower. Treat biennials as perennials.

✔ **Bindweed.** *Convolvulus arvensis.* Spreading from underground roots, this vining perennial can snake around your garden and wrap itself around your plants. The leaves are shaped like an arrowhead and the flowers resemble morning glories, a more appreciated cousin. Beware, however, that if you allow bindweed to flower, you greatly compound your problem. The seeds have been found to be viable after 50 years. Use a digging fork to remove the plants rather than a spade, which can divide the roots into pieces that will each grow new plants.

Repeated *flaming* is an effective control strategy for bindweed. Cook your weeds to death. With a propane torch in hand, you can kill weeds in $1/10$ of a second by boiling the water in the plant's cells until they burst. Flaming is most effective in spring and early summer against annual weeds. Perennial weeds may require several treatments. Follow all safety precautions, of course, if you use this method.

✓ **Bermuda grass.** *Cynodon dactylon.* This wiry perennial grass (see Figure 16-8) has thin blades with creases down the center. Its creeping stems travel quickly, rooting at the nodes. Any piece of stem or root left behind after you weed can establish a new plant. Bermuda grass has a secret weapon to reduce competition from nearby plants: It releases a chemical to impede their growth. Flaming provides good control.

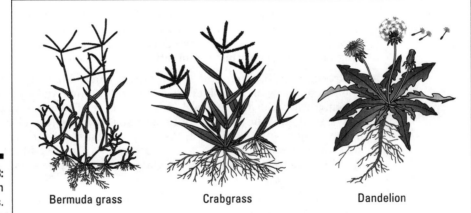

Figure 16-8:
Common
weeds.

Bermuda grass   Crabgrass   Dandelion

✓ **Chickweed.** *Stellaria media.* You can easily spot this densely matting annual weed in late winter and early spring, when the stems of $1/2$-inch (1.2 cm), oval leaves reach toward the sun. The tiny white flowers open fully on sunny days. Broken stems can root if dropped on the ground.

✓ **Crabgrass.** *Digitaria.* Most common in dry, sandy soil, this annual has leaves with bluish cast and spreading stems that root at the nodes. (Refer to Figure 16-8.) It's easy to grab hold of the clump and pull it up. Mulch effectively smothers crabgrass. Control by maintaining a vigorous lawn and by applying corn gluten meal in early spring.

✓ **Curly dock.** *Rumex crispus.* Perennial curly dock often arrives in gardens courtesy of manure. Left alone, it grows to 4 feet (1.2 m) tall with clusters of heart-shaped, reddish brown seed pods. The taproot can extend 2 feet (60 cm) underground, but if you can remove just the top 5 inches (12.5 cm), the root dies. Corn gluten herbicide prevents seeds from sprouting.

✔ **Dandelion.** *Taraxacum officinale*. The first leaves of this perennial, which emerge in early spring, are low and oval. Later leaves are arrow-shaped with deep lopes. The unmistakable yellow flowers quickly go to seed, so pick them early. The edible flowers are reported to be tasty when battered and fried. Long-handled weeders seem made to remove this common weed from lawns and gardens. Remove as much of the taproot as possible because the plant regrows from any portion that's left. Corn gluten herbicide prevents seed germination, and Weed Eraser can kill adult weeds.

✔ **Lamb's-quarters.** *Chenopodium album*. This upright-growing annual is distinctive for the white sparkles on the surfaces of young leaves. Leaf undersides are dusty white. Adding to the rather attractive display, the stems are often red or lighter green. Frequent hand-pulling and hoeing can keep the rapidly growing weed under control. Prevent seed germination with corn gluten herbicide.

✔ **Oxalis.** This is a perennial weed notable for its clover-like leaves and bright yellow flowers. Control by repeated cultivations or flaming and applications of corn gluten herbicide. Use the corn gluten later to minimize or prevent seed germination.

✔ **Redroot pigweed.** *Amaranthus retroflexus*. The reddish stems of this annual can grow up to 10 feet (3m) tall, with oblong, pointy leaves. Green, upright flowers resemble a bottle brush. These plants are quite easy to pull, but they also reroot easily so uprooting them leaving them in the garden won't help much. As for all annuals, slice them off at the surface with a sharp scuffle hoe. Or use Safer's SuperFast herbicide or Weed Eraser to kill pigweed. Corn gluten herbicide prevents its seeds from germinating.

✔ **Purslane.** *Portulaca oleracea*. Think of the popular bedding plant called portulaca and you'll be able to identify annual purslane. The succulent leaves are prostrate and branching, forming dense mats. Pulling and cultivation help, but plants reroot readily. Or use Safer's SuperFast soap herbicide to spray. Corn gluten herbicide prevents seed growth.

✔ **Shepherd's purse.** *Capsella bursa-pastoris*. Seed pods of this annual are thought to resemble the purses carried by early shepherds. These tiny green triangles perch on thin stalks all along upright stems that emerge from the base of the plant, which resembles a dandelion. Remove seed pods before they drop seeds or you'll never get rid of these weeds.

✔ **Spotted (or prostrate) spurge.** This very low growing and spreading annual weed loves hot weather and compacted soil. Eliminate by cultivating, flaming, or soap herbicide. Prevent seed germination with corn gluten herbicide.

When planning your garden, think in three dimensions. Use trees, shrubs, and vines to create your overhead and vertical spaces. Flowering trees, such as these blooming dogwood trees, add visual punch to an otherwise green landscape.

Loebner magnolia
Magnolia 'Leonard Messel'
20-foot tree, zones 4-9

Black tupelo
Nyssa sylvatica
30-to-50-foot tree, zones 5-8

Paperbark maple
Acer griseum
20-to-30-foot tree, zones 5-8

Staghorn sumac
Rhus typhina
15-to-25-foot tree, zones 4-8

Flowering dogwood
Cornus florida
20-foot tree, zones 6-9

Higan (spring) cherry
Prunus subhirtella
25-foot tree, zones 5-8

English hawthorn
Crataegus laevigata
20-foot tree, zones 4-7

Chinese fringetree
Chionanthus retusus
20-foot tree, zones 6-9

Trees

Color 3-4

Sugar or hard maple
Acer saccharum
60-foot, zones 4-8

Saucer magnolia
Magnolia soulangiana
25-foot tree, zones 5-9

Bailey acacia *Acacia baileyana*, **15-foot tree, zones 9-10**

Bowles golden grass
Carex elata 'Bowles Golden'
Perennial, zones 6-9

Border forsythia
Forsythia intermedia
Shrub, zones 4-8

Rosemary
Rosmarinus officinalis 'Huntington carpet'
Shrub and herb, zones 8-10

Smoke tree
Cotinus coggygria 'Royal Purple'
Shrub, zones 4-10

Threadleaf false cypress
Chamaecyparis pisifera 'Filifera'
Shrub, zones 4-7

Purple beautyberry
Callicarpa japonica
Shrub, zones 5-8

Eastern white cedar
Arborvitae 'Rheingold'
Shrub, zones 5-7

Butterfly bush (white) *Buddleia davidii* **with bee balm**
Shrub, zones 5-9

Common winterberry
Ilex verticillata
Shrub, zones 3-9

Lilac
Syringia vulgaris
Shrub, zones 3-7

This spring garden features blooming rhododendron and dogwoods, and also conifers and maples.

Rhododendron
Rhododendron catawbiense 'Roseum Pink'
Shrub, zones 4-9

Morning glory
Ipomoea tricolor
'Heavenly Blue'
Annual vine

Clematis
Clematis jackmanii
Perennial vine, zones 4-9

Black-eyed Susan vine
Thunbergia alata
Annual vine

White potato vine
Solanum jasminoides 'Alba'
Perennial, zones 9-11

Chapter 17

Tools of the Trade

● ●

In This Chapter

▶ Looking at the seven most essential and the five handiest hand tools

▶ Finding the right lawn mower

▶ Using string trimmers

▶ Getting to know tillers and garden grinders

▶ Knowing where — and how — to shop for garden tools

● ●

Gardening really doesn't require a shed full of tools. In fact, we recommend starting with just a few essential tools and then building your collection as specific jobs call for more-specialized tools. But having the right tool for the job often makes the difference between a pleasurable experience and a frustrating chore, or between a job well done or not. That's what this chapter is all about: choosing the right tool for the job.

Hand Tools

To save money over the long haul, buy high-quality, durable tools. Generally, forged-steel tools hold up better than welded types. Relatively new on the market are tools with fiberglass handles, which are stronger than wood. Hardware stores and garden centers offer what you need to get started. Mail-order garden supply catalogs, such as A. M. Leonard, Inc., offer more-specialized tools. (See Appendix B.)

The magnificent seven tools

Following is a list of the tools that you absolutely must have:

> ✔ **Garden hose.** Buy a top-quality hose with a lifetime guarantee. A good hose coils easily, resists kinking, and remains flexible even in cold weather. Choose one long enough to reach all corners of your garden.

✔ **Hand trowel.** A hand trowel is important for transplanting seedlings, scooping soil into containers, and doing close-up weeding jobs. Buy one that fits your hand and is light enough to be comfortable.

✔ **Hoe.** Forgo the conventional garden hoe designed to chop at the soil; buy a *scuffle hoe* instead. This type of hoe is easier to use — instead of chopping, you push the hoe along the soil's surface. A scuffle hoe is indispensable for weeding on packed, level surfaces such as garden paths. Although scuffle hoes vary in design, all work with a push-pull motion. Some cut and scrape the tops off weeds on both strokes. Our favorite, the *oscillating* or *action* hoe, has a hinged blade that moves back and forth as it cuts.

✔ **Lawn rake.** Nothing works better than a bamboo, polypropylene, or metal rake with long, flexible tines for gathering up lawn clippings, leaves, and even small rocks on both paved and natural surfaces. (See Figure 17-1.)

✔ **Pruners.** Once you own a pair of pruners that you can hold comfortably and that produces a clean cut with little effort, you'll find it hard to imagine gardening without them. Most gardeners favor *by-pass pruners*, which cut like scissors. *Anvil pruners* that cut by pressing a blade into a soft metal anvil are less expensive. Use either type to cut soft and woody stems up to about $1/2$ inch (1.3 cm) thick. Use this tool to clip flowers, harvest vegetables, groom shrubs, and prune trees.

✔ **Shovel.** A regular round-nose shovel, as shown in Figure 17-1, is the single most versatile tool you can own. You need it for digging, turning, and scooping. When used in a chopping motion, the shovel effectively breaks up clods of earth. Choose a length and weight that's comfortable.

✔ **Stiff-tined rake.** The first rake you should buy is a *stiff-tined* or *steel bow* rake, as shown in Figure 17-1. This rake is an important tool for spreading and leveling soil and for gathering organic materials. The rake also is a good tool for breaking up small clods of earth. Use both the *tines* (the thin, pointed prongs) and the back edge of the rake for building and smoothing raised garden beds: Keep the tines facing downward when breaking up lumps of soil or collecting stones, and keep the flat edge of the head downward when leveling.

Hand-tool maintenance

Take care of your hand tools — they'll last longer and work better. Try to clean and dry your tools each time you finish your gardening chores, but also know that primary maintenance consists of keeping

✔ Wood handles smooth and sound

✔ Metal tool heads rust-free

✔ Blades sharp

Figure 17-1:
The lawn rake is effective for gathering leaves and lawn clippings. The round-nose shovel can dig, scoop, turn, and chop. A stiff-tined rake is useful for spreading and leveling soil.

When wooden tool handles show wear, sand off the factory varnish and apply boiled linseed oil. Apply several coats, allowing the oil to soak in each time. Clean metal tool heads with a wire brush and sharpen edges with a file. Protect the metal by coating with rust-proof primer followed by a coat of rust-proof paint. Many by-pass pruners have replacement cutting blades that are easy to install. You can also sharpen pruners (the beveled side of the curved blade only) with a fine-grit diamond file.

Replace worn hand tool grips with a liquid plastic, sold in most hardware stores. The best tool lubricants are synthetic oils that lubricate, repel dust, protect against rust, and leave only a light film. Our favorite is Corona's CLP Shear Maintenance Oil, available from A. M. Leonard. See Appendix B.

Five more tools to buy

After you invest in the seven essential tools — and if you still have space in your shed or garage — here's what to buy next. Though not as critical as the seven essential tools, these all-purpose tools are very useful to most gardeners. Which tools you need to own depends entirely upon the jobs that you're trying to accomplish. If, for example, you've just moved into a home with a garden that includes massive, overgrown shrubs, buy loppers before a trowel.

- ✔ **Garden cart.** A lightweight, well-balanced cart that maneuvers easily makes daunting tasks a cinch. With a cart, a gardener can haul big, heavy loads of soil, compost, plants, containers, or wood with little effort.

- ✔ **Gardening gloves.** Sooner or later, you'll wish you had a good pair of gloves. Gloves should fit well and be thick enough to protect your hands, yet not so clunky that you can't maneuver small objects. Cloth gloves with leather reinforcement hold up well to general garden tasks. Gloves with extra-long cuffs help protect your wrists from branches and thorns.

  Glove materials and their best uses are cotton/polyester and leather — general garden chores; synthetics such as Spectra and Kevlar — working with saws and knives; latex or PVC — working with and around water; chemical-resistant nitrile or neoprene — working with chemicals.

- ✔ **Lopping shears.** When you get serious about pruning trees and shrubs, loppers are a must. These tools cut easily through branches an inch or more in diameter. Figure 17-2 shows a pole lopper, which allows you to prune branches that are well above your head.

- ✔ **Tape measure.** A metal tape measure is essential for laying out garden beds and helpful in spacing plants. When staking out an entire landscape, a 100-foot (30 m) length helps you measure precisely.

- ✔ **Water wand.** This hose-end attachment is great for watering containers, garden seedlings, and seedbeds. Choose one with a shut-off valve. The wand should provide a full but gentle flow that doesn't wash away soil and seeds.

Powering Up Your Tools

Which is it for you: "That cursed internal combustion contraption!" or "Praise be the internal combustion!" Does anyone really *need* power equipment of some kind? In our experience, most gardeners use at least one of these tools from time to time.

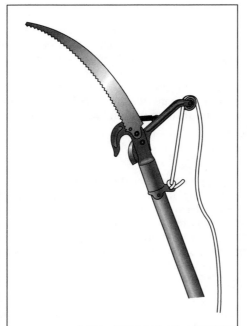

Figure 17-2:
A pole lopper allows you to prune branches above your head.

Lawn mowers

Lawns may not be the most politically correct corner of the garden, but most of us have one — or wish we did. (For more about lawn care, see Chapter 6.)

One of the reasons that people get fed up with lawns is that lawns require this regular, monotonous maintenance called *cutting the grass,* which, for some of you, may conjure up memories of noisy, dirty, hard-to-start engines. We're here to tell you that times have changed! You have so many more choices now that you're more likely to find the mower that's right for you. New lawn mowers are quieter, better working, less polluting, and safer to use.

Choose a lawn mower according to the size of your lawn, the type of grass, your tolerance (or not) of noise, and your desire for exercise. Allow about an hour to mow 2,500 square feet (232 m²) of grass, using a 20-inch-wide (50 cm) rotary mower. The wider the mower or the faster it moves, the more quickly you can get the job done.

Push-reel mowers

The original teenager's nightmare, push-reel mowers have been rediscovered, reinvented, and improved. Guess what? These mowers are good for the environment and for your body, too. Push-reel mowers are quiet and completely nonpolluting, they give your body a workout that equals a session (at the least) with a treadmill. If your lawn is 1,000 square feet (93 m²) or less and composed mostly of soft grasses such as fescue, Kentucky bluegrass, or ryegrass, this type of mower is a serious option. Most cost around $100, but fancy ones can be twice that.

Power-reel mowers

The power-reel mower is the type of mower that professional gardeners and greenskeepers use. In all cases, the engine drives both the cutting blades and the wheels, but some types throw clippings to the front, and others throw to the rear. These mowers are much more expensive than rotary mowers ($300 and up), but they are unsurpassed at providing a close, even cut, even of dense, thick grasses such as Bermuda grass or zoysia.

Push rotary power mowers

Push rotary power is the type of mower that America uses to cut its grass. You provide the push power, but the engine and the spinning blade do the grass cutting. This type is relatively inexpensive ($200–$400, depending on features) and easy to operate. One decision you need to make is choosing between _side_ or _rear bagging_. Side-baggers are cheaper; they are slightly less convenient (because you can cut close on one side of the mower only) but work just as well.

Don't buy a push rotary power mower that doesn't include a blade break system, colorfully termed a _deadman switch_. This device makes the spinning blade stop within 3 seconds after the operator releases a lever on the handle. This makes the mowers more expensive, but reduces mower-caused injuries.

Self-propelled and mulching rotary mowers

Self-propelled and mulching rotary mowers are basically the same as push rotary power mowers but with added features. Naturally, the price is steeper: $500–$700, usually. The _self-propelled_ feature is plain enough: Pulleys and gears link the engine to the front wheels. The mulching concept is a bit more involved: The mower is basically the same, but the cutting blade and deck are redesigned to cut and recut the grass and leaves, resulting in smaller pieces. These mowers also have no exit chute on the side or rear (or it's optional).

Mulching mowers chop grass blades small enough that the grass filters back down into the lawn. As the cut blades decompose, they release nutrients to the growing lawn, and you don't have to bag and send clippings to the landfill.

Electric rotary mowers

Electric rotary mowers are great, especially if you live next to a hospital or absolutely refuse to deal with anything gasoline-powered. The machines are virtually silent — all you hear is the low hum of the spinning blade. And these mowers are easy to start — you turn a switch, and the blade spins. Electric rotary mowers do have a downside, though. A long cord, usually of a maximum length, restricts your movements (and how much lawn you can cut); the umbilical-free, battery-powered kinds are a bit heavy and pricey. A variety of solar-powered mowers are available now, but these are expensive and not practical in many situations.

Lawn mowers that you can sit on

This category is broad. The simplest are correctly called *riding mowers,* which do nothing but cut grass. Typically, the engine is in the rear, the mowing deck out in front, and you sit somewhere in between. The mowing deck is 30–42 inches (76–106 cm) wide, and engines are 8–13 horsepower. Prices range from $700 to $1,000.

Lawn-and-garden tractors

Lawn-and-garden tractors are somewhat larger than sit-down lawn mowers and look a bit more like real farm tractors. You sit and look out over a hood that covers the engine, and the mowing deck is right below your chair. Most have a channel steel frame and front axle, and most have 12–18 horsepower. These mowers cut 38–48 inches (96 cm–1.2 m) of grass in one swipe. Some models take attachments such as tillers and snowthrowers. Some even offer cruise control! The lawn-and-garden tractor is the type for a homeowner with a large property. Cost? Expect to pay anywhere from $1,000 to $4,000.

Don't buy more horsepower than you need. Lawn-and-garden tractors with 14 horsepower are enough to cut several acres of grass and occasionally till the soil.

Garden tractors

Garden tractors are actual, scaled-down versions of farm tractors. Equally heavy-duty as their full-size brethren, their frames are heavy, 10-gauge steel, and both front and rear axles are cast iron. These machines use anywhere from 12 to 20 horsepower and cut 38–60 inches (96 cm–1.5 m) of grass at once. The benefit of a garden tractor over a lawn tractor is that the garden tractor can accept a variety of attachments, such as rototillers, chippers, and snowblowers. A garden tractor is a good tool for a weekend farmer who needs to do lots of chores. Expect to pay at least $3,000 and as much as $10,000.

Trimmers

The string trimmer is (after lawn mowers) the most widely used power tool. Some are electric (power cord or battery), and some are gas powered. Most of the gas-powered kinds use two-stroke engines. This type of engine requires that you mix special oil into the gasoline. A few manufacturers now offer quieter and less polluting 4-stroke engines on their trimmers. Gas-powered trimmers are louder than electric versions.

Most trimmers cut soft grass and weeds with a spinning nylon cord. Some use a solid nylon disk, and some can accept other, heavy duty cutting blades. For a basic string trimmer, look for one with an automatic or semiautomatic "feed" system for the nylon whip. Some trimmers force you to stop the engine and lengthen the string or whip by hand every time the string wears down.

Electric trimmers

Electric trimmers with power cords are the least expensive kind. These trimmers enable you to work 50–100 feet (15–30 m) from an outlet, they're lightweight, and they're quiet. Prices start at about $50. Models powered by batteries allow you to roam more freely but limit you to about 45 minutes of continuous trimming. They cost a bit more, about $100.

Gasoline-powered trimmers

Trimmers with gas power work roughly the same as the electric models, but they give you more power, need more maintenance, make more noise, and let you do more work in less time.

Even though the spinning whip of cord is safer than a whirling blade, it can damage the bark of young trees and shrubs (not to mention hands and feet). If you use this type of trimmer around trees, protect the lower trunk with a heavy plastic collar (available at garden centers). Or better yet, add a ring of mulch around the tree and eliminate the need for close trimming!

Tillers and grinders

Most tillers and grinders (also known as "chipper-shredders") are hefty machines. Weight begins at about 70 pounds (32 kg) and goes up to a few hundred pounds. Engine horsepower begins at 3, but some have 8 or more. The cost begins at around $500 and ranges upward to $1,600. As big and heavy as they are, both are big time-savers. If you regularly garden a quarter acre or more, both may be smart investments.

A tiller consists of an engine that provides the power to a transmission that channels the power to the wheels and the tiller. Tillers with the tines in front don't have powered wheels, so the transmission has only to drive the tiller.

If you need a tiller or chipper just once or twice a year, buying your own may not make good economic sense (and where would you store it?). Renting one for a day or two is a sensible option.

All rotary tillers are categorized as either *front tine* or *rear tine*. Front-tine rotary tillers are lighter in weight and cheaper; consider them medium-duty machines. If the soil you're tilling is relatively loose, these are very effective. These tillers, however, are not as efficient if the soil is compacted or rocky. The tines pull the tiller forward; so if the tines connect with a big stone or root, the machine lurches forward. The other downside of front-tine tillers is that you must walk directly behind them, through the freshly fluffed soil.

Heavy-duty tillers have the engine in front and the tines in the rear. Expert gardeners prefer rear-tine tillers because they're much easier and less jarring to operate (even though heavier). The tines dig down into the soil rather than force the machine to lurch forward, and the operator doesn't need to walk through freshly tilled soil.

As the tines turn

Most tines rotate in the direction of travel. The resistance of the soil on the blades causes the tiller to drive itself forward. You need to restrain this driving force to ensure even tilling of the soil.

Tillers offer several kinds of tines, with many different functions. By far, the most common kind of tine is the *bolo* tine, which is shaped like an *L* and is sharpened on the cutting edge. The bottom of the *L* is twisted slightly so that the soil lifts up and away as the tine turns. Some tines are further bent so that they can enter the soil more easily.

The higher the tine speed, the more easily and more finely you can prepare the seedbed. A higher tine speed is also necessary to adequately chop up crop residues or compost and incorporate them into the soil. The common tine speed for front-tine tillers is 100–175 rotations per minute. Commercial tillers often allow you to vary the tine speed for different uses. The throttle setting also affects tine speed.

Mini-tillers

Also referred to as *lightweight tiller/cultivators, hand-held tiller/cultivators,* and *power cultivators,* mini-tillers are 20- to 30-pound (9–13 kg), gasoline-powered (usually two-cycle) machines. In most designs, the horizontally mounted engine (1–1¹/₂ horsepower) sits directly above the tines. Connected to this engine and tine unit are handlebars with a lever for throttle control and an on/off switch. The cost of mini-tillers varies with the number of attachments you buy, but expect to pay around $300.

Mini-tiller tines are made of sharper-edged spring steel and spin faster than the heavier tines of large tillers. The patented Mantis tines are star-shaped, so they tend to slice into the soil. The others have conventional, L-shaped tines that dig like a hoe.

On small patches of ground that are in good condition, hand tools are probably just as quick and efficient. Additionally, hand tools are not as damaging to soil structure as tillers, which tend to pulverize particles more than plants need for good root growth. Tillers of any kind may create a layer of packed and hardened soil at the bottom of their cultivating depth — the so-called *plow sole*. But on larger stretches of relatively stone-free ground, the mini-tillers can be worthwhile. They dig about twice as fast as a person skillful with a fork and spade and require much less bending than working the soil with hand tools does.

An automatic clutch activates the tines, which control forward motion. A lever on either the right or left handlebar controls engine speed. At idle, the tines don't move. As you squeeze the lever, the engine speeds up, and the tines engage.

Tines work soil to a depth of 3–10 inches (7.5–25 cm). An average working depth after two passes through an average soil is probably about 6 inches, but by working the machine back and forth, you make it dig deeper. Some gardeners use mini-tillers for digging trenches and planting holes for trees.

Here's what you should use a mini-tiller for:

- ✔ Tilling loamy, stone-free soil
- ✔ Tilling soil in small or raised beds
- ✔ Cultivating compacted, weedy soil between rows of vegetables
- ✔ Cultivating soil in narrow, tight locations
- ✔ Weeding in compacted walkways
- ✔ Mixing compost and amendments into planting beds
- ✔ Digging planting holes for trees, shrubs, and perennials

Garden grinders

Most garden grinders available today are part chipper and part shredder. The former consists of a 3–4-inch (7.5–10 cm) hardened steel blade inserted into the main flywheel of the machine. You feed material — branches or corn stalks for instance — to it via a narrow tube. The shredder part is a larger opening designed to accept armloads of preferably dry leaves. The opening leads to a chamber in which a number of 2-inch (5 cm) long flails spin and "shred" the material. One manufacturer, Troy-Bilt, currently produces a chipper that is essentially a scaled-down version of commercial, tree-company chippers. Instead of a blade spinning in a flywheel, it has larger blades mounted in a drum. This version has no flails or shredding chamber.

Electric motors, gasoline engines, or power-take-off (PTO) connections of garden tractors supply power to grinders. Electric grinders are suitable for chipping small prunings up to an inch or so in diameter. Gasoline-powered grinders have 3–12 horsepower engines and a manual or automatic clutch.

Garden grinders are among the most dangerous tools gardeners regularly use. Wear goggles or protective glasses at all times and avoid loose-fitting clothing. Follow all the safety precautions carefully, and always turn the engine off and wait for it to stop completely before reaching in to unclog.

Where to Shop for Garden Tools

All plants are not created equal, nor are tools, potting mixes, and most gardening implements. So to get what you want for your garden — the best quality, a true bargain, or something really strange (like an electric bulb-planting drill) — you need to know where to shop.

By the way, you can order an electric bulb-planting drill from Park Seed Co. (See Appendix B for the address.)

Nurseries

In addition to plants and information, larger nurseries offer seeds, bulbs, soil amendments, bark mulches, containers, fertilizers, pesticides, tools, irrigation supplies, and even garden ornaments.

Other sources for tools and garden supplies

Shop at hardware stores and home-building centers for garden tools. Also look to these places for materials to build garden structures, such as lumber, nails, and twine for trellises.

If you live in rural areas, turn to farm and feed stores. These stores are a great source for seeds, tools, soil amendments, fertilizers, pesticides, fencing, and irrigation supplies.

If you know a quality product by brand name or know how to judge the quality of a product, then you are well-positioned to find a true bargain at a discount store. But just because something is inexpensive doesn't mean it's a bargain. Heed this warning: Know what you're paying for.

Shopping by mail greatly broadens your choice of seeds, plants, tools, and supplies. However, besides having to wait for delivery, the downside of shopping by mail is not being able to see what you're buying. That's why it's especially important to know that your sources, especially nurseries, are reliable. Appendix B lists some reliable mail-order catalogs. Look for the Source icon throughout this book for more.

Part VI
Special Gardens

The 5th Wave   By Rich Tennant

"Something's about to die in your cactus container."

In this part . . .

A garden may be in a teacup or a barrel, or it may cover an acre or more. What makes a garden is the interest and intent of the gardener, not grandeur or super plantsmanship.

Inevitably, many gardeners adopt specialties. Some like to grow their own food; others cultivate only flowers. For some, a garden must be neat and orderly; for others, the more casual, the better.

Here are four of our favorite gardens from gardens in containers, to food gardens, to gardens that attract birds and butterflies. But remember that countless other types of gardens exist.

Chapter 18

Food Gardens

In This Chapter

▶ Making a vegetable garden

▶ Choosing your favorite vegetables

▶ Squeezing in herbs

▶ Getting started with fruits

▶ Looking at favorite fruits and berries

*I*f you have a bit of farmer in you — or even if you don't — you can get a lot of satisfaction out of growing good things to eat. Vegetables, herbs, fruits, and berries can make your yard productive as well as good looking.

Surprisingly, most edible plants (especially vegetables) are easy to grow. You don't need a lot of space either. Gardening has no rule that says you must lay out vegetables in long rows — many of them grow better in beds. You can even mix vegetables, herbs, fruits, and flowers together and end up with a garden that pleases all your senses.

Planning a Vegetable Garden

Vegetable gardening can be downright simple if you follow a few guidelines. Planting at the right time is key, and to do that, you need to know a little about both the vegetables you want to grow and your climate.

Pay especially close attention to the seasons. (Why do you think farmers are always talking about the weather?) Most vegetables are annuals. Their lives begin and end within the scope of one "season." Exactly when that season begins and ends is the rub.

Seasonal preferences

Regarding season, vegetables are broadly categorized as either "warm season" or "cool season." Warm-season vegetables like warmth and they don't like cold. Their season is pretty much bracketed by frosts: the last one in spring and the first one in fall. The days or months between those two markers are the season for warmth-loving vegetables such as corn, peppers, and tomatoes. (See Figure 18-1.)

Figure 18-1: Plant warm-season vegetables after all danger of frost has passed.

Now you can guess about cool-season vegetables (see Figure 18-2) such as peas, lettuce, and radishes: They like cool weather; many also can withstand a little bit (sometimes a lot) of frost.

Figure 18-2: Cool-season vegetables stand up to colder weather, but avoid frost!

Vegetable garden calendar

Suppose you live in an area like Kansas City and your last spring frost comes around April 15. (See Chapter 2 for details on frost dates.) A couple weeks before that, you kick off the planting season with three cool-season vegetables: lettuce (because it's easy), carrots (because they're pretty), and broccoli (because it's good for you).

To celebrate filing your taxes, you cruise through the garden center and pick up some tomato and pepper plants. As soon as you get the feeling in your bones that the last frost is a done deal, into the ground they go.

Now it's a beautiful weekend in May. You sow seeds of bush beans, sweet corn, and cucumbers. Stash a few basil plants where you see gaps, and sow some dill seeds where the lettuce didn't come up. Now you have a diversified garden going. Keep it more or less weeded and mulched, and the garden will behave while you're on vacation.

Summer's midpoint has passed, so you start some crops like spinach and more lettuce from the cool-season list and get them going. By the time frost comes in fall, you've had your fill of squash and tomatoes anyway, and the spinach will taste a bit better after being touched by frost.

The last piece of information you need — before actually planting — is the pattern of cool and warm temperatures where you live and how that pattern relates to vegetables. Chapter 2 gives lots of details about how this pattern works, but this section offers some examples specifically for vegetables.

For most Northern Hemisphere gardeners, the timing is pretty simple: The last frost in spring usually occurs sometime between March and May. Plant cool-season crops a couple weeks before that date; warm-season crops one or two weeks after. The first frost in fall occurs sometime between September and November. Any warm-season crops die then, but cool-season crops keep on growing, sometimes until December.

This pattern however, gets turned around for gardeners in a really warm climate, such as Phoenix, Arizona, or Miami, Florida. The overall weather pattern is the same, with the cool season starting in the fall. But that's when the climate finally cools enough for what the rest of us know as *warm-season* crops.

Similarly, in mild-winter regions, such as much of coastal California, southeast Texas, and the Gulf Coast, the cool-season crops won't grow at all during the hot summers. You have to wait until September or October to get these plants started. And in the far north, the cold season is too severe for much of anything to grow and the warm (or frost-free) season is relatively cool — meaning you grow just about all vegetables at the same time.

Choose the right location

Most vegetables need six to eight hours of direct sun daily for best results. Leafy greens, like spinach and lettuce, can thrive with a bit less. Fruit-producing vegetables like tomatoes, peppers, pumpkins, and squash need more. Be mindful of nearby trees. Deciduous trees allow much light to pass through in winter and early spring, and cast increasingly dense shade as the season progresses.

If possible, locate the garden so that access to and from the kitchen is easy and convenient — you'll be more apt to notice what needs to be tended and to take full advantage of the harvest.

In many areas, the foundations of houses are drenched with pesticides to keep termites from eating the footings. Instead of growing edible plants right next to your exterior walls where their roots can contact death-wish chemicals, use those places for inedible flowers and shrubs.

Make the garden the right size

Start small. A 20-x-30-foot (6 x 9 m) garden may be average, but a 10-x-20-foot (3 x 6 m) plot is sufficient for a garden sampler that will yield a variety of greens, some herbs, a few tomatoes and peppers, beans, cucumbers, and even edible flowers such as nasturtiums for garnishes.

A 20-x-30-foot (6 x 9 m) garden gives you room to grow a wide range of crops, including some tasty space hogs like corn and winter squash. By growing plants in succession and using 3-foot-wide (91 cm) beds with 18-inch (46 cm) paths, you should have plenty of luscious vegetables for fresh eating — even extras for friends.

Designing the garden

The process of designing a vegetable garden is both practical and creative. You need to give plants enough room to grow and arrange them so that taller vegetables don't shade lower-growing types. You also need to be aware of the appropriate planting techniques that fit the growth habits of different kinds of vegetables. How you will water your garden is also a strong influence on the garden design. And you should also think about access — how will you get to your plants to harvest, weed, or water? How will you keep out deer and other creatures?

Following are three basic planting arrangements for vegetables:

- ✔ **Rows.** You can plant any vegetable in rows, but this approach works best with plants that need quite a bit of room, such as tomatoes, cabbage, corn, potatoes, melons, and squash.

- ✔ **Beds.** Beds are kind of like wide, flat-topped rows of soil, usually at least 2 feet (60 cm) wide and at least 6 inches (15 cm) high. You can install permanent borders of wood or other material, which makes maintaining edges easy. You can also concentrate all your amendments and fertilizers in the bed more easily and without waste. Beds are ideal for smaller vegetables that don't mind living in close quarters — such as lettuce, carrots, radishes, and turnips — but any vegetable can thrive. Plant the vegetables in a random pattern in the bed or in closely spaced rows.

- ✔ **Containers**. Of course you can grow vegetables in containers. In fact, containers are ideal for apartment dwellers who may have only a patio or balcony to use for outdoor living. You can find more about container gardening in Chapter 19.

- ✔ **Hills.** Hills are best for vining crops like cucumbers, melons, and squash. You create a 1-foot (30 cm) wide, flat-topped mound for heavy soil, or just a circle at ground level for sandy soil, surrounded by a moat-like ring for watering. Plant two or three evenly spaced plants on each hill. Space the hills at the recommended distance for between rows.

Proper plant spacing is a compromise of sometimes competing needs. Gardeners want to squeeze as many plants into the available space to maximize harvest or appearance. Plants need enough physical room (in soil for roots, too) to grow and spread. Also, leave enough space between plants for you to get in to inspect, water, and harvest. Check the catalog or seed packet for mature plant size and planting distance recommendations.

Sketching out your plan on paper can help you purchase the right amount of seeds or transplants and use space more efficiently.

Drawing out the design is a good way to see the possibilities for *succession planting* (following one crop with another) and *interplanting* (planting a crop that matures quickly next to a slower-maturing one and harvesting the two before they compete for space). For example, you may see that you can follow your late peas with a crop of broccoli, and you'll be ready with transplants in July. Or you may see that the garden still has space for you to tuck in a few lettuce plants among your tomatoes while the vines are still small.

Improving the soil

The ideal garden location has loose soil that drains well. If you haven't had your soil tested to determine the pH, do so now. Most vegetables require a pH between 6.0 and 6.8. (See Chapter 11 for more on soil testing and adjusting the pH.)

In most gardens, vegetable garden soil can stand some improvement. Apply several inches of compost or natural fertilizers like decomposed chicken manure over the surface and work it into the soil with a rake.

If your soil is hopeless or if you like convenience, consider growing vegetables in *raised beds* — actually just any planting area that rises above the surrounding ground level. The bed simply can be a normal bed with the soil piled 5 or 6 inches (12.5 or 15 cm) high, or it can be a large containerlike structure with wood, stone, or masonry sides. Wooden raised beds should be made of rot-resistant redwood or cedar or recycled plastic timbers. If you put in several raised beds, leave at least 3 to 4 feet (91 cm–1.2 m) for access paths between them.

What to start with

Many vegetables are best started from seeds sown directly in the ground *(direct-sown)*; others go in as young plants called *seedlings*. You can grow your own seedlings or buy them. (See Chapter 13 for specifics on raising your own seedlings and transplanting.)

Two of your best sources of information about seeds and seedlings are free: seed packets and seed catalogs. To acquire several seed catalogs for free, you can subscribe to a garden magazine; you will begin receiving a selection of catalogs almost immediately. (You can find discount coupons for *National Gardening* magazine in the back of this book.) Or you can mail in the coupons found inside the magazines.

Other sources that you can use, which may be a little bit faster than U.S. mail, are the computer and phone. Use magazines to get Web addresses or toll-free phone numbers, or see Appendixes A and B.

It's all in the timing

The key date in vegetable planting timing is the average date of the last spring *frost* (when all danger of frost has passed). Though frost may not always kill your young plants, it is damaging to most kinds of vegetables. If you don't know the date for your region, check with your local extension office or nursery.

Table 18-1 lists "tough" crops that you can plant two to four weeks before the last frost date.

Table 18-1	Frost-Resistant Crops
Direct-sow	*Transplant*
Beets	Broccoli *
Carrots	Brussels sprouts *
Dill	Cabbage *
Onions *	
Peas *	Parsley *
Radishes *	
Salad greens *	
Spinach *	

* You can sow these crops again later in the season: in midsummer for an autumn harvest; and, in mild-winter climates, in autumn for a winter garden. These plants also are some of the easiest and best for fall vegetable gardens.

Table 18-2 shows examples of "tender" crops to go into the garden after danger of frost is past:

Table 18-2	Frost-Tender Crops
Direct-sow	*Transplant*
Basil **	Eggplant
Beans	Peppers
Cucumbers	Tomatoes
Melons **	
Squash	

** In areas with a short growing season, these crops are often transplanted as seedlings to give them a head start.

Raise them right

Successfully planting seeds in the ground hinges on two factors: depth and moisture. The general rule: Plant the seeds twice as deep as they are wide. So you plant really big seeds like beans and squash 1 to 2 inches (2.5–5 cm) deep, medium-sized seeds like corn 1 inch (2.5 cm) deep, small seeds like beets and spinach $1/2$ inch (1.3 cm) deep, and itty-bitty lettuce, carrot, and turnip seeds no more than $1/4$ inch (0.6 cm) below the surface. You can also buy strips of paper with small seeds glued on at exactly the right spacing. You plant these strips, called *seed tapes,* and eliminate thinning. Most seed catalogs offer seed tapes.

Keep the seeds moist. Water helps soften the seed's coat or shell so that the sprout can break through more easily. Either set up a sprinkler to help keep newly seeded beds moist or cover the bed with an old sheet in between daily watering. As long as the soil isn't clammy (cold and wet), the seeds should sprout within a week.

Whether you set out plants or sow seeds, weeds will appear all over your garden about three weeks after you plant. This is a natural occurrence, but you do have to stifle those wild invaders. Get a comfortable pad to sit on and hand-weed right around your plants. Then use a hoe to clear weeds from large areas of bare soil.

After you finish weeding, mulch over the weeded space to keep more weeds from taking the places of the ones you killed. You can use rolls of fabric mulch material, chopped leaves, grass clippings, hay, newspapers covered with enough leaves or grass clippings to keep them from blowing away, and even old carpeting. (See Chapter 11 for more on mulching.)

Have a happy harvest

If you plant what you like to eat, you'll have to hold yourself back to keep from picking your vegetables too early. Fortunately, most veggies are best when picked on the young side, especially leafy greens, snap beans, peas, cucumbers, and squash. With some other vegetables, especially root vegetables, the old-timers taste better. Wait for carrots to reach full size — that's when they are full of flavor; and tomatoes and peppers are best when allowed to hang on the plants until they're very ripe.

When in question, take a bite! If you don't like what you taste, spit it out, wait a few days, and try again. You'll probably be enthralled with the superior taste of really fresh, ripe vegetables from your own garden.

You Can't Go Wrong with These

Following is a top-ten list of easy-to-grow vegetables, along with a few tips on planting them and recommended varieties. For much more detail about vegetable gardening and especially good home garden varieties, see *Vegetable Gardening For Dummies* by Charlie Nardozzi and the Editors of the National Gardening Association (IDG Books Worldwide, Inc.).

- ✔ **Carrot.** Plant seeds several times throughout the growing season, early spring into fall for a continuous harvest. Soil should be loose and deep. Varieties: 'Nantes', 'Chantenay', 'Touchon', 'Short n' Sweet'.

- ✔ **Cucumber.** Wait until warm weather to plant seeds. Varieties: 'Sweet Success', 'Fanfare', 'Lemon'.

- ✔ **Green Beans.** Plant seeds after frost danger. Bush types are easier to manage, but pole types are more productive in an equal space (because they're taller!). Varieties: 'Blue Lake', 'Contender', 'Kentucky Wonder'.

- ✔ **Lettuce.** Plant seeds as soon as soil can be worked — hot weather ruins the plants. Varieties: 'Black Seeded Simpson', 'Buttercrunch', 'Deer Tongue', 'Nevada'.

- ✔ **Onion.** Timing the planting of seeds or the miniature onion bulbs called *sets* can be tricky. Also consider mail-order onion seedlings. Check locally for availability.

- ✔ **Peas.** Sow seeds early in spring as soon as you can work the soil. Varieties: 'Alderman', 'Sugar Snap', 'Oregon Trail', 'Super Sugar Mel'.

- ✔ **Radish.** Sow seeds during the short, cool days of spring and fall. During these times, radishes are perhaps the easiest and fastest vegetable to grow. Varieties: 'Cherry Belle', 'White Icicle', 'Scarlet Globe'.

- ✔ **Summer Squash.** Sow seeds after weather warms up. Grow bush types to save space. Varieties: 'Sunburst', 'Yellow Crookneck', 'Scallopini'.

- ✔ **Sweet Pepper.** Plant seedlings in warm weather along with tomatoes. Varieties: 'Bell Boy', 'California Wonder', 'Sweet Banana', 'Gypsy'.

- ✔ **Tomato.** Set out seedlings after the air and soil have warmed up. Tomatoes come in countless varieties; among the best: 'Celebrity', 'Big Rainbow', 'Brandywine', and 'Enchantment'.

Tomatoes are one of those rare plants that actually benefit if seedlings are planted deeper than they grew in the nursery pot. Plants will be more anchored and sturdier, and roots will develop along the buried portion of the stem. Pinch off lower leaves, and plant as shown in Figure 18-3.

What about Hybrids and Heirlooms?

As you look through seed catalogs or read seed packets, you may notice the words *hybrid* and *heirloom*. *Hybrid vegetables* are the result of a cross (where pollen from one flower fertilizes another, resulting in seed) of selected groups of plants of the same kind. Hybrid plants may show what's called *hybrid vigor* — a significant increase in qualities such as early and uniform maturity and increased disease resistance. The increased vigor and predictably good performance make hybrids worth the extra cost to many gardeners.

If you choose hybrid seeds, you need to buy a new batch every season rather than save your own. When hybrid plants cross with themselves and form seeds, these seeds lose the specific combination of genetic information that gave the hybrid its predictable qualities. If you plant seed from hybrids, you end up with a very mixed bag of plants.

Figure 18-3:
Planting tomatoes deeply provides stability and forces roots to develop along the buried stem.

At the other end from hybrid varieties are *open pollinated varieties*. These plants are basically inbred lines that are allowed to pollinate each other in open fields. The resulting seeds are pretty predictable, but you won't have the consistency of hybrids.

Heirloom vegetables, like the varieties your grandparents grew, have been open-pollinated for years. Heirlooms are enjoying quite a revival because of the variety of fruit colors, tastes, and forms. Many heirlooms are selected for and perform best in specific regions. If you live where these varieties were grown and selected over many years, then the plants should thrive.

Neither hybrid nor heirloom is necessarily better than the other. Try all kinds of vegetables, especially ones that sound promising to you. Then see what works best, what you like most, and plant more of them.

Squeezing in Herbs

You can always use for fresh herbs in the kitchen, so always try to squeeze a few into a vegetable garden — or into pots or even a flower garden.

Many herbs are annuals (like marigolds) which require full sun and a long warm season. Some, like chives and parsley, are biennials; and several, such as oregano and thyme, are perennials. Most all herbs grow best in soil that is not too rich and that drains water quickly.

The following are among the easiest and most useful herbs to grow:

- ✔ **Basil.** This annual is easy to start from seed or transplants. In short season areas, sow seeds indoors six to eight weeks before the last frost; plant outdoors, in full sun, only after danger of frost has passed. Plants grow 12–18 inches (30–46 cm) high. Pick leaves as you need them; six plants are plenty for most gardeners.

- ✔ **Chives.** Start plants from seeds or clumps. Plant in early spring as soon as the soil is workable, in full sun or partial shade. Plants grow about 12 inches (30 cm) high and produce round, pinkish flowers in early summer. Use scissors to snip leaf tips as needed. Divide slowly expanding clumps every three years or so.

- ✔ **Garlic.** Start with bulbs from the market, nursery, or mail-order supplier (the latter can provide extensive variety selection). Plant in fall. Separate bulbs into individual cloves; leaving the papery membrane in place. Set cloves pointed end up, 2 inches (5 cm) deep and 3 inches (7.5 cm) apart. Harvest all types in midsummer when the tops are mostly brown.

- ✔ **Mints.** These tremendously varied plants all have leaves that are rich with aromatic oils, and all share a love of moist soil. Peppermint (*Mentha piperita*) is a favorite. You can snip the tip of a branch, pour hot water over it, and have instant peppermint tea. Plants grow about 12 inches (30 cm) high.

- ✔ **Oregano and marjoram.** We place these two plants together here because they are so closely related and so often confused. Oregano (*Origanum vulgare*) is a 3-foot (91 cm) tall hardy perennial, and marjoram (*O. majorana*) is a 2-foot (60 cm) tall tender annual. Both are strongly aromatic and flavorful, but marjoram is a little sweeter and milder. The best way to start either plant in your garden is to buy plants from your nursery or by mail.

- ✔ **Parsley.** This herb is so familiar as a restaurant garnish it's possible to overlook how attractive and useful it is in the garden. The rich green of the leaves is a perfect foil to spring daffodils or pansies. Snip or pinch a few leaves whenever you need it for a recipe. Start from seeds or plants, but we recommend the latter because gardeners often have trouble starting the seeds.

- ✔ **Rosemary.** Gardeners anywhere can grow this resinous, aromatic shrub in summer. But if you live where winters aren't too cold, like zone 8 and warmer, rosemary is a perfectly behaved landscape shrub that you can also harvest for the kitchen and barbecue. Many named varieties of rosemary are available, but all have flavorful leaves and stems. They differ primarily in growth habit: Some trail and some are upright. All have blue flowers and need full sun and well-drained soil. Buy rosemary plants at your local nursery or from mail-order suppliers.

✔ **Sage.** This plant is a hardy perennial (*Salvia officinalis*) that gardeners anywhere can have in their gardens for years. They are ornamental: Several kinds have variously colored leaves, but all have the same distinctive flavor that cooks desire. Sage grows 24–30 inches (60–76 cm) high and produces violet flowers in early summer. Plant in full sun and well-drained soil. Start with plants from your local or mail-order nursery.

✔ **Thyme.** These hardy perennials are mostly low growing (a few very low growing). Some are ornamental only with just faint flavor. Most, however, have leaves and stems that are rich with fragrant oils. Common thyme (*Thymus vulgaris*) grows 6–8 inches (15–20 cm) high and is the form that cooks prefer. But lemon thyme (*T. citriodorus*), with its citrus scent, runs a close second. Mother-of-thyme (*T. praecox arcticus*) grows only about 2 inches (5 cm) high and is excellent growing between stepping-stones where an occasional step releases the wonderful scent.

Is There Fruit in Your Future?

If you have just ¼ acre (100 x 100 feet, or 30 x 30 m) in your backyard or side yard, you can grow the full range of temperate tree fruits (apples, pears, cherries, peaches, and plums), plus berries and brambles. Of course your climate will impose a few restrictions. For instance, apples are a problem if you live too far south where winters are hardly cold at all, and peaches are pushing their ability to withstand cold in zones 5 and 6 in the north. Nevertheless, don't think "orchard." Instead, think in terms of a fruit *garden* — you really need only a handful of trees to get more than enough fruit. One full-grown peach tree, for example, gives you three or more bushels.

Apples are available as true dwarf varieties, so you can plant a large number of individual varieties without outpacing your ability to use the fruit. With careful pruning, you can keep the trees as small as 6 feet (1.8 m) tall. Spaced 2 feet (60 cm) apart — each tree can yield between 10 and 15 pounds (4.5 and 6.8 kg) of fruit.

Also check with your local Master Gardeners — and perhaps become one yourself. You can learn about the program through your local extension office. For more information about Master Gardeners, see Appendix A.

Get an agent

Extension office agents are people employed by your home state at county offices. They are gold mines of helpful information for farmers and home gardeners like you (and the information is usually free — you've already paid for it with your taxes). They don't have time to provide individual tutoring but will gladly give you literature on crucial topics like the following:

✔ Average first and last frost dates for your area

✔ Home vegetable garden guide, including recommended varieties

✔ Home fruit production guide, including recommended varieties

Six steps to a fruit tree harvest

You don't need to don a tin-pot hat, à la Johnny Appleseed, to grow fruit trees. Just take a look at the following general tips:

✔ **Be patient.** Most fruit trees require at least five to eight years from planting to the first harvest. But if you're in a hurry, plant dwarf trees. They'll bear fruit much quicker.

✔ **Plant varieties adapted to your climate.** Most gardening comes down to matching the plant with your climate and fruit gardening is no different. If you live where winters are 25°F (–4°C) or colder, guess what? You can't grow mangoes. Likewise, if you live where winters never drop below 40°F (4°C), you may not be able to grow apples.

Most deciduous fruit trees, particularly apples, need a minimum amount of *chill,* or number of hours below 45°F (7°C), while the tree is dormant in winter. The chill period helps the tree to grow and fruit well the following season. In the north, this chill requirement isn't an issue, but in southern and western regions, gardeners need to choose varieties that have a low chill requirement. Even though the plant is perfectly hardy and will grow well, check to make sure the variety you choose will also produce a good crop where you live.

✔ **Provide pollinizers.** Many fruit trees need the pollen from a different but compatible variety — called *cross-pollination* — to produce a crop of fruit. Apples, pears, sweet cherries, and Japanese plums are in this category. Exceptions include most peaches, figs, and sour cherries. Apples need cross-pollination, but ornamental crab apples can serve too, so you can get by with only one apple tree if you live where apples (and crab apples) are abundant.

✔ **Plant in the right place.** A good site means full sun and fertile, well-drained soil. If you live in an area with strong winds, plant trees in protected locations. If spring frosts threaten developing buds and flowers, plant on a gentle slope so that cold air travels downhill and away from the trees.

✔ **Keep trees well watered and fertilized.** Water trees deeply every two weeks. The soil should be moist down to at least 2 feet (60 cm) for dwarf trees and 3–4 feet (91 cm–1.2 m) for full-sized trees. Use mulch, such as compost or straw, to help maintain even soil moisture. Apply an organic fertilizer, like compost or aged manure, or a complete commercial fertilizer, like 10-4-4, if growth is poor. But be aware that too much fertilizer can cause bland, soft fruit that is susceptible to brown rot.

✔ **Prune and thin.** The primary objectives of pruning fruit trees are to create a strong tree form and maximize the harvest. Check with local experts or your extension office for specifics on pruning various types of fruit trees.

Thin the number of fruits that the tree sets after flowering to get larger, higher-quality fruit and to encourage steady, year-to-year production. The best time to thin most fruit trees is when fruits reach $1/2$–1 inch (1.3–2.5 cm) in diameter. In most cases, thin to allow 6 to 8 inches (15–20 cm) between fruits. For apples and Japanese plums, thin to one fruit per cluster.

Planning a fruit garden

Your fruit garden needs lots of sun, at least six hours at midday in summer. Orient the rows north to south, if you can. That way, shade in the morning and evening falls on adjacent walkways rather than on adjacent trees. Plan to maintain walkways that are at least 4 feet (1.2 m) wide between rows of trees. As for aesthetics, put lush, free-growing plants like peaches and apricots up front. Plan for as long a harvest season as you can by planting different kinds of fruit. And if you want fruit plantings nearer the house and among the vegetables, stick to the berries. They rarely need spraying, and they give you the earliest fruit.

Fruits for the home garden

The following sections describe some good choices for your mini fruit orchard. We list just hardy fruits — no citrus or other tropicals, which are suitable only for mild climates.

Apples

Apples are easiest to grow and harvest when you buy dwarf varieties, which grow 6–8 feet (1.8–2.4 m). (See Figure 18-4.) Plant several varieties to provide a range of flavors and ripening times. Because apples need spraying

Figure 18-4:
Comparing the size of full-size and dwarf apple trees.

more than other fruits, isolate these trees from vegetable gardens, patios, and pools. The yield of apple trees is 1–3 bushels (35–105 liters) per tree (late summer through autumn). Some apples are hardy through zone 2.

Scab is the most common disease problem of apples, especially in regions that get plenty of rainfall in summer. The following varieties are immune or resistant to scab, and they have excellent flavors: 'Dayton', 'Enterprise', 'Freedom', 'Gold Rush', 'Jonafree', 'Liberty', 'Macfree', 'McShay', 'Nova Easygro', 'Novamac', 'Prima', 'Priscilla', 'Pristine', 'Redfree', 'Sir Prize', and 'Williams' Pride'.

Peaches

Peaches can be tricky but are worth the effort. Peach trees get big, so put them where you'll enjoy their profile and glossy green foliage. Mulch to thwart grass and nourish trees. Where the climate is too cold for peaches (zone 5 and lower), consider sour cherries or apricots for this spot in the landscape. The yield is 3–5 bushels (105–175 liters) of peaches per tree (mid- to late summer).

Pears

Pears are a bit easier to grow than apples. On dwarfing rootstock, pears reach 8–10 feet (2.4–3 m) tall. Train them as small pyramidal trees. Oriental pears, which are better adapted to the warmer regions, get one-third larger. You need two or more compatible varieties for pollination. The yield is 3–4 bushels (105–140 liters) per tree (late summer through autumn). Full-size pears produce reliably through zone 3; dwarf pear trees are hardy through zone 5.

Cherries

Sweet cherries become medium to large trees. Tart cherries on a dwarf rootstock are scarcely larger than a bush, and because they're self-fertile, one is enough. The yield for sweet cherries is 30 quarts (31 liters), and for tart, 15 quarts (15.2 liters) (early summer). Cherries produce reliably through zone 5; tart or sour cherries through zone 4.

Plums

Plums make nice small- to medium-size trees for a yard. Japanese and Japanese-American hybrids need cross-pollination by another variety from either group. Most European plums need another European pollinator; a few are self-fertile. The yield is 2–3 bushels (70–105 liters) (mid- to late summer). Plums regularly produce through zone 4.

Strawberries

Strawberries are the first fruits of the season, which may be why people treasure them so. An early and a late variety provide strawberries for two to three weeks. Grow them in 3- to 4-foot (91 cm–1.2 m) wide beds and be ready to lay netting over the plants to keep out the birds. You need to renovate strawberry beds every two or three years. The yield is 1 quart (1 liter) per plant (late spring to early summer). Strawberries are hardy to all zones.

Grapes

Grapes on a trellis are good for masking a fence or for making a windbreak for vegetables or other tender plants. Traditionally, gardeners train the vines over arbors or trellises, but putting the vines so far overhead makes pruning and picking tough to do. The most-productive types of grapes yield up to 15 pounds (7 kg) per plant (late summer to early autumn). Grapes are productive through zone 3.

Blueberries

Blueberries are a good candidate for a hedge because they grow in bushes. You need two varieties for cross-pollination — three or more are better and can extend the blueberry harvest to two months. Some blueberries can grow nearly anywhere in North America if you can provide acid soil rich in organic matter. The yield is 4 quarts (4 liters) per plant (mid- to late summer). Blueberries are productive through zone 4.

Bramble fruits

Bramble fruits — red and black raspberries and blackberries — are best grown as rambling hedges on large properties or trained to a wall or trellis on small properties. Of the group, raspberries are best adapted to cooler areas, and blackberries can grow in hotter areas. In temperate regions where all types grow, the bramble harvest can stretch from early summer into autumn. To get the most from red raspberries, plant at least two kinds: a main-crop variety for heavy, early summer harvests and an autumn (or everbearing) type to close out the berry harvest. Bramble fruits are productive throughout all zones. The yield is 2 quarts (2 liters) per plant.

Chapter 19

Container Gardens

In This Chapter

▶ Choosing pots to plant in

▶ Designing with container plants

▶ Matching up pots and plants

▶ Offering just the right soil mix

▶ Providing special care

Some people grow plants in containers (or pots or planters) because that's the only suitable place they can find — maybe their garden soil is too horrible or their space too limited. Others who have abundant garden space are just as motivated to grow plants in pots — container plants can add height, charm, and surprise to a garden.

Whatever your reason, you can't find a better way to observe plants up close and to get to know them. Growing plants in pots can bring out different sides of your personality: the artist (Should I put the yellow pansy with the red tulips?) and the scientist (How do I lower the pH of this soil mix?).

Welcome to the fun and challenge of container plants. If you enjoy what you see in this chapter or want to learn more about planting in pots, take a look at *Container Gardening for Dummies,* by Bill Marken and the Editors of the National Gardening Association (IDG Books Worldwide, Inc.).

Choosing the Right Pots

Containers come in a huge variety of materials — especially if you start making your own or finding them. As you look, be sure you consider at least two key factors: porosity and drainage.

✔ **Porosity.** Some materials used to create containers are more porous than others and allow moisture and air to penetrate more readily. For example, unglazed terra cotta, wood, and paper pulp dry out faster than nonporous material, but also allow soil to cool by evaporation and to *breathe* (roots need oxygen). Porosity has the effect of drawing away excess water, thereby preventing waterlogged soil. Nonporous materials such as glazed terra cotta, plastic, and cans hold soil moisture better, which helps to reduce watering frequency. That characteristic, however, may make the plants vulnerable to waterlogged soil.

✔ **Drainage.** For healthy root development, soil must drain water properly and have enough space for air. Soil that is too heavy or dense can slow drainage — so can lack of a drain hole or a blocked drain hole. If drainage is slow or nonexistent, water may collect at the bottom (where it can stagnate and smell bad); roots can rot, and the plant can die. Look for drain holes when selecting containers. If you have a container you love but it has no drainage hole, you can *double-pot* (place a container within a larger container) so that the inner pot can drain into the larger one; or drill drain holes by using a carbide-tipped drill.

The following list contains the materials used most often for making containers these days. Each has its strengths and weaknesses.

✔ **Terra cotta (or unglazed clay).** Unglazed clay, or terra cotta (which means *baked earth* in Italian), is usually reddish orange but comes in other colors as well — tan, cream, black, and chocolate brown. These pots come in many shapes and sizes, as shown in Figure 19-1. Higher-quality pots — those with thick walls and fired in high heat — last longer. Pots fired at low heat have a more grainy texture and weather away more quickly.

Unglazed clay pots generally offer good value for the money. Their earthy colors and natural surface make the pots look comfortable in almost any garden situation, from rustic to formal. The porosity in unglazed clay enables plant roots to breathe and excess moisture to evaporate — all desirable for many plants. Porosity also means soil dries out quickly so plants in such pots are likely to need more frequent watering.

In cold climates, terra cotta pot sides can crack when moist soil freezes and expands inside the pot. Empty the container and store it in a garage or basement until spring.

✔ **Glazed clay.** Usually inexpensive, these pots come in many more colors than unglazed ones — bright to dark, and some with patterns. Many are made in Asia and fit nicely in Japanese-style gardens. Glazed clay containers are great in formal situations and can liven up a grouping of plain clay pots. Although glazed pots are less porous than unglazed and hold moisture better, they are also breakable.

Figure 19-1:
Terra cotta pots come in many shapes and sizes.

✔ **Wood.** Square and rectangular boxes and round tubs come in many styles and usually made of rot-resistant redwood and cedar. Wood containers are heavy, durable, and stand up well to cold weather. Appearance is usually rustic, at home on decks and other informal situations. Wood provides good soil insulation, keeping roots cooler than terra cotta. Evaporation is also slower than with clay pots. Thicker lumber is better — at least ⁷/₈ inch (2.25 cm). Bottoms may rot if they stay too moist; raise containers at least an inch off the ground with stands or saucers.

To make wood last longer, treat the insides with wood preservative such as a copper-based wood preservative. Or use wood that has been pressure-injected with CCA or ACQ preservatives to build your planter (the latter is less toxic, but harder to find). For more details about landscaping lumber, check out *Decks & Patios For Dummies*, by Robert Beckstrom and the Editors of the National Gardening Association (IDG Books Worldwide, Inc.).

✔ **Plastic.** Many plastic pots imitate the look of standard terra cotta pots. Plastic is less expensive, easier to clean, and weighs less than terra cotta. This material is nonporous, so soil doesn't dry out as quickly as with terra cotta — be careful that you don't overwater. Watch for poor quality plastic pots, which can fade in the sun and become brittle.

✔ **Other materials.** *Cast concrete* is durable, heavy, and cold-resistant. *Paper pulp* is compressed recycled paper that degrades in several years. You actually can plant pot and all directly in the ground, and the roots grow through the sides as the paper decomposes. Inexpensive and lightweight but not particularly handsome, paper pulp pots also are candidates for slipping into larger, more attractive containers. Use pulp pots where looks don't matter. *Metal* is a favorite choice for antique and Asian planters. Look for iron, aluminum, and other metal containers at boutiques and antique shops. Make sure that a metal pot provides drainage.

✔ **Improvised containers.** Turning mundane items — wheelbarrows, wagons, old boots, whatever — into plant containers is fun. The only thing a plant container absolutely *must* have is a drainage hole in the bottom.

Designing with Container Plants

Does *designing* sound pretentious for determining what plants to put in which pots, how to combine different plants in the same pots, and how to combine different types of pots? Whatever designs you come up with, they should make sense in terms of maintenance. Whatever designs you create, be sure to combine plants or pots that have similar maintenance requirements. For example, you wouldn't plant a water-loving plant with a cactus, nor a shade-lover with one that needs eight hours of sun.

One plant in a container standing alone can be stunning — it had better be if that is all you have space for. However, combining several or many container plants creates a fuller, lusher effect, almost like a garden growing in the ground. Containers can do all the things that a whole garden can: announce the seasons, flash bright color, and create miniature slices of nature.

Style points

Talking about style and taste is never easy — there are seldom any definite answers. We give you a few reminders about style, anyway, to keep in mind when creating container plantings:

✔ **Work with what you already have.** Use container plants to complement your home or garden. In an informal setting, for example, you may want to use tubs of mixed summer annuals. Cacti in shallow bowls lend a dramatic note to a contemporary setting.

✔ **Think about color.** Using mostly green or white creates a cooling effect. Bright, hot colors (zinnias, for instance) heat things up.

✔ **Consider the different shapes of the plants you're using** — whether they're in individual containers, mixed plantings, or multiple containers. Think about the shapes of the plants and use shape to complement and contrast with each other. Plant shapes fall into several categories. For example:

- **Tall, spiky plants:** Snapdragons, New Zealand flax

- **Round, mounded shapes:** Impatiens, lavender

- **Trailers:** Lobelia, ivy

✔ **Think about formality.** Topiary is formal. So are symmetrical plantings — two boxwoods in classical urns flanking the front door or tree roses lining a walk, for instance. Containers with flowers all in the same color are formal. A more casual look would be mixed-color annuals, or groups of containers of different sizes, materials, and shapes.

✔ **Decide on something old or something new.** A sleek, contemporary atmosphere in your garden calls for uncluttered, geometric lines in the shapes of your containers and plants. A few boldly shaped containers can be effective filled with bromeliads, cacti, or papyrus.

If you prefer an always-been-there look, choose used containers that show a bit of wear and tear. One speedy way to "age" a new concrete or terra cotta pot is to paint a combination of buttermilk or yogurt and a little live moss onto the outsides. The buttermilk (or yogurt) helps promote moss growth, quickly creating a nice "old" patina.

✔ **Remember the value of repetition.** Repeat the same colors or plants. For example, use yellow marigolds in a cluster of pots near the beginning of a front walk and again on the front porch. Of course, moderation is important. Going overboard on repetition — for instance, a long border of alternating red and white impatiens — can end up looking like a giant candy cane.

✔ **Scale is a big subject.** Big spaces demand large containers — with an opening at least 20–24 inches (50–61 cm) in diameter. If you cluster pots, make sure to include at least one good-sized container with a taller plant in it.

One special plant

Hundreds of plants — annuals, cacti, fruit trees, even eggplant — can make special showings in individual pots. This approach is *elemental container gardening:* one plant in one pot, or several plants of the same type (five pansies, for example) in one pot.

As a rule for goods looks, the plant should be at least as tall as the container. This rule applies most consistently to annuals. Put 12-inch (30.5 cm) tall snapdragons in a pot that is no more than 12 inches tall. Don't put 6-inch (15 cm) pansies in a 12-inch pot — it won't look good, you have our word.

That rule of height also applies to succulents or bonsai; these low-growing, mound-shaped plants look best in low or shallow containers. Don't follow the rule with big shrubs and trees, which can be much taller in proportion, or with bulbs which are often planted in relatively shallow containers known as *bulb, azalea,* or *fern* pots.

Combining plants in containers

Mixed annuals, annuals with perennials, perennials with bulbs — depending on your climate, you can combine different types of plants in the same container. Keep this basic strategy in mind:

If you live where it's safe to leave containers outside all year (zones 8–11), you can have a garden in a pot. Start with one dominant plant (Japanese maple, snapdragons, delphiniums, whatever), and then place compatible mounding or trailing plants (lobelia, impatiens, and many others) around it.

How to arrange containers

Arranging groups of container plants is like hanging pictures or moving furniture. Don't be afraid to experiment, to move around your plant-filled containers again and again. Remember the most important thing: The results should look good to you.

The most visually effective groupings use a minimum of three plants and up to dozens. (As a rule of composition, an uneven number of items usually looks better than an even number.)

A few basic rules apply for grouping container plants:

- ✔ Start by using matching types of containers (for example, terra cotta) in different sizes. Make one or two pots a lot larger than the others. If you want, throw in a maverick, like a glazed pot.

- ✔ For a big deck or expanse of paving, use lots of pots and mix sizes, styles, and shapes.

- ✔ Mix plants of different textures, colors, and heights, as shown in Figure 19-2. Think about the basic categories of shapes described in "Style points" in this chapter.

- ✔ Group identical pots with identical plants. Nothing looks more smashing in spring than three 14-inch (35.5 cm) terra cotta pots stuffed to the gills with red tulips.

- ✔ Raise some containers higher than others; provide a lift with a couple of bricks underneath or use plant stands. The height adds emphasis and puts the plants at a better viewing level.

- ✔ Be careful when placing small plants by themselves. People can overlook or trip over them. Use small containers to accompany bigger ones.

Figure 19-2:
Vary the
height,
color, and
texture in a
container
planting.

✔ Try to place containers where people gather — a seating area, for instance — and can view plants up close and appreciate their beauty and fragrance.

✔ In large gardens, place containers near the house where you can easily notice them often. Selectively scatter container plants along garden paths. Another good spot is in the transition zone between a patio and lawn or between lawn and wild garden.

✔ Hang your containers. There's no easier and quicker way to get favorite plants up to eye level. Use wood, plastic, or moss-lined wire frames. Make sure supports are strong because a plant gains weight as it grows, not to mention the weight after watering. See Figure 19-3.

Putting It All Together

As you think about the possibilities of designing with containers, consider the following suggestions for growing and displaying them effectively in your garden — making use of the principles we discuss in the section titled "Designing for Container Plants" in this chapter.

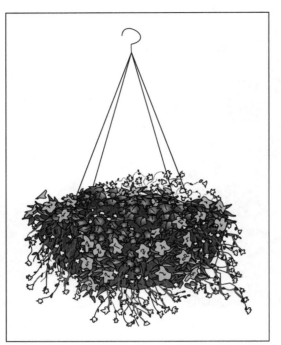

Figure 19-3:
A hanging
basket can
add color
and height
to an empty
spot.

- Put a single, golden-barrel cactus in a low, 12-inch (30.5 cm) diameter bowl. Make a drainage hole if necessary. The cactus will grow slowly. Let it fill the pot.

- Circle a small tree, where roots don't allow anything to grow, with eight or so terra cotta containers overflowing with white impatiens. Plant eight impatiens seedlings in each 12-inch container (30.5 cm).

- On a balcony (mild climate permitting), create a privacy screen with containers of bamboo or English laurel.

- By your front door, where shade can make growing conditions tough, use a pair of topiary ivy balls in matching containers to greet visitors in a formal way.

- Announce spring with a window box full of sun-loving, early blooming pansies and snapdragons.

- For the holiday season, buy gallon size (4.5 liter) cans of spruce, pine, or other conifer trees available in your area, transplant them to terra cotta or glazed pots, and decorate them with tiny glass balls for table-top decorations. These plants will do well indoors for a few weeks.

- If you live where Japanese maples thrive, you can't find a better choice for a striking specimen tree in a container. For all-year good looks, choose colorful-leaf types (like 'Oshio Beni', or even colorful-bark varieties (such as 'Sango Kaku').

✔ Lead the way up front steps by flanking steps with big pots of white marguerites — one plant per each 14-inch (35.5 cm) pot.

✔ At the edge of a sunny patio overhead, hang baskets of bougainvillea — normally a vine, but a vivid-blooming trailer when grown in a hanging basket.

✔ On a blank, shady wall, attach wire half-baskets — at least three, staggered at different heights — filled with blooming begonias and impatiens, plus ferns for greenery.

Favorite Container Combos

Wondering what to plant in containers? Because summer annuals and bulbs are downright easy to grow in pots, why not start with one or both of them? We throw in some edible ideas as well.

Annuals all summer

The flowers in Table 19-1 are team players that also make good solo performers if planted alone. Match numbers to find plants that combine well in containers. For example, combine alyssum (number 1 in this table) with fibrous begonia, celosia, lobelia, and pansies (numbers 2, 3, 7, and 8, respectively). If you're combining different plants, place the tallest, most upright ones in the center and surround it with lower-growing or trailing plants.

Table 19-1		**Annuals to Combine in Pots**	
Number	*Flower*	*Combinations*	*Uses*
1	Alyssum	(2, 3, 5, 7, 8, 10)	Pots, boxes, baskets
2	Begonia (fibrous)	(1, 4, 7)	Pots, boxes
3	Celosia (plume)	(1, 9, 10)	Pots, boxes
4	Coleus	(1, 2, 6, 7)	Pots, boxes, baskets
5	Geraniums	(1, 7, 9, 10)	Pots, boxes, baskets
6	Impatiens	(4, 7)	Pots, boxes, baskets
7	Lobelia	(1, 2, 4, 5, 6, 7, 8, 9)	Pots, boxes, baskets
8	Pansy	(1, 7)	Pots, boxes, baskets
9	Petunia	(3, 5, 7)	Pots, boxes, baskets
10	Verbena	(1, 3, 5)	Pots, boxes, baskets

Perennial accents

To have year-round fun in a mild-winter (zones 8–11), all-container garden, you need some evergreens to hold the fort from autumn to spring. As long as you use big pots (more than 14 inches, or 35.5 cm, wide at the top), dwarf conifers, spreading junipers, dwarf boxwoods, and other small shrubs are happy to serve as permanent features. Around the base of the evergreens plant a few little bulbs (such as crocus or grape hyacinth) or "pave" over the soil with ivy.

In cold climates — zones 7 and colder — perennials and bulbs can't survive through the winter in a container outdoors. If possible, move the pots into an attached garage or basement that stays cool but protects the plants from frigid outdoor temperatures and winds.

Of course, you can grow tender plants outdoors in containers during warm weather and then winter them indoors near a bright window. Hibiscus and lemon trees commonly grow like this in regions far colder than their native ones. Additionally, many plants live long lives in containers in zones 8–11. These include shrubs, living Christmas trees, and large perennial plants.

Delectable edibles

Your adventures in containers don't need to stop with flowers and ever-greens. Try some tastier side trips: Carrots, red- and green-leaf lettuces, dwarf or cherry tomatoes, peppers, and radishes are some suggestions. Herbs — chives, marjoram, parsley, and thyme — are also good choices.

Growing just about any vegetable in a container is possible, but a giant pumpkin or something similarly huge may not be worth the effort (although it is possible!). Look for "container friendly" vegetable varieties. These are the ones described as "compact" or "bush-type."

Container gardening with vegetables makes good sense for many gardeners, not the least of which is that a yard is not required. With containers, you can have a vegetable garden on a balcony, patio, or even a rooftop. Also, maintaining a few vegetables in some pots is much easier than a traditional garden, and you can move the containers out of the way after harvest.

For more about growing vegetables in containers, see *Container Gardening for Dummies*, by Bill Marken and the Editors of the National Gardening Association (IDG Books Worldwide, Inc.).

Container Plants for Four Seasons

Depending on your climate, you can find appealing container plants at almost any time of year. (Of course, you have limited options during the winter in cold climates.) Table 19-2 lists just a few of the many annuals, perennials, bulbs, and permanent plants that perform particularly well outdoors at various seasons.

Table 19-2	Container Plants for Various Seasons		
Spring	*Summer*	*Fall*	*Winter*
Azalea	Geranium	Aster	Camellia
Calendula	Dahlia	Chrysanthemum	Cyclamen
Columbine	Daylily	Dwarf pomegranate	Holly
Daffodils	Sunflower (dwarf)	Flowering cabbage	Pyracantha
Felicia	Hibiscus	Heavenly bamboo	Primrose
Iceland poppy	Impatiens	Japanese maple	Colorado spruce (living Christmas tree)
Primrose	Coleus	Pansy	Dwarf Alberta spruce (living Christmas tree)
Rose	Marigold	Rose	Noble fir (living Christmas tree)
Snapdragon	Petunia	Sasanqua camellia	Scotch pine (living Christmas tree)
Tulips	Zinnia	Sweet olive	White fir (living Christmas tree)

A Primer on Soil for Pots

Plants in containers are especially dependent on the soil or growing mix in which they grow simply because the roots have so much less soil area to explore in the confines of the pots. So to keep your plants happy and healthy, you need to first take care of the roots — and that means growing them in the right stuff.

Finding the ideal soil mix for container gardening isn't difficult. Fortunately for the rest of us, a whole lot of people have studied just what plants in containers need. You can go into just about any nursery or garden center and find an aisle with packages marked with something like "growing mix." (To get a better understanding of what all plants need from soil, dip into Chapter 11.)

You can find a whole slew of soil mixes for containers on the market under a variety of brand names and companies. Some mixes consist of special formulas for starting seedlings, potting up transplants, or growing nursery stock. However, if you take a look at the ingredients, one of the first things you may notice is that the mixture has very little real soil, if any, listed.

Why not use ordinary garden soil to grow your prize plants in containers? After all, many of the plants that you grow in containers on your patios and decks also grow successfully in the open ground. Why can't you just take a shovelful of soil and dump it in a pot?

Although you may think that a good soil in the garden would make a good soil in a pot or planter, it just isn't so. When you lift the soil from the garden, the soil loses its structure. Also, as garden soil settles in a shallow container (which is much different from the natural depth of the soil in a field), it forms a dense mass that roots can't penetrate. The soil drains poorly, saturating the roots. As a result, not enough oxygen reaches the root zone, and the roots suffocate. Plus, garden soil harbors disease-causing organisms that can devastate container plantings; and it could have weed seeds and insect eggs, as well.

Plants in containers have different soil and water requirements than plants in the ground, and they need a special soil mix that meets those needs. The following list provides a rundown of the particular needs of container plants:

- ✔ **Fast water infiltration and optimal drainage.** In garden soil, water gets pulled down to the roots by gravity; capillary action; and the attraction of small, clay particles for water also dictate how water moves in soil. The water keeps moving through the soil in a continuous column, acting in the same manner that a hose siphon works or a blotter of ink. Each drop needs another drop of water behind it to continue the flow. Because the soil in a container is so confined, the soil needs to have a loose, open structure to encourage this flow of water.

- ✔ **Plenty of air spaces in soil.** This soil condition goes hand in hand with the requirement for good drainage. Air space is actually the most important requirement for a good container mix. Container plantings must have plenty of air in the soil after drainage because they require air for growth and to keep roots healthy. (Disease organisms abound in the absence of oxygen.) For more about the importance of good air circulation in soil, see Chapter 11.

✔ **Water retention.** You're probably thinking, "Hey, hold it now. You just said that container plants need plenty of air and good drainage. Doesn't that go against holding onto moisture?" This point is where mixtures get tricky. This last requirement is a trade-off, because the soil mix that holds onto the most water and drains slowest also has less room for air.

Although you may hear that you can improve drainage in pots by putting a layer of pea gravel or other potting shards in the bottom of your container to improve drainage, don't do it! A drainage layer may sound logical, but using pea gravel in the bottom of a pot actually results in *less* air for the plant's roots and *more* water in the bottom of the pot. Instead, cover the drainage hole at the bottom with just one or two pieces of shard, or a bit of hardware cloth or screen as shown in Figure 19-5. Next, fill the entire container with the same soil mix. You can also put the smaller, soil-filled pot in a larger decorative pot that has gravel in the bottom.

Figure 19-4:
Cover just the drainage hole with hardware cloth or screen or a bit of potting shard.

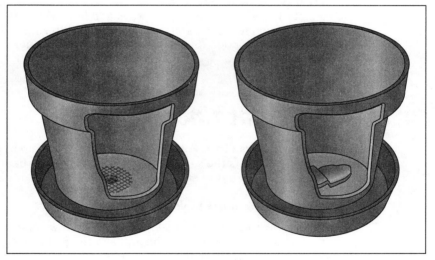

Most people who grow plants in containers use bagged potting soils or *soilless* mixtures made up of *peat moss* plus *perlite* or *vermiculite*. These products are (or should be) free of microorganisms that cause plant diseases; already have their pH corrected with the appropriate addition of lime; and hold just the right amount of moisture. The downside is that soilless mixtures contain few plant nutrients, so you must feed your plants regularly with some kind of fertilizer.

Would you rather make your own potting soil? Sooner or later, you may delve into creating special mixtures for ferns, cacti, or some other plants that have strange tastes in soil. The following list describes your basic ingredients and the flavor that each one brings to the stew:

✔ **Peat moss.** Basically rotted moss, peat moss is soft-textured and almost never hosts diseases — and it's like a feather bed to delicate plant roots. The final content of peat in a potting mixture can run as high as 80 percent (for ferns), or 40–75 percent for other plants. Peat has an acidic pH and contains negligible plant nutrients. Be sure to moisten the peat to make it easier to work with.

✔ **Sand.** Sand drains quickly and doesn't hold water worth a flip, which makes it a good addition to pots planted with cacti, herbs, and bulbs. The sand content of the mixture rarely, if ever, exceeds 20 percent.

✔ **Vermiculite or perlite.** These popcornlike mineral particles lighten up a mixture and help keep it porous yet damp. For potted plants, 20 percent of one or the other of the 'lites is right, or maybe use a little of each material.

✔ **Lime.** Ground-up *dolomitic limestone* corrects the acidic pH of peat; and plants that prefer neutral-to-alkaline conditions (such as wallflowers and clematis) need an extra dose. Always add lime with restraint. Use too much and you make the soil too alkaline, the flip side of a soil that is too acid. One teaspoon (5 ml) of dolomitic limestone per gallon of potting mix is the max.

How to Plant Containers

Ready to get your fingers dirty? Follow these steps to plant a pot, one step at a time. The procedure is the same whether you're planting bedding plants (annuals and perennials sold as small seedlings), vegetables, or herbs:

1. **Cover the drainage holes in your container.**

   If you cover the holes with a small section of window screen, water can't puddle up in the bottom of the pot, and the soil won't gush out through the holes. Note the difference between *covering* holes and plugging them up. Avoid the outdated practice of putting a layer of gravel in the bottom of the container.

2. **Fill the container about ²/₃ full with soil.**

3. **Remove the plant from container.**

   If you're working with lightweight plastic containers, simply push on the bottom of the container until the seedling pops out. Or use one hand to turn the container upside down while supporting the plant with the other hand. Gently pull out the plant. Whatever method you use to remove a plant from its container, try to keep the root ball intact. A moist root ball doesn't fall apart as easily as a dry one, so water the plant at least an hour before you plant.

4. **Plant plants at the same depth they grew in their previous pots, adding more soil almost to the top of the pot.**

Don't add soil up to the brim of the pot. Leave some space at the top of the pot to hold water.

5. **Place the whole container in a small tub (or your kid's wagon) and water the plant thoroughly. Next, add water ¹/₂ inch (1.25 cm) deep to the tub (or wagon).**

   Letting the pot soak ensures that all the soil, top to bottom, is wetted.

6. **Wait 15 minutes and then water your plants again.**

7. **Finally, set the container on the ground and let it drip dry.**

Is Everybody Happy?

Plants growing in containers can't let their roots wander about in search of food and water, so you must take care of these needs.

You can make watering as scientific as you want (including the use of a drip irrigation system designed for container plants), but we'll leave our advice at this for now:

In mild spring weather, you probably don't need to water your plants more than once a week, but as temperatures rise and the plants get bigger, you may need to water almost every day. Big plants need more water than little ones do (but big containers hold more water, too).

A fertilizing plan

Plants growing in containers need more water than those growing in the ground. The more you water, the more you flush nutrients from the soil, and the more often you have to fertilize.

You can offset some of this constant loss of nutrients by mixing slow-release fertilizers into the soil mix before planting. But we also like to take the approach of less food, more often — the best looking container plants we've seen are on a constant-feed program. In other words, you give plants a little liquid fertilizer every time, or every other time, you water. Of course this means using less, sometimes a lot less, fertilizer with each water. Some fertilizer products will include directions for *constant* (same as *every time*) feeding, which you need to follow. Wait until you see the results!

If that method is too much hassle for you, use a liquid or water-soluble fertilizer once every week or two. Follow the rates recommended on the label. Your container plants will still do great.

You can use granular fertilizers on container plants. Just beware, it's not a very precise technique, and you may burn plants if you put on too much.

What about repotting?

The time may come (definitely it will) when a plant outgrows its container, and it's time for repotting. How can you tell?

Any plant that has restricted roots obviously needs more space. If you see lots of roots coming through the drain hole or find matted roots near the soil surface, it's time for a move. Repotting can involve long-term plants, annuals that you start from seed, or small transplants that need space for more and more roots. How often do plants need repotting? Good question. A general rule is repot every few years with permanent plants. Seasonal plants like annuals and most vegetables don't need repotting because they don't stay in the container that long.

Repot permanent plants when growth is slow or when the plant is dormant — usually well before or after flowering. (Camellias are one notable exception: They're most dormant when in bloom.) With this timing, plants have a chance to recover from these rather dramatic changes. Repot spring-blooming permanent plants in fall, evergreens in spring or fall, and spring-flowering bulbs in fall. For summer-flowering bulbs, repot in winter or spring. With bedding plants and annuals, repot as needed through the growing season before the full flush of flowering hits.

If you want to increase growth, you need to give plants more room for roots by transplanting into larger pots. How much larger do the pots need to be? Moving up little by little to a new pot that's only a few inches (about 5 cm) larger in diameter is best, as shown in Figure 19-6. If you want to control growth and keep the plant from getting too big, you can trim the roots and return the plant to a pot of the same size.

To repot a plant, just follow these steps:

1. **Turn the container upside down, tap the rim, and slide the plant out.**
   If you're repotting something prickly or otherwise unwieldy, like a cactus, wrap the plant with heavy cloth so that you can handle it safely.

2. **Inspect the roots; then separate and trim the roots (if needed).**

   You may have to trim off large roots poking through the drain hole. For plants going into larger containers, gently pull apart tangled roots.

3. **Prune roots (if needed).**

   Some permanent plants require *root-pruning*, which refers to using hand pruners to cut away root growth. This step is necessary if, once exposed, you can see that roots are a dense, circling mass. Prune the roots of plants that have reached a desired size and have become pot-bound. Root-pruning controls growth and forces plants to grow new roots, leading to limited but healthy new growth.

A vegetable garden harvest can include many things. This harvest of potatoes is practical and nutritious, as well as beautiful.

A vegetable garden this large can produce
enough for more than one family.

Neatly straw-mulched garden rows
evoke an old-time country farm.

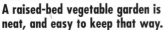

A raised-bed vegetable garden is
neat, and easy to keep that way.

A deer-excluding fence is the only sure protection from vegetable-loving
wildlife in many suburban and country gardens.

Apple 'Red Jonagold'

Ripe raspberries

Broccoli 'Purple Sprouting'

A perfectly ripe bunch of cherries.

Ripe peaches in a home garden.

Strawberries

Peas

Green and purple kale with rhubarb chard

Red oriental poppies and lupine bloom alongside pea seedlings set to scramble up bamboo teepees.

Tale of two colors:
Lettuces 'Red Ruby' and 'Salad Bowl'

Thriving garlic produces pungent heads in this drip-watered, raised-bed garden.

Heirloom garden tomatoes come in a variety of sizes, shapes, and colors.

Pathway weaves through exuberant beds of perennial plants to shady gazebo.

A variety of annuals and perennials means lots of flowers for cutting and sharing.

Instead of a lawn: zinnias! Sounds good to us.

Miniature rose thrives in a pot.

In a southwestern garden, prickly pear in background contrasts golden barrel cactus in container.

Corn flourishes in raised beds.

Garden acid test: Does the cat approve?

An oasis in a small city garden is made with tall screening plants and the refreshing look and soothing sounds of water.

A water garden need not be big and expensive. All you need is a single pot.

Large-leaved Gunnera shades a pond with water lilies and koi. Is there a better image of paradise?

Water lilies add color to a water garden.

To root-prune properly, remove about a quarter of the soil and untangle as much of the root mass as you can. Using shears, cut between $^1/_4$ and $^1/_3$ of the roots. For tightly balled roots, slice off $^1/_4$ inch (0.6 cm) all around the outside of the root ball, and make vertical cuts from top to bottom of the root ball in several places. After root pruning, lightly prune top growth to help maintain some balance between leaves and roots.

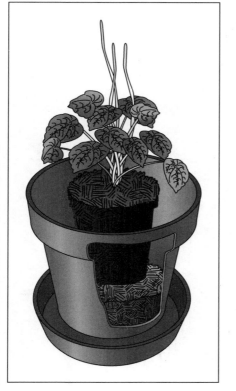

Figure 19-5:
Place your plant in a new container that measures about 2 inches (5 cm) more in both depth and diameter than its nursery pot.

4. **Set the plant in its new pot or in its newly filled existing pot.** Add soil to the height of the original root ball, and make sure to allow at least $^1/_2$ inch (1.25 cm) from soil to pot rim (more for larger plants).

Chapter 20

Gardens for Birds, Bees, and Butterflies

● ●

In This Chapter

▶ Understanding why you want to attract birds, bees, and butterflies

▶ Taking in some bird-friendly tips

▶ Boosting the butterfly population

▶ Encouraging pollinators

● ●

*I*f you plant a garden, the birds will come. Butterflies and bees will show up too, and so will lots of other insects for the birds to eat, which, of course, brings the birds back for more.

All this garden life, of course, is a good thing. Birds love to talk, and their chatter and songs bring sound to the garden. Butterflies' flitting movements put the garden scene in motion.

The engaging little shows that birds and butterflies stage change with the seasons. Butterflies, being solar-powered creatures, perform only during warm months, whereas the bird circus is most evident in the autumn, winter, and spring. This seasonal sequence of wildlife activity is the first angle to exploit when attracting birds, bees, and butterflies to your yard. And because birds, bees, and butterflies, like other creatures, mostly hang around places where they can meet their needs for food, water, and shelter, then providing these three necessities is your primary means for attracting them.

After you manage to attract these friendly visitors, you may notice some other changes. Your garden may come closer to the balance found in nature, which means that the creatures start to take charge more and you may have less work to do in controlling unfriendly pests.

Making Birds an Offer They Can't Refuse

North American birds, and birds in other parts of the world, are in crisis; sprawling towns and cities have taken away many of the trees and natural habitat the birds used as homes. Sparrows, blackbirds, and a few other species rolled with the punches and adapted by constructing their nests in buildings and power switchboxes. Most other birds, however, *must* have trees to survive.

Birds face a food shortage, too. For finches, finding thistle and weed seeds in a condominium complex isn't easy, and chickadees can't survive in a concrete jungle where there are few insects to eat. You can help solve the housing and food shortage by planting or preserving bird-friendly trees and bushes, particularly native species that host native birds. From a bird's-eye point of view, here are some of the best trees and shrubs:

✔ **Trees.** Pines and other evergreens (whatever species grow best in your area), wild cherries, serviceberries (*Amelanchier* species), hawthorns, cedars, and mulberries.

   Be careful not to plant trees that produce juicy berries close to your house, deck, and walkways, or you'll get berry goo all over your shoes.

✔ **Shrubs.** Junipers, hollies, native viburnums, and cotoneaster — when planted in clumps or hedges — provide habitat and food for birds.

Hungry birds are not finicky eaters. Almost every species loves black oil sunflower seeds (the common type sold as birdfeed), so a feeder stocked with these seeds gets birds interested in your yard in a hurry. When birds get used to finding sunflower seeds at your feeder, they go to great lengths to find acceptable nesting sites in or near your yard.

When summer comes, you can ease up on the birdseed; most birds crave protein-rich insects while raising their young, and they can probably find plenty of palatable creatures in and around your garden. On the other hand, if you want to attract woodpeckers year-round, keep a supply of commercial suet in your yard, as shown in Figure 20-1.

Also, provide a yearlong supply of water for birds in a birdbath or set out shallow dishes of water. If your house is near a pond, stream, or river, don't worry too much about water — the birds will know where to go.

Depending on how cold it gets in your region, you can keep the water in the birdbath ice-free either by changing it frequently or by using an immersion water heater (shown in Figure 20-2) designed for outdoor use.

Figure 20-1:
Suet attracts insect-eating birds such as woodpeckers.

Figure 20-2:
Birds need water year-round. In cold-winter areas, keep the water thawed in the birdbath by using an immersion-type heater.

WARNING

Feeders and watering sites for birds can be plain or fancy, but you must place them out of reach of cats and squirrels. Your beloved Kitty is probably adept at assassinating birds, and you don't want to be an accomplice to such crimes. Suspend feeders from secure limbs or place them atop a smooth, stout pole that Kitty can't climb.

Squirrels are another matter — plenty cute in their own right, but downright confounding when it comes to keeping them from emptying a bird feeder. Use a feeder that opens only for a lightweight bird and closes immediately with the squirrel's weight. Alternately, use a birdfeeder that includes an attached baffle or that has a funnel-shaped top. When you have the right feeder, be sure to hang or support the feeder with wire or something the squirrels can't chew. For good measure, situate the feeder 8–10 feet, (2.5–3 m) (just further than squirrels are likely to jump) from buildings and tree branches.

Keeping pesky birds at bay

The pleasing sounds and movements that birds bring to your garden sometimes come at a cost. If you plan to grow fruits, you must take precautions to keep birds from devouring them. Birds especially love berries, and some eat corn and tomatoes. Effective deterrents include the following:

✔ **Polyester bird netting.** Sold at most garden centers, this barrier is by far the most reliable way to protect fruits and vegetables. Drape the netting over fruit-bearing plants as soon as fruits begin to ripen.

✔ **Birdscare flash tape.** This tape looks like metallic ribbon. Decorate the tops of plants with the stuff and trick birds into thinking the plant is on fire.

✔ **Fake predators.** These fool-the-eye figures include artificial snakes, and owls, and good old scarecrows. Rearrange these phony spooks often to keep the birds baffled.

✔ **Noisemakers.** The devices include wind chimes, bells, rattling aluminum pie pans, and other items that make sounds when bumped by birds or jostled by the wind (just use your imagination).

Different types of birds live in different places, and you can network with other bird lovers to learn more about helping the winged ones that live in your area. Check your telephone directory or ask your Chamber of Commerce for information about local bird-watching clubs. You can also find a local chapter of the National Audubon Society; the address for the society's headquarters is 700 Broadway, New York, NY 10003; 212-979-3000. The Internet address is www.audubon.org. You can also take your binoculars to *Bird Watching For Dummies* by Bill Thompson III, published by IDG Books Worldwide, Inc.

Beckoning Butterflies to Your Garden

Inviting butterflies (and moths) into your yard is as easy as growing flowers. Both probably will find your yard no matter what kinds of flowers or plants you grow, but you can choose from many easy ways to make sure they'll flit in your direction.

First, you need some sun. Butterflies can feed in shade, but they must have sun to charge their energy batteries. On cool mornings, have you noticed how butterflies stand around, slowly opening and closing their wings, and how they don't fly away when your 6-year-old grabs at them? This inactivity is called *basking,* and it's how cold-blooded butterflies gather solar energy. If your yard is basically shady, put some flat, dark colored stones in a spot that gets morning sun and watch the butterflies use the sun-warmed stones as their warm-up room.

Next, grow flowers that produce nectar. Butterflies and moths consume the juices of flowers, and flower nectar is becoming a rare commodity these days. Like native birds, native butterflies and moths are struggling amid burgeoning urbanization. The weeds, clovers, and wildflowers they used to find everywhere are in increasingly short supply. You can help set things right by growing flowers that butterflies like a lot and by planting the flowers in ways that make it impossible for butterflies to miss them.

Plants that are native to your region not only are more likely to grow and survive but also provide the specific foods that native birds and butterflies rely on. By using native plants, you help sustain native wildlife.

A butterfly sips flower nectar by sticking its long tongue (properly called a *proboscis*) down the throats of nectar-rich flowers. Some flowers are much more "slurpable" than others, both because they have a lot of nectar and because the flowers are shaped just right. No butterfly garden should be without at least one of the following three plants — your aces-in-the-hole for attracting butterflies:

- ✔ **Butterfly weed.** *Asclepias tuberosa.* This native perennial weed is hardy through zone 3. The seeds are hard to sprout, so nursery-propagated plants are a better choice. Butterfly weed needs plenty of sun, blooms orange from midsummer onward, and seldom grows more than 1–2 feet (30–60 cm) tall. Once planted, it likes to stay put.

- ✔ **Butterfly bush.** *Buddleia davidii.* This hardy shrub has become so popular that nursery-grown plants are easy to find. They are hardy through zone 5; come in many shades of purple, pink, and white; and, depending on conditions, grow 3–10 feet (91cm–3 m) tall. When they freeze, you may cut them down to the ground; they'll revive to grow and bloom again.

- ✔ **Lantana.** *Lantana camara.* This tender perennial survives winter only in zones 8–10; in other zones, you can buy bedding plants in the spring and grow them as summer annuals. Plant in full sun. Almost all butterflies like lantana.

Okay, so you don't have all three of the butterfly biggies. As long as your garden includes plenty of flowers, preferably the nectar-rich types with fewer petals (properly called *single* flowers), you will still see plenty of butterflies.

Butterflies prefer single flowers (as opposed to the double-petal type) because when a blossom is jam-packed with petals, butterflies have a hard time getting to the nectar hidden in the middle. Single flowers that are relatively flat give butterflies a solid place to land and easy access to nectar. Among easy annuals, single cosmos, marigolds, and zinnias are of great interest to butterflies. Where you can use more height, try tithonia, also known as Mexican sunflower or torch flower.

Some other good plants to incorporate into your butterfly haven include any type of verbena, salvia, cosmos, phlox, coneflower, and rudbeckia. Always keep your eyes peeled for flowers that attract butterflies in your area — butterflies often show strong regional preferences for certain plants.

The last thing we need to say is that birds eat butterflies. But don't worry — making your yard bird-friendly does not sentence your butterflies to certain death. Your garden probably has plenty of other insects that birds would rather eat, and they'll bypass a dozen butterflies to get at a feeder filled with sunflower seeds.

Designing for butterflies

If you splash flower color around in broad strokes, butterflies have an easier time finding the flowers. The color of the flowers is not as important as the size of the clump, which should include at least three plants of any individual flower.

For a long time, gardeners were advised to use bright reds and oranges to lure butterflies, but it turns out that pink, purple, lavender, and yellow work just as well. The key is to keep similar colors more or less together. Butterflies are not very smart. A big jolt of color or fragrance is often necessary to get their attention.

Most buddleias produce lavender or purple flowers, so use that hue as a starting point for choosing the colors of your other flowers. Orange or yellow contrasts nicely with purple, and many butterfly gardens use either purple and yellow or purple and orange as the basic color scheme.

Mixing a butterfly cocktail

If you're a butterfly, you don't want to hang out around deep or moving water, where a good gust of wind may turn your beautiful wings into a sopping mess. But you and your friends like to get together for a drink, so you're always on the lookout for a nice watering hole. Your idea of a friendly bar is an almost-puddle of soaked soil, where you can stand firmly (without getting your feet too wet) and slurp up soupy water by sticking your proboscis in the ground.

One fact of butterfly life is that males (and an occasional female) like to drink together in puddle clubs. To create such a pub in your butterfly garden, mix some sand, soil, and pebbles and use the mixture to fill a small shallow basin lined with smooth stones. From time to time, fill the basin with water until it's puddly. Neon signs are not necessary — the butterflies will find the water on their own.

Catching up with caterpillars

Oh, those squirmy, creepy caterpillars! All caterpillars chomp on leaves, but not all are undesirable. When winter comes, most butterflies have already ensured the welfare of the next generation: Swallowtails lay dormant eggs (which become caterpillars); monarchs migrate to California, Mexico, and beyond; and several species wrap themselves in leaves and sleep through winter as mummylike larvae, called *hibernaculi*. A few butterflies wait out winter as adults, hidden away in tree crevices or perhaps your attic.

To encourage butterflies to stay in your garden, you need to know the difference between the caterpillar stage of a monarch or swallowtail butterfly and a pest like the tomato hornworm. To help you do that, *National Gardening* magazine, with artist Amy Bartlett Wright, created a 16 x 24-inch (40 x 60 cm) poster of the eight most common, nonpest garden butterflies in North America and their caterpillar stage. The poster is available for $10. Write to Butterfly Poster, *National Gardening* magazine, 180 Flynn Ave., Burlington, VT 05401, or call 800-LETSGRO (800-538-7476).

The long-time favorite pesticide of organic gardeners, *Bacillus thuringiensis* (Bt), is deadly to all caterpillars — pest and nonpest. That's why we think handpicking selected caterpillars is the best control method. (Most pesticides are toxic to butterflies, which is one reason to use gentle biological controls for pest management and to use them only when absolutely necessary. See Chapter 16 for more information on wise use of garden pesticides.)

Bees and Pollination

When you make your garden more favorable to birds and butterflies, you're also making it friendlier to honeybees and other pollinators. These insects are important (especially for gardeners who grow vegetables and fruit) because we rely upon insect pollination to set abundant and healthy crops. Moreover, the numbers of our most familiar pollinator, honeybees, have declined in recent years.

Pollination occurs when insects move pollen from the (male) anther of one flower to the (female) stigma of another flower. Two-thirds of all flowering plants depend on pollinating insects for this service. More than 3,800 species of bees exist in the United States, and most of them collect nectar and pollen. All adult bees eat protein-rich pollen and feed it to their young.

In recent years, the Varroa mite *(V. jacobsonii)* has destroyed honeybee populations in many regions of the Northeast and central Midwest (Illinois, Iowa, Kansas, and Nebraska). *Foulbrood* — a bacterial infection that kills bees' larvae — and several other diseases also afflict colonies. When honeybee populations suffer, pollination of cultivated crops is in jeopardy.

The current but temporary decline of honeybee populations is a perfect time to learn more about other pollinators, particularly considering that pollinators are an essential link in the food chain.

Although the honeybee is an extremely valuable pollinating species, wild bees and other insects not often recognized as pollinators are also vital to your garden's well-being. Spraying pesticides destroys all insects — harmful, beneficial, and pollinating, so think twice before using such sprays.

Gardeners can encourage the proliferation of the beneficial and pollinating insects by providing nesting sites, especially for solitary bees, by following these tips:

- ✔ **Turn flowerpots upside down** so bottom holes face up, to attract bumblebees. In early spring, partially bury the pot in an out-of-the-way spot — ideally near a favored bumblebee food source.

- ✔ **Cut some plants and leave the stems alone.** Cutting stems exposes soft tissues into which bees bore to make a home. Rose growers often complain about "rose cane borers" that drill down into canes causing the cane to die back. (The remedy is to seal the cut surface with a daub of white glue or similar material.) Various insects will bore into rose canes from time to time, but often it is one of the solitary bees, such as carpenter bees or mason bees (also known as orchard bees).

- ✔ **Set out blocks of wood or logs drilled with holes** to attract mason and leafcutter bees to make your yard. Use a ⁵/₁₆-inch drill and space the holes about ³/₄-inch (2 cm) apart. Drill 3–6 inches (7.5–15 cm) deep. The wood provides convenient nesting sites when placed in a protected area.

- ✔ **Bundle a dozen or so partially rotted plant stems,** like raspberry canes, to lure solitary bees into your yard. Secure the stems with twine and place the bundles in protected locations such as under fence or balcony rails. (Creative gardeners have also been known to bundle soda straws for the same purpose.)

Chapter 21

Gardening in Tight Spaces

• •

In This Chapter

▶ Designing in limited space

▶ Making small seem big

▶ Discovering hidden growing spots

▶ Finding gems for small spaces

• •

*J*ust because your outdoor space is small doesn't mean you have to give up your dreams of having a truly satisfying garden. In fact, if you've ever lingered in a small garden that is well-planned and carefully put together, you've probably noticed that the garden has a sense of intimacy and enclosure that most large, sprawling landscapes lack.

Smallness need not dictate the type of gardening that you do. Whether you are aiming for a serene Japanese-style meditation garden or the country charm of an English cottage garden, the basic techniques for successful small-space gardening are the same.

The following tips and techniques can help you on your way; but before you start digging, review Part I of this book on garden planning. Because all available space is critical in small gardens (and every element is seen close-up), starting with a cohesive plan is doubly important.

And think about container gardening (see Chapter 19) — often the best answer for growing plants on a patio, deck, balcony, or anyplace where every inch or centimeter counts.

Simple Pleasures

A small garden feels most spacious and harmonious when the design is simple and all the elements work together. Choose a single style or theme for your garden and use this style to connect all the parts, from paving to plants and structures and ornaments. Just imagine how distracting a spewing Goliath of a fountain would be in a tiny, contemplative Japanese-style garden. In contrast, a bamboo spout trickling water onto stone would feel soothing and appear quite natural in such a setting.

To help keep things simple and avoid a hodgepodge, repeat garden elements. For example, rather than planting a wide assortment, use a few types of plants repeatedly in different areas of the garden. Rely on two or three colors that best express the garden's mood. Choose one or two types of paving for walkways and use those same materials throughout the garden to create a visual, as well as physical, connection.

Details Make the Difference

In a little garden, everything shows. Each plant, ornament, structure, and surface becomes an integral part of the whole. One goal of small-garden design is to create interest and intrigue without adding extraneous *stuff*.

One of the advantages of smallness is that it encourages you to focus on quality rather than quantity. Just a few carefully chosen and well-placed plants or ornaments can transform an otherwise bland plot into an evocative haven. Consider using the following lures (and invent some of your own) to attract attention and to keep the viewer from taking in your entire garden in one glance:

- Bent-willow chair flanked by a large pot of tulips in bloom
- Wall-mounted fountain (saves more space than a freestanding one)
- Ornamental waterspout protruding from a wall and flowing onto a pebble surface
- Small pond in a large antique ceramic pot
- Stone sculpture
- Clipped boxwood topiary
- Single raised urn set in brick paving and filled with white daisylike marguerites and geraniums at the urn's base
- Apple tree trained to a decorative pattern against a fence or wall

Illusions of Grandeur

Visual trickery lies at the very heart of successful small-space gardening. Employ the following strategies to help defy garden boundaries and make your small space feel larger:

✔ **Use plants to blur walls and fences.** Doing so ensures that your eye doesn't abruptly stop at the garden's boundaries.

✔ **Construct gently curving paths.** By curving your paths, you can make them "disappear" at the garden's edge (perhaps at a false gate in a fence) to suggest that more lies beyond.

✔ **Vary levels.** Add vertical texture to the garden by using berms, steps, or terraces. Changes in levels add dimension and lengthen the route through the garden, which makes the space appear bigger. Level changes also divert the eye from the garden's boundaries and add an element of surprise as you move through the garden.

✔ **Create depth.** Layer plants at the garden's periphery. Put light-colored or variegated plants in front of taller, darker green ones. Or place shrubs or small trees in front of a vine-covered wall or fence.

✔ **Position cool colors.** Use cool colors, such as blue and violet, toward the farthest edges of the garden. These colors tend to recede and give an impression of distance.

✔ **Install a wall-mounted mirror.** Such a mirror can reflect an intriguing view.

✔ **Draw attention inward and downward.** Use decorative paving or an eye-catching living ground cover.

✔ **Borrow a view.** Expand the boundaries of your garden visually to incorporate a view beyond your property line into your garden design. If, for example, your neighbor has a gorgeous flowering shade tree, situate a bench in your yard to take advantage of the view.

Finding Space Where It Doesn't Exist

Take a cue from dandelions: They make room for themselves in the cracks of asphalt-surfaced parking lots. If you feel as though you have no growing space, then create some — on walls and overhead, in containers and window boxes, between pavers, and in raised beds. Here's how.

✔ **Plant in gaps.** Gardening in the crevices between bricks or stone not only gives you more growing space but also softens the hard look of these surfaces. Plants growing between paving create a visual link, connecting the hard surfaces with adjacent flower beds or other plantings.

Good gap-plant choices provide a thick, low carpet of greenery that stands up to some foot traffic. Certain ground covers add flowers or fragrance, as well. See the sidebar "Top gap plants" in this chapter for information about plants best suited for gaps.

✔ **Create window boxes.** These wall-hung minigardens provide a view from inside and outside your window. Mix in a few sweet-scented plants and enjoy the wafting fragrance, as well. (See Figure 21-1.)

✔ **Build raised beds.** When space is at a premium, room for large flower beds and borders may be unavailable. Rather than plant large beds and borders, squeeze in a few raised beds spilling over with annuals, perennials, or even vegetables.

✔ **Cover up with climbers.** Save valuable ground space by growing plants vertically. Use annual or perennial climbers or use wall shrubs — shrubs you can prune until they are nearly flat against a wall. For ideas on how to choose and train climbing vines, see Chapter 10. For information about good wall shrubs, turn to Chapter 8.

✔ **Plant overhead.** Encourage plants up and over arbors and arches to create a cool, green ceiling or a dramatic canopy of blooms. Deciduous plants provide welcome filtered shade in summer and let the warming sun shine through in winter.

Start with simple, sturdy structures that can support the weight and bulk of heavy, woody vines at maturity. A classic plant for garden ceilings is wisteria with its fragrant violet flowers in 1½-foot-long (46 cm) clusters. Among edibles, the kiwi vine (with branches to 30 feet, or 9 m, long) is a favorite patio cover. Keep in mind that both of these vines are rampant growers, so they require sturdy supports. Check Chapter 10 for additional ideas.

Figure 21-1:
Space-saving window boxes add charm.

Use lightweight containers to suspend plants from tree branches or overhead structures. Chapter 19 explains container gardening in detail.

Little Precious Gems

Select plants for your small garden as though you were choosing gems for your lover. A plant with the right style, fit, size, and color has the potential to dazzle, just as an inappropriate choice will look and feel awkward. When you select plants, consider the big picture — consider how each plant will contribute to the whole. Bear in mind the following tips when making your choices:

- Choose plants that fit your soil type, site (shady, sunny, wet, dry), and climate.

- Choose plants in proportion to your house and garden.

- Consider the mature size of plants so that, eventually, you don't have to face either constant shearing or a huge tree devouring the entire garden.

- Select plants with well-mannered roots that won't rob their neighbors of garden space, water, and nutrients.

- Because flowers are transitory, use them as color accents in a garden well-clothed in trees, shrubs, and vines that remain attractive year-round.

- Consider plant forms. Rounded shrubs are good backdrops for spiky accent plants. Pendulous or weeping plants direct attention downward. Use pyramidal or columnar plants for height.

- Limit the number of plant varieties and plant forms, and plant in groups to give your garden order.

- At the garden's edges, group plants of different sizes, shapes, and textures to create a sensation of depth.

- Because too many plants with strong personalities can make the garden's space appear cluttered, choose a few show-offs as accents.

Even with room for only a few containers and a chair, your garden can be inspiring and satisfying. So go forth and seek out the nooks and crannies.

Top gap plants

Excellent plants for planting in crevices are ajuga (*Ajuga reptans*, zones 4–8), blue star creeper (*Laurentia fluviatilis*, zones 8–10), creeping speedwell (*Veronica repens*, zones 6-10), crane's bill (*Erodium chamaedryoides*, zone 5 with snow cover, zone 7–9 without), dichondra (*Dichondra micrantha*, zones 9–10), Indian mock strawberry (*Duchesnea indica*, zones 4–10), moneywort (*Lysimachia nummularia*, zones 4–10), partridgeberry (*Mitchella repens*, zones 3–8), sandwort (*Arenaria montana*, zones 3–10), and spring cinquefoil (*Potentilla neumanniana*, zones 4–10).

For fragrance underfoot, thymes are quite reliable. Plant gray-green woolly thyme (*Thymus pseudolanuginosus*, zones 4–10), lemon thyme (*T. citriodorus*, zones 4–10), or mother-of-thyme (*T. praecox arcticus*, zones 4–10). Other fragrant choices include chamomile (*Chamaemelum nobile*, all zones), Corsican mint (*Mentha requienii*, zones 8–11), and yerba buena (*Satureja douglasii*, zones 8–10).

Part VII
The Part of Tens

The 5th Wave   By Rich Tennant

WE PLANT OUR PERENNIALS UP HERE SO THAT BY THE END OF MUD SEASON THEY'RE COMING UP IN OUR BACKYARD.

In this part . . .

List, list, O, list! —The ghost to Hamlet (Hamlet I, V)

Throughout this book, we give you lots of lists: lists of
can't miss annuals; lists of our favorite perennials; and
lists of our favorite trees, shrubs, and more. Well, here we
are in a part dedicated to lists.

In this part, you can find a couple more useful lists,
though we weren't necessarily constrained by the number
ten. You can find a list of great garden projects and even a
list of perfumed gardens here.

Then, don't miss the appendixes, which are pretty
substantial lists themselves — far exceeding the number
ten. These helpful references point you to other gardening
resources (whether books, magazines, or the Web) and to
mail-order gardening suppliers.

We hope you enjoy our part of gar-tens.

Chapter 22
Ten Quick Projects

In This Chapter

▶ Enjoying your herb and flower harvest

▶ Bringing the little beauties indoors

▶ Creating a water garden in a tub

▶ Making a salad basket

▶ Building a rustic trellis from prunings

*W*e can't say it enough: Gardening is fun. And the more you learn and do, the more fun it is. If you have gardening fever, the easy projects we describe here will enable you to enjoy the plants you are growing now or inspire you to grow even more.

Cooking Up Herb Vinegars

Herb vinegars are so easy to make at home that it should be illegal for food companies to sell them. You can flavor and mellow vinegars with many kinds of fresh garden herbs — fennel, sage, rosemary, garlic, and chives, to name a few. Our favorite herb vinegar is made with purple basil. In addition to its spicy basil flavor, this vinegar turns a gorgeous orchid pink.

As a general guide, use 1 cup of fresh-picked herbs to flavor 1 (1 liter) quart of vinegar. Depending on your taste, use white, cider, or wine vinegar. (White vinegar works best with purple basil.)

Here's all there is to it, though the variations are endless:

1. **Loosely fill a clean glass jar with clean herbs.**

2. **Fill with vinegar to cover the herbs and cap with plastic or a cork. (Don't use metal.)**

3. **Store in a cool, dark place for two to six weeks. The longer the time period, the stronger the herb flavor.**

4. **Strain to remove the herbs when the flavor satisfies your taste.**

Use flavored vinegars any way you would a wine vinegar, but consider reserving them for salads. The herb flavors make a subtle and very effective accent to any vinaigrette dressing. Add a whole sprig of the herb to the bottle for visual interest and to help identify the flavor; its presence won't hurt anything. Before presenting as a gift, wrap a bit of ribbon or raffia around the neck. Consider, too, a pretty, hand-printed label that identifies the flavor, date, and maker.

Making Cut Flowers Last

If you're cutting flowers for arrangements, care in harvesting and handling helps them last. Remember the following tips:

- ✔ Use sharp shears and cut the flowers in the early morning (before too much moisture has transpired from the plant).

- ✔ As you cut, put stems directly into water — carry a water-filled bucket into the garden with you.

- ✔ As soon as you bring the flowers indoors, remove the lower leaves that will be below the water in your vase. Submerged leaves rot and cloud the water, and can give off an unpleasant odor.

- ✔ Recut stems under water before placing them in the vase.

- ✔ Adding floral preservative to the vase water provides nutrients, acidifies the water, and slows respiration — all of which serve to lengthen the life of the flower.

- ✔ Change the vase water every couple of days.

- ✔ Place your bouquet in a cool spot, out of direct sunlight and away from heating vents.

Some large flowers with hollow stems, such as delphiniums and amaryllis, last longer if you first hold the stems upside down and pour water into them. Then plug the base of the stem with cotton.

Certain flowers, including Iceland poppies, euphorbias, and hollyhocks, need to have their stems sealed by searing to prevent them from drooping. Immediately after cutting, hold each stem over a flame for a few seconds or dip the stems in boiling water for 1 or 1 1/2 minutes.

For roses, fill a clean sink or large baking dish with lukewarm water and lay the roses in flat. Soak the roses for 10–20 minutes before arranging or to revive fading flowers. The process might even restore drooping flower heads.

Plants with woody stems, such as lilacs, forsythias, and pussy willows, require a slightly different treatment. You need to split or smash the stems to help with the uptake of water. One way to accomplish this is to pound the bottom few inches of each stem with a hammer. Alternatively, use a sharp knife or clippers to cut several times into the stem.

Drying Flowers

You can easily preserve the essence of summer when you pick a bunch of flowers and hang them to dry for winter bouquets.

Air-dry the annuals listed here simply by hanging them upside down in bundles, from the ceiling, or from a drying rack. Remove the foliage, group them in small bunches, and secure the bunches with a rubber band. Keep the drying flowers in a warm, dark place with good ventilation. Most flowers are dry when the stems snap. Store dried flowers in covered boxes or paper bags (away from dust and light).

Some dried flowers, such as strawflowers, have weak stems and you must wrap the stem with florist's wire to provide additional support if you want to use them in arrangements.

Following are a dozen annuals that you can count on to hold their shape and color:

- ✔ **Winged everlasting.** *Ammobium alatum* 'Grandiflorum'. Flowers are white and yellow with yellow centers. Cut when buds start to open.

- ✔ **Safflower.** *Carthamus tinctorius* 'Lasting Orange'. Cut yellow-orange flowers in bud or just at peak color.

- ✔ **Cockscomb.** *Celosia argentea* 'Chief' or Kurume series. Colors are intense and warm. Cut when heads reach full color.

- ✔ **Larkspur.** *Consolida ambigua*, Giant Imperial series. Colors are pink, blue, purple, and white. Cut stems when about two-thirds of the flowers are open and one-third are in bud.

- ✔ **Globe amaranth.** *Gomphrena globosa*. Colors are orange, white, pink, purple, and red. Cut when heads are plump and in full color.

- **Strawflower.** *Helichrysum bracteatum,* 'Bright Bikini' hybrids. Colors are mixed and vibrant. Cut when buds start to open.

- **Pink paper daisy.** *Helipterum roseum* (also called *Acrolineum roseum*). Colors in shades of pink and white. Cut partially open blooms.

- **Statice.** *Limonium sinuatum* 'American Beauty Rose', 'Art Shades', or 'Market Blue'. Colors range from purple to orange. Cut when most of the florets are open.

- **Love-in-a-mist.** *Nigella damascena* 'Miss Jekyll' hybrids. Grown for attractive seedpod. Cut when mature.

- **Pink pokers (or Russian statice).** *Psylliostachys suworowii.* Cut lavender pink flowers when fully open.

- **Starflower.** *Scabiosa stellata* 'Drumstick'. Cut decorative seedpods as soon as petals fade.

- **Immortelle.** *Xeranthemum annuum.* Colors are lavender, white, and shades of pink and purple. Cut open flowers after they show full color.

Making a Flowering Centerpiece

For a picnic table in summer, consider mixing begonias, ageratum, and sweet alyssum, the combination that we've based this set of steps on. A winter centerpiece for indoor decoration could include moth orchids and African violets with ivy and diminutive ferns. You may need a small bag of potting soil to fill in gaps between plants. If need be, put loose perlite (that white, light, popcornlike soil amendment you can get at nurseries) underneath plant pots to raise them up in the basket.

1. **Choose an oblong basket about 15–20 inches long, 8–10 inches wide, and 4 or so inches high (38–50 cm long, 20–25 cm wide, 10 cm high).**

2. **Line the basket with a heavy plastic trash bag and trim the edges.**

3. **Fill the basket with a combination of flowering and foliage plants in small, 2–4-inch (5–10 cm) containers.**

   Place the tallest plants (like begonias) in the center and the lower-growing plants (like ageratum and sweet alyssum) toward the outside. At the edges, you can squeeze in trailing plants, including small-leafed ivies. Fill all gaps with potting soil. Use Spanish moss to hide pots.

4. **To maintain the centerpiece, water plants individually, using a narrow-spouted watering can.**

   Fertilize the plants regularly, especially during summer when most plants grow fastest. Refresh the centerpiece with new plants as needed.

For a very full look, squeeze in more plants by removing some of the smaller ones from their containers and slipping the root ball of each plant into a zipped sandwich bag (partially close the bag around the base of the plant). Then gently squeeze the bagged plants between the potted plants. Water the plants just enough to keep them moist.

Creating an Autumn Harvest Wreath

You don't need to be an artist to pull off this craft project successfully. After just a couple of hours of collecting and arranging leaves, seedpods, and fruits from your garden and grocery store, you have a beautiful wreath for your harvest celebration. It lasts anywhere from several days to several months, depending on the plants you use.

The object is to cover a polystyrene foam wreath base (available at craft and floral supply stores) with garden goodies. You need about 2 large grocery bags full of plant material to cover a 12-inch (30.5 cm) wreath. Combine foliage such as magnolia, eucalyptus, and dusty miller leaves with colorful accents like rose hips, seedpods, and pyracantha berries. If you're short on home-grown plants, use accent material like baby corn, lady apples, and miniature pumpkins or gourds purchased from your grocery store.

Here's what you do:

1. **Attach a wire to the wreath base to hang the wreath.**

   Slide the wire through the base, leaving a looped hook on top; twist and cut the ends of the wire.

2. **Cover the wreath base with dry leaves, using hairpins to hold it in place.**

   Work in one direction around the base from the inside of the wreath outward. Attach thin-stemmed leaves in clusters and large leaves individually. For pizzazz, combine foliage of different colors and textures.

3. **After you cover the base, add accents.**

   Secure small fruits and berries with hairpins or glue. Secure larger fruits, such as baby pumpkins or lady apples, by using floral picks (available at craft and floral supply stores). Place these larger items sparingly as focal points.

Forcing Narcissus Indoors

On blustery winter days when the garden is dull and quiet, a pot of home-grown bulbs gracing the dining room table is truly gratifying. Setting up narcissus to bloom takes little effort. All they need are water and several weeks to work their magic.

The two varieties of narcissus that are most available and reliable for water culture are paperwhites and yellow 'Soleil D'Or'. Paperwhites flower only five to six weeks after planting; 'Soleil D'Or' takes a bit longer.

Here's what you do:

1. **Choose a fairly shallow waterproof bowl or pot, at least twice as deep as the size of the bulbs.**

2. **Fill the container to within several inches from the top with pebbles.**

3. **Set the bulbs on the pebbles about $1/2$ inch (1.3 cm) apart with the broad ends down.**

4. **Fill the container with water so that the water just touches the bottom of the bulbs.**

5. **To hold the bulbs in place, fill the spaces between them with more pebbles.**

6. **Put the planted container in a cool, dark place to encourage root growth.**

7. **In two to three weeks, when the leaves are about 3 inches (7.5 cm) high, move the container to a warmer, bright location.**

8. **As the plants develop, add water from time to time, keeping it at the base of the bulbs.**

If you want blooms for Thanksgiving, start paperwhites about the middle of September. For Christmas blooms, start them in mid-November. For continuous flowering throughout winter, start the first pot of bulbs in late October and continue planting at two- to three-week intervals.

Creating a Water Garden in a Tub

The thought of building a traditional garden pond can be overwhelming, but creating a soothing water feature in a tub is quite achievable. This garden is a functioning ecosystem, meaning you don't need to filter or change water, as for a fish tank. Though small in scale, your tub garden will teem with life: fish, flowers that you start, and even birds that come to drink.

Display the water garden where it can receive two to three hours of shade during the hottest part of the day.

Here are the materials you need:

- Sturdy plastic, or glazed ceramic pot without a drainage hole
- New, durable faux terra cotta containers. Choose one about 30 inches (76 cm) in diameter and about 20 inches (50 cm) high.
- An assortment of water plants:
  - One water iris
  - One water lily
  - One free-floating water hyacinth
  - A clump of parrots feather, a common water plant
- Half-dozen fish:
  - Mosquito fish
  - Minnows
  - Goldfish
- Empty 5-gallon (19 liters) plastic pot

Here's what you do:

1. **Fill the large tub about ²/₃ full with water and place the 5-gallon pot (19 liters), inverted, to one side of the tub.**

2. **Place the iris on top of the inverted pot.**

3. **Place the water lily, in its own container, on the bottom of the tub.**

   The water lily's leaves and flowers will rise above the water surface.

4. **Plant the clump of parrots feather in the soil in the iris container.**

5. **Add the floating water hyacinth and fill the tub with water.**

6. **Acclimatize fish by placing them — still in their plastic bag — in the water for about 20 minutes. Release the fish from the bag.**

   You don't need to give the fish supplemental food — they'll feed on algae and insect larvae in the water.

Aquatic plants are becoming more readily available at nurseries. If you can't find them locally, order them by mail. (See Appendix B for mail-order sources.)

Preparing a Salad Basket

You're probably familiar with *mesclun* — those expensive mixes of tender gourmet salad greens. Why buy mesclun when you can easily grow it? Why grow it in a garden when you can have it in a basket? That's what we thought.

Many mesclun greens germinate just a few days after planting and are ready for harvesting in two to four weeks. More good news for gardeners: After you cut mesclun greens, they grow back for a repeat harvest.

You can buy a premixed mesclun seed blend or mix your own by combining your favorite greens. Typical ingredients include loose-leaf lettuces, arugula, chicories, mizuna, red mustard, and curly cress.

Here's how to grow a basket of mesclun that you can harvest after three weeks:

1. **Choose a large, sturdy basket that can support the weight of wet soil.**

   Line the basket with a heavyweight black plastic trash bag. To provide drainage, use scissors to poke holes through the plastic at the bottom of the basket.

2. **Fill the basket with moistened peat moss and perlite-type potting mix (several kinds are available commercially) to 2 inches (5 cm) below the rim. (Trim off any plastic that extends beyond the rim.)**

3. **Scatter seeds thinly over the soil surface, cover with about 1/4 inch (0.6 cm) of potting mix, and then water gently.**

4. **Cover the basket with a piece of water-retaining plastic or food wrap and keep in a 65°–70°F (18°–21°C) location until the seeds germinate.**

5. **When seeds sprout, remove the plastic and move the basket to a sunny location.**

   Keep the soil moist as the plants grow and fertilize weekly with a complete liquid fertilizer.

6. **Start harvesting when the seedlings are about 3 inches tall by cutting with scissors 1/2 inch (1.3 cm) above the soil surface.**

Finding Treasures from Twigs

Consider yourself lucky if you are trimming a vine, grooming a hedge, or pruning a tree here and there and find yourself with a few piles of twigs and branches. These bits of woody materials have many uses in the home and garden, both utilitarian and aesthetic.

- **Brush cuttings.** Use prunings that are about $^1/_4$–$^1/_2$ inch (0.6–1.3 cm) thick at the base to support bush peas.

- **Straight branches.** Branches about 3 feet (1 m) long and $^1/_2$ inch (0.6 cm) wide make sturdy plant supports. To keep blooms of large-flowering perennials such as peonies from toppling over, drive stakes into the ground to form a ring around the plant. Connect the stakes with twine tied at the appropriate height to support top-heavy stems.

  You can also handcraft rustic trellises from straight, sturdy branches. Allow 18 inches (46 cm) at the base to push into the soil for support. Weave rope or twine as shown to connect the branches and provide supports for plants.

- **Tall stems.** Use wispy, branching stems about 24 inches (61 cm) long to support stems of paperwhite narcissus growing in pebbles and water.

- **Twigs.** Use thin twigs to support cut flowers in arrangements. Place groups of twigs at different angles in the vase and then insert flowers.

- **Vines.** To form decorative wreaths, bend and weave together fresh-cut vines from dormant grapes, bittersweet, or willow (not a vine, but flexible enough stems to use like one). Bind the ends together with wire and let the vines dry out.

Cleaning Containers

By cleaning used containers before replanting, you help prevent the spread of plant diseases and pests. Because they are porous, terra cotta containers need cleaning more often than plastic.

Using a stiff wire brush, scrape off soil and fertilizer residue, algae, and salt crust inside and outside the pot. Then scrub the pots with a 10-percent bleach solution and rinse well.

If you've had a perennial or a shrub growing in the same container for several seasons, the outside surface of the container may be dirty and discolored. To freshen it up, brush the surface and, using an old rag, rub on linseed oil.

On the other hand, if the container has acquired the attractive patina of age and the plant inside it is growing well, you can leave the container as is.

Chapter 23

Perfumed Garden Flowers

· ·

In This Chapter

▶ Planning your perfumery

▶ Discovering the most fragrant annuals and perennials

▶ Finding surprises after dark

▶ Deciding which trees, vines, and shrubs to grow for fragrance

▶ Exploring sweet-scented bulbs

▶ Enjoying the essence of roses

· ·

*G*rowing fragrant plants is a sure way to lift our spirits and stir good memories.

Sweet scents come with all types of plants — from annuals to shrubs to vines and trees. We tend to focus on flowers when we think of scent, yet many garden plants have luscious-smelling leaves — certainly the fragrant foliage of lemon verbena or a mint-scented geranium rivals that of many a rose. Although flower fragrances waft on high, you often need to seek out leaf fragrance. Only when you rub or crush the leaves of such fragrant delights as Corsican mint or rosemary do they release their aromas.

Think of your favorite flower and foliage fragrances when you plan and plant your garden. Including them is easy.

Getting the Most for Your Whiff

Much current garden literature encourages readers to cluster fragrant plants together in a collection. But the most sensual gardens of all are infused with perfumed plants through and through. Cultivate sweet-scented plants in prime locations so that you are certain to catch their drift. Target the following areas:

- ✔ **Locate potted plants under windows or on your balcony** so that you can enjoy the aromas indoors and out. Perfumed annuals (such as sweet alyssum, carnations, and stocks, which release their fragrance at night) or bulbs (such as freesias and paperwhite narcissus) are excellent choices.

- ✔ **Frame your front door or garden entrance** with a sweet-smelling vine, such as Arabian jasmine or goldflame honeysuckle. Or plant the strongly perfumed thornless climbing rose 'Zephirine Drouhin'.

- ✔ **Cover a sturdy arbor or patio** with a robust climber like the old-fashioned wisteria; its fragrant blooms in 1- to 2-foot (30–60 cm) pendulous clusters are legendary.

- ✔ **Edge pathways** with fragrant herbs (like lavender and thyme), annuals (mignonette, for example), and perennials (such as chocolate cosmos and lemon daylily).

Flowers Most Possessed with Scent

In a single gardening season, you can work perfume magic simply by planting fast-growing annuals and perennials. Enjoy their instant fragrance gratification while your slower-growing perfumed trees and shrubs become established.

- ✔ **Sweet sultan.** *Centaurea moschata* (annual, all zones). This plant has erect branching stems to 2 feet (60 cm) with thistlelike, 2-inch (5 cm), musk-scented flower heads. Common colors include lilac, rose, yellow, and white.

- ✔ **Chocolate cosmos.** *Cosmos atrosanguineus* (annual, all zones). Deep brownish-red fragrant flowers adorn this perennial. The flowers, nearly 2 inches (5 cm) wide, appear on top of stems that grow up to 2$\frac{1}{2}$ feet (45 cm). Some say the fragrance is chocolate — others say vanilla!

- ✔ **Pink.** *Dianthus* (perennial, zones 3–9). Several kinds of strongly fragrant perennial pinks, or border carnations, are available. Tops for fragrance are cheddar pink *(D. gratianopolitanus)*, cottage pink *(D. plumarius)*, maiden pink *(D. deltoides)*, D. 'Rose Bowl', and D. 'Tiny Rubies'.

- ✔ **Carnations.** *Dianthus caryophyllus* (perennial, zones 8–10; annual, all zones). Choose spicy-sweet border carnations, which are bushier and more compact than the florist type. Some varieties to look for are 14-inch-high (35 cm) 'Fragrance' in shades of crimson, rose, pink, and white; 1-foot-tall (30 cm) 'Juliet' with scarlet flowers; and 2-foot-tall (60 cm) 'Luminette', also with scarlet flowers.

- ✔ **Common heliotrope.** *Heliotropium arborescens* (perennial, zone 11; annual, all zones). This plant's delightful sweet fragrance comes from clusters of rich purple flowers on 1–4 foot (1.2 m) stems (taller in warmer, long-season regions).

- ✔ **Sweet pea.** *Lathyrus odoratus* (annual, all zones). The old-fashioned varieties are the most fragrant by far. Look for 'Old Spice' and 'Painted Lady'. Other truly fragrant sweet peas are 'Mammoth Mix' and the 'Old Royal' series.

- ✔ **Stock.** *Matthiola incana* (annual, all zones). Spicy-sweet flowers cluster along erect stems, which are 1–3 feet (30 cm–1 m) tall, depending on variety. Stock is good for cutting.

- ✔ **Mignonette.** *Reseda odorata* (annual, all zones). Old-fashioned and considered one of the most fragrant of all flowers, mignonette has been described as possessing a sweet pea-raspberry-tangerine scent. The plant reaches from 1 to $1^1/_2$ feet (30–45 cm) with inconspicuous flowers in dense, spikelike clusters. Compact forms are the most fragrant.

- ✔ **Sweet violet.** *Viola odorata* (perennial, zones 5–10). This plant has been long cherished for its sweet oils, which were extracted for perfumes. It has dark green, heart-shaped leaves and, depending on the variety, grows from 2 to 12 inches (5–30 cm). Sweet violet spreads by runners near the soil surface, and in mild climates it can become a pest.

Some types of flowers are not usually sought after for fragrance, yet particular species or varieties among them are quite nicely scented. So if you're planting peonies, for example, look for 'Myrtle Gentry' with its exceptional tea rose fragrance. Daylilies noted for fragrance include the lemon daylily *(Hemerocallis lilioasphodelus)* and hybrids such as 'Fragrant Light', 'Hyperion', 'Ida Jane', and 'Citrina'. Among tulips, some single early types have a sweet scent. Examples are butter-yellow 'Bellona' and golden-orange 'General de Wet'. Also, the multiflowered *Tulipa sylvestris* has a pleasant, sweet fragrance.

Fragrance after Dark

Certain plants release their heady scents only near or after dark. Plant them near the spots where you hang out on summer nights — close to porches and bedroom windows and next to your most comfy garden bench.

- ✔ **Dame's rocket.** *Hesperis matronalis* (annual, all zones). This plant is excellent for the wild garden where it often self-sows. Its branching plants reach 2–4 feet (60 cm–1.2 m) high with rounded clusters of richly fragrant phloxlike blooms in lavender or purple.

- ✔ **Moonflower.** *Ipomoea alba* (annual, all zones). A perennial vine grown as a summer annual, moonflower's fragrant white trumpet blooms open to 6 inches (15 cm) wide at sunset.

- ✔ **Evening stock.** *Mathiola longipetala bicornis* (annual, all zones). Only 3–12 inches (7.5–30.5 cm) tall, this inconspicuous annual with small purplish flowers is extraordinarily fragrant.

- ✔ **Flowering tobacco.** *Nicotiana alata* (annual, all zones). This wild species has large white flowers that open toward evening on 2–3 foot (60 cm–1 m) stems. 'Grandiflora' is exceptionally fragrant.

- ✔ **Fragrant evening primrose.** *Oenothera caespitosa* (perennial, zones 4–7). Low-growing with gray-green fuzzy leaves, this primrose has white, 4-inch (10 cm) blooms.

- ✔ **Night phlox.** *Zaluzianskya capensis* (perennial, zones 9–11; or annual, all zones). Fragrant, 2-inch (5 cm) flowers are dark red with white interiors.

The Most Aromatic Herbs

Following is a sampling of some of the best herbs for fragrant foliage. In addition to smelling great, thyme, lavender, and rosemary are extremely useful and rugged landscape plants.

- ✔ **Lemon verbena.** *Aloysia triphylla.* Zones 8–11.

- ✔ **Chamomile.** *Chamaemelum nobile.* All zones.

- ✔ **Lavender.** *Lavandula.* Zones 5–10.

- ✔ **Corsican mint.** *Mentha requienii.* Zones 8–11.

- ✔ **Scented geraniums.** *Pelargonium* species, including *P. citrosum, P. graveolens, P. nervosum, P. odoratissimum, P. quercifolium,* and *P. tomentosum.* All zones.

- ✔ **Rosemary.** *Rosmarinus officinalis.* Zones 7–11.

- ✔ **Thyme.** *Thymus.* Zones 4–10.

Heavenly Scented Trees, Shrubs, and Vines

We conducted an informal survey among our trusty garden gurus across the country, asking them to name the most pleasantly fragrant trees, shrubs, and vines they grow. Here are 11 of their favorite perfume-packed plants:

- ✔ **Butterfly bush.** *Buddleia davidii* (zones 6–11). Sometimes called summer lilac, this deciduous or semievergreen shrub grows quickly to 10 feet (3 m). In summer, small fragrant flowers develop in arching, spikelike clusters to 12 inches (30 cm) long.

✔ **Daphne.** *Daphne* species (zones 5–10, varies by species). These shrubs can be a bit temperamental, but the flowers' seductive scent encourages serious fragrance fanciers to persist. You can choose from several species, including *D. burkwoodii* (white flowers fading to pink), *D. cneorum* (rosy-pink flowers), *D. mantensiana* (purple flowers), and *D. odora* (flowers pink to deep red with creamy pink throats).

All parts of the daphne are safe to handle but poisonous if ingested.

✔ **Gardenia.** *Gardenia jasminoides* (zones 8–11). The creamy white blossom is the classic corsage flower. Depending on variety, these evergreen shrubs grow from 3 feet to 8 feet high (1–2.4 m). Gardenias tolerate temperatures of 20°F (–6°C) or even lower, but they need summer heat to grow and bloom well.

✔ **Arabian jasmine.** *Jasminum sambac* (zones 10–11). A tender shrub that's hardy at best to 25°F (–4°C), it is among the most highly scented plants. Known as *pikaki* in Hawaii, Arabian jasmine blossoms appear in leis, and its essence distilled to make perfumes. The plant grows to about 5 feet (1.5 m) high, and the white flowers are ³/₄ to 1 inch (2–2.5 cm) wide.

✔ **Goldflame honeysuckle.** *Lonicera heckrottii* (zones 6–10). This sweet-smelling vine grows up to 12 feet (3.7 m) and displays rose-pink and pale yellow flowers.

✔ **Michelia.** *Michelia champaca* (zones 9–11). Deliciously fragrant, 3-inch (7.5 cm), pale orange flowers highlight this evergreen tree that grows to 30 feet (9 m) high. Michelia leaves are large and glossy.

✔ **Banana shrub.** *Michelia figo* (zones 8–10). This slow-growing evergreen shrub reaches 8 feet (2.5 m) or more. Small creamy-yellow flowers with purplish shading exude a powerful fruity fragrance resembling the smell of ripe bananas.

✔ **Sweet olive.** *Osmanthus fragrans* (zones 8–10). Tiny, inconspicuous white flowers exude a powerfully sweet apricot-like fragrance on this evergreen shrub that grows up to 10 feet (3 m) or more.

✔ **Plumeria.** *Plumeria rubra* (zones 10–11). This tender, deciduous shrub or small tree has long, pointed leaves and clusters of 2–2¹/₂-inch-wide (5–6 cm) fragrant flowers. Depending on the variety, plumeria flowers may be red, purple, pink, yellow, or white.

✔ **Cleveland sage.** *Salvia clevelandii* (zones 9–10). A rounded, drought-tolerant shrub, Cleveland sage grows to 4 feet (1.2 m) and has intensely fragrant gray-green foliage — plus fragrant lavender-blue flowers.

✔ **Lilac.** *Syringa vulgaris* (zones 2–9). Common lilac includes many named varieties. In northern climates it is a common, and fragrant, landscape shrub.

Best Bulbs for Fragrance

You can find some of the most highly scented flowers among bulbs. For more information about bulbs, see Chapter 6.

- **Naked lady.** *Amaryllis belladonna* (zones 8–10). Evocatively named because 3-foot-high (1 m) flowering stalks emerge in later summer, but not leaves. Its pink, trumpet-shaped flowers are about 3 inches (7.5 cm) in diameter.

- **Lily-of-the-valley.** *Convallaria majalis* (zones 2–9). Starting this hardy and resilient bulb in your own garden is easy. The tiny, hanging, bell-shaped flowers that appear in early spring are wonderfully scented.

- **Freesia.** *Freesia* (zones 9–10 or all zones in containers). Not all are fragrant, but 'Safari' (yellow), 'Snowdon' (double white), and the red and yellow *Tecolote* hybrids emit the strong, spicy-sweet scent associated with these spring bloomers.

- **Hyacinth.** *Hyacinthus orientalis* (zones 5–10, or all zones in containers). You can easily force these large bulbs indoors (see Chapter 6 for details on forcing bulbs), and you can get special vases to fit the bulbs. Several colors are available, and all are equally fragrant. One flowering hyacinth is enough to perfume an entire house. Or plant outdoors in clumps or in containers.

- **Lily.** *Lilium* (all zones). Lily species include gold-banded lily (*L. auratum*), Madonna lily (*L. candidum*), and trumpet lily (*L. longiflorum*), as well as Oriental lilies, such as 'American Eagle', 'Blushing Pink', 'Imperial Silver', 'Journey's End', and 'Everest'.

- **Grape hyacinth.** *Muscari azureum* (zones 4–10). You put your nose up to the blue flower spikes and smell a glass of fresh grape juice.

- **Narcissus.** *Narcissus jonquilla* (zones 4–10) and *N. tazetta* (zones 7–10). Jonquils are the shorter narcissus that produce two to four flowers per flowering stalk. The tazettas include the pure white paperwhites and the golden 'Soleil d'Or'. As is often the case with these highly scented flowers, a single paperwhite can perfume a whole room or more, but it's not a universally loved scent. Try it for yourself.

- **Tuberose.** *Polianthes tuberosa* (zones 9–11 or all zones in containers). Flowers of this tender summer-to-fall tuber are heavy and waxy — almost unreal looking. The scent is equally unbelievable. Plant in spring, after frost danger is past.

- **Tulip 'Bellona'** (all zones as fall-planted annuals). This bright-yellow, single early tulip hybrid grows about 12 inches (30 cm) tall.

Redolent Roses

Nothing is quite like sniffing an old rose (meaning an antique type) for the most intense floral-fragrance experience. Fragrance aficionados can even identify the class of old rose — Tea, China, Damask, and Bourbon, for example — by its characteristic perfume. Entire books are devoted to old roses, and we recommend in particular *Roses for Dummies* by Lance Walheim and the Editors of the National Gardening Association.

Modern roses are another story. In their quest for improved flower color and growth habits in modern roses, breeders have sacrificed the fragrance of the older varieties. Some dedicated rose lovers, however, have managed to develop garden rose varieties with the attributes of a modern rose *and* a delicious fragrance. The following modern roses (all hardy in zones 6–10 without protection) have received awards for their intense fragrance. (See Chapter 7 for more about hardiness and the definition of these rose types):

- ✔ **'Chrysler Imperial'**. Hybrid tea; rich crimson with darker shadings.
- ✔ **'Crimson Glory'**. Hybrid tea; deep crimson aging to purplish.
- ✔ **'Double Delight'**. Hybrid tea; cherry-red surrounding creamy center.
- ✔ **'Fragrant Cloud'**. Hybrid tea; orange-red.
- ✔ **'Granada'**. Hybrid tea; yellow flushed with pink and red.
- ✔ **'Papa Meilland'**. Hybrid tea; bright, dark crimson.
- ✔ **'Sundowner'**. Grandiflora; orange and salmon-pink.
- ✔ **'Sunsprite'**. Floribunda; yellow.
- ✔ **'Sutter's Gold'**. Hybrid tea; yellow with red shading on outer petals.
- ✔ **'Tiffany'**. Hybrid tea; soft pink with yellow at the petal base.

One last note here on experiencing your favorite floral fragrance: A flower's perfume is usually strongest on warm and humid days and weakest when the weather is hot and dry. For an intense rush of flower fragrance, bring the blossom to your face and lightly breathe into it before inhaling. The warmth of your breath releases the flower's volatile oils.

Appendix A
Gardening Resources

• •

*L*earning about gardening is an endless pursuit. Anyone can spend a lifetime learning (and many have) and never know everything about gardening. But if you're just getting started and want to learn more, this appendix is for you. Here we tell you about gardening books, magazines, software, and the Internet.

If you want to learn more even after exploring all the resources here, consider taking classes at a local college, or becoming a certified Master Gardener. Your local cooperative extension office sponsors the Master Gardener program. Call the extension office for more information. Or check with the umbrella organization for all the regional programs, Master Gardeners International, 424 North River Dr., Woodstock, Virginia 22664; fax 540-459-9797, or e-mail mgic@capaccess.org.

Books and Magazines about Gardening

Sooner or later, most gardeners get hooked on books and magazines. You can find publications for all types of gardeners, from novices to specialists. Those specialists can focus on a particular type of plant, such as rhododendrons, orchids, or wildflowers; or a particular type of gardening, such as edible landscaping, rock gardening, or indoor gardening. Because the natures of books and magazines differ, each type of publication tends to treat the various gardening topics in different but complementary ways. Books are ideal for treating broad subjects in depth and for bringing together in one place information that otherwise would be scattered. Magazines are ideal for reporting new trends and seasonal topics and for approaching specific topics from interesting and unusual angles. Using books and magazines together, you easily can form an impressive knowledge base.

The resources included in this appendix are predominantly North American, the territory we know best. On every continent — not to mention in every region — you can find gardening information that directly targets plants and conditions there. Also, international trade rules are still complex enough to discourage easy exchange: All the prices noted here are in U.S. dollars and assume U.S. delivery. We encourage you to seek out the resources where you live, beginning perhaps at local botanical gardens.

Books

Gardening books fall into two basic categories: practical and inspirational. *Inspirational* books are those that stimulate and invite you to stretch your thinking. These books feed your dreams. Inspiration can be visual, with books of exciting full-color photographs, or literary, with works that capture the imagination through the excellence of the writing.

Practical books include how-to books that show you how to do the basic tasks of gardening and reference books that you can refer to over and over. Essential reference books include encyclopedias of plants, dictionaries of gardening terms and practices, and directories of sources. Sources include nurseries and mail-order companies for obtaining seeds and plants, lists of organizations that provide information, and descriptions and addresses of gardens to visit and events to attend.

Gardens are very personal, and your favorite books will be a very personal selection also. Nevertheless, you should watch for the following points when considering the practical type of book:

- ✔ **Plant requirements.** Make sure that any book of plants you buy includes the light, moisture, soil type, and temperature requirements for growing them successfully. You can be frustrated if you discover belatedly that the "perfect" plant in terms of size, shape, color, and seemingly every other aspect is not cold-hardy or heat-tolerant for your area.

- ✔ **Plant names.** Beginning gardeners are intimidated by botanical names of plants and find it much easier to use common names. However, common names of plants are so ambiguous that planning gardens or buying plants based on common names alone isn't wise. Don't buy a book of plants that doesn't also give the Latin name, or you'll never be sure of getting the plant that you saw in the book.

- ✔ **Conditions in your geographical region.** Climate, soil, and temperature vary; thus, the plants that grow well and the cultivation methods gardeners use to make them flourish will also vary. A book that tells you how and particularly *when* to do tasks such as planting and mulching must address your particular region.

- ✔ **Qualifications of the author.** Look for authors who have experience in the type of gardening that you want to do or the style of garden that you want to create. But ultimately, what's important is an author's ability to communicate and provide useful information to you.

- ✔ **Quality and number of illustrations.** Are gardening steps illustrated and clearly labeled? Are photographs in focus and true to color? Do photos illustrate the subject, or are they merely big, beautiful pictures? Do captions accompany illustrations? If the book is on garden design, does the book include design plans? Do the plans have labels? Do they show plant names? Is the scale clear?

✔ **Size and type of index.** Good books have indexes, usually at the back of the book. The best indexes include names of gardens, organizations, nurseries, people, and plants, as well as the topics mentioned in the book. Dictionaries and encyclopedias preclude the need for an index by arranging entries in alphabetical order.

We recommend that beginning gardeners start with one or two general how-to books and a few reference books. As your skill level progresses and your tastes develop, you can branch out and read in-depth treatments of your specific subjects. We selected the practical books in this list because they are both easy for beginners to understand and have content substantial enough to be useful as your gardening skill grows.

Where-to-find-it books

Take a look at the following reference guides.

✔ *Gardening by Mail: A Source Book, 5th Edition.* Written by Barbara J. Barton and Ginny Hunt. Houghton Mifflin, 1997. $24 (paperback). If you can afford only one source guide, this is it. Through this book, you can find enough information to support any kind of gardening: plant and seed sources, garden suppliers and services, professional societies, trade associations, conservation and umbrella groups, horticultural and plant societies, magazines and newsletters, libraries, and books.

✔ *The Garden Tourist: A Guide to Garden Tours, Garden Days, Shows and Special Events.* Edited by Lois G. Rosenfeld. Annual. $17. This book is a handy compilation of all the garden shows and events in the country, organized by state. Order from The Garden Tourist Press, 330 West 72nd St, Suite 12B, New York, NY 10023. Phone 212-874-6211; fax 212-799-7094; or e-mail Gardentour@aol.com.

Basic gardening primers: ...For Dummies!

Of course we're convinced that the best gardening primers on the planet are our own ...*For Dummies* gardening books. The titles include the following:

✔ *Perennials For Dummies,* 1997, with Denver-based garden guru Marcia Tatroe

✔ *Roses For Dummies,* 1997, with central California's most famous gardener, Lance Walheim

✔ *Lawn Care For Dummies,* 1997, again with Lance Walheim

✔ *Annuals For Dummies,* 1997, with San Francisco-based gardener and editor Bill Marken

✔ *Container Gardening For Dummies,* 1997, also with Bill Marken

✔ *Decks & Patios For Dummies,* 1998, with Napa Valley contractor and editor Robert Beckstrom

- *Flowering Bulbs For Dummies,* 1998, with New York Botanical Garden's horticulture instructor and international bulb expert, Judy Glattstein

- *Houseplants For Dummies,* 1998, with Quebec City's own one-person horticultural tour de force, Larry Hodgson

- *Landscaping For Dummies,* 1999, with Venice, California-based landscape contractor Philip Giroux

- *Vegetable Gardening For Dummies,* 1999, with National Gardening Association senior horticulturist, vegetable gardening expert, and TV personality, Charlie Nardozzi

A word about British books

British gardens and British gardeners have a definite cachet. Great Britain, with good reason, has been called the garden capital of the world. Gardens around the world emulate British gardens, and some of the best gardeners and garden writers are British.

Gardening in Great Britain, however, is not like gardening in the United States, Australia, Canada, South Africa, or anywhere else, for that matter. Some differences include climate, soil, pests, diseases, light, and availability of plants, and how and when best to perform garden tasks. Indoor conditions are different, too. For example, in winter, people in the United States tend to keep their houses hotter and drier. We also use different terminology.

Beginning gardeners find some of the how-to advice in British books confusing and the results disappointing. Novices who seek how-to books should buy books by authors familiar with the conditions where they will be gardening. Experienced gardeners are better able to filter out advice not appropriate to their situations and, thus, to benefit from exposure to new ideas and different ways of doing things. As you gain gardening skills, we recommend that you do explore the full and wonderful world of garden books, but be cautious at first.

The British excel in matters of taste, plant collecting, and plant breeding. British books on gardens, garden history, garden design, garden ornamentation, floral arrangement, plant exploration, plant breeding and propagation, biography, and essays can be used with far fewer caveats than books whose main intent is to show you how to do something, like plant a vegetable garden, yourself.

Magazines

Magazines are important sources of both information and inspiration and are good values for the money. Magazines publish feature-length articles that cover a wide variety of topics and situations. These publications usually also give very practical information, such as sources for obtaining plants or seeds, and generally have illustrations such as full-color photographs, plot plans, diagrams, and botanical drawings. Many magazines offer reviews of garden books, a very useful service in helping you decide which books are right for you. Other features can include regular columns for presenting news, discussing trends, or answering readers' questions. Magazines are published frequently, so articles are often more up-to-date than books.

Hundreds of periodicals publish articles about plants and gardens. Like books, a magazine exists for every skill level and type and style of garden imaginable. Start with a few of the most popular national magazines and then add subscriptions to specialty periodicals as you find appropriate. You can write or call any of the following magazines directly, or subscribe online at www.enews.com on the Internet.

Some of the leading national gardening magazines in North America are

- *American Gardener.* Published bimonthly. American Horticultural Society, 7931 E. Boulevard Dr., Alexandria, VA 22308-1300; phone 703-768-5700; Web site www.ahs.org. Available with $25 membership.

- *Brooklyn Botanic Garden: Handbook.* Published quarterly. Brooklyn Botanic Garden, 1000 Washington Ave., Brooklyn, NY 11225; phone 718-622-4433; Web site www.bbg.org. Each issue covers a different topic. Available with $35 membership.

- *Fine Gardening.* Published bimonthly. The Taunton Press, 63 S. Main St., P.O. Box 5506, Newtown, CT 06470-5506; phone 800-283-7252 or 203-426-8171; Web site www.taunton.com. Articles about flowers and ornamental gardens. Subscriptions are $32.

- *Garden Design.* Published eight times a year. Meigher Communications, 100 Avenue of the Americas, New York, NY 10013; phone 212-334-1212. For subscriptions, write to: P.O. Box 55458, Boulder, CO 80322-5458; phone 800-234-5118. For style-oriented, upscale readers. Subscriptions are $28.

- *Garden Gate.* Published bimonthly. August Home Corp., 2200 Grand Ave., Des Moines, Iowa 50312; phone 800-978-9631; Web site www.augusthome.com/gardeng.htm. Articles about home gardening and design. Subscriptions are $19.95.

✔ *Horticulture*. Published ten times a year. Horticulture, 98 N. Washington St., Boston, MA 02114; phone 617-742-5600; Web site `www.hortmag.com`. Subscriptions are $26.

✔ *National Gardening*. Published bimonthly by the National Gardening Association, the largest nonprofit association of home gardeners in the United States (and the authors of this book!), 180 Flynn Ave, Burlington, VT 05401; phone 802-863-1308; Web site `www.garden.org`. See the coupon at the back of this book for a special subscription offer. Subscriptions are $18.

✔ *Organic Gardening*. Published bimonthly. Rodale Press, 33 E. Minor St., Emmaus, PA, 18098; phone 215-967-5171; Web site `www.organicgardening.com`. $20.

✔ *Rebecca's Garden*. Published quarterly. Hearst Communications, Inc., Box 7476, Red Oak, IA 51591-0476; Web site `www.rebeccasgarden.com`. Based on Rebecca Kolls's syndicated television show. $10 for six issues.

Most gardening magazines publish annual indexes to articles appearing in their own magazines. For instance, a detailed four-year cumulative index (1995 through 1998) of *National Gardening* magazine is available for $10 by writing to NG Magazine/Index, 180 Flynn Ave., Burlington, VT 05401. Or go online at `www2.garden.org/nga/EDIT/home.html` to retrieve the same index for free.

You can also purchase indexes that cover several magazines. One such index is *Garden Literature: An Index to Periodical Articles and Book Reviews* (Garden Literature Press, 398 Columbus Ave, Suite 181, Boston MA 02116; phone 617-424-1784; Web site `www.gardennet.com/gardenliterature`.

Gardening Online

Ask gardeners, "What's your favorite gardening tool?" and they'll tell you about a favorite old pair of oft-sharpened pruners or a nicely balanced watering can or how they finally splurged and bought a really good spade. Not one of them will say, "My computer." But a computer is probably one of the most versatile tools a gardener can own.

With a computer and access to the Internet, you can select the right plants for your particular climate and site, design and lay out a new garden, learn more about plants and their care, find authoritative answers to gardening questions, join in discussions or live chats with other gardeners, read magazine articles, find information on garden catalogs or browse through online catalogs, do your shopping online, and just plain have fun browsing.

The World Wide Web

Way back in 1996, when we wrote the first edition of *Gardening For Dummies,* it was possible to offer a comprehensive listing of all gardening-related sites on the World Wide Web. Such sites numbered in the dozens. Now they number in the many thousands, and keeping track of them all is no longer possible.

In selecting Web sites for inclusion in this section, we looked for well-designed, well-maintained sites with substantial content and demonstrated staying power on the ever-growing Web.

For help getting started, check out *The Internet For Dummies,* 5th Edition, by John Levine, Carol Baroudi, and Margaret Levine Young; or *Netscape and the World Wide Web For Dummies,* 2nd Edition, by Paul Hoffman (both published by IDG Books Worldwide, Inc.).

Most (but not all) Internet addresses begin with the characters `http://`. But you can save a few keystrokes simply by beginning the address with "`www`" and letting your browser automatically add the `http://`. That's why in most of the addresses that follow we dropped the `http://`.

Where to look for answers

The secret to finding what you're looking for among the many millions of Web pages is knowing where to start. Are you looking for an authoritative answer to a specific gardening question? Illustrated plant information? Web sites on a particular topic? Regional information? Tips and tricks from fellow gardeners? It's all out there if you know how and where to look.

When should I divide my irises? Is fresh horse manure safe for my plants? How do I dry and store my herbs? Every week, gardeners around the country phone in thousands of questions like these to Cooperative Extension offices. State Cooperative Extensions Services are treasure troves of publications on a wide range of horticultural topics. Following is a sampling of Extension Service Web sites:

- *Factsheet Database* (Ohio State University). Check out the Web site at `www.hcs.ohio-state.edu/factsheet.html`. If every gardener could have only one bookmark, this would be it. OSU's specialized search engine searches only through the fact-filled publications of university and Cooperative Extension Web sites around the country.

- *Horticulture Solutions* (Illinois Cooperative Extension Service). Web site `www.ag.uiuc.edu/~robsond/solutions/hort.html`. Quick answers to common gardening questions; organized by topic. Includes a glossary.

If you've done some homework but still haven't found an answer and would like to ask a real live person, you can first try your local Cooperative Extension office. Many have a horticulture specialist on staff. A number of Web sites also offer question-and-answer services for free. But just as you wouldn't go out in the street and ask just anyone, don't go out on the Web and ask just anyone. The following Web site offers answers from professional horticulturists: National Gardening Association, `www2.garden.org/nga/ngaqua/home.html`.

If you are looking for Web sites on particular topics, a number of sites provide organized collections of links. Here are some of the best in terms of coverage and organization:

- **Dig the Net (Virtual Garden Toolshed),** `www.digthenet.com`. The considerable resources of Time Life are behind this well-organized site. Individual sites are briefly reviewed.

- **Gardening (Miningco),** `http://gardening.miningco.com/`. Unlike most sites that use frames to keep you on their site, Miningco has made it possible to bookmark other Web sites you visit.

- **GardenNet,** `www.gardennet.com/`. It's one of the oldest garden Web sites and contains book reviews, gardener roundtables, links to other garden sites, and links to many companies.

- **Internet Directory for Botany: Gardening,** `www.helsinki.fi/kmus/bothort.html`. All gardening Web sites are simply lumped under "Gardening," but this listing is still worth a visit. The collection is searchable.

- **LookSmart (AltaVista),** `www.looksmart.com`. Under Hobbies and Interests: Gardening, you will find a good selection of Web sites, each with a one- or two-line description.

- **The Garden Gate,** `www.prairienet.org/garden-gate`. One of the few remaining noncommercial directories, The Garden Gate offers gardeners and nature lovers a carefully selected and well-organized collection of links to informative and interesting horticulture sites around the world.

- **Yahoo!,** `www.yahoo.com/Recreation/Home_and_Garden/Gardening`. One of the oldest directories on the Web, Yahoo! organizes its listings by topic. Site owners provide brief descriptions of their own sites, and so a site's charms may be a bit overstated.

Global search engines like AltaVista, Infoseek, Hotbot, and Lycos can indeed find a needle in a haystack. The problem is that they will find all the needles in all the haystacks in the world. Then, it's up to you to find a needle in a needlestack. In other words, the more general your topic or search term, the more widely occurring it is and the harder it is going to be to zero in on the right information. Try searching for *gardening* and then for *air-layering* to see the difference.

Web search engines number in the hundreds, but the following are the largest and most extensive:

- ✔ **AltaVista,** www.altavista.digital.com. One nice feature of AltaVista is that you can enter natural language queries. For instance, "What is compost?" brings up pages that address that question.

- ✔ **Excite!** www.excite.com. The results of your search are ranked by relevance, with the most likely page presented first.

- ✔ **Hotbot,** www.hotbot.com. A dropdown menu of choices makes it easy to specify whether you are searching for an exact phrase, all, or any of the words you've entered.

- ✔ **Infoseek,** www.infoseek.com. An excellent Advanced Search page makes it easy for you to zero in on the information you're seeking.

- ✔ **Lycos,** www.lycos.com. In addition to offering a powerful search engine, Lycos also provides a selection of reviewed and rated Web sites covering a number of gardening topics. Look for Gardening under "Home/Family."

- ✔ **Yahoo!** www.yahoo.com. Yahoo!'s searchable directory is organized hierarchically by topic.

Each search engine uses its own unique search syntax. For example, a search for *horticulture therapy* at AltaVista returns a few hundred sites that discuss this topic, whereas Infoseek returns a list of over 1 million pages that contain either the word *horticulture* or the word *therapy*. Pick two or three search engines and take a little time to read through their online help and learn the syntax for each one. Your searches will be far more efficient if you speak the search language.

Plant information

Even experienced gardeners unwittingly kill plants by choosing the wrong plant and planting it the wrong place. Plant databases offer you something even the best plant book can't: the ability to select the right plants for a particular site based on a variety of criteria. Most databases let you search by a combination of criteria, such as USDA zone, soil type, light and water requirements, and soil pH, as well as flower and foliage color, blooming period, and special uses such as butterfly gardens or rock gardens. Databases generally provide color photos or botanical illustrations of plants along with information on their planting and care.

For information on CD-ROM databases that you can use on your own computer, see the section "Gardening Software" in this appendix.

- ✔ **Garden Encyclopedia,** www.sierra.com/sierrahome/gardening/encyc/. An online sampler of the *Sierra Garden Encyclopedia*. (See later under Gardening Software.)

✔ **Houseplant Pavilion** (Time Life), www.pathfinder.com/vg/timelife/houseplants. For help with selection and care of houseplants.

✔ **Interactive Plant List** (Ohio State University), www.hcs.ohio-state.edu/hort/plantlist.html. Search both the Plant Dictionary and the Factsheet Database for comprehensive information about a particular plant. Includes: annuals, bulbs, grasses, ground covers, perennials, shrubs, trees, and vines.

✔ **Plant Dictionary** (Ohio State University), www.hcs.ohio-state.edu/hcs/TMI/TR2/pmTOC.html. A searchable database of almost 3,000 high-quality images depicting ornamental plants and accompanying pests and diseases.

✔ **Plant Encyclopedia** (Time Life), www.pathfinder.com/cgi-bin/VG/vg. This searchable plant database features the lovely botanical illustrations by Allianora Rosse that have graced the pages of *The Time-Life Encyclopedia of Gardening* through many editions. (When the Time Life site was first being developed, the Web masters tracked down the original watercolors and saved them in the nick of time from an Indiana warehouse where they were about to be discarded.)

✔ **Plant Information Online** (University of Minnesota), plantinfo@jaws.umn.edu. This site lists mail-order sources of 60,000 plants, a detailed source information on 1,000 North American nursery and seed catalogs, and an index of 75,000 plant images. Access is to members only, $40 per individual.

For a more detailed look at finding answers, see The Garden Gate's Gardener's Guide to Finding Answers on the Internet, at www.prairienet.org/garden-gate/answers.htm online

Shopping

The true harbinger of spring isn't the robin. The true harbinger of spring is that first mail-order gardening catalog that always seems to arrive right around the winter solstice, just as the days are beginning to get longer again. The winter solstice may mark the first day of winter, but with the help of that catalog, the gardener is already thinking spring.

✔ **Barbara Barton's Gardening by Mail,** www.pathfinder.com/vg/gbm. A searchable collection of gardening catalogs from The High Priestess of Catalog Junkies, whose book *Gardening by Mail* (see "Where to Find It," earlier in this chapter) is a source for mail-order information.

✔ **Cyndi's Catalog of Catalogs,** www.cog.brown.edu/gardening/cat.html. Cyndi's catalog is organized by topic and comprises a collection of almost 2,000 mail-order sources for just about any gardening interest you can imagine.

✔ **Garden Escape,** www.garden.com. Although this site is very much aimed at selling you things, and its claim at being "the ultimate source for everything gardening" is a bit much, it is still worth a visit. If your Web browser is Java-capable, you can try your hand at online garden design.

✔ **Garden Solutions,** www.gardensolutions.com. This is the Web site of four well-known garden catalogs — Breck's Bulbs, Springhill Nursery, Stark Bros., and Vermont Wildflower Farm.

Many people naturally are concerned about the security of online credit card transactions. Electronic mail offers little security, so it is inadvisable to send credit card information via e-mail. Unless you are on a Web site with a secure server and feel confident that you are dealing with an established, reputable company, do not provide your credit card number or other personal information online. A secure server encrypts transmissions over the Internet, making it safer to send sensitive information. Most new Web browsers can detect when you are on a secure server. Watch for a blue border and a closed lock in the lower left-hand corner. When in doubt, however, do your mail-order shopping the old-fashioned way: via phone or postal mail.

A number of seed companies and mail-order nurseries have their catalogs online:

✔ **Association of Online Growers and Suppliers** (Garden Web), www.gardenweb.com/aogs.

✔ **Online Buyer's Guide** (National Gardening Association), www2.garden.org/nga/CENTER/home.html.

✔ **Online Gardening Catalogs** (Miningco.com), http://gardening.miningco.com/msub5.htm.

Some online catalogs you might enjoy browsing include the following:

✔ **Burpee Seeds,** garden.burpee.com.

✔ **The Cook's Garden,** www.cooksgarden.com.

✔ **Johnny's Selected Seeds,** www.johnnyseeds.com.

✔ **Shepherd's Seeds,** www.shepherdseeds.com.

✔ **Thompson and Morgan,** www.thompson-morgan.com.

✔ **Wayside Gardens,** www.waysidegardens.com

✔ **White Flower Farm,** www.whiteflowerfarm.com.

Just browsing

The Web also can be just plain fun, a pleasant entertainment on a chilly winter's afternoon. The following sites offer lots of useful information as well as some enjoyable bells and whistles.

- ✔ **Gardening at Miningco.com,** `http://gardening.miningco.com`. An informative mix of articles and well-organized collections of links on a wide range of gardening topics.

- ✔ **Horticulture Online,** `www.hortmag.com`. *Horticulture* magazine online. Articles, live chat, resources. Shares plant finder and online garden design with Garden Escape.

- ✔ **National Gardening Association,** `www2.garden.org/nga`. Includes more than 500 gardening articles in its searchable online library: `www.nga.nga.gendat.com/article.html`.

- ✔ **The Garden Web,** `www.gardenweb.com`. Garden forums, articles, directories of resources, calendar of gardening events.

- ✔ **Virtual Garden** (Time Life), `www.pathfinder.com/vg`. This site has a lot to offer and it's easy to get lost as you navigate. For an overview, check out the Virtual Garden At a Glance: `www.pathfinder.com/vg/ataglance`.

Discussion groups

The Internet offers many ways to communicate with your fellow gardeners. Newsgroups are like electronic bulletin boards. Anyone can post a message and anyone can read it.

Newsgroups

The following minitable lists newsgroups that are available to gardeners around the world:

`rec.gardens`	Gardening, methods, and results
`rec.gardens.ecosystems`	Ecosystems and organic gardening
`rec.gardens.edible`	Edible gardening topics
`rec.gardens.orchids`	Growing, hybridizing, and general care of orchids
`rec.gardens.roses`	Gardening information related to roses

In the past year or two, many new regional newsgroups have been springing up. You can check for newsgroups for your region at `liszt.bluemarble.net/news`, **Liszt's Usenet Newsgroups Directory.**

If you are unfamiliar with newsgroups and how they work, the easiest way to start is to use the newsreader that is part of your Web browser. (Newer versions of Netscape and Microsoft Internet Explorer have a newsreader built in.) Check with your Internet Service Provider (ISP), because you need to enter the name of their news server in your Web browser's setup before you start.

If checking out the discussion on a newsgroup or finding discussions on a given topic interests you, visit the searchable news archives at Deja News, www.dejanews.com. If you have some time on your hands, you can also browse the newsgroups: www.dejanews.com/home_bg.shtml.

Most ISPs carry only a subset of all the newsgroups that are available. If you find a newsgroup that interests you, most ISPs will add an existing newsgroup upon request. Be sure to give the full name of the newsgroup in your request.

Mailing lists

Electronic mailing lists are growing steadily in popularity as a way for groups of like-minded people to discuss topics of mutual interest. Mailing lists come in many flavors: open forums; moderated lists where a moderator approves each post before being distributed to the subscribers; and one-way lists used for announcements and newsletters. A good mailing list can develop into a friendly community with people sharing information on a favorite topic.

Programs called *mailing lists managers* (MLMs) run electronic mailing lists, which run on the list host. You may encounter different brand names such as listserv, listproc, majordomo, or smartlist. The MLM automatically handles tasks such as distributing messages to subscriber lists and adding and deleting subscribers upon request. Each list has a human list owner. The list owner is responsible for managing the list and providing assistance to list subscribers. The list owner often is the person who has the last word on list policy.

If you aren't already in the habit of checking your e-mail regularly, you may be better off with newsgroups and other online discussion forums. A busy mailing list can pile up unwanted messages in your mailbox pretty quickly.

When you first subscribe to a mailing list, you will receive a welcome message. Save this message for future reference. It will usually give the list's purpose and scope, posting guidelines, and the list owner's address, as well as information on unsubscribing or changing your list setting.

If you prefer to receive list mail as a single larger post, check your welcome file for instructions on how to set your setting to "digest."

Be aware that some lists, especially general-interest ones, can generate very high volume, delivering over a hundred messages a day.

If you are new to mailing lists, check out the Introduction to Mailing Lists (Liszt.com), www.liszt.com/intro.html. You'll find lists of mailing lists at the following sites:

✔ **Mailing Lists for Gardeners** (The Garden Gate),`www.prairienet.org/` `garden-gate/maillist.htm`. Choose from a selection of established mailing lists from A for Alpine to W for Woody Plants.

✔ **Publicly Accessible Mailing Lists,** `www.neosoft.com/internet/` `paml/`. Lists are organized alphabetically and by topic. Look for lists under gardening, botany, and horticulture:

```
www.neosoft.com/internet/paml/bysubj-gardening.html
www.neosoft.com/internet/paml/bysubj-botany.html
www.neosoft.com/internet/paml/bysubj-horticulture.html
```

✔ **Liszt, the mailing list directory,** `www.liszt.com`.

New mailing lists come online every day. Liszt offers a searchable database of tens of thousands of lists.

Web forums and live chat

Some live chat sites are open around the clock. Some are open only for specially scheduled chats by gardening experts.

✔ **GardenWeb Forums,** `www.gardenweb.com/forums`. GardenWeb offers dozens of Web-based discussion forums on a wide variety of garden topics.

✔ **Gardentown,** `www.gardentown.com`. Several forums, as well as live Web-based chat.

✔ **Compuserve and AOL.** If you are a member of AOL or Compuserve, you can take advantage of members-only forums offered by these services. Forums also host chats with gardening experts and celebrities.

✔ **Live Chat at Miningco.com,** `http://gardening.miningco.com/` `mpchat.htm`.

✔ **Virtual Garden Chat,** `www.pathfinder.com/vg/Info/Chats/`.

New forums and chats are popping up every month. Forum One keeps track of them in a searchable database: `www.forumone.com`.

Gardening software

The last few years have seen a proliferation of gardening software programs, which fall into three categories:

✔ Garden design

✔ Plant selection and care

✔ Troubleshooting

Be familiar with your computer's configuration, its processor type and speed, hard-disk size, amount of memory, sound and video capability, and CD-ROM drive speed. Always check its configuration against the requirements of a particular software program before you buy to be sure you can run the program you're buying.

Gardening software programs probably number in the hundreds by now. We selected a few programs in each category that are suitable for beginning gardeners.

Garden design software

Design programs naturally are going to be graphical, allowing you to lay out your garden plan. Additional information is available for each of the programs from the company Web sites.

Plant graphics can be the abstract symbols used by landscape architects, more colorful symbols that look more like the plant they represent, or even photographic representations of plants.

- ✔ **Flowerscape** (Windows, Macintosh), Voudette Software, `www.fscape.com`. Flowerscape is an attractive and easy-to-use program that uses photo-real images of plants. The layout interface is clear and straightforward. You can easily master the program without referring to the documentation. Some satisfied users report that their small children play with it, calling it "the flower game."

  The searchable plant database is relatively limited but contains a good selection of plants that you would expect to find at your neighborhood garden center. A seasonal feature lets you see how the garden will look through the year, so you can plant a garden with year-round interest! If you have a newer computer, Flowerscape does have a drawback in that it requires you to step down your color display to 256 colors.

- ✔ **LandDesigner 3D** (Windows 95), Sierra Online, `www.sierra.com`. LandDesigner is a far more full-featured program than Flowerscape, with an extensive plant database provided by White Flower Farm. Because of its relative complexity, however, mastering this software fully requires a time commitment, and for that reason we don't recommend it for the beginning computer user. If you are familiar with other drawing programs, LandDesigner may appeal to you for its flexibility and wide range of built-in symbols for trees, shrubs, flowers, and vegetables, as well as "hardscaping" like walls, ponds, patios, fences, and so on. Like many graphics-intensive programs, LandDesigner can be temperamental. The 3-D feature in particular does not work reliably, even on a high-end computer.

Plant selection and care

Both of these programs offer searchable plant databases with color photos of plants and information on their care:

- ✔ **Garden Companion** (Windows 3.1, Windows 95), Lifestyle Software Group, www.lifeware.com/catalog.

- ✔ **Garden Encyclopedia** (Windows 95), Sierra Online, www.sierra.com.

Troubleshooting

One of the keys to good gardening is learning how to nip problems in the bud, so to speak. An excellent resource is Ortho's Home Gardening Problem Solver (Windows 95, with book). The CD-ROM comes with the book but also is sold separately. It's available from www.ortho.com/content/books.

Gardening software is available from a number of sources, as well as direct from the companies via their Web pages. A few reliable mail-order and Internet sources for gardening software include:

- ✔ PC Connection, www.pcconnection.com, 800-800-0009.

- ✔ Computer Discount Warehouse, www.cdw.com, 800-840-4239.

- ✔ Amazon.com, www.amazon.com.

- ✔ Retailers such as Best Buy and Office Depot often carry gardening titles.

If you are looking for a particular gardening resource online and haven't been able to find it, check out The Garden Gate's "Gardener's Guide to Finding Answers on the Internet," www.prairienet.org/garden-gate/answers.htm.

If you're still striking out, you're welcome to e-mail The Garden Gate at garden-gate@prairienet.org. Please identify yourself as a reader of *Gardening For Dummies,* 2nd Edition. Due to time constraints, we can't answer actual gardening questions but will be happy to try to help you find online gardening resources.

Appendix B
Mail-Order Resources

• •

More than any other type of garden literature, seed and nursery catalogs inspire, cajole, inform, enthuse, sell, and, in general overflow with the sometimes singular plant passions of their owners.

Of course those of us lucky enough to live near a home center or a great garden center can find just about everything we need to make and keep a garden. And buying locally has one significant virtue: Plants are more likely to be better adapted to your climate. Another plus is if you have problems with the plant, you can take it back to the nursery. Even the biggest home store in the biggest city, however, cannot match the variety of plants and products available through the resources below.

Catalog and online shopping are essential for gardeners who live in remote areas or for those who seek a plant or product that isn't mainstream — and those products include most of the nifty stuff that makes gardens and gardening fun. If you're looking for something special, you'll love the companies in this appendix.

Even though we think most catalogs make great reading, we assembled this descriptive listing so that you can quickly find what you're looking for. First we created categories, such as "Bulbs" and "Flowers and Vegetables," to narrow choices. We also provide brief descriptions of the company and products, enough hopefully to steer you right toward what you need. Want to make sure to have vegetable varieties adapted to your area? Try Kilgore's Florida Planting Guide (Florida and Gulf Coast), Johnny's Selected Seeds (northeast), or Territorial Seed Company (northwest). Or what about antique varieties of apples? Organic seeds? Check out Seeds of Change and Territorial Seed Co., or go straight to Sonoma Antique Apple Nursery.

Beyond the hundreds of mail-order gardening suppliers that appear in this appendix, still more exist. You can find sources for gardening products (including seeds, bulbs, plants, tools, supplies, and accessories) by visiting the Mailorder Gardening Association Web site. For a copy of the MGA's Garden Catalog Guide, which contains descriptions of more than 125 gardening catalogs and magazines, send a $2 check or money order to Mailorder Gardening Association, Dept. GFD, P.O. Box 2129, Columbia, MD 21045.

Note: In the lists that follow, we indicate which suppliers charge a fee to send a catalog. Most refund the catalog cost with your first order. If we don't list a fee, then the catalog is free.

Bulbs

Antonelli Brothers Begonia Gardens, 2545 Capitola Rd., Santa Cruz, CA 95062; phone 408-475-5222; fax 408-475-7066; Web site www.infopoint.com/sc/market/antnelli. Antonelli Brothers is one of the largest retail growers of tuberous begonias in North America.

Breck's, 6523 N. Galena Rd., Peoria, IL 61656-1757; phone 800-722-9069; fax 800-996-2852; Web site www.gardensolutions.com. Breck's features bulbs direct from Holland.

Brent & Becky's Bulbs, 7463 Heath Trail, Gloucester, VA 23061; phone 804-693-3966; fax 804-693-9436; Web site www.brentandbeckysbulbs.com. This third-generation bulb grower offers several special varieties.

Caladium World, Box 629, Sebring, FL 33871; phone 941-385-7661; fax 941-385-5836. Caladium World offers more than 20 varieties of fancy strap- and dwarf-leaf varieties.

Connell's Dahlias, 10616 Waller Rd. E., Tacoma, WA 98446; phone 206-531-0292; fax 206-536-7725. Catalog $2. Choose from more than 350 varieties from this dahlia specialist.

Cooley's Gardens Inc., Box 126, Silverton, OR 97381; phone 800-225-5391; fax 503-873-5812; Web site www.cooleysgardens.com. Catalog $5. The world's largest iris nursery offers more than 400 varieties of bearded iris.

Cruickshank's Inc., 780 Birchmount Rd., Unit 16, Scarborough, Ontario, Canada M1K 5H4; phone 800-665-5605; fax 416-750-8522. Cruickshank's is Canada's leading bulb and rare plant specialist.

Dutch Gardens, Box 200, Adelphia, NJ 07710; phone 800-818-3861; fax 732-780-7720. This company offers more than 200 varieties of flower bulbs at close to wholesale prices.

John Scheepers, 23 Tulip Dr., Bantam, CT 06750; phone 860-567-0838; fax 860-567-5323; Web site www.johnscheepers.com. John Scheepers sells tulips, daffodils, allium, lilies, amaryllis, and hard-to-find bulbs.

McClure & Zimmerman, 108 W. Winnebago, Box 368, Friesland, WI 53935; phone 800-883-6998 or 920-326-4220; fax 800-692-5864; Web site www.mzbulb.com. You can find a wide selection of spring- and autumn-blooming bulbs at this company.

Michigan Bulb Co., 1950 Waldorf N.W., Grand Rapids, MI 49550, phone 616-453-5401; fax 616-735-2628; Web site www.gardensolutions.com. Order bulbs, perennials, and horticultural products from this gardening mainstay.

Roozengaarde, 1587 Beaver Marsh Rd., Mt. Vernon, WA 98273; phone 800-732-3266; fax 360-424-3113; Web site www.tulips.com. Roozengaarde offers top-quality tulips, daffodils, irises, and more.

Schipper and Company USA, Box 7584, Greenwich, CT 06836; phone 888-TIP-TOES; fax 203-862-8909; Web site www.colorblends.com. Catalog $1. Order classic color combinations of tulips from this company.

Swan Island Dahlias, Box 700, Canby, OR 97013; phone 503-266-7711; fax 503-266-8768. Catalog $3. Swan Island offers more than 250 varieties of dahlias.

Van Bourgondien Brothers, 245 Farmingdale Rd., Box 1000, Babylon, NY 11702; phone 800-622-9997 (orders) or 800-622-9959 (customer service); fax 516-669-1228; Web site www.dutchbulbs.com. Van Bourgondien Brothers imports and distributes bulbs and perennials.

Van Dyck's Flower Farms, Inc., Box 430, Brightwaters, NY 11718-0403; phone 800-248-2852; fax 516-669-3518. Order quality Dutch bulbs and perennials from this grower.

Veldheer Tulip Garden, 12755 Quincy St., Holland, MI 49424-9259, phone 616-399-1900; fax 616-399-1270; Web site www.veldheertulip.com. Veldheer offers more than 2,000 top quality domestic and imported bulbs, roots, and perennials.

Flowers and Vegetables

Abundant Life Seed Foundation, Box 772, Port Townsend, WA 98368; phone 360-385-5660; Web site http://csf.colorado.edu/perma/abundant/index.html. Contact these specialists for heirloom, open-pollinated varieties of vegetables.

Bethlehem Seed Co., P.O. Box 1351, Bethlehem, PA 18018; phone 610-954-5443; Web site www.bethlehemseed.com. You can choose from broad selections of vegetables and flower seeds at inexpensive prices.

W. Atlee Burpee & Co., 300 Park Ave., Warminster, PA 18974; phone 800-888-1447; fax 800-487-5530; Web site www.burpee.com. This granddaddy of gardening sells a wide selection of flower and vegetable seeds and supplies.

Bountiful Gardens, 18001 Shafer Ranch Rd., Willits, CA 95490; phone or fax 707-459-6410; e-mail bountiful@zapcom.net. Bountiful Gardens, a nonprofit entity, specializes in untreated, unusual varieties of vegetables, cover crops, herbs, and grains. It sells no hybrids.

Burrell Seed Co., Box 150, Rocky Ford, CO 81067; phone 719-254-3318; fax 719-254-3319. Burrell Seed has a complete line of vegetables, and specializes in cantaloupes and watermelons.

The Cook's Garden, Box 535, Londonderry, VT 05148; phone 800-457-9703; fax 800-547-9705; Web site www.cooksgarden.com. You can choose from a wide selection of culinary vegetables, herbs, and flowers, including European and hard-to-find salad greens.

William Dam Seeds, Box 8400, Dundas, Ontario, Canada L9H 6M1; phone 905-628-6641; fax 905-627-1729. This company has a full line of vegetable, flower, and wildflower seeds and some products for northern gardeners.

DeGiorgi Seed Co., 6011 'N' St., Omaha, NE 68117-1634; phone 800-858-2580; fax 402-731-8475. DeGiorgi offers a full line of vegetables, flowers, herbs, and grasses.

Dill's Atlantic Giant Pumpkins, Howard Dill, 400 College Rd., Windsor, Nova Scotia, Canada B0N 2T0; phone 902-798-2728. You can buy seed for the world's largest pumpkins, such as 'Atlantic Giant' and other varieties.

Dixondale Farms, P.O. Box 127, 2007 N. 1st St., Carrizo Springs, TX 78834; phone 830-876-2430; fax 888-876-9640. Dixondale Farms specializes in sweet-onion plants.

Evergreen Y.H. Enterprises, P.O. Box 17538, Anaheim, CA 92817; phone and fax 714-637-5769; e-mail wshwang@aol.com. This company specializes in Asian vegetables.

Fedco Seeds, P.O. Box 520, Waterville, ME 04903-0520; phone 207-873-7333. Fedco offers a full line of vegetables, including a good selection of potatoes. The company also sells books, tools, and garden products.

Ferry-Morse Seeds, Box 488, Fulton, KY 42041; phone 800-283-6400; fax 800-283-2700; Web site www.ferry-morse.com. Ferry-Morse sells a wide selection of un-treated hybrid and nonhybrid seeds.

Heirloom Seeds, P.O. Box 245, W. Elizabeth, PA 15088-0245; Catalog $1. This small company specializes in heirloom seeds.

Henry Field's Seed & Nursery Co., 415 North Burnett St., Shenandoah, IA 51601-1063; phone 605-665-9391; fax 605-665-2601. This company offers a complete line of vegetables, flowers, and fruit trees, plus growing aids and supplies.

High Altitude Gardens, P.O. Box 1048, Hailey, ID 83333-1048; phone 208-788-4363; fax 208-788-3452, Web site www.seedsave.org. You can choose from more than 180 varieties of open-pollinated vegetables for high-altitude gardens. High Altitude Gardens also has a good selection of Russian heirloom tomatoes, herbs, flowers, and tools.

Filaree Farm, 182 Conconully Hwy., Okanogan, WA 98840; phone 509-422-6940. Catalog $2. Filaree Farm offers more than 350 varieties of garlic.

Fragrant Path, Box 328, Fort Calhoun, NE 68023. Catalog $2. You can find seeds of fragrant, rare, and old-fashioned plants at Fragrant Path.

Garden City Seeds, 778 Hwy. 93 N., Hamilton, MT 59840; phone 406-961-4837; fax 406-961-4877; e-mail gcseeds@aol.com or gdnctysd@cyberport.net. Garden City sells a wide selection of seeds, and specializes in open-pollinated, short-season vegetable seeds.

Gurney Seed and Nursery Company, 110 Capital St., Yankton, SD 57079; phone 605-665-1930; fax 605-665-9718. This is a full-line seed and nursery catalog.

Harris Seeds, 60 Saginaw Dr., Box 22960, Rochester, NY 14692-2960; phone 800-514-4441; fax 716-442-9386; Web site www.harrisseeds.com. Harris Seeds offers vegetable and flower seeds and gardening accessories.

Johnny's Selected Seeds, Foss Hill Rd., RR1, Box 2580, Albion, ME 04910; phone 207-437-4301; fax 800-437-4290; Web site www.johnnyseeds.com. Find top quality vegetable, herb, and flower seeds and other accessories at Johnny's Selected Seeds. It also specializes in seeds for shorter growing seasons.

J.W. Jung Seed Co., 335 S. High St., Randolph, WI 53957; phone 800-247-5864; fax 800-692-5864; Web site www.jungseed.com. Wide selection of garden plants, seeds, and products.

Kilgore Seed Co., 1400 W First St., Sanford, FL 32771, phone 407-323-6630. Kilgore Seed sells a complete line of vegetable and flower seeds for Florida and the Gulf Coast, as well as garden supplies and tools.

Liberty Seed Company, 461 Robinson Rd., New Philadelphia, OH 44663-0806; phone 800-541-6022; fax 330-364-6415; Web site www.libertyseed.com. Liberty Seed sells more than 1,000 varieties of annual and perennial flowers and vegetables.

Lockhart Seeds Inc., P.O. Box 1361, Stockton, CA 95205; phone 209-466-4401. Lockhart offers a full line of vegetable and cover crops seeds, especially varieties adapted for California.

Native Seeds/SEARCH, 526 North 4th Ave., Tucson, AZ 85705; phone 520-622-5561; fax 520-622-5591; Web site http://desert.net/seeds. Contact this specialist if you're seeking Native American varieties of vegetables adapted to the desert Southwest.

Nichols Garden Nursery Inc., 1190 N. Pacific Hwy., Albany, OR 97321-4598; phone 541-928-9280; fax 541-967-8406; Web site www.gardennursery.com. This company offers Asian and unusual vegetables and herbs.

Nourse Farms, Inc., 41 River Rd., South Deerfield, MA 01373; phone 413-665-2658; Web site www.noursefarms.com. You can find a good selection of small fruits and asparagus at this company.

Park Seed Co., 1 Parkton Ave., Greenwood, SC 29647; phone 800-845-3369; fax 800-275-9941; Web site www.parkseed.com. The park Seed Company sells more than 1,800 kinds of bulbs and seeds.

The Pepper Gal, Box 23006, Ft. Lauderdale, FL 33307-3006. Catalog $2. Phone 954-537-5540; fax 954-566-2208. The Pepper Gal offers more than 250 varieties of sweet and hot peppers.

Piedmont Plant Co., Box 424, Albany, GA 31702; phone 800-541-5185; fax 912-432-2888; e-mail piedmont@surfsouth.com. Choose from a wide selection of field-grown vegetable transplants.

Pinetree Garden Seeds, Box 300, New Gloucester, ME 04260; phone 207-926-3400; fax 888-527-3337; e-mail superseeds@worldnet.att.net; Web site www.superseeds.com. Pinetree sells more than 800 varieties of seeds, and also offers tools and books.

Redwood City Seeds, Box 361, Redwood City, CA 94064; phone 650-325-7333; Web site www.batnet.com/rwc-seed/.

Ronniger's Seed & Potatoes Co., Box 307, Ellensburg, WA 98926; phone 509-925-6025; Web site www.angelfire.com/biz2/ronnigers/index.html. At Ronniger's, you can find more than 60 varieties of potatoes, plus garlic, onions, and horseradish.

Santa Barbara Heirloom Nursery, P.O. Box 4235, Santa Barbara, CA 93140; phone 805-968-5444; fax 805-562-1248; Web site www.silcom.com/heirloom/index.html. This nursery offers a wide selection of heirloom vegetable varieties, sold and shipped as transplants.

Seed Dreams, P.O. Box 1476, Santa Cruz, CA 95061-1476; phone 408-458-9252. This small company specializes in heirloom vegetables and grains.

Seed Savers Heritage Farm, 3076 North Winn Rd., Decorah, IA 52101; phone 319-382-5990; fax 319-382-5872. Seed Savers has a good selection of heirloom vegetable varieties from the United States and U.S. and Europe. It is associated with the largest, nonprofit, group seed saving organization in the United States Seed Savers Exchange.

Seeds Blüm, HC 33, Idaho City Stage, Boise, ID 83706; phone 800-528-3658; Web site www.seedsblum.com. This company is a pioneer in the rediscovery and development of heirloom, open-pollinated vegetable varieties.

Seeds of Change, Box 15700, Santa Fe, NM 87506-5700; phone 888-762-7333; fax 505-438-7052; Web site www.seedsofchange.com. Seeds of Change sells organic, open-pollinated vegetable, flower, and herb seeds.

Select Seeds Antique Flowers, 180 Stickney Rd., Union, CT 06076; phone 860-684-9310; fax 860-684-9224; Web site www.selectseeds.com. Catalog $1. The company sells vintage flowers for color or cutting and vines for arbors.

Seymour's Selected Seeds, Dept. 92, Box 1346, Sussex, VA 23884-0346; phone 803-663-9771; fax 803-663-9772. Seymour's sells seeds from cottage garden plants from England.

Shepherd's Garden Seeds, 30 Irene St., Torrington, CT 06790; phone 860-482-3638; fax 860-482-0532; Web site www.sheperdseeds.com. The catalog features European and Asian gourmet vegetables, herbs, recipes, and old-fashioned flower varieties.

R. H. Shumway's, Box 1, Graniteville, SC 29829; phone 803-663-7271. Shumway's has a wide selection of vegetable seeds.

Southern Exposure Seed Exchange, Box 170, Earlysville, VA 22936; phone 804-973-4703; fax 804-973-8717; Web site www.southernexposure.com. Catalog $2. You can choose from more than 500 varieties of heirloom and traditional vegetables, flowers, and herbs.

Stokes Seeds, Inc., Box 548, Buffalo, NY 14240; phone 800-263-7233, fax 905-684-8411; Web site www.stokeseeds.com. The catalog has a complete listing of flower and vegetable seeds, including cultural information.

Sunrise Enterprises, P.O. Box 1960, Chesterfield, VA 23832. Catalog $2. Phone 804-796-5796; fax 804-796-6735, http://commercial.visi.net/sunrise/. Sunrise specializes in Asian vegetable seeds.

Territorial Seed Co., Box 157, Cottage Grove, OR 97424; phone 541-942-9547; fax 888-657-3131; Web site www.territorial-seed.com. Contact Territorial Seed if you need vegetable, herb, and flower seeds — including varieties suited to the Pacific Northwest and Canada.

Thompson & Morgan Seed Co., Box 1308, Jackson, NJ 08527-0308; phone 800-274-7333; fax 888-466-4769; Web site www.thompson-morgan.com. Thompson & Morgan offers a wide selection of rare and unusual flower and vegetable seeds.

Tomato Growers Supply Co., Box 2237, Fort Myers, FL 33902; phone 941-768-1119; fax 941-768-3476. Choose from more than 375 kinds of tomatoes and peppers.

Totally Tomatoes, Dept. 84, Box 1626, Augusta, GA 30903; phone 803-663-0016; fax 803-663-9772. This company sells more than 350 varieties of tomatoes and peppers.

Vermont Bean Seed Company, 32 Garden Ln., Fair Haven, VT 05743; phone 800-345-5977. The selection includes more than 100 varieties of beans, plus other vegetable seeds.

Vesey's Seed Ltd., Box 9000, Charlottetown, Prince Edward Island, Canada C1A 8K6; phone 800-363-7333; fax 800-686-0329; Web site www.veseys.com. Vesey's wide selection of vegetable and flower seeds are adapted for short growing season conditions.

Wild Garden Seeds, Shoulder to Shoulder Farm, Box 1509, Philomath, OR 97370. Catalog $4. Phone 541-929-4068. Choose from a selection of vegetables and insect-attracting plants bred on the farm.

Willhite Seed Inc., Box 23, Poolville, TX 76487; phone 800-828-1840; fax 817-599-5843; Web site www.willhiteseed.com. Willhite specializes in melon seeds plus all types of vegetable seeds, with varieties from France and India. Seeds are available in small packets or bulk.

Wood Prairie Farm, RFD 1, 164, Bridgewater, ME 04375; phone 800-829-9765. Wood Prairie offers a wide selection of potato varieties.

Herbs

Al's Farm, Box 1282, Crystal Beach, TX 77650; fax 409-684-8201. This company's selections include herb, spice, and pepper seeds.

Companion Plants, 7247 N. Coolville Ridge Rd., Athens, OH 45701; phone 614-592-4643. Catalog $3. You can choose from a wide selection of plants and seeds.

Hole's Greenhouse and Gardens, 101 Bellerose Dr., St. Albert, Alberta T8N 8N8, Canada; phone 403-419-6800; fax 403-459-6042; Web site www.telusplanet.net-public-holes or www.icangarden.com/holes.htm. Hole's offers herbs, vegetables, ornamental grasses, and more.

Miles Estate Herb & Berry Farm, 4308 Marthaler Rd. NE, Woodburn, OR 97071; phone 888-810-0196; fax 503-792-3899; Web site www.herbs-spices-flowers.com. Miles Estate sells high-quality herbs, dried herbs, exotic plants, and gifts.

Rasland Farms, NC 82 at US 13, Godwin, NC 28344; phone 910-567-2705. Catalog $3. The selections include herb plants and products for potpourri, teas, and baths.

Richters Herb Company, Goodwood, ONT LOC 1AO, Canada; phone 905-640-6677; Web site www.richters.com. You can choose from an extensive selection of herb seeds, plants, books, and products.

The Rosemary House and Gardens, 120 S. Market St., Mechanicsburg, PA 17055; phone 717-697-5111, e-mail rosemaryhs@aol.com. Catalog $3. The Rosemary House sells everything for and about herbs.

Sandy Mush Herb Nursery, 316 Surrett Cove Rd., Leicester, NC 28748-9622; phone 704-683-2014. Catalog $4. This company offers unusual culinary herbs and fragrant and native plants.

The Thyme Garden, 20546-N Alsea Hwy., Alsea, OR 97324; phone 541-487-8671. Catalog $2. You can select from more than 460 varieties of herb seeds and plants.

Well-Sweep Herb Farm, 205 Mt. Bethel Rd., Port Murray, NJ 07865; phone 908-852-5390. Catalog $2. This source offers unusual and old-fashioned herbs and flowering perennials.

Fruits and Berries

Brittingham Plant Farms, P.O. Box 2538, Salisbury, MD 21801; phone 410-749-5153; fax 800-749-5148. This grower offers more than 25 varieties of certified, virus-free strawberry plants. It also has blueberries, asparagus, raspberries (four colors), blackberries, and grapes.

Hartman's Plant Co., Box 100, Lacota, MI 49063; phone 616-253-4281. Hartman's specialty is blueberries.

Indiana Berry & Plant Co., 5218 W. 500 South, Huntingburg, IN 47542; phone 800-295-2226; fax 812-683-2004. The name says it all: Strawberries, blueberries, raspberries, blackberries, rhubarb, asparagus, and grapes.

Ison's Nursery & Vineyards, 6855 Newnan Hwy., Brooks, GA 30205; phone 800-733-0324; fax 770-599-6970. You can choose Mucho muscadines (grapes for warmer climates), plus dozens of other fruits, large and small.

Lawson's Nursery, 2730 Yellow Creek Rd., Ball Ground, GA 30107; phone 770-893-2141. Lawson's grows a wide selection of apples, cherries, peaches, pears, and plums.

Lewis Strawberry Nursery, Inc., 3500 Hwy 133, Rocky Point, NC 28457; phone 800-453-5346; fax 910-602-3106. This nursery has 30 million scientifically grown strawberry plants inspected by the North Carolina State University.

Miller Nurseries, 5060 West Lake Rd., Canandaigua, NY 14424; phone 800-836-9630; fax 716-396-2154; Web site www.millernurseries.com. Miller has a complete selection of fruiting plants, including many varieties of antique dwarf apples.

Northwoods Retail Nursery, 27635 S. Oglesby Rd., Canby, OR 97013; phone 503-266-5432; fax 503-266-5431. The catalog includes unique fruits and ornamentals.

One Green World, 28696 S. Cramer Road, Molalla, OR 97038; phone 503-651-3005; fax 800-418-9983. One Green World sells unique fruiting and ornamental plants from around the world. It specializes in hardy plants from Russia and Eastern Europe.

Pacific Tree Farms, 4301 Lynwood Dr., Chula Vista, CA 91910; phone 619-422-2400. Catalog $2. You can choose from an extensive collection of citrus, other exotic fruit plants, and rare and unusual trees and shrubs.

Raintree Nursery, 391 Butts Rd., Morton, WA 98356; phone 360-496-6400; fax 360-496-6465; Web site www.raintreenursery.com. Raintree offers fruits, nuts, berries, bamboo, and unusual edibles.

Sonoma Antique Apple Nursery, 4395 Westside Rd., Healdsburg, CA 95448; phone 707-433-6420, fax 707-433-6479, e-mail tuyt20b@prodigy.com.. Sonoma offers a wide selection of heirloom apples.

Stark Bro's. Nursery, Box 10, Louisiana, MO 63353; phone 800-325-4180; fax 573-754-5290; Web site www.starkbros.com. This nursery offers fruit trees and landscape plants.

Womacks Nursery, Rt. 1, Box 80, DeLeon, TX 76444-9631; phone 817-893-6497; fax 817-893-3400. Check out Womacks' fruit and pecan trees.

Perennial and Specialist Plants

Ambergate Gardens, 8015 Krey Ave., Waconia, MN 55387-9616; phone 612-443-2248; fax 612-443-2248. Catalog $2. You can choose from many new hardy perennials.

Andre Viette Farm & Nursery, Rt. 1, Box 16, Fishersville, VA 22939; phone 540-943-2315; fax 540-943-0782. Catalog/resource guide/landscaping kit $5. This resource sells top perennials from around the world.

B&D Lilies, Box 2007, Port Townsend, WA 98368; phone 360-385-1738; fax 360-385-9996; Web site www.bdlilies.com. Choose spectacular blooms from North America's largest garden lily supplier.

Bluestone Perennials, 7211 Middle Ridge Rd., Madison, OH 44057; phone 800-852-5243; fax 440-428-7198; Web site www.bluestoneperennials.com. Bluestone offers more than 800 perennials.

Busse Gardens, 5873 Oliver Ave. S.W., Cokato, MN 55321-4229; phone 612-286-2654; fax 612-286-6601. Catalog $2. Busse Gardens offers cold-hardy and unusual perennials and native plants.

Carroll Gardens, 444 East Main St., Box 310, Westminster, MD 21158; phone 800-638-6334 or 410-876-7336; fax 410-857-4112. Catalog $3. Carroll Gardens offers a wide selection of rare and unusual perennials, herbs, vines, roses, and shrubs.

Davidson-Wilson Greenhouse, Inc., Department 10, Rural Route 2, Box 168, Crawfordsville, IN 47933-9426; phone 765-364-0556; fax 800-276-3691; Web site www.davidson-wilson.com. Davidson-Wilson is a specialist in scented geraniums, and sells succulents, begonias, and other plants.

Gilson Gardens, 3059 Rt. 20, Box 277, Perry, OH 44081; phone 216-259-4845; fax 216-259-2378. Gibson Gardens sells perennials, ornamental grasses, and ground covers.

Goodwin Creek Gardens, Box 83, Williams, OR 97544; phone 541-846-7357; fax 541-846-7357. Catalog $1. Goodwin Creek offers herbs, everlastings, scented geraniums, plants, and seeds that attract hummingbirds and butterflies.

Heronswood Nursery, Ltd., 7530 N.E. 288th St., Kingston, WA 98346; phone 360-297-4172; fax 360-297-8321; Web site www.heronswood.com. Catalog $4. Heronswood offers rare and hard-to-find trees, shrubs, vines, and perennials.

Klehm Nursery, 4210 N. Duncan Rd., Champaign, IL 61821; phone 800-553-3715; fax 217-373-8403; Web site www.klehm.com. This nursery specializes in peonies.

Kurt Bluemel, 2740 Greene Ln., Baldwin, MD 21013-9523; phone 410-557-7229. Catalog $3. Contact Kurt Bluemel for bamboo, ferns, ornamental grasses, perennials, and water plants.

Logee's Greenhouses, 141 North St., Danielson, CT 06239; phone 888-330-8038; Web site www.logees.com. Logee's offers a wide variety of rare and specialist exotic plants.

Milaeger's Gardens, 4838 Douglas Ave., Racine, WI 53402-2498; phone 800-669-9956 or 414-639-2371. Catalog $1. Milaeger's sells many varieties of hostas, daylilies, and other perennials.

Northstar Nurseries, Inc., 13450 Willandale Road, Rogers, MN 55374-9585; phone 612-428-7601. Northstar specializes in daylilies for the northern gardener.

Peter Paul's Nurseries, 4665 Chapin Road, Canandaigua, NY 14424-8713; phone 716-394-7397; fax 716-394-4122; Web site www.peterpauls.com. Check out this nursery for carnivorous plants, seeds, supplies, and live sphagnum moss.

Shady Oaks Nursery, 112 10th Ave. S.E., Waseca, MN 56093; phone 800-504-8006; fax 507-835-8772. This nursery specializes in hostas and other shade perennials.

Southern Perennials & Herbs, 98 Bridges Rd., Tylertown, MS 39667; phone 800-774-0079; Web site www.s-p-h.com.

Spring Hill Nurseries, 6523 N. Galena Rd., Peoria, IL 61656; phone 800-582-8527; fax 800-991-2852; Web site www.gardensolutions.com. Spring Hill offers perennials, roses, shrubs, and vines.

Stokes Tropicals, Box 9868, New Iberia, LA 70562; phone 800-624-9706; fax 318-365-6991; Web site www.stokestropicals.com. Stokes offers an extensive collection of bananas, heliconias, plumerias, bromeliads, and other exotics.

Teas Nursery Company, Inc., P.O. Box 1603, Bellaire, TX 77402; phone 800-446-7723 or 664-4400 X211; fax (713) 295-5170; Web site www.teasnursery.com. Teas Nursery grows orchids and other exotic plants. It has a complete supply catalog, including a full range of hard-to-get specialty items.

Wayside Gardens, 1 Garden Lane, Hodges, SC 29695-0001; phone 800-845-1124; fax 800-457-9712; Web site www.waysidegardens.com. Wayside has bulbs, perennials, roses, trees, and shrubs.

Weiss Brothers Nursery, 11690 Colfax Hwy., Grass Valley, CA 95945; 916-272-7657; fax 916-272-3578. Check out Weiss Brothers' more than 400 varieties of perennials and herbs.

White Flower Farm, Box 50, Litchfield, CT 06759-0050; phone 800-503-9624; fax 860-496-1418; Web site www.whiteflowerfarm.com. This lavishly illustrated catalog includes more than 700 varieties of annuals, perennials, bulbs, and shrubs.

Roses

Antique Rose Emporium, 9300 Lueckemeyer Rd., Brenham, TX 77833; phone 800-441-0002; fax 409-836-0928. This specialist offers easy-to-grow old garden roses.

Arena Rose Co., Box 3096, Paso Robles, CA 93447; phone 805-227-4094. Arena carries old-fashioned and heritage roses.

Blossoms & Bloomers, E. 11415 Krueger Ln., Spokane, WA 99207; phone 509-922-1344. Catalog $1. This company sells old roses, perennials, and plants that attract birds.

Edmunds' Roses, 6235 S.W. Kahle Rd., Wilsonville, OR 97070; phone 888-481-7673; fax 503-682-1275; Web site www.edmundsroses.com. This company specializes in exhibition and European varieties of modern roses.

Heirloom Old Garden Roses, 24062 NE Riverside Dr., St. Paul, OR 97137, phone 503-538-1576.

Jackson & Perkins, Box 1028, Medford, OR 97501; phone 800-292-4769; fax 800-242-0329; Web site `www.jacksonandperkins.com`. J&P is one of the world's largest producers of new roses.

Justice Miniature Roses, 5947 S.W. Kahle Rd., Wilsonville, OR 97070; phone 503-682-2370. The company specializes in miniature roses.

Lowe's Own-Root Roses, 6 Sheffield Rd., Nashua, NH 03062-0328; phone 603-888-2214; fax 603-888-6112. Catalog $2. The company offers many kinds of roses, including climbers and rare varieties.

Nor'East Miniature Roses, Inc., 58 Hammond St., Box 307, Rowley, MA 01969; phone 800-426-6485 or 508-948-7964. Also: Box 473, Ontario, CA 91762; phone 800-662-9669 or 909-984-2223. Take a look at this company's large selection of miniature roses.

The Roseraie at Bayfields, Box R, Waldoboro, ME 04572; phone 207-832-6330; fax 800-933-4508, `http://pbmfaq.dvol.com/list/roseraiebay.html`. Free consultations by nursery staff and $6 video available. This specialist has practical roses for hard places.

Roses of Yesterday and Today, 803 Browns Valley Rd., Watsonville, CA 95076; phone 408-724-3537; fax 800-980-7673. Catalog $3. Take a look at this company's old, rare, and unusual roses.

Royall River Roses, Box 370, Yarmouth, ME 04097; phone 800-820-5830; fax 207-846-7603; Web site `www.royallriverroses.com`. Royall River sells 250 varieties of hardy bare-root roses.

Tools and Supplies

Bozeman Biotech, Box 3146, Bozeman, MT 59772; phone 800-289-6656 or 406-587-5891; fax 406-587-0223, e-mail `ewayne@pop.mcn.net`. Bozeman offers environmentally friendly products for your lawn, garden, and farm.

Beaty Fertilizer Co., Inc., Box 2878, Cleveland, TN 37320; phone 800-845-2325; fax 800-845-2325; Web site `www.wingnet.net/~beaty`. This company is the maker of Magic Mills Rose Mix.

Charley's Greenhouse Supply, 17979 State Route 536, Memorial Hwy, Mt. Vernon, WA 98273; phone 800-322-4707 or 360-428-2626; fax 800-233-3078; Web site `www.charleysgreenhouse.com`. The hobby greenhouse experts have been in business for 22 years.

Deerbuster, 9735a Bethel Rd, Frederick, MD 21702-2017; phone 800-248-DEER; fax 301-694-9254. Deerbuster sells a full line of deer fencing, repellents, scaring devices, and other pest control products.

Drip Rite Irrigation Products, 4235 Pacific Street, Suite H, Rocklin, CA 95677; phone 916-652-1008; fax 916-652-1017; Web site www.DripIrr.com. You can buy drip-irrigation products at discount prices.

The Earth Box, P.O. Box 1966, St. Petersburg, FL 33731; phone 800-821-8838 or 727-823-5900; fax 727-823-1100; Web site www.earthbox.com. The Earth Box is a self-watering, self-feeding container system designed to grow vegetables and herbs without the usual guesswork and maintenance needed for conventional gardens.

Earthmade, 1502 Meridian Road, P.O. Box 609, Jasper, IN 47547; phone 800-843-1819; fax 800-817-8251; Web site www.earthmade.com. Earthmade offers a wide array of useful and top quality tools and accessories, including power equipment, greenhouses, and indoor gardening supplies.

Garden Trellises, Inc., Box 105N, LaFayette, NY 13084; phone 315-498-9003. The company offers galvanized steel trellises for vegetables and perennials.

Gardener's Eden, Box 7307, San Francisco, CA 94120-7307; phone 800-822-9600. Turn to Gardener's Eden for stylish garden supplies and accessories.

Gardener's Supply Company, 128 Intervale Rd., Burlington, VT 05401; phone 800-863-1700; fax 802-660-4600; Web site www.gardeners.com. The catalog contains hundreds of innovative tools and products for gardeners.

GardenStyles, 10740 Lyndale Ave. S., Ste. 9W, Bloomington, MN 55420; phone 800-203-6409; fax 612-948-0409; Web site www.gardenstyles.com. The company offers more than 20 Juliana hobby greenhouse models and carries cold frames and accessories.

Gardens Alive!, 5100 Schenley Pl., Dept. 5672, Lawrenceburg, IN 47025; phone 812-537-8650; fax 812-537-5108. Gardens Alive! is one of the largest organic pest control and fertilizer suppliers.

Gempler's, 100 Countryside Dr., Box 270, Belleville, WI 53508; phone 800-382-8473; Web site www.gemplers.com. Gempler's sells hard-to-find, industrial-grade tools for horticulture.

Harmony Farm Supply, Box 460, Graton, CA 95444; phone 707-823-9125; fax 707-823-1734; Web site www.harmonyfarm.com. Catalog $2. Turn to Harmony for drip and sprinkler irrigation equipment, organic fertilizers, beneficial insects, power tools, and composting supplies.

Hoop House Greenhouse Kits, Dept. N, 1358 Rt. 28, South Yarmouth, MA 02664; phone 800-760-5192; fax 508-760-5244; Web site www.hoophouse.com. Check out this company's greenhouse solutions — Hoop House kits.

Hydrofarm, 755 Southpoint Blvd, Petaluma, CA 94954; phone 707-765-9990; fax 707-555-1234; Web site `www.growlights.com`. Hydrofarm makes high-intensity grow lights and hydroponic supplies.

IPM Labs, Box 300, Locke, NY 13092-0300; phone 315-497-2063. This lab is a specialist in beneficial insects.

Kinsman Company, River Rd., FH, Point Pleasant, PA 18950; phone 800-733-4146; fax 215-297-0450. The Kinsman Company offers gardening supplies and fine-quality tools.

Langenbach, Box 1420, Lawndale, CA 90260-6320; phone 800-362-1991; fax 800-362-4490. Langenbach sells fine-quality tools and garden gifts.

Lee Valley Tools, Box 1780, Ogdensburg, NY 13669; phone 800-871-8158; Web site `www.leevalley.com/lvtmain.htm`. Lee Valley offers a wide variety of tools for home gardeners.

A. M. Leonard, Inc., Box 816, Piqua, OH 45356; phone 800-543-8955; fax 800-433-0633. See this source for professional nursery and gardening supplies.

Mantis, 1028 Street Road, Southampton, PA 18966; phone 800-366-6268; fax 215-364-1409; Web site `www.mantisgardentools.com`. Mantis manufactures minitillers and other specialized equipment for gardeners.

Mellinger's, Inc., 2310 W. South Range Rd., North Lima, OH 44452-9731; phone 800-321-7444; fax 330-549-3716; Web site `www.mellingers.com`. This company offers a broad selection of gardening tools, supplies, fertilizers, and pest controls, as well as plants.

Natural Gardening, 217 San Anselmo Ave., San Anselmo, CA 94960; phone 707-766-9303; fax 707-766-9747. Natural Gardening offers organic gardening supplies and tomato seedlings.

PBM Group, Inc., 160 Koser Rd, Lititz, PA 17543; phone 717-627-4300; fax 717-626-2424. PBM is an exclusive marketer of composting systems and other gardening tools.

Peaceful Valley Farm Supply, Box 2209 #NG, Grass Valley, CA 95945; phone 916-272-4769; fax 916-272-4794; Web site `www.groworganic.com`. Check out Peaceful Valley's organic gardening supplies and fine-quality tools.

Plow & Hearth, Box 5000, Madison, VA 22727; phone 800-627-1712; fax 800-843-2509. Plow & Hearth sells a wide variety of products for home and garden.

Smith & Hawken, 2 Arbor Ln., Box 6900, Florence, KY 41022-6900; phone 800-776-3336; fax 606-727-1166; Web site `www.smith-hawken.com`. The catalog showcases a wide selection of high-end tools, furniture, plants, and outdoor clothing.

Spray-N-Grow, Box 2137, Rockport, TX 78381; phone 800-288-6505; Web site www.spray-n-grow.com. Check out the company's line of environmentally safe horticulture products.

Snow Pond Farm Supply, RR 2, Box 1009, Belgrade, ME 03917; phone 800-768-9998.

The Urban Farmer Store, 2833 Vicente St., San Francisco, CA 94116; phone 800-753-3747 or 415-661-2204. Catalog $1. TheUrban Farmer offers drip-irrigation supplies.

Walt Nicke Co., Box 433, Topsfield, MA 01983; phone 800-822-4114; fax 508-887-9853. You can find a good selection of gardening tools at Walt Nicke.

Watermiser Drip Irrigation, 4335 Eastlake Blvd., Carson City, NV 89704-9102; phone 800-332-1570 or 702-331-1570; fax 702- 849-2540; Web site www.watermiser.com. Watermiser offers a line of high-quality irrigation products at low prices.

Trees, Shrubs, and Vines

Appalachian Gardens, Box 82, Waynesboro, PA 17268; phone 888-327-5483 or 717-762-4312; fax 717-762-7532. Appalachian Gardens sells scarce, unusual, hardy ornamental trees and shrubs, including many native plants.

Fairweather Gardens, Box 330, Greenwich, NJ 08323; phone 609-451-6261; fax 609-451-6261. Catalog $3. Fairweather Gardens' offerings include trees and shrubs. It also has a large selection of camellias, witch hazel, magnolia, holly, and viburnum.

Forestfarm, 990 Tetherow Rd., Williams, OR 97544-9599; phone 541-846-7269; fax 541-846-6963. Catalog $3. Forestfarm offers more than 4,000 varieties of native and rare plants, with particular emphasis on plants for wildlife.

Gossler Farms Nursery, 1200 Weaver Rd., Springfield, OR 97478; phone 541-746-3922. Gardeners can choose from a good selection of magnolias and other choice shrubs. Catalog $2.

Greer Gardens, 1280 Goodpasture Island Rd., Eugene, OR 97401-1794; phone 800-548-0111 or 541-686-8266; fax 541-686-0910. Catalog $3. This specialist in rhododendrons also offers rare and unusual plants.

Hughes Nursery, Box 7705, Olympia, WA 98507-7705; phone 360-352-4725; fax 360-352-1921 or 360-249-5580. Catalog $1.30. Hughes Nursery is a specialist in dwarf, Japanese, and other maples.

Kelly Nurseries, 1700 Morrissey Dr., Bloomington, IL 61704; phone 309-662-3511. Choose from a broad line of trees, ornamental plants, and roses.

Musser Forests, Inc., Box 340, Indiana, PA 15701-0340; phone 800-643-8319; fax 724-465-9893; Web site www.musserforests.com. Musser Forests' line comprises Northern Hemisphere-grown ornamental shrubs, nut trees, evergreen trees, and hardwood trees.

New Growth, Inc., P.O. Box 522, Hubbard, OR 97032; phone 800-605-7457; fax 800-264-7911; Web site www.newgrowth.com. New Growth sells Douglas fir, giant sequoia, red-leaf Japanese maple, and more.

Owen Farms, 2951 Curve-Nankipoo Rd., Ripley, TN 38063-6653; phone 901-635-1588. Owen Farms offers trees, shrubs, and perennials — including many named varieties — container-grown at the nursery.

Rock Spray Nursery, Box 693, Truro, MA 02666-0693; phone 508-349-6769; fax 508-349-2732; Web site www.rockspray.com. Find dwarf conifers and hardy heaths, and heathers at Rock Spray.

Roslyn Nursery, 211 Burrs Ln., Dix Hills, NY 11746; phone 516-643-9347; fax 516-484-1555. Catalog $3. Roslyn offers many rare and unusual plants.

Siskiyou Rare Plant Nursery, 2825 Cummings Rd., Medford, OR 97501; phone 541-772-6846; fax 541-772-4917. Catalog $3. Check out the hardy perennials, shrubs, and smaller conifers; and alpine and rock garden plants at Siskiyou.

Water Garden Plants and Supplies

Crystal Palace Perennials, Ltd., Box 154, St. John, IN 46373; phone 219-374-9419; fax 219-374-9052; Web site www.crystalpalaceperennial.com. This company offers one of the largest selections of water plants in the country, plus supplies. The catalog is $3, but free from the Web.

Lilypons Water Gardens, 6800 Lilypons Rd., Box 10, Buckeystown, MD 21717-0010; phone 800-999-5459; fax 800-879-5459; Web site www.lilypons.com. Lilypons specializes in all aspects of water gardening.

Paradise Water Gardens, 14 May St., Whitman, MA 02382; phone 800-955-0161; fax 800-966-4591; Web site http://users.aol.com/PStet82980/paradise.html. You can find just about everything for starting a water garden.

Slocum Water Gardens, 1101 Cypress Gardens Blvd., Winter Haven, FL 33884-1932; phone 941-293-7151; fax 800-322-1896 or 941-299-1896. Catalog $3. Slocum is a nursery of aquatic plants.

VanNess Water Gardens, 2460 N. Euclid Ave., Upland, CA 91784-1199; phone 800-205-2425 or 909-982-7217. Choose from a wide selection of water plants and supplies.

Wildflowers

Agua Viva Seed Ranch, Rt. 1, Box 8, Taos, NM 87571; phone 800-248-9080 or 505-758-4520. Agua Viva sells hardy perennials and bulbs, in addition to wildflowers.

Clyde Robin Seed Company, Box 2366, Castro Valley, CA 94546; phone 800-647-6475; fax 510-785-6463; Web site www.clyderobin.com. Catalog $2. Clyde Robin Seed Co. is a wildflower specialist.

High Country Gardens, 2902 Rufina Street, Santa Fe, NM 87505-2929; phone 800-925-9387; fax 800-925-0097. The full color catalog highlights water-thrifty wildflowers, winter hardy perennials, native shrubs, and cold hardy cacti and succulents.

Moon Mountain Wildflowers, Box 725, Carpinteria, CA 93014-0725; phone 805-684-2565. Catalog $3. Moon Mountain sells wildflower mixes and individual annual and perennial varieties.

Native Gardens, 5737 Fisher Ln., Greenback, TN 37742; phone and fax 423-856-0220; e-mail rcopallina@aol.com. Catalog $2. Gardeners can choose from a selection of native perennials.

Prairie Moon Nursery, Rt. 3, Box 163, Winona, MN; phone 507-452-1362. Catalog $2. Prairie Moon sells native plants and seeds for wetlands, prairies, and woodlands.

Vermont Wildflower Farm, Box 5, Rt. 7, Charlotte, VT 05445-0005; phone 802-425-3500; fax 802-425-3504. Vermont Wildflower Farm offers seeds of meadow and prairie wildflowers.

Wildseed Farms Ltd., Box 3000, Fredericksburg, TX 78624; phone 800-848-0078; fax 830-990-8090; Web site www.wildseedfarms.com. You can buy wildflower seeds by the packet or pound.

Index

• A •

A. densiflorus (asparagus fern), container plant use, 64
A. frikartii (aster), 69
A. M. Leonard, Corona's CLP Shear Maintenance Oil, 269
A. palmatum (Japanese maple) deciduous tree, 113
A. platanoides (Norway maple) deciduous tree, 113
A. rubrum (red maple) deciduous tree, 113
A. saccharinum (silver maple) deciduous tree, 113
A. saccharum (sugar maple) deciduous tree, 113
A. setaceus (asparagus fern), container plant use, 64
Aaron's-beard (Hypericum calycinum) ground cover, 150
AARS (All-American Rose Selections), healthy rose indicator, 98
Abelia grandiflora (glossy abelia) shrub, 121
Acacia baileyana (Bailey acacia), 3-4
accent, shrub designs, 119
Acer griseum (paperbark maple), 3-2
Acer saccharum (sugar or hard maple), 3-4
Acer species (maple) deciduous tree, 113
Achillea (yarrow), cutting plant, 64
Achillea millefolium (Daylily with purple yarrow), 1-7
Achillea species (yarrow), 68–69
Achillea tomentosa (woolly yarrow) ground cover, 149
acid soils
    pH level testing, 174
    raising pH level with ground dolomitic limestone, 134, 178
action hoe, uses, 268
activators, composting, 225
activities, deciding which area of yard to use, 33
African daisy (Osteospermum barberae), 72–73, 149
African lily (Agapanthus), container plant use, 64
Agapanthus (lily of the Nile), 64
ageratum, edging uses, 56
Ageratum houstonianum (Floss flower), 1-2

aggregate, 40
air spaces, container garden requirements, 310
Ajuga reptans (carpet bugle) ground cover, 149
alba (Rosa alba) shrub rose, 94
alkaline soil
    lowering pH level with elemental sulfur, 134, 178
    pH level testing, 174
Aloysia truphylla (lemon verbena), 346
alyssum, 51, 56
A-maizing Lawn, nontoxic herbicide, 264
Amaranthus (love-lies-bleeding), border uses, 54
Amelanchier species (serviceberries), bird habitat, 318
amending the soil, 167
American Forests, Global ReLeaf campaign, 111
American Horticultural Society's Plant Heat-Zone Map, 20–21
American Rose magazine, rose growing information source, 96
American Rose Society, rose growing information source, 96
anaerobic containers, 225
animals
    bulb protection ideas, 81
    deer, 262
    gophers, 262
    groundhogs (woodchucks), 262
    outwitting techniques, 262
    winter damage plant risk avoidance, 28
annual chrysanthemum (Chrysanthemum p.), 58
annual chrysanthemum (Leucanthemum paludosum), 58
annual grasses, textured variety, 54
annual rye, cover crop use, 263
annual vinca (Catharanthus roseus), 59
annual vines, varieties, 162–164
annuals
    bicolor flower type, 49
    butterfly varieties, 322
    color variations, 53
    container garden varieties, 307
    container growing, 56
    cool-season types, 49, 57–59

deadheading, 57
described, 47–49
designing for fragrance, 54–55
direct sowing varieties, 188–189
double flower type, 48
drift planting, 197
dwarf varieties, 48
en masse plantings, 55–56
fertilizer program, 56
flower types, 48–49
fully double flower type, 49
height variations, 53–54
heirloom variety fragrance advantages versus modern hybrids, 54
life span, 47–48
maintenance guidelines, 35, 56–57
picotee flower type, 49
planting methods, 51
purchasing guidelines, 51–52
reseeding from existing plants, 51
scrim plants, 53
shape variations, 53–54
single flower type, 48
star flower type, 49
structure variations, 53–54
sun/shade effects on, 50–51
trailers, 48
transplant advantages, 51
uses for, 52–56
variegated varieties, 53
versus perennials, 47
warm-season varieties, 50, 59–60
when to water, 56
year round growing season areas, 50
anthracnose disease, 114, 257
Antirrhinum majus (snapdragon), 57
antitranspirants, animal damage risk avoidance, 28
anvil pruners, uses, 268
aphids, 243
APHIS (Plant Health Inspection Service), foreign pest control, 247
apical bud, described, 230
apple maggot, described, 243
apple scab, treatment, 257
apples, varieties, 258, 294–295
    'Red Jonagold', 4-3
Aquilegia species (columbine), 68
Arapanthus orientalis (lily-of-the-Nile) bulb, 84
arboretums, tree variety source, 109
arbors, 160, 328–329
Arborvitae 'Rheingold' (Eastern white cedar), 3-6

Arctostaphylos species (bear-
    berry), 128
Arctostaphylos species (manza-
    nita), 128
Arctostaphylos uva-ursi
    (kinnikinnick) ground
    cover, 149
argyanthemum frutescens
    (marguerite daisy), 70
Argyranthemum frutescens (golden
    marguerite), cutting plant, 64
aromatic herbs, 346
artemisia (*Artemisia* species), 68
artemisias herb, midsummer rose
    garden partner, 96
Asclepias tuberosa (butterfly
    weed), butterfly
    attractor, 321
ash (*Fraxinus* species) deciduous
    tree, 114
Asiatic hybrid lily (*Lilium*),
    'Apricot Beauty', **1-8**
asparagus fern (*A. densiflorus*), 64
asparagus fern (*A. setaceus*), 64
aster (*A. frikartii*), 69
aster (*Aster* species), 69
Athyrium nipponicum (Japanese
    painted fern), **2-4**
Aurinia saxatilis (basket-of-gold), 69
Austin, David, David Austin
    (English) rose breeder,
    91–92
authors, e-mail address, 5
automated irrigation system, low
    maintenance landscape, 36
automated watering systems, 213
Autumn Fern (*Dryopteris
    erythrosora*), **2-4**
autumn gardening, frost avoid-
    ance techniques, 25–26
autumn harvest wreath,
    creating, 337
azaleas (*Rhododendron* species)
    shrub, 126–127

• *B* •

B. mentorensis (evergreen
    barberry) shrub, 121
B. microphylla japonica (Japanese
    boxwood) shrub, 121
B. sempervirens (English box-
    wood) shrub, 121
B. t. kurstaki, caterpillar treat-
    ment, 252
B. t. tenebrionis, Colorado potato
    beetle treatment, 252
B. thunbergii ('Crimson Pygmy')
    ground cover, 149
B. thunbergii (Japanese barberry)
    shrub, 121
baby gladiolus (*G. colvillei*)
    bulb, 85

backgrounds, 63, 119
backyards, use guidelines, 37
bacterial insecticides, 251
Bahia grass, 133
Bailey acacia (*Acacia baileyana*),
    3-4
baked earth (terra cotta)
    containers, 300
balled-and-burlapped plants, 195
bamboo stakes, tall perennials,
    67–68
bamboo teepees, vine support
    structure, 157–158
barberries (*Berberis* species)
    shrub, 121, 127, 149
bare-root plants, 195, 204–205
barriers, 119, 245
basil herb, 188, 291
basket-of-gold (*Aurinia saxatilis*), 69
basking, butterfly activity, 321
bean leaf beetle, 244
bearberry (*Arctostaphylos*),
    drought-tolerant shrub, 128
bearberry cotoneaster (*C.
    dammeri*) ground cover, 149
Bearded Iris (*Iris*), **1-7**
bedding begonias (*Begonia
    semperflorens*), 59
bedding begonias (*Begonia
    semperflorens-cultorum*), **1-2**
beds, 185, 285
Bee Balm (*Monarda didyma*), **1-7**
beer trap, snail/slug treatment, 248
bees, 323–324
Begonia semperflorens (bedding
    begonia), 59
Begonia semperflorens-cultorum
    (bedding begonias), **1-2**
Begonia tuberhybrida (begonia)
    bulb, 84
begonias (*Begonia tuberhybrida*)
    bulb
    described, 84
    easy to root plants, 237
    summer-blooming bulb, 78
bellflower (*Campanula* species),
    69–70
bells of Ireland (*Moluccella
    laevis*), 193
beneficial insects, 245, 251–252
Berberis (barberries) ground
    cover, 149
Berberis species (barberries)
    shrub, 121
Bermuda grass (*Cynodon
    dactylon*), 133, 265
berries, mail order, 375–376
Betula pendula (European white
    birch) deciduous tree, 114
bicolor flower type, 49
bigleaf hydrangea (*H.
    macrophylla*) shrub, 123
bindweed (*Convolvulus arvensis*)
    weed, 264–265

bins, compost, 222–223
birch borers, controlling, 114
birch trees, white bark, 109
birdbath, bird attractor, 318–319
birdfeeders, squirrel resistant
    designs 318–319
birds, 318–320
birdscare flash tape, garden
    protector, 320
Bishop's hat (*Epimedium rubrum*),
    2-4
black plastic, soil clearing
    method, 169
black spot disease, 102, 259
Black tupelo (*Nyssa sylvatica*), **3-2**
black vine weevil, 244
black-eyed coneflower (*Rudbeckia
    fulgida*), 64
black-eyed Susan (*Rudbeckia
    hirta*), 73
black-eyed Susan (*Thunbergia
    alata*) vine, 173, 188, **3-8**
blanket flower (*Gaillardia
    grandiflora*), 71
Bleeding Heart (*Dicentra*), **1-5**
blood-red geranium (*Geranium
    sanguineum*), 71
blue fescue (*festuca glauca*)
    ground cover, 150
blue grama grass, meadowlike
    landscaping, 152
blue oat grass (*Helictotrichon
    sempervirens*), 72
blue salvias, midsummer rose
    garden partner, 96
blueberries, 296
blue-leaf plantain lily (*H.
    sieboldiana*), 71
board scraper, lawn leveling
    tool, 136
bolo tine, tillers, 275
Bordeaux mixture, 257, 261
border flower bed, 62
borders, 62–63
borers, 244
boron, 216
Boston ivy (*P. tricuspidata*) vine,
    153, 154, 162
botanical gardens, tree variety
    source, 109
botanical insecticides, 251
botanical names, 14
botrytis blight, treatment, 259
Bougainvillea (*Bougainvillea*
    species) vine, 161, 237
bourbon shrub rose, 94
Bowles golden grass (*Carex elata*),
    'Bowles Golden', **3-5**
boxwood (*Buxus* species) shrubs,
    121
bramble fruits, 297

branch collar, tree pruning, 232
Brassica species (flowering cabbage), 57
Brassica species (flowering kale), 57
bridal wreath spiraea (*S. vanhouttei*) shrub, 127
British books, cautions, 354
Broccoli, 'Purple Sprouting', **4-3**
brown rot, treatment, 259
brush cuttings, using, 341
Bt (*Bacillus thuringiensis*)
    advantages/disadvantages, 252–253
    butterfly caterpillar cautions, 323
    caterpillar treatment, 244
    codling moth treatment, 244
    Colorado potato beetle, 245
    corn earworm treatment, 245
    described, 251
    gypsy moth treatment, 246
    tomato hornworm treatment, 250
buckwheat, cover crop use, 263
Buddleia davidii (Butterfly bush) 121, 321, **3-6**
buffalo grass, 133, 152
bulb bark, 83
bulb pans, 83
bulbs
    container growing process, 82–83
    described, 75–76
    design styles, 80
    dividing, 82
    drying process, 81
    fertilizing, 81
    forcing, 82–83
    fragrant, 348
    mail order, 368–369
    maintenance guidelines, 81–82
    naturalizing design style, 80
    perennialize design style, 80
    pips, 84
    planting process, 79–81
    propagating, 82
    protecting from animals, 81
    purchasing guidelines, 76–79
    quality testing, 78
    replanting every year, 82
    rhizomes, 84
    size issues, 78
    spring-blooming bulb purchasing/planting guidelines, 77
    storage process, 81
    summer-blooming bulb purchasing/planting guidelines, 78
    uses for, 76
    varieties, 84–86
    when to dig, 81
    wire mesh baskets, 81
burlap screens, winter hardiness technique, 28
burlap-wrapped root ball plants, 205–206

burrowing animals, wire mesh bulb baskets, 81
bush cinquefoil (*Potentilla fruticosa*) shrub, 124
butterflies, 320–323
Butterfly bush (*Buddleia davidii*), 121, 321, **3-6**
butterfly weed (*Asclepias tuberosa*), butterfly attractor, 321
Buxus species (boxwood) shrubs, 121
by-pass pruners, uses, 268

• C •

C. aramandi (evergreen clematis) vine, 161
D. caryophyllus (carnation), 71
C. dammeri (bearberry cotoneaster) ground cover, 149
C. divaricatus shrub, 122
C. grandiflora (coreopsis), 70
C. horizontalis (rock cotoneaster) ground cover, 149–150
C. japonica (Japanese camellia) shrub, 122
C. lacteus (Parney cotoneaster) shrub, 122
C. microphyllus (rockspray cotoneaster) ground cover, 150
C. oleifera shrub, 122
C. persicifolia (peach-leaf bellflower), 69
C. plumosa (celosia), indoor starting annuals, 193
C. poscharskyana (Serbian bellflower), 69
C. sasanqua (sasanqua camellias) shrub, 122
C. sulphureus, 59
Caenothus species (wild lilac), 128
Caladium bicolor (Fancy-leaved caladium), **1-8**
Caladium hortulanum (fancy-leafed caladium) bulb, 84
Calcium, 216
calendula (*Calendula officinalis*), 49, 51, 193
Calendula officinalis (pot marigold), 57
caliche, soil layer, 173
California poppy (*Eschscholzia californica*), 58
calla lily (*Zantedeschia* species) bulb, 86
callicarpa japonica (Purple beautyberry), **3-6**
Camellia species (camellias) shrub, 122
camellias (*Camellia* species) shrub, 122

Campanula species (bellflower), 69–70
camphor (*Cinnamomum camphora*) evergreen tree, 116
canary creeper (*Tropaeolum peregrinum*) vine, 163
candytuft (*Iberis sempervirens*), 72, 237
canna (*Canna* species) bulb, 78, 84
Canna species (canna) bulb, 84
caraway, lacewing attractor, 252
Carex elata (Bowles golden grass), **3-5**
carnation (*D. caryophyllus*), 71, 344, 237
Carolina cherry laurel (*P. caroliniana*) shrub, 124–125
carpet bugle (*Ajuga reptans*) ground cover, 149
carrier, fertilizers, 217
carrots
    direct sowing patterns, 186–188
    raised bed process, 181–182
    varieties, 288
cassia (*Cassia* species), drought-tolerant shrub, 128
cast concrete containers, 301
catalogs, 79, 184–185, 367–384
caterpillars, 244, 323
Catharanthus roseus (annual vinca), 59
Catharanthus roseus (Madagascar periwinkle), 59, **1-4**
Catharanthus roseus (vinca rosea), 59
cedar tree, bird habitat, 318
celosia (*C. plumosa*), indoor starting annual, 193
celosia (*Celosia cristata*), 50, 193
Celosia argentea (cockscomb), **1-2**
Celosia cristata (celosia), indoor starting annual, 193
Centaurea cineraria (dusty miller), 57
Centaurea moschata (sweet sultan), 344
centerpieces, making, 336–337
centifolia (*Rosa centifolia*) shrub rose, 94
centipede grass, 133
Cercis canadensis (eastern redbud) deciduous tree, 114
Chaenomeles (flowering quince) shrub, 122
chain stores, summer-blooming bulb purchasing guidelines, 78
chain-link fences, vine support structure, 158
chamomile (*Chamaemelum nobile*) ground cover, 149
Chanaecyparis pisifera (Threadleaf false cypress), **3-6**

chelated micronutrients, 217
cherries, photos, **4-3**
cherry trees, 296
chickweed (*Stellaria media*)
    weed, 265
children's areas, 13, 34
chill, deciduous fruit tree
    temperatures, 293
China (*R. chinensis*) shrub rose, 94
China asters, textured variety, 54
chinch bug, 244
Chinese forget-me-not
    (*Cynoglossum amabile*), 58
Chinese fringetree (*Chionanthus
    retusus*), **3-3**
Chinese jasmine (*Jasminum
    polyanthum*) vine, 161
Chinese juniper (*J. chinensis*)
    shrub, 124
Chinese pistache (*Pistacia
    chinensis*) deciduous
    tree, 115
Chinese praying mantis, beneficial
    insect, 251
Chinese wisteria (*Wisteria sinensis*)
    vine, 162
Chionanthus retusus (Chinese
    fringetree), **3-3**
chipper-shredders, 276–277
chives herb, 291
chlorine, 216
chlorophyll, 216
chocolate cosmos (*Cosmos
    atrosanguineus*), scented
    flower, 344
chrysanthemum, easy to root
    plants, 237
Chrysanthemum p. (annual
    chrysanthemum), 58
chrysanthemum, 70
Cinnamomum camphora (cam-
    phor) evergreen tree, 116
Cistus species (rockroses)
    shrub, 122
clay soils, 170–171, 173
clematis (*Clematis jackmanii*), **3-8**
clematis (*Clematis* species)
    vine, 161
Clematis jackmanii (Clematis), **3-8**
cleome, direct sowing annual, 188
climate, 10, 210
climbers, small garden
    technique, 328
climbing roses (*Rosa* species)
    vine, 90, 154, 162
clinging vines, 153, 155
coast live oak (*Q. agrifolia*)
    evergreen tree, 117
cockscomb (*Celosia argentea*), **1-2**
codling moth, 244
cold frames, 23–24
cold hardy, 18
coleus (*Coleus hybridus*), 53, 59

collars
    branch. trimming, 232
    cutworm prevention, 245
    pest barriers, 250
Colorado potato beetle, 245
colors
    container garden design
        concepts, 302
    cool, 53
    fruit trees, 109
    hot, 53
    multi-season shrub varieties, 127
    plant design characteristic, 42
    repetition concept, 40
    trees for all seasons, 108
    variegated annuals, 53
columbine (*Aquilegia* species), 68
columnar shape, trees, 110
commercial compost bins, 224–225
common mondo grass
    (*Ophiopogon japonicus*)
    ground cover, 150
Common winterberry (*Ilex
    vertocollata*), **3-7**
complete fertilizer, 178, 217
components, book sections, **2-5**
compost, 176
compost bins, 221–225
compost tea, recipe for, 242
composted manure, 176–177
composting, 221–225
cone shape, trees, 110
Confederate vine (*T. asiaticum*)
    ground cover, 150
conifers, 116
conserving water, 215
Consolida ambigua (larkspur), 57
container gardens
    annual varieties, 307
    arrangement guidelines, 304–307
    combining plants, 304
    design concepts, 302–305
    elemental container gardening
        concept, 303–304
    fertilizing, 313
    pea gravel cautions, 311
    perennial varieties, 308
    photo, **4-7**
    planting process, 312–313
    pot materials, 299–302
    potting soil mixtures, 311–312
    repotting issues, 314–315
    root-pruning, 314
    seasonal guidelines, 309
    single plant, 303–304
    soils, 309–312
    style points, 302–303
    vegetable varieties, 308
container-grown trees/shrubs,
    200–204
containers
    aged versus new look, 303
    annual varieties, 56

bulb pans, 83
cast concrete, 301
cleaning, 341–342
drainage factor, 300
glazed clay, 300
improvised, 302
metal, 302
miniature roses, 90–91
paper pulp, 301
plastic, 301
porosity factor, 300
recycling, 201
starting seeds indoors, 189–193
terra cotta (unglazed clay), 300
vegetable garden planting
    arrangement, 285
wood, 301
Convallaria majalis (lily-of-the-
    valley) bulb, 84
cool colors, 53
coolibah (*E. microtheca*) ever-
    green tree, 117
cool-season
    annuals, 49, 57–59
    grass, 131–132
    plants, 23–26
    vegetables, when to plant, 282
copper, 216
copper, disease treatment, 261
copper strips, slug/snail barrier,
    248, 250
coral bells (*Heuchera*), 64, 71
coreopsis (*C. grandiflora*), 67, 70
coreopsis (*Coreopsis* species), 70
coring machine, lawn tool, 146
cork oak (*Q. suber*) evergreen
    tree, 117
corn earworm, 245
corn gluten weed killer, nontoxic
    herbicide, 144, 264
Cornus florida (flowering
    dogwood) deciduous tree,
    114, **3-3**
Corona's CLP Shear Maintenance
    Oil, tool lubricant, 269
cosmos (*Cosmos bipannatus*)
    direct sowing annual, 188
    photo, 102
    reseeding volunteer, 51
    warm-season variety, 59
Cosmos atrosanguineus (chocolate
    cosmos), 344
Cosmos bipannatus (Cosmos), 51,
    59, **1-2**
Cotinus coggygria (Smoke tree), **3-5**
cotoneaster (*Cotoneaster* species)
    shrub
    bird habitat, 318
    described, 122
    fireblight disease, 122
    ground cover uses, 149
    multi-season color, 127
cotyledon, 186

county parks, tree variety source, 109
cover crops, 178, 263
crab apple trees, 109, 258
crabgrass (*Digitaria*) weed, 265
crape myrtle (*Lagerstroemia indica*) deciduous tree, 108, 115
Crataegus laevigata (English hawthorn), **3-3**
Crategus species (hawthorn) deciduous tree, 114
creeping fig (Ficus pumila) vine, 161
creeping lily turf (*Liriope spicata*) ground cover, 150
creeping phlox, spring rose garden partner, 96
creeping St. John's-wort (*Hypericum calycinum*) ground cover, 150
creeping thyme (*Thymus praecox arcticus*) ground cover, 150
crocus bulbs, 77, 80, 96
Crocus vermus (Dutch crocus), **2-4**
cross-pollination, fruit trees, 293
cucumber beetle, 245
cucumbers, 288
cultivated variety (cultivar), 14
cultivation, weed control, 263
cultivators, 275–276
cultural heritage, landscape planning considerations, 35
curculio, 245
curly dock (*Rumex crispus*) weed, 265
cuttings, 237–238
cutworm collars, 250
cutworms, 245
Cynoglossum amabile (Chinese forget-me-not), 58
cytospora canker, treatment, 259

• D •

D. barbatus (sweet William), 71
Daffodil (*Narcissus*) bulb
 'King Alfred', 86
 animal dislike, 81
 described, 86
 double-nosed shaped, 78
 forcing candidate, 82–83
 naturalistic design style candidate, 80
 photo, **1-8**
 round shaped, 78
 spring-blooming, 77
 spring rose garden partner, 96
dahlia (*Dahlia* species) bulb, 78, 84
damask (*R. damascena*) shrub rose, 94
dame's rocket (*Hesperis matronalis*), scented flower, 345

damping-off, treatment, 259
dandelion (*Taraxacum officinale*) weed, 266
David Austin (English) roses, 91–92
daylily (*Hemerocallis* species), 71–72
Daylily with purple yarrow (*Achillea millefolium*), 'Rubra', **1-7**
Daylily with purple yarrow (*Hemerocallis*), 'Little Grapette', **1-7**
deadheading, 57, 66–67
deadman switch, power mowers, 272
deciduous, described, 62
deciduous fruit trees, chill temperatures, 293
deciduous holly shrubs, 123
deciduous plants, pruning, 234
deciduous trees
 described, 108, 112
 varieties, 112–116
deciduous viburnum (*V. plicatum*) shrub, 128
decks, maintenance considerations, 36
deer, outwitting, 262
deer-excluding fence, **4-2**
delphinium, 67
Dendranthema (*Hardy chrysanthemum*), **1-6**
Dendranthema grandiflora (garden mum), 70
dianthus (*Dianthus* species), 71
Dianthus (pinks), cutting plant, 64, 237, 344
Dianthus caryophyllus (carnations), 71, 344
diatomaceous earth, 245, 253
Dicentra (Bleeding Heart), **1-5**
Digitalis purpurea (Purple foxglove), **1-6**
dill herb, lacewing attractor, 252
direct sowing, 185–188
discount stores, tool purchasing source, 277
discussion groups, 362–364
diseases
 anthrancose, 257
 avoiding conditions that promote problems, 241
 black spot, 259
 botrytis blight, 259
 brown rot, 259
 cytospora canker, 259
 damage identification techniques, 241–242
 damping-off, 259
 fusarium wilt, 261
 least-toxic remedies, 261
 mildew, 259–260
 milky spore, 246

peach leaf curl, 260
phytophthora blight, 260
prevention techniques, 256–257
rust, 260
solarization treatment, 257
sooty mold, 260
types, 257–261
verticillium wilt, 261
wilt, 261
dividing, 67, 82
division, 238
Dodonea viscosa (hop bush), drought-tolerant shrub, 128
dog runs, site analysis consideration, 34
dolomitic limestone, potting soil ingredient, 312
dormant buds, 230
dormant oil, 244–249
double digging, 181
double flower type, 49
double-nosed daffodil bulb, flower potential, 78
drainage
 container considerations, 300
 including in site analysis drawings, 31
 preventive maintenance advantages, 240
drawings
 field testing, 44
 final plan creation, 42–44
 goose egg area representations, 32
 plot plan advantages, 36
 scale drawing process, 38
 site analysis draft, 30–33
 vegetable garden succession planting uses, 285
drifts, 197
drip irrigation
 described, 186, 212–213
 water conservation, 215
Drosanthemum floribundum (rosea ice plant) ground cover, 150
drought-tolerant shrubs, varieties, 128
drying flowers, 335–336
Dryopteris erythrosora (Autumn Fern), **2-4**
Dustin-Mizer, dust applicator, 253
dusty miller (*Centaurea cineraria*), 57
Dutch crocus (*Crocus vermus*), **2-4**
dwarf daylily, midsummer rose garden partner, 96
dwarf flowering almond (*P. gladulosa*) shrub, 125
dwarf periwinkle (*Vinca minor*) ground cover, 150
dwarfs, described, 48

• E •

E. alata (winged euonymus) shrub, 123

E. europaea (European spindle tree) shrub, 123

E. fortunei (evergreen euonymus) shrub, 123

E. japonica (evergreen euonymus) shrub, 123

E. microtheca (coolibah) evergreen tree, 117

E. nicholii (Nichol's willow-leaf peppermint) evergreen tree, 117

early season plant varieties, frost-beating gardening, 26

eastern redbud (Cercis canadensis) deciduous tree, 114

Eastern white cedar (Arborvitae)'Rheingold', 3-6

easy to root plants, 237

Echinacea purpurea (purple coneflower), 71, 1-6

Elaeagnus angustifolia (Russian olive) deciduous tree, 114

electric grinders, 276–277

electric rotary mowers, 273

electric trimmers, 274

elemental container gardening, 303–304

elemental sulfur, lowering alkaline soil pH level, 134

e-mail addresses
    author's, 5
    Master Gardeners International, 351

emitters, drip irrigation systems, 212–213

endophyte, natural pest repellent, 132

English boxwood (B. sempervirens) shrub, 121

English hawthorn (Crataegus laevigata), 3-3

English holly (Ilex acquifolium) shrub, 124

English ivy (Hedera helix) vine, 150, 153, 155, 161

English laurel (P. laurocerasus) shrub, 124–125

English oak (Q. robur) deciduous tree, 116

English primrose (P. polyantha), 58

entertainment area, garden use, 13

Epimedium rubrum (Bishop's hat), 2-4

Eschscholzia californica (California poppy), 58

eucalyptus (Eucalyptus species) evergreen tree, 116–117

euonymus (Euonymus species) shrub, 123, 127

Euonymus fortunei (winter creeper) ground cover, 150

European spindle tree (E. europaea) shrub, 123

European white birch (Betula pendula) deciduous tree, 114

evapotranspiration, 214

evapotranspiration rate, 214

evening primrose, beneficial insect attractor, 252

evening stock (Mathiola longipetala bicornis), scented flower, 346

ever-blooming, hybrid tea roses, 88

evergreen barberry (B. mentorensis) shrub, 121

evergreen clematis (C. aramandi) vine, 161

evergreen euonymus (E. fortunei) shrub, 123

evergreen euonymus (E. japonica) shrub, 123

evergreen holly shrubs, 124

evergreen pear (Pyrus kawakamii) evergreen tree, 117

evergreen perennials, 62

evergreen shrubs, winter rose garden partner, 96

evergreen trees, 112, 116

evergreen viburnum (V. tinus) shrub, 127

existing plants
    container garden design concepts, 302
    including in site analysis drawings, 30

extension office
    fruit growing information source, 293
    local frost date resource, 26
    soil testing, 174–175
    tree variety source, 109
    Web sites, 357

• F •

face-lifts, lawn care, 146

Fairy primrose (P. malacoides), 58

fake predators, pesky bird discourager, 320

fan trellises, vine support structure, 159

fancy-leafed caladium (Caladium hortulanum) bulb, 84

fancy-leaved caladium (Caladium bicolor), 1-8

fastigate shape, trees, 110

feed stores, tool purchasing source, 277

feeders, bird, 318–319

fences
    deer-excluding, 4-2
    maintenance considerations, 36
    vine cautions, 155

fennel, lacewing attractor, 252

fern, container plant use, 64

fertile mulch, 227–228

fertilizer
    annual guidelines, 56
    bulbs, 81
    carrier, 217
    complete, 178, 217
    container gardens, 313
    fruit trees, 294
    lawn guidelines, 145
    liquid, 219
    organic, 219–221
    perennials, 65–66
    Rose Food, 100
    roses, 100–101
    slow-release, 219
    spreader, 218
    terms, 217–219
    types for various plants, 219–220

festuca glauca (blue fescue) ground cover, 150

Ficus pumila (creeping fig) vine, 161

field testing, site analysis drawings, 44

final plan, 42–44

Finale, nonselective herbicide, 168

fine fescue, 132

fireblight disease
    cotoneaster shrubs, 122
    firethorn shrubs, 126
    Hawthorn tree, 114

firethorn (Pyracantha species) shrub, 126–127

flaming, bindweed treatment, 265

flat spade, sod stripping tool, 168

flea beetles, 246

floating row covers, 24–25, 250

floribunda roses, 89

floss flower (Ageratum houstonianum), 1-2

flour, outlining sites, 167

flower arrangements, keeping fresh, 334–335

flower beds, types, 62

flowering cabbage (Brassica species), 57

flowering cherry (P. serrulata) deciduous tree, 'Kwanzan', 116

flowering crab apples (Malus species) deciduous tree, 115

flowering dogwood (Cornus florida) deciduous tree, 114, 3-3

flowering fruit (Prunus species) deciduous tree, 116
    shrub, 124, 127

flowering kale (Brassica species), 57
flowering quince (*Chaenomeles*) shrub, 122
flowering tobacco (*Nicotiana alata*), 60, 346
Flowerscape, garden design software, 365
fluorescent bulbs, starting seeds indoors, 192
foliage mixing, border design, 63
folier fertilizer, 218
...For Dummies resource books, 353–354
forcing, 82–83
forget-me-not (*Myosotis sylvatica*), 51, 58
form, plant design characteristic, 41
formality, container garden design concepts, 303
forums, 364
foundation plantings, shrub designs, 118–119
foxglove, accent uses, 54
fragrant evening primrose (*Oenothera caespitosa*), 346
fragrant gardens, photos, **4-6**
Fraxinus oxycarpa (Raywood ash) deciduous tree, 114
Fraxinus species (ash) deciduous tree, 114
free plants, 237–238
freesia (*Freesia* species) bulb, 85
front tine tillers, 275
front yards, use guidelines, 36–37
frost, vegetable garden planting dates, 283
frost hardy, 18
frost-free days, 21–22
frost-resistant crops, varieties, 287
frost-tender crops, varieties, 287
frost-tender plants, 23–26
fruit and vegetable gardens, **4-2–4-5**
fruit gardens
 apples, 294–295
 blueberries, 296
 bramble fruits, 297
 described, 292
 extension office information source, 293
 grapes, 296
 peaches, 295
 pears, 296
 planning, 294
 plums, 296
 strawberries, 296
 sweet cherries, 296
 tree fruit planting/harvest guidelines, 293–294
 varieties, 294–297
 versus orchards, 292
fruit trees, 293–296
fruits, mail order, 375–376

fuchsia, easy to root plants, 237
fully double flower type, 49
fungicides, least-toxic disease remedies, 261
furrow irrigation, 211–212
furrows, 211–212
fusarium wilt, treatment, 261

• *G* •

G. colvillei (baby gladiolus) bulb, 85
G. elwesii (giant snowdrop) bulb, 85
Gaillardia grandiflora (blanket flower), 67, 71
Galanthus species (snowdrops) bulb, 85
gallica (*R. gallica*) shrub rose, 94
gap planting, 327
garden cart, uses, 270
Garden Companion, plant selection/care software, 365
Garden Encyclopedia, plant selection/care software, 365
garden grinders, 276–277
garden hose, uses, 267
garden mums (*Dendranthema grandiflora*), 70
garden penstemon (*Penstemon gloxinioides*), 73
garden season, stretching techniques, 22–26
garden software, 364–365
garden tomatoes, Heirloom, **4-5**
garden tractors, 273
Garden Verbena (*Verbena hybrida*), **1-4**
gardenia (*Gardenia jasminoides*) shrub, 123, 237
gardening gloves, uses, 270
gardens
 bee attractor plant types, 323–324
 bird attracting plant types, 318–320
 butterfly attracting plant types, 320–323
 common conceptions, 1
 container, 299–315, **4-7**
 fragrant, **4-6**
 fruit, 292–297
 herb, 290–292
 limited space techniques, 325–330
 perfumed, 343–349
 raised bed, 181–182
 uses for, 12–13
 vegetable, 281–290
 water, **4-8**
garlic herb
 described, 291
 raised bed garden, **4-5**
gasoline-powered trimmers, 274
gazanias (*Gazania*) ground cover, 149

generosa roses, 92
genetic disposition of plants, watering factors, 210
genus, 14
geranium (*Pelargonium* species), 58, 237
geranium, midsummer rose garden partner, 96
Geranium sanguineum (blood-red geranium), 71
germander (*Tecrium* species), drought-tolerant shrub, 128
germination percentage, lawn seed purchasing guideline, 135
giant snowdrop (*G. elwesii*) bulb, 85
girdling, 28
gladiolus (*Gladious* species) bulb, 85
glazed clay containers, 300
Global ReLeaf, tree planting campaign, 111
globe amaranth (*Gomphrena*), 193
globe shape, trees, 110
Gloriosa daisy (*Rudbeckia fulgida*), 'Goldsturm', **1-5**
gloriosa daisy (*Rudbeckia hirta*), 73
glossy abelia (*Abelia grandiflora*) shrub, 121
golden marguerite (*Argyranthemum frutescens*), cutting plant, 64
Golden Prayers plantain lily (*Hosta*), **1-5**
goldenrod (*Solidago*), 65, 252
Gomphrena (glove amaranth), indoor starting, 193
goose eggs, site analysis rough draft drawing area representations, 32
gophers, outwitting, 262
grandiflora roses, 90
granular fertilizer, 218
grape (*Vitis* species) vine, 154, 162, 296
grape hyacinth (*Muscari* species) bulb, 86
gray-foliaged plants, border design, 63
green beans, 289
green kale, photo, **4-4**
green lacewing, 251
green manure crops, 178
grinders, 276–277
groundcover
 described, 147
 low maintenance landscape, 35
 photo, **2-4–2-5**
 planting process, 147–148
 shearing, 148
 shrub uses, 119
 varieties, 149–152
 versus lawns, 147

ground dolomitic limestone
  direct sowing place marker, 188
  raising acidic soil pH level,
    134, 178
ground-cover roses, 92
groundhogs (woodchucks),
    outwitting, 262
groupings, border design, 63
growing season
  autumn frost avoidance
    techniques, 25–26
  described, 21
  early planting methods, 23–25
  last frost date by geographic
    areas, 283
  length of, 17
  stretching techniques, 22–26
  year-round gardening tech-
    niques, 26
gypsum, direct sowing place
    marker, 188
gypsy moths, 246

• *H* •

H. arborescens (smooth hydran-
    gea) shrub, 123
H. macrophylla (bigleaf hydran-
    gea) shrub, 123
H. paniculata (peegee hydrangea)
    shrub, 123
H. quercifolia (oakleaf hydrangea)
    shrub, 123
H. sieboldiana (blue-leaf plantain
    lily), 71
hand hoeing/pulling, weed
    control, 264
hand pruner, 235
hand saw, 235
hand tools, types, 267–270
hand trowel, uses, 268
hand watering, 211
hand-held tiller/cultivators,
    275–276
hard maple (*Acer saccharum*), **3-4**
hardening off, 65, 193
hardpan, clay soil layer, 173
hardscape materials
  described, 39–40
  frugal substitution ideas, 40–41
  low maintenance landscape, 35
  repetition concept, 40
  scavenging for, 39
hardware stores, tool purchasing
    source, 277
Hardy chrysanthemum
    (*Dendranthema*), 'Clara
    Curtis', **1-6**
hardy roses, 93
hawthorn (*Crataegus* species)
    deciduous tree, 109, 114, 318
heading cuts, pruning, 231–232

heather, easy to root plants, 237
heavenly bamboo (*Nandina
    domestica*) shrub, 124, 127
heavy clay soil, watering
    factors, 210
Hedera helix (English ivy)
    ground cover, 150
    vine, 161
hedges, shrub uses, 119
height, annual design layout
    considerations, 53–54
heirloom vegetables, advantages/
    disadvantages, 290
Helianthus annuus (sunflower),
    warm-season variety, 60
Helichrysum (strawflower), indoor
    starting annual, 194
Helictotrichon sempervirens (blue
    oat grass), 72
heliotrope (*Heliotropium
    arborescens*), 54, 345
Heliotropium arborescens
    (common heliotrope), 345
Hemerocallis (Daylily with purple
    yarrow), **1-7**
Hemerocallis lilioasphodelus
    (lemon daylily), 345
Hemerocallis species (daylily),
    71–72
herb gardens
  basil, 291
  chives, 291
  combining with vegetable
    gardens, 290
  garlic, 291
  lemon thyme (T. citriodorus), 292
  marjoram (*O. marjorana*), 291
  mints, 291
  mother-of-thyme (*T. praecox
    arcticus*), 292
  oregano (*Origanum vulgare*), 291
  parsley, 291
  peppermint (*Mehtha piperita*), 291
  rosemary, 291
  sage (*Salvia officinalis*), 292
  thyme (*Thymus vsulgari*), 292
  varieties, 291
herb vinegars, 333–334
herbaceous flowering perennials, 62
herbicides, weed control, 264
herbs, 346, 374–375
Hesperis matronalis (dame's
    rocket), 345
Heteromeles arbutifolia (toyon),
    drought-tolerant shrub, 128
Heuchera (coral bells), 64
Heuchera sanguinea (coral bells), 71
hibernaculi, 323
Higan (spring) cherry (*Prunus
    subhirtella*), **3-3**
hills, vegetable garden planting
    arrangement, 285
historical heritage, landscape
    planning considerations, 35

hoeing, weed control, 264
hoes, uses, 268
hollies (*Ilex* species) shrub, 123–124
holly oak (*Q. ilex*) evergreen
    tree, 117
holly shrub
  bird habitat, 318
  multi-season color, 127
home-building centers, tool
    purchasing source, 277
homes, 35, 155
honeybees, gardening for, 323–324
honeysuckle, easy to root
    plants, 237
hop bush (*Dodonea viscosa*),
    shrub, 128
horizontal spread shape, trees, 110
horizontally spreading plants,
    design uses, 41
horticultural oil
  advantages/disadvantages,
    253–254
  mealybug treatment, 247
  Mexican bean beetle
    treatment, 248
  scale treatment, 248
  whitefly treatment, 250
hose-end sprayer, 218
Hosta (plantain lily)
  container plant use, 64
  described, 71
  Golden Prayers plantain lily
    photo, **1-5**
hot beds, 24
hot caps, 24
hot colors, 53
humus, 172, 177
hyacinth (*Hyacinthus orientalis*)
  bulb described, 85
  forcing candidate, 82–83
  spring-blooming, 77
Hyacinth bean, direct sowing
    annual, 188
Hyacinthus orientalis (hyacinth)
    bulb, 85
hybrid musk roses, 93
hybrid perpetual shrub rose, 94
hybrid tea roses, 88–89, 102
Hybrid tulip, **1-8**
hybrid vegetables, advantages/
    disadvantages, 289–290
hybrid vigor, 289
hydrangea (*Hydrangea* species)
    shrub, 123, 127
Hypericum calycinum (Aaron's-
    beard) ground cover, 150
Hypericum calycinum (creeping St.
    John's-wort) ground
    cover, 150

• I •

I. meserveae (Meserve hybrid
hollies) shrub, 124
I. verticillata (winterberry)
shrub, 123
Iberis sempervirens (candytuft), 72
ice plants ground cover, 150
Iceland poppies, cool-season
plant, 50
Ichiban Japanese eggplant, 61 day
growing cycle, 26
Ilex acquifolium (English holly)
shrub, 124
Ilex species (hollies) shrubs,
123–124
Ilex verticillata (Common
winterberry), **3-7**
imidan, curculio treatment, 245
immersion water heater, birdbath
temperature control,
318–319
impatiens (Impatiens wallerana),
50, 60, **1-3**
improvised containers, 302
Indian hawthorn (Rhaphiolepis
indica) shrub, 126
indoor planting, growing season
stretching technique, 23
indoor views, site analysis
considerations, 31
informal globe shape, trees, 110
inoculants, composting, 225
inorganic mulch, 227
insect traps, 250
insecticidal soap
advantages/disadvantages, 254
aphid treatment, 243
bean leaf beetle, 244
spider mite treatment, 249
whitefly treatment, 250
insecticides
B. t. kurstaki, 252
B. t. tenebrionis, 252–253
bacterial, 251
botanical, 251
Bt (Bacillus thuringinesis), 244–
246, 250–253
diatomaceous earth, 245, 253
dormant oil, 249
horticultural oil, 247–248, 250,
253–254
imidan, 245
insecticidal soap, 243–244, 249–
250, 254
mineral oil, 245
neem tree (Azadirachta indica),
244–247, 254–255
oil-based leaf shine product, 247
pyrethrins (Tanacetum
cinerarifolium), 248, 250,
255–256

Rotenone, 256
rubbing alcohol, 248
insects
aphids, 243
apple maggot, 243
bean leaf beetle, 244
birch borers, 114
black vine weevil, 244
borers, 114, 244
caterpillars, 244
chinch bug, 244
codling moth, 244
Colorado potato beetle, 245
corn earworm, 245
cucumber beetle, 245
curculio, 245
cutworms, 245
encouraging beneficial
species, 240
flea beetles, 246
foreign invasion prevention
issues, 247
gypsy moths, 246
IPM (integrated pest management), 250–256
Japanese beetles, 246–247
leaf miners, 247
lygus bugs (tarnished plant
bugs), 249
mealybugs, 247
Mexican bean beetles, 248
oriental fruit moths, 248
pest promotion conditions, 241
pheromones, 245
root maggots, 248
scale, 248
slugs, 248–249
snails, 248–249
spider mites, 249
tarnished plant bugs (lygus
bugs), 249
tent caterpillars, 250
tomato hornworm, 250
types, 243–250
Varro mite (V. jacobosonii), 324
whiteflies, 250
inspirational books, 352
Internet addresses, characters
used, 357
interplanting, vegetable
gardens, 285
IPM (integrated pest management)
described, 250
bacterial insecticides, 251
barrier types, 250
disease prevention techniques,
256–257
encouraging good insects, 251–
252
pest chemicals, 252–256
water blasting pests, 250
Ipomoea alba (moonflower), 345
Ipomoea imperialis (morning
glory) vine, 163

Ipomoea tricolor (Morning glory),
3-8
Iris (Bearded Iris), **1-7**
iris (Iris species) bulb, 85
iron, 216
irrigation systems, automated, 36
island flower bed, 62
ivy, easy to root plants, 237

• J •

J. chinensis ('San Jose') juniper
ground cover, 151
J. chinensis (Chinese juniper)
shrub, 124
J. horizontalis ground cover, 150
Japanese barberry (B. thunbergii)
shrub, 121
Japanese beetle traps, cautions/
concerns, 246–247
Japanese beetles, 246–247
Japanese boxwood (B. microphylla
japonica) shrub, 121
Japanese camellia (C. japonica)
shrub, 122
Japanese maple (A. palmatum)
deciduous tree, 113
Japanese painted fern (Athyrium
nipponicum), **2-4**
Japanese photinia (P. glabra)
shrub, 124
Japanese spurge (Pachysandra
terminalis) ground cover, 150
jar method, soil texture test,
171–172
Jasminum polyanthum (Chinese
jasmine) vine, 161
juniper ground cover, winter rose
garden partner, 96
juniper shrub, bird habitat, 318
junipers (Juniperus species)
shrub, 124
junipers (Juniperus) ground
cover, 150
junk, protecting plants from
unexpected frost, 24

• K •

Kentucky bluegrass, 132
kinnikinnick (Arctostaphylos
uva-ursi) ground cover, 149
Korean spice viburnum (V.
carlesii) shrub, 128
Kwanzan flowering cherry
deciduous tree, 116

• L •

L. muscari ground cover, 150
Ladd trap, apple maggot treatment, 243
ladder and pole pruner, 235–236
lady beetles See ladybugs
ladybugs, friendly insect, 251
Lagerstroemia indica (crape myrtle) deciduous tree, 115
lamb's ears (Stachys byzantina), 74, 96
lamb's-quarters (Chenopodium album) weed, 266
Lampranthus spectabilis (trailing ice plant) ground cover, 150
LandDesigner CD, garden design software, 365
landscapes
   area defining techniques, 38–39
   described, 29
   historical/cultural heritage considerations, 35
   home resale value effects, 35
   photos, 2-2–2-3
   repetition concept, 40
   site analysis, 30–33
   unit concept, 40
   wish list items, 33–34
landscape fabric, 228
landscaping software, final plan creation tool, 43–44
lantana (Lantana camara), butterfly attractor, 321
larkspur (Consolida ambigua), 57, 188
Lathyrus (sweet peas) vine, 164
Lathyrus odoratus (sweet pea), 58, 345
latticework trellises, vine support structure, 159
lavender (Lavandula species)
   aromatic herb, 346
   container plant use, 64
   drought-tolerant shrub, 128
lawn mowers, 271–273
lawn rake, uses, 268–269
lawn roller, lawn seed planting tool, 136
lawn spreader, lawn seeding tool, 136
lawn-and-garden mowers, 273
lawns
   cool-season varieties, 131–132
   coring machine, 146
   cost considerations, 130
   coverage per square feet guidelines, 135–136
   face-lift methods, 146
   fertilizing guidelines, 145
   laying sod, 134
   maintenance guidelines, 129, 143–146

meadowlike landscaping, 152
mowing guidelines, 144
native grasses, 152
overseeding, 146
photos, 2-4–2-5
planting tools, 136
plug planting process, 143
plugs, 131
power rake, 146
seed germination percentage, 135
seed purchasing guidelines, 135–136
seeding process, 134–139
seeding versus sodding, 134
sizing, 130
sod laying process, 131, 140–142
soil pH testing, 134
sprig planting process, 131, 143
thatch removal, 146
topdressing, 146
tune-up methods, 146
turfgrass varieties, 131–133
versus ground covers, 147
warm-season grass varieties, 131, 133
weeding, 144
winter overseeding, 146
laying sod, 134
leading bud, 230
leaf buds, 102
leaf miners, 247
leaf shine product, mealybug treatment, 247
legumes, green manure/cover crops, 179
lemon daylily (Hemerocallis lilioasphodelus), 345
lemon thyme (T. citriodorus) herb, 292
lemon verbena (Aloysia truphylla), aromatic herb, 346
length of growing season, zone concept, 17
lettuce, 186–188, 289, 4-5
Leucanthemum maximum (Shasta daisy), 58
Leucanthemum paludosum (annual chrysanthemum), 58
Leucojum species (snowflake) bulb, 85
Liatris (Yellow coreopsis), 1-7
light, seed growing requirements, 184
lighting
   site analysis considerations, 31
   starting seeds indoors, 192
lightweight/tiller cultivators, 275–276
lilac (Syringa vulgaris) shrub, 127, 3-7
lilies (Lilium species) bulb, 85
Lilium (Asiatic hybrid lily), 1-8
lily of the Nile (Agapanthus), container plant use, 64, 84

lily turf (Ophiopogon) ground cover, 150
lily-of-the-valley (Convallaria majalis) bulb, 84
limbs, sawing, 233
lime, potting soil ingredient, 312
lime sulfur, disease treatment, 261
Limonium (statice), indoor starting, 194
liquid fertilizer, 219
Liquidambar (sweet gum) deciduous tree, 108, 115
Liriope (mondo grass) ground cover, 150
Liriope spicata (creeping lily turf) ground cover, 150
live chat, 364
loam soils, 170–171
lobelia (Lobelia erinus), 56, 60
Lobularia maritima (sweet alyssum), 58, 194
location, watering factors, 210
Loebner magnolia (Magnolia), 'Leonard Messel', 3-2
lopper, 235
lopping shears, uses, 270
Love-in-a mist (Nigella damascena), 54, 1-3
love-lies-bleeding (Amaranthus), texture uses, 54
low spreading plants, design uses, 41
Lycopersicum esculentum (tomatoes), 194
lygus bugs (tarnished plant bugs), 249

• M •

M. sargentii (Sargent crab apple) deciduous tree, 115
M. sieboldii zumi deciduous tree, 115
M. soulangiana (saucer magnolia) deciduous tree, 115
macronutrients, 216
Madagascar periwinkle (Catharanthus roseus), 59, 1-4
magnesium, 216
Magnolia (Loebner magnolia), 3-2
magnolia (Magnolia species) deciduous tree, 115
Magnolia grandiflora (southern magnolia) evergreen tree, 117
Magnolia soulangiana (saucer magnolia), 3-4
mahonia (Mahonia species), drought-tolerant shrub, 128
mail-order
   beneficial insect source, 251

berries, 375–376
bulbs, 77–78, 368–369
catalog pointers, 79
flowers, 369–374
fruits, 375–376
perennial plants, 376–378
resources, 367–384
roses, 378–379
seed purchasing guidelines, 184–185
specialist plants, 376–378
supplies, 379–382
tools, 278, 379–382
trees, 382–383
vegetable, 369–374
water garden plants/supplies, 383–384
wildflowers, 384
mailing list managers (MLM), 363
mailing lists, 363–364
maintenance, site analysis considerations, 35–36
Malus species (flowering crab apples) deciduous tree, 115
manganese, 216
manzanita (*Arctostaphylos*), drought-tolerant shrub, 128
maple (*Acer* species) deciduous tree, 113
marguerite daisy (*Argyanthemum frutescens*), 70
marigold (*Tagetes*)
  direct sowing, 188
  indoor starting, 194
  reseeding volunteer, 51
  warm-season plant, 50, 60
marjoram (*O. marjorana*) herb, 291
masonry, low maintenance landscape, 36
Master Gardeners, fruit garden source, 292
Master Gardeners International, 351
Mathiola longipetala bicornis (evening stock), 346
Matthiola incana (stock), 58, 345
meadow lawns, native grass landscaping, 152
mealybugs, 247
melampodium, direct sowing annual, 189
mesclun, salad basket, 340
Meserve hybrid hollies (*I. meserveae*) shrub, 124
metal containers, 302
metal trellises, vine support structure, 158
metal-rod method, soil structure testing, 172–173
Mexican bean beetles, 248
Mexican sunflower (*Tithonia rotundifolia*), 194, **1-3**

microclimates, plant growth factor, 10
micronutrients, 216–217
mignonette (*Reseda odorata*), 54, 345
mildew, treatment, 259–260
milky spore disease, Japanese beetle treatment, 246
mineral oil, corn earworm treatment, 245
miniature roses, 91
mints herb, 291
Miscanthus sinesis (variegated eulalia grass), 72
mixed border, 63
moisture, seed growing requirements, 184
Moluccella laevis (bells of Ireland), 193
molybdenum, 216
Monarda didyma (Bee Balm), **1-7**
mondo grass (*liriope*) ground cover, 150
moonflower (*Ipomoea alba*), scented flower, 345
moonflower vine, sweet scented, 54
morning glory (*Ipomoea imperialis*) vine, 163, **3-8**
morning glory, direct sowing, 189
moss rose (*Portulaca*), midsummer rose garden partner, 96
mother-of-thyme (*T. praecox arcticus*) herb, 292
mowing, lawn maintenance guidelines, 144
mugho pine (*Pinus mugo*) shrub, 124
mulberry tree, bird habitat, 318
mulch
  contents, 227
  described, 226
  fertile, 227–228
  inorganic, 227
  lawn seed planting tool, 136
  newspaper, 228
  water conservation, 215
  weed control, 263
  winter hardiness technique, 27
Mulch Plus, landscape fabric, 263
mulching mowers, 272
muscari bulbs, spring rose garden partner, 96
Muscari species (grape hyacinth) bulb, 86
Myosotis sylvatica (forget-me-not), 58

• *N* •

Nandina domestica (heavenly bamboo) shrub, 124
Nanking cherry (*P. tomentosa*) shrub, 125

Narcissus species (daffodils) bulb, 86, 338, **1-8**
nasturtium (*Tropaeolum majus*), 54, 59, 189, **1-3**
vine, 163
National Audubon Society, bird-watching club source, 320
National Gardening magazine
  caterpillar identification poster, 323
  subscription coupons, 286
  USDA Plant Hardiness Zone Map reliance, 19
native grasses, meadowlike landscaping, 152
native plants, growth advantages, 12
natural features, site analysis considerations, 31
naturalizing, bulb design style, 80
neem tree (*Azadirachta indica*) insecticide
  advantages/disadvantages, 254–255
  chinch bug treatment, 244
  Colorado potato beetle, 245
  flea beetles, 246
  gypsy moths, 246
  Japanese beetle treatment, 246
  leaf miner treatment, 247
  mealybug treatment, 247
  Mexican bean beetle treatment, 248
neighbors, site analysis considerations, 35
Nerium oleander (oleander) shrub, 124
Newport purple-leaf plum (*P. cerasifera*) deciduous tree, 116
newsgroups, 362–363
newspaper
  as mulch, 228
  soil clearing method, 169
Nichol's willow-leaf peppermint (*E. nicholii*) evergreen tree, 117
Nicotiana alata (flowering tobacco), 60, 194, 346
Nicotiana sylvestris (woodland tobacco), accent plant, 54–55
Nigella (love-in-a-mist), border uses, 54
Nigella damascena (Love-in-a-mist), **1-3**
night phlox (*Zaluzianskya capensis*), scented flower, 346
night-scented stock, clove scented, 55
Nitrogen (N), 216–217
noise, site analysis considerations, 31

noisemakers, pesky bird discourager, 320
non-grafted roses, zonal guidelines, 100
non toxic herbicides, weed control, 264
nonlegumes, green manure/cover crops, 179
nonselective herbicide, site clearing, 168
north side plantings, winter hardiness technique, 27
Norway maple (*A. platanoides*) deciduous tree, 113
nurseries
  bulb purchasing guidelines, 77–78
  tool purchasing source, 277
  tree variety source, 109
nutrients, adding to soil, 178
nylon hosiery, supporting vining plants, 156
Nyssa sylvatica (Black tupelo), **3-2**

• O •

oakleaf hydrangea (*H. quercifolia*) shrub, 123
oaks (*Quercus* species) deciduous tree, 116
oaks (*Quercus* species) evergreen tree, 117
odors (smell), site analysis considerations, 31
Oenothera caespitosa (fragrant evening primrose), 346
offsets, 82
old garden roses, 94–95
oleander (*Nerium oleander*) shrub, toxin cautions, 124
onion, 289
online resources, 356–366
open irregular shape, trees, 110
open pollinated varieties, vegetable plants, 290
Ophiopogon (lily turf) ground cover, 150
Ophiopogon japonicus (common mondo grass) ground cover, 150
orchards, versus fruit gardens, 292
order, plant design characteristic, 42
oregano (*Origanum vulgare*) herb, 291
organic fertilizer, 219–221
organic foods, garden use, 13
organic matter, 172, 175–176
oriental fruit moths, 248
ornamental corn, screening uses, 53
ornamental gardens, 72, 181–182

ornamental grasses, winter rose garden partner, 96
ornamental pear (*Pyrus calleryana*) deciduous tree, 116
oscillating hoe, uses, 268
Osteospermum (trailing African daisy) ground cover, 149
Osteospermum barberae (African daisy), 72–73
outdoor sink, site analysis consideration, 34
overseeding, 146
own-root roses, zonal guidelines, 100
oxalis, 266

• P •

P. caroliniana (Carolina cherry laurel) shrub, 124
P. cerasifera ('Newport' purple-leaf plum) deciduous tree, 116
P. cistena (purple-leafed sand cherry) shrub, 125
P. coccinea ('Lalandei') shrub, 126
P. fraseri shrub, 124
P. glabra (Japanese photinia) shrub, 124
P. gladulosa (dwarf flowering almond) shrub, 125
P. laurocerasus (English laurel) shrub, 124
P. lusitanica (Portugal laurel) shrub, 124
P. malacoides (Fairy primrose), 58
P. polyantha (English primrose), 58
P. quinquefolia (Virginia creeper) vine, 162
P. serrulata ('Kwanzan' flowering cherry) deciduous tree, 116
P. tabernaemontanii (Spring cinquefoil) ground cover, 150
P. tomentosa(Nanking cherry) shrub, 125
P. tricuspidata (Boston ivy) vine, 162
P. verna (Spring cinquefoil) ground cover, 150
Pachysandra terminalis (Japanese spurge) ground cover, 150
Paeonia (peonies), cutting plant, 64
Paeonia lactiflora (West Elkton peony), **1-6**
painted daisy (*Tanacetum coccineum*), 70
pansy (Viola species)
  cool-season variety, 49–50, 59
  reseeding volunteer, 51
pansy (*Viola wittrockiana*), **1-4**
paper pulp containers, 301
paperbark maple (*Acer griseum*), **3-2**

parasitic nematodes, 244, 246, 251
parks, tree variety source, 109
Parney cotoneaster (*C. lacteus*) shrub, 122
parsley herb, 291
parsnips, raised bed process, 181–182
pathways, defining, 38–39
patterns, direct sowing, 185–188
pea gravel, container garden cautions, 311
peach leaf curl, treatment, 260
peaches, 295, **4-4**
peach-leaf bellflower (*C. persicifolia*), 69
pears, 296
peas, 289, **4-4**
peat moss, 177, 312
peegee hydrangea (*H. paniculata*) shrub, 123
Pelargonium (geraniums), 58, 237, 346
Pennisetum setaceum (purple fountain grass), 64, 72
Penstemon gloxinioides (garden penstemon), 73
penstemon, easy to root plants, 237
peonies (*Paeonia*), 64, 67–68
peppermint (*Mentha piperita*) herb, 291
percolation method, soil structure testing, 172–173
percolation rate, 173
perennial border, designing, 62–65
perennial plants, mail order, 376–378
perennial ryegrass, 132
perennialize design style, bulbs, 80
perennials
  border designs, 63–65
  border use, 62–63
  container garden varieties, 308
  cutting varieties, 64–65
  deciduous type, 62
  described, 61–62
  dividing to propagate, 67
  dry climate varieties dormancy period, 65
  easy to root, 237
  evergreen type, 62
  feeding (fertilizing), 65–66
  hardening off, 65
  low maintenance landscape, 35
  maintenance, 65–67
  ornamental grasses, 72
  pinching (deadheading), 66–67
  planting process, 65
  potting varieties, 64
  pruning, 66–67
  single bloom season, 62
  staking taller varieties, 67–68
  types, 62

versus annuals, 47, 61
watering guidelines, 65–66
perfumed gardens, 343–349
perlite, potting soil ingredient, 312
Perma-Guard Inc., Spritzer tube
 duster, 253
Persian buttercup (*Rannuclus
 asiaticus*) bulb, 86
personal likes/dislikes, landscape
 design considerations, 30
pests, 241–242 *See also* insects
pet area, garden use, 13
Petunia (*Petunia hybrida*), 60, **1-4**
pH (negative logarithm of
 hydrogen ion concentra-
 tion)
 adjusting with amendments, 178
 described, 174
 soil testing, 134, 174
 vegetable garden improvements,
 285–286
pheromones, 245
pheromone traps
 codling moth treatment, 244
 Japanese beetle cautions/
 concerns, 246
 oriental fruit moths, 248
Phlox paniculata (summer
 phlox), 73
phlox, easy to root plants, 237
Phosphorus (P), 216–217
photinia (*Photinia* species) shrub,
 124–125, 127
photosynthesis, 216
phytophthora blight, treatment, 260
picotee flower type, 49
pillar roses, 160
pillars, vine support structure, 160
pinching, 231–232
pincushion flower (*Scabiosa*),
 cutting plant, 64
pinks (*Dianthus*), 64, 237, 344
Pinus mugo (mugho) shrub, 124
pips, 84
Pistacia chinensis (Chinese
 pistache) deciduous tree, 115
pitchfork, composting, 226
Pittosporum tobira (tobira)
 shrub, 124
plant groupings, perennial border
 design, 63
plant growth factors, 10–12, 230
plant hardiness, 18
plant hardiness zone maps, **2-6–2-8**
plant recognition factor, direct
 sowing issue, 185
plant shapes, container garden
 design concepts, 302–303
plant ties, 160
plant timing, water conservation, 215
plantain lily (*Hosta* species), 64, 71
plants
 animal damage risk avoidance, 28

areas to place for most scent
 effect, 344
bare-root planting process, 195,
 204–205
botanical naming conventions,
 14–15
burlap-wrapped root ball, 195,
 205–206
common naming conventions, 15
container-grown root-bound
 condition, 200
design characteristics, 41–42
for free, 237
growth factors, 10–12
needing water, 214–215
pH levels, 174
raising from seeds, 183–194
repetition concept, 40
rotating crops to lessen pest/
 disease effects, 240
seedlings, 195
small garden selection guidelines, 329
starting indoors to increase
 growing season, 23
transplants, 195
types of fertilizer needed,
 219–220
plastic collars, animal damage risk
 avoidance, 28
plastic containers, 301
plastic netting, vine support
 structure, 159
plot plans, site analysis drawing
 advantages, 36
plow pan, 180
plow sole, tillers, 276
plugs, 131, 143
plums, 296
pole beans, direct sowing
 annual, 189
pole lopper, uses, 271
pollination, bees importance,
 323–324
polyantha roses, floribunda rose
 cross, 89
polyester bird netting, garden
 protector, 320
poppies, direct sowing annual, 189
porosity, container considerations, 300
Portland shrub roses, 95
Portugal laurel (*P. lusitanica*)
 shrub, 124
pot marigold (*Calendula
 officinalis*), 57
Potassium (K), 216–217
Potentilla fruticosa (bush
 cinquefoil) shrub, 124
Potentilla neumanniana (Spring
 cinquefoil) ground
 cover, 150

potting soils, container gardens,
 311–312
power cultivators, 275–276
power rake, lawn thatch removal
 tool, 146
power tools, types, 270–277
power-reel mowers, 272
practical books, 352–353
pressure pan, 180
prevailing winds, including in site
 analysis drawings, 31
preventative maintenance, 240–
 242, 268–269
primary nutrients, 216
primroses (*Primula* species), 58
private getaway, garden use, 12
problem areas, site analysis
 determinations, 30
proboscis, butterfly tongue, 321
projects
 autumn harvest wreaths, 337
 centerpiece, 335
 cleaning containers, 341–342
 drying flowers, 335–336
 forcing narcissus indoors, 338
 herb vinegars, 333–334
 making cut flowers last, 334–335
 salad basket, 340
 using garden trimmings, 341
 water gardens in a tub, 338–339
propagating, 229, 237–238
prostrate (spotted) spurge
 weed, 266
pruners, uses, 268
pruning
 branch angle for flower
 production, 231
 described, 229–230
 effect on plant growth, 230
 for desired effect, 234–235
 for health of plant, 230
 fruit trees, 294
 heading cuts, 231–232
 perennial guidelines, 66–67
 pinching, 231–232
 roses, 102
 rules of limb, 234
 shearing, 231–232
 summer, 234–235
 thinning cuts, 231–232
 timing, 230, 234–235
 tools, 235–236
 treat tree wounds, 233
 trees, 232–233
 vines, 156
 winter, 234
pruning tools, 235–236
pruning trees, 232–233
Prunus species (flowering fruit)
 deciduous tree, 116
 shrub, 124
Prunus subhirtella (Higan (spring)
 cherry), **3-3**

publications
  Annuals For Dummies, 353
  Bird Watching For Dummies, 320
  Container Gardening For Dummies, 299, 308, 353
  Decks & Patios For Dummies, 301, 353
  Flowering Bulbs For Dummies, 76, 354
  The Garden Tourist: A Guide to Garden Tours, Garden Days and Special Events, 353
  Gardening by Mail: A Source Book, 5th Ed, 353
  Houseplants For Dummies, 354
  Internet For Dummies, 357
  Landscaping For Dummies, 29, 354
  Lawn Care For Dummies, 131, 143, 353
  Netscape and the World Wide Web For Dummies, 357
  Ortho's Home Gardening Problem Solver, 366
  Perennials For Dummies, 238, 353
  Roses For Dummies, 353
  Sunset Western Garden Book, 20
  Vegetable Gardening For Dummies, 21, 288, 354
Purple beautyberry (*callicarpa japonica*), **3-6**
purple coneflower (*Echinacea purpurea*), 71, **1-6**
purple fountain grass (*Pennisetum setaceum*), 64, 72
Purple foxglove (*Digitalis purpurea*), **1-6**
purple kale, photo, **4-4**
purple-leafed sand cherry (*P. cistena*) shrub, 125
purslane (*Portulaca oleracea*) weed, 266
push rotary power mowers, 272
push-reel mowers, environmentally friendly, 272
Pyracantha species (firethorn) shrub, 126, 237
pyrethrins (*Tanacetum cinerarifolium*) insecticide
  advantages/disadvantages, 255–256
  cucumber beetle treatment, 245
  Mexican bean beetle treatment, 248
  whitefly treatment, 250
Pyrus calleryana (ornamental pear) deciduous tree, 116
Pyrus kawakamii (evergreen pear) evergreen tree, 117

• Q •

Q. agrifolia (coast live oak) evergreen tree, 117
Q. ilex (holly oak) evergreen tree, 117
Q. robur (English oak) deciduous tree, 116
Q. rubra (red oak) deciduous tree, 116
Q. suber (cork oak) evergreen tree, 117
Q. virginiana (southern live oak) evergreen tree, 117
Queen Anne's lace, beneficial insect attractor, 252
Quercus (oaks species) evergreen tree, 117
Quercus species (oaks) deciduous tree, 116

• R •

R. chinensis (China) shrub rose, 94
R. damascena (damask) shrub rose, 94
R. gallica (gallica) shrub rose, 94
radish, 289
rainfall, measuring to aid water conservation, 15
rainwater, water conservation, 215
raised beds
  creating, 181–182
  small garden technique, 328
  vegetable garden alternative, 286
rake, lawn seed planting tool, 136
Ranunculus asiaticus (Persian buttercup) bulb, 86
raspberries, photo, **4-3**
Raywood ash (*Fraxinus oxycarpa*) deciduous tree, 114
rear bagging mowers, 272
rear tine tillers, 275
records, perennial border design, 63
red maple (*A. rubrum*) deciduous tree, 113
red oak (*Q. rubra*) deciduous tree, 116
redroot pigweed (*Amaranthus retroflexus*) weed, 266
relaxation area, garden use, 13
remedy fungicide, disease treatment, 261
repeat bloom, floribunda roses, 89
repeat cultivation, 169
repeated tilling method, 169
repetition, 40, 303
repotting, container plants, 314–315
resale value, site analysis considerations, 35
Reseda odorata (*mignonette*), bold fragrance, 54
resources
  books, 351–354
  magazines, 355–356
  mail order, 367–384
  online, 356–366
Rhaphiolepis indica (Indian hawthorn) shrub, 126
Rhizobium, nitrogen-fixing bacteria, 179
rhizomes, 84
Rhododendron (*Rhododendron catawbiense*), 'Roseum Pink', **3-7**
Rhododendron species (azaleas) shrub, 126
Rhododendron species (rhododendrons) shrub, 126
rhubarb chard, photo, **4-4**
Rhus typhina (Staghorn sumac), **3-2**
ribbons-and-bows method, soil texture test, 171
riding mowers, 273
rock cotoneaster (*C. horizontalis*) ground cover, 149–150
rockroses (*Cistus* species) shrub, 122
rockspray cotoneaster (*C. microphyllus*) ground cover, 150
rodent repellents, animal damage risk avoidance, 28
romantica shrub roses, 95
root flare, 206
root maggots, 248
root-bound, 200
root-pruning, container plants, 314
rooting hormone, 237
Rosa alba (alba) shrub rose, 94
'Rosa Bianca' eggplant, 75 day growing cycle, 26
Rosa centifolia (centifolia) shrub rose, 94
Rosa rugosa (rugosa) shrub roses, 95
Rosa species (climbing roses) vine, 162
Rosa species (roses) shrubs, 126
Rose Food, rose fertilizer, 100
rosea ice plant (*Drosanthemum floribundum*) ground cover, 150
rosemary (*Rosmarinus officialis*) herb
  aromatic, 346
  described, 291
  drought-tolerant shrub, 128
  'Huntington carpet', **3-5**
  midsummer rose garden partner, 96
roses
  AARS (All-American Rose Selections), 98
  black spot disease, 102
  climbing varieties, 90

David Austin (English) varieties, 91–92
described, 87
fertilizing/watering guidelines, 100–101
floribundas varieties, 89
fragrant, 349
generosa varieties, 92
grading, 97
grandiflora varieties, 90
ground-cover varieties, 92
hardy varieties, 93
healthy plant indicators, 97–98
hybrid musk varieties, 93
hybrid teas, 88–89
landscaping uses, 96–97
leaf buds, 102
mail order, 378–379
midsummer landscape design, 96
miniature varieties, 90–91
non-grafted, 100
old garden varieties, 94–95
own-root, 100
planting process, 99–100
pruning guidelines, 102
purchasing guidelines, 97–98
raised bed process, 181–182
Rose Food fertilizer, 100
shrub rose varieties, 91–96, 127
Smooth Touch throttles, 96
spring landscape design, 96
standards, 91
types, 88–96
underground branch pruning, 102
uses for, 97
winter landscape design, 96
roses (*Rosa* species) shrub, 126
Rosmarinus officinalis (rosemary) shrub
described, 346
drought-tolerant, 128
photo, **3-5**
Rotenone insecticide, advantages/disadvantages, 256
rototiller, 136, 179–180, 274–276
round-shaped daffodil bulb, flower potential, 78
Roundup, nonselective herbicide, 168
row covers, 24–25
rows, vegetable garden planting arrangement, 285
rubbing alcohol, scale treatment, 248
Rudbeckia fulgida (black-eyed coneflower), cutting plant, 64
Rudbeckia fulgida (Gloriosa daisy), **1-5**
Rudbeckia hirta (black-eyed Susan), 73
Rudbeckia hirta (gloriosa daisy), 73
rugosa (*Rosa rugosa*) shrub roses, 95

Russian olive (*Elaeagnus angustifolia*) deciduous tree, 114
rust disease, Hawthorn tree, 114
rust, treatment, 260

• S •

S. azurea grandiflora, 73
S. bumalda ('Anthony Waterer') shrub, 127
S. superba perennial, 73
S. vanhouttei (bridal wreath spiraea) shrub, 127
sage (*Salvia* species), 60, 237
sage (*Salvia officinalis*) herb, 292
salad basket, preparing, 340
salvia (*Salvia* species), 73
salvia (*Salvia*), indoor starting annual, 194
Salvia species (sage), warm-season variety, 60
sand, potting soil ingredient, 312
sandy soil, 170–171, 210
Sargent crab apple (*M. sargentii*) deciduous tree, 115
sasanqua camellias (*C. sasanqua*) shrub, 122
saucer magnolia (*M. soulangiana*) deciduous tree, 115, **3-4**
Scabiosa (pincushion flower), cutting plant, 64
scale drawings, creating, 38
scale of garden, 248, 303
scales, 82
scent, releasing from leaves, 343
scented geraniums (*Pelargonium* species), aromatic herb, 346
scented leafed geranium, scent varieties, 55
screens, shrub uses, 119
scrim plants, 53
scuffle hoe, uses, 268
sculpting for decorative reasons, 230
search engines, 358–359
seasonal preferences, vegetable garden planning, 282–283
secondary nutrients, 216
security concerns, online shopping, 361
sedum (*Sedum*), 'Autumn Joy', **1-5**
sedum, easy to root plants, 237
seed companies, 184–185, 361
seed leaves, 186
seed packets, label guidelines, 186
seed tapes, planting methods, 287–288
seedlings
described, 195
hardening off process, 192–193

pest types, 242
planting process, 196–199
purchasing guidelines, 196
thinning, 186
vegetable garden planting method, 286
seeds
advantages of starting plants from, 183
direct sowing techniques, 185–188
germination percentage, 135
light requirements, 184
moisture requirements, 184
purchasing guidelines, 184–185
soil temperature requirements, 184
starting indoors, 189–193
vegetable garden planting methods, 287–288
self-propelled rotary mowers, 272
Senecio cineraria, 57
Serbian bellflower (*C. poscharskyana*), 69
serviceberries (*Amelanchier* species), bird habitat, 318
shade areas, 11, 30–31, 50–51
shape
annual design layout considerations, 53–54
container garden design concepts, 302–303
repetition concept, 40
shaping trees, 230
Shasta daisy (*Leucanthemum maximum*), 70
shearing, 148, 231–232
shepherd's purse (*Capsella bursa-pastoris*) weed, 266
shopping Web sites, 360–362
short season plant varieties, frost-beating gardening, 26
shovels, uses, 268–269
shrub roses, 91–95
shrubs
bird habitat types, 318
container-grown purchasing guidelines, 200
described, 117–118
drought-tolerant varieties, 128
fragrant, 346–347
landscape design considerations, 118–119
mail order, 382–383
multi-season color varieties, 127
organizing by height, 119–120
photos, **3-5–3-7**
varieties, 121–128
side yards, use guidelines, 37
side-bagging mowers, 272
Sierra Online, Complete LandDesigner program, 44
silver maple (*A. saccharinum*) deciduous tree, 113

single digging, 179–180
single flower type, 48
site analysis
    activity by yard area planning, 33
    area defining techniques, 38–39
    backyard use guidelines, 37
    barbecue area placement, 34
    children's areas, 34
    current strengths/weaknesses, 30
    described, 30–33
    dog run placement, 34
    drainage considerations, 31
    existing plants, 30
    field testing drawings, 44
    final plan creation, 42–44
    front yard use guidelines, 36–37
    hardscape elements, 39–40
    historical/cultural heritage
        considerations, 35
    indoor view angles, 31
    lighting issues, 31
    maintenance considerations,
        35–36
    natural features, 31
    neighbor concerns, 35
    noise levels, 31
    personal likes/dislikes, 30
    plant forms, 41–42
    plot plan drawing advantages, 36
    problem area determinations, 30
    rough draft drawing, 30–33
    scale drawing process, 38
    side yard use guidelines, 37
    slope considerations, 31
    smells (odors), 31
    soil types, 31
    sun/shade areas, 30–31
    use timing considerations, 34
    user considerations, 34
    vegetable garden location, 284
    vegetable garden placement, 34
    view considerations, 31
    wish list items, 33–34
sites, clearing process, 167–169
size, plant design character-
    istic, 41
slope, 31, 148
slow-release fertilizer, 219
slugs, 248–249
small gardens
    attention diverter techniques, 326
    climbing plants, 328
    design concepts, 325–326
    detail importance, 326
    gap plant varieties, 330
    gap planting, 327
    overhead arbors, 328–329
    plant selection guidelines, 329
    raised beds, 328
    visual enlargement techniques,
        326–327
    window boxes, 328
smells (odors), site analysis
    considerations, 31

Smoke tree (*Cotinus coggygria*),
    'Royal Purple', **3-5**
smooth hydrangea (*H.
    arborescens*) shrub, 123
Smooth Touch rose, thornless
    variety, 96
snails, 248–249
snapdragon (*Antirrhinum majus*),
    49, 57
snowdrop bulbs, animal dislike, 81
snowdrops (*Galanthus* species)
    bulb, 85
snowflake (*Leucojum* species)
    bulb, 85
soaker hose, 186
sod
    described, 131
    laying process, 140–142
    purchasing guidelines, 140
    stripping existing, 168–169
sod cutter, sod stripping tool,
    168–169
softer moss (*R. centifolia*) shrub
    rose 95
software, 44, 364 365
softwood stem cuttings, 237
soil amendments, 136, 175–178
soil structure, 172–173
soil temperature, seed require-
    ments, 184
soils
    alternate clearing methods, 169
    amending, 167
    amendment materials, 175–179
    black plastic clearing method, 169
    clay type, 170–171
    container garden guidelines,
        309–312
    double digging process, 181
    improvement materials, 175–179
    jar texture test, 171–172
    loam type, 170–171
    loosening techniques, 179–182
    newspaper clearing method, 169
    perennial border design, 63
    pH level testing, 174
    pH testing, 134
    plant growth factor, 11
    potting mixtures, 311–312
    professional testing sources,
        174–175
    raised bed creation, 181–182
    repeat cultivation clearing
        method, 169
    ribbons-and-bows texture test,
        171
    sandy type, 170–171
    single digging process, 179–180
    site analysis considerations, 31
    texture types, 170–172
    type as factor in watering, 210
    when to work, 179
Solanum jasminoides (White
    Potato vine), **3-8**

solarization, 257, 264
Solidago (goldenrod), cutting
    plant, 65
sooty mold, treatment, 260
southern live oak (*Q. virginiana*)
    evergreen tree, 117
southern magnolia (*Magnolia
    grandiflora*) evergreen
    tree, 117
spade, single digging process,
    179–180
Spanish jasmine (*Jasminum
    grandiflorum*) vine, 150
specialist plants, mail order,
    376–378
species, 14
speedwell (*Veronica*), cutting
    plant, 65
spider mites, 249
spiky (upright) plants, design
    uses, 41
spiraea (*Spiraea* species)
    shrub, 127
spotted (or prostrate) spurge, 266
sprawling vines, 154
spray paint, outlining sites, 167
spreader, fertilizer, 218
sprigs, 131, 143
Spring cinquefoil (*P.
    tabernaemontanii*) ground
    cover, 150
Spring cinquefoil (*P. verna*)
    ground cover, 150
Spring cinquefoil (*Potentilla
    neumanniana*) ground
    cover, 150
spring garden, photo, **3-7**
spring-blooming bulbs, purchas-
    ing/planting guidelines, 77
sprinklers, 26, 211, 214
Spritzer tube duster, DE (diatoma-
    ceous earth) dispenser, 253
squirrels, birdfeeder guide-
    lines, 319
St. Augustine grass, 133
Stachys byzantina (lamb's ears), 74
Staghorn sumac (*Rhus typhina*), **3-2**
stakes, 67–68, 202–203
standards, rose varieties, 91
star flower type, 49
star jasmine (*Trachelospermum
    jasminoides*) ground
    cover, 150
star jasmine (*Trachelospermum
    jasminoides*) vine
    described, 159, 162
    easy to root plants, 237
    twining vine, 154
statice (*Limonium*), indoor
    starting annual, 194
steel bow rake, uses, 268
stem cuttings, 236–237
stick pest barriers, 246

stiffer moss (*R. centifolia*) shrub rose, 'Henri Martin', 95
stiffer moss (*R. damascena*) shrub rose, 95
stiff-tined rake, uses, 268–269
stock (*Matthiola incana*), 58, 345
'Stokes' aster (*Stokesia laevis*), cutting plant, 65
straight branches, using, 341
strawberries, 296, **4-4**
strawflower (*Helichrysum*), 194, 335
string lines, direct sowing aide, 188
string trimmers, 274
structure, annual design layout considerations, 53–54
succession of blooms, border design, 63
succession planting, vegetable gardens, 285
suckers, 234
suet, bird attractor, 318–319
sugar maple (*A. saccharum*) deciduous tree113, **3-4**
sulfur
    changing alkaline soil pH level, 178
    described, 216
    disease treatment, 261
summer phlox (*Phlox paniculata*), 73
summer pruning, 234–235
summer squash, 289
summer-blooming bulbs, purchasing/planting guidelines, 78
sun areas
    effects on annual plants, 50–51
    including in site analysis drawings, 30–31
    plant growth factor, 11
sunflower (*Helianthus annus*), 51, 53, 60, 189
supermarkets, summer-blooming bulb purchasing guidelines, 78
supplies, mail order, 379–382
sweet alyssum (*Lobularia maritima*)
    cool-season variety, 58
    diminutive size, 53
    edging plant use, 55
    indoor starting annual, 194
sweet cherries, 296
sweet gum (*Liquidambar styraciflua*) deciduous tree, 108, 115
sweet pea (*Lathyrus odoratus*)
    cool-season variety, 58
    direct sowing annual, 189
    perfume scented, 54–55
    scented flower, 345
sweet peas (*Lathyrus*) vine, 164
sweet peppers, 289

sweet sultan (*Centaurea moschata*), scented flower, 344
sweet violet (*Viola odorata*), scented flower, 345
sweet William (*D. barbatus*), 55, 71
Syringa vulgaris (common lilac) shrub, 127, **3-7**

● **T** ●

T. asiaticum (Confederate vine) ground cover, 150
T. clusiana bulb, 86
Tagetes species (marigold), 60, 194
taking cuttings, propagating, 236–237
tall stems, using, 341
Tanacetum coccineum (painted daisy), 70
tape measure, uses, 270
tarnished plant bugs (lygus bugs), 249
tea shrub roses, 95
Tecrium species (germander), drought-tolerant shrub, 128
tendrils, 154
tent caterpillars, 250
terra cota (unglazed clay) containers, 300
texture
    plant design characteristic, 41–42
    soil types, 170–172
thatch, 146
thermometers, compost, 225
thin metal wire loop stakes, bushy perennial plants, 67–68
thinning cuts, pruning, 231–232
thinning out process, seedlings, 186
Threadleaf false cypress (*Chamaecyparis pisifera*), 'Fillifera', **3-6**
thunbergia (*Thunbergia alata*) vine, 163, **3-8**
thyme (*Thymus vulgaris*) herb
    aromatic herb, 346
    described, 292
    midsummer rose garden partner, 96
Thymus (thyme), 346
Thymus praecox arcticus (creeping thyme) ground cover, 150
tickseed (*Coreopsis grandiflora*), 64
tillers. *See* rototillers
time of day/year, site analysis considerations, 34
timers, water conservation, 215
tines, 268
tip bud, 230
Tithonia rotundifolia (Mexican sunflower), 194, **1-3**
tobira (*Pittosporum tobira*) shrub, 124–125, 127

tomato hornworm, 250
tomatoes (*Lycopersicum esculentum*), 194, 289, 405
tools
    compost aerating, 225
    compost sifter, 225
    computer, 356
    grinders, 274, 276–277
    hand, 267–270
    hose-end sprayer, 218
    lawn seed planting, 136
    mail order, 379–382
    pitchfork, 226
    power, 270–277
    purchasing sources, 277–278
    renting versus owning, 136
    spreader, 218
    tillers, 274–276
    trimmers, 274
topdressing, 146
topsoil, 177
toxins, oleander (*Nerium oleander*) shrub, 124
toyon (*Heteromeles arbutifolia*), drought-tolerant shrub, 128
Trachelospermum (star jasmine) ground cover, 150
Trachelospermum jasminoides (star jasmine) vine, 150, 162
trailers, 48
trailing African daisy (*Osteospermum*) ground cover, 149
trailing ice plant (*Lampranthus spectabilis*) ground cover, 150
transpiration, water loss, 214
transplants
    container-grown trees/shrubs, 201–204
    described, 195
    drift planting, 197
    spacing issues, 196–197
traps
    beer, 248
    described, 250
    pheromone, 244–245
trees
    attractive bark varieties, 109
    birch borers, 114
    bird habitat types, 318
    colorful fruit, 109
    conifers, 116
    container-grown purchasing guidelines, 200
    crab apple, 109
    crape myrtles, 108
    deciduous, 108, 112–116
    evergreen, 112, 116–117
    fragrant, 346–347
    Global ReLeaf campaign, 111
    hawthorns, 109
    healthy tree indicators, 113
    heating/cooling expense advantages, 108

(continued)

trees *(continued)*
   landscaping advantages,
     107–109
   mail-order, 382–383
   ornamental characteristics,
     108–109
   photos, **3-2–3-3**
   planting guidelines, 111–112
   pruning, 232–233
   rose standards, 91
   seasonal colors, 108
   selection guidelines, 109–111
   shapes, 110
   shaping, 230
   sweet gum (Liquidambar), 108
   treating pruning wounds, 233
   understory, 53
   windbreaks for energy conserva-
     tion, 108
trichogramma wasps, 245, 251
trimmings, 341
Tropaeolum majus (nasturtium),
   59, 163, **1-3**
Tropaeolum peregrinum (canary
   creeper) vine, 163
troubleshooting, software, 366
tulip (*Tulilpa sylvestris*), scented
   flower, 345
tulips (*Tulipa* species) bulb
   described, 86
   forcing candidate, 82–83
   naturalistic design style
     candidate, 80
   spring-blooming bulb, 77
tumblers, compost bins, 224
tune-ups, lawn care, 146
turfgrass, 131–134
turf-type tall fescue, 132
twigs, using, 341
twine wrapping, winter hardiness
   technique, 27
twining vines, 154
Typar, landscape fabric, 263

• U •

understory trees, 53
unity, 40, 119
university campus, tree variety
   source, 109
upright (spiky) plants, design
   uses, 41
USDA Plant Hardiness Zone Map,
   19–20, **2-6–2-8**
users, site analysis considerations, 34
utilities, locating before digging, 201

• V •

V. carlesii (Korean spice viburnum) shrub, 128

V. plicatum (deciduous viburnum)
   shrub, 128
V. tinus (evergreen viburnum)
   shrub, 127
variegated, described, 53
variegated eulalia grass
   (*Miscanthus sinesis*), 72
variety, described, 14
Varro mite (*V. jacobosonii*),
   honeybee population, 324
vase shape, trees, 110
vegetable gardens
   beds, 285
   calendar for, 283
   carrot, 288
   combining with herb gardens, 290
   containers, 285
   cool-season varieties, 282
   cucumber, 288
   direct-sown planting method, 286
   frost timing, 286–287
   frost-resistant crops, 287
   frost-tender crops, 287
   green beans, 289
   harvesting, 288
   heirloom vegetable advantages/
     disadvantages, 290
   hills, 285
   hybrid variety advantages/
     disadvantages, 289–290
   hybrid vigor, 289
   interplanting, 285
   last frost dates, 283
   lettuce, 289
   locating, 284
   onion, 289
   open pollinated varieties, 290
   peas, 289
   photos, **4-2–4-8**
   planning, 281–288
   plant spacing importance, 285
   planting arrangements, 284–285
   radish, 289
   raised bed process, 181–182
   rows, 285
   seasonal preferences, 282–283
   seed planting methods, 287–288
   seed tape planting, 287–288
   seedling planting method, 286
   site analysis considerations, 34
   sizing, 284
   soil improvement techniques,
     285–286
   succession planting, 285
   summer squash, 289
   sweet pepper, 289
   tomato, 289
   varieties, 288–289
   warm-season varieties, 282
vegetables
   container garden varieties, 308
   direct sowing, 185–188
   growing season issues, 21–22

seedling pest types, 242
verbena (*Verbena hybrida*), 60, **1-4**
Verbena bonariensis, scrim plant
   uses, 53
vermiculite, potting soil ingredient, 312
Veronica (speedwell), cutting
   plant, 65
vertical gardening, climbing
   plants, 328
verticillium wilt, treatment, 261
viburnum (*Viburnum* species)
   shrub, 127–128
views, including in site analysis
   drawings, 31
vinca, reseeding volunteer, 51
Vinca minor (dwarf periwinkle)
   ground cover, 150
vinca rosea (*Catharanthus roseus*),
   50, 59
vinegars, herb, 333–334
vines
   annual varieties, 162–164
   arbors, 160
   bamboo teepees, 157–158
   chain-link fences, 158
   clinging varieties, 153
   described, 153
   fan trellises, 159
   fragrant, 346–347
   latticework trellises, 159
   mail order, 382–383
   metal trellises, 158
   photos, **3-8**
   pillars, 160
   plant ties, 160
   plastic netting, 159
   pruning guidelines, 156
   sprawling varieties, 154
   support types, 155–160
   tendrils, 154
   types, 153–154
   using, 341
   using effectively, 155–156
   varieties, 161–162
   wall-mounted supports, 160
viola (*Viola* species), 51, 59
Viola odorata (sweet violet), 345
Viola species (pansy), 59
Viola species (viola), 59
Viola wittrockiana (Pansy), **1-4**
Virginia creeper (*P. quinquefolia*)
   vine, 155, 162
Vitis (grape) vine, 162
volunteers, reseeding technique, 51

• W •

wall-mounted supports, vine
   structure, 160
walls, vine cautions, 155

warm-season annuals, 50
warm-season grass, 131–133
warm-season vegetables, when to
    plant, 282
water
    bird attractor, 318–319
    blasting pests off plants with a
        hose, 250
    container garden requirements,
        310–311
    conservation, 215
    direct sowing guidelines, 186
    early morning advantages, 241
    fruit tree needs, 294
    plant growth factor, 11
    rose guidelines, 100–101
    starting seeds indoors, 191
    winter hardiness technique, 28
water drainage, percolation
    test, 173
water gardens, 338–339,
    383–384, **4-8**
water wand, uses, 270
water-filled cloche, 24
watering
    conserve water, 215
    determining amount and timing,
        213–215
    do early to aid in
        conservation, 215
    factors in how much, 210
    when plants need, 214–215
watering depth, water conserva-
    tion, 215
watering methods, 211–213
watersprouts, 234
weather, watering concerns, 210
Web sites
    AHS Plant Heat-Zone Map, 21
    American Forests, 111
    American Gardener, 355
    AOL (America Online), 364
    APHIS (Plant Health Inspection
        Service), 247
    ARS (American Rose Society), 96
    Association of Online Growers
        and Suppliers, 361
    Barbara Barton's Gardening by
        Mail, 360
    Brooklyn Botanic Garden:
        Handbook, 355
    Burpee Seeds, 361
    Compuserve, 364
    Cook's Garden, 361
    Cyndi's Catalog of Catalogs, 360
    Dig the Net (Virtual Garden
        Toolshed), 358
    Factsheet Database, 357
    Forum One, 364
    forums, 364
    Fun gardening, 355
    Garden Encyclopedia, 359
    Garden Escape, 361

Garden Gate, 355, 358, 360, 366
Garden Literature Press, 356
Garden Solutions, 360
Garden Web, 362
Garden Web Forums, 364
Gardening at Mingco.com,
    358, 362
GardenNet, 358
Gardentown, 364
    herbs, 374–375
Horticulture, 356
Horticulture Online, 362
Horticulture Solutions, 357
Houseplant Pavilion, 360
Interactive Plant List, 360
Internet Directory for Botany:
    Gardening, 360
Johnny's Selected Seeds, 361
Lawn Talk at Illinois Cooperative
    Extension Service, 134
Liszt, the mailing list
    directory, 364
Live Chat at Miningco.com, 364
Look Smart (AltaVista), 358
mail-order sites, 367–384
mailing lists, 363–364
Mailing Lists for Gardeners, 363
National Audubon Society, 320
National Gardening Association,
    356, 358, 362
National Turfgrass Evaluation
    Program, 134
newsgroups, 362–363
Online Buyer's Guide, 361
Online Gardening Catalogs, 361
Organic Gardening, 356
Plant Dictionary, 360
Plant Encyclopedia, 360
plant information, 359–360
Plant Information Online, 360
Publicly Accessible Mailing
    Lists, 364
Rebecca's Garden, 356
search engines, 359
security concerns, 361
Shepherd's Seeds, 361
shopping, 360–362
shrubs, 382–383
Sierra Online, 44
Sunset, 20
Thompson and Morgan, 361
Turf Information Center at
    Michigan State
    University, 134
vines, 382–383
Virtual Garden, 362
Virtual Garden Chat, 364
Wayside Gardens, 361
White Flower Farm, 361
Yahoo!, 358–359
Weed Block, landscape fabric, 263
Weed Eraser, non toxic
    herbicide, 264

weeding, direct sown seeds, 186
weeds
    Bermuda grass (*Cynodon
        dactylon*), 265
    bindweed (*Convolvulus
        arvensis*), 264–265
    chickweed (*Stellaria media*), 265
    controlling, 148, 263–266
    corn gluten meal
        preventative, 144
    cover crops, 263
    crabgrass (*Digitaria*), 265
    cultivation effects, 263
    curly dock (*Rumex crispus*), 265
    dandelion (*Taraxacum
        officinale*), 266
    flaming control strategy, 265
    hand hoeing/pulling, 264
    lamb's-quarters (*Chenopodium
        album*), 266
    landscape fabric controls, 263
    mulch uses, 263
    nontoxic herbicides, 264
    oxalis, 266
    purslane (*Portulaca oleracea*), 266
    redroot pigweed (*Amaranthus
        retroflexus*), 266
    shepherd's purse (*Capsella
        bursa-pastoris*), 266
    solarization, 264
    spotted (or prostrate) spurge, 266
    varieties, 264–266
    water conservation, 215
Weed-X, landscape fabric, 263
WeedzSTOP, non toxic
    herbicide, 264
weeping shape, trees, 110
West Elkton peony (*Paeonia
    lactiflora*), 'West Elkton', **1-6**
western North America, sunset
    zone information sources, 20
wheat grass, meadowlike
    landscaping, 152
white ground limestone, outlining
    sites, 167
White Potato vine (*Solanum
    jasminoides*), 'Alba', **3-8**
whiteflies, 250
wild cherry tree, bird habitat, 318
wild lilac (*Caenothus* species), 128
wildflower mixes, 152, 384
willow, easy to root plants, 237
wilt, treatment, 261
windbreaks, trees as energy
    conservation, 108
window boxes, small garden
    technique, 328
winds, prevailing, 31
winged euonymus (*E. alata*)
    shrub, 123
winter creeper (*Euonymus
    fortunei*) ground cover, 150
winter gardening, techniques, 26

winter hardiness, described, 18,
27–28
winter jasmine (*Jasminum
nudiflorum*) vine, 150
winter overseeding, lawn care, 146
winter pruning, 234
winterberry (*I. verticillata*) shrub,
123
wire loop stakes, bushy perennial
plants, 67–68
wire mesh, direct sowing aide, 188
wire mesh bulb baskets, burrowing animal protection, 81
wish list, site analysis considerations, 33–34
Wisteria sinenis (Chinese wisteria)
vine, 162
wood, maintenance considerations, 36
wood containers, 301
woodchucks (groundhogs),
outwitting, 262
wooden compost bins, 223–224
woodland tobacco (*Nicotiana
sylvestris*), accent plant,
54–55
woodpeckers, suet attractors,
318–319
woody plants, easy to root, 237
woolly yarrow (*Achillea
tomentosa*) ground cover, 149
work areas, garden use, 13
World Wide Web, resource, 357
WOW (With-out-weeds), nontoxic
herbicide, 264

• *Y* •

yards, activity area planning, 33
yarrow (*A. filipendulina*),
'Moonshine', 68
yarrow (*Achillea* species), 64,
68–69
Yellow coreopsis (*Liatris*),
'September Glory', 1-7

• *Z* •

Zaluzianskya capensis (night
phlox), 346
Zantedeschia species (calla lily)
bulb, 86
zinc, 216
zinnia (*Zinnia elegans*), 50–51, 60,
188, 4-6
zone maps, 2-6–2-8
zones
American Horticultural Society's
Plant Heat-Zone Map, 20–21
described, 17
length of growing season, 17

Sunset Western Garden Book, 20
USDA Plant Hardiness Zone Map,
19–20, 22
zoysia grass, 133

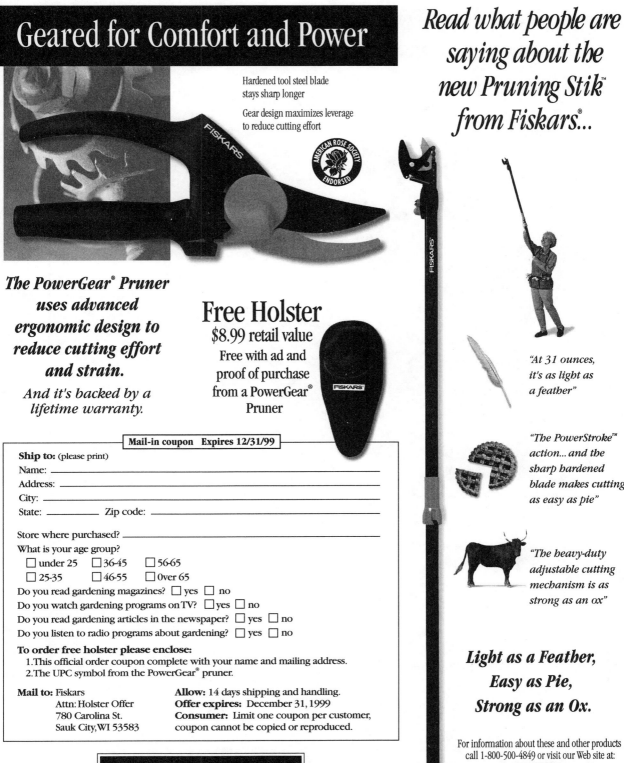

YOUR ONLINE RESOURCE
WWW.DUMMIES.COM

Discover Dummies™ Online!

The *Dummies* Web Site is your fun and friendly online resource for the latest information about *...For Dummies®* books on all your favorite topics. From cars to computers, wine to Windows, and investing to the Internet, we've got a shelf full of *...For Dummies* books waiting for you!

Ten Fun and Useful Things You Can Do at www.dummies.com

1. Register this book and win!
2. Find and buy the *...For Dummies* books you want online.
3. Get ten great *Dummies Tips™* every week.
4. Chat with your favorite *...For Dummies* authors.
5. Subscribe free to *The Dummies Dispatch™* newsletter.
6. Enter our sweepstakes and win cool stuff.
7. Send a free cartoon postcard to a friend.
8. Download free software.
9. Sample a book before you buy.
10. Talk to us. Make comments, ask questions, and get answers!

Jump online to these ten fun and useful things at
http://www.dummies.com/10useful

SURF THE NET
WWW.DUMMIES.COM

For other technology titles from IDG Books Worldwide, go to
www.idgbooks.com

Not online yet? It's easy to get started with *The Internet For Dummies®,* 5th Edition, or *Dummies 101®: The Internet For Windows® 98,* available at local retailers everywhere.

IDG BOOKS WORLDWIDE

Find other *...For Dummies* books on these topics:
Business • Careers • Databases • Food & Beverages • Games • Gardening • Graphics • Hardware
Health & Fitness • Internet and the World Wide Web • Networking • Office Suites
Operating Systems • Personal Finance • Pets • Programming • Recreation • Sports
Spreadsheets • Teacher Resources • Test Prep • Word Processing

IDG BOOKS WORLDWIDE
BOOK REGISTRATION

Register This Book and Win!

We want to hear from you!

Visit **http://my2cents.dummies.com** to register this book and tell us how you liked it!

- Get entered in our monthly prize giveaway.

- Give us feedback about this book — tell us what you like best, what you like least, or maybe what you'd like to ask the author and us to change!

- Let us know any other ...*For Dummies*® topics that interest you.

Your feedback helps us determine what books to publish, tells us what coverage to add as we revise our books, and lets us know whether we're meeting your needs as a ...*For Dummies* reader. You're our most valuable resource, and what you have to say is important to us!

Not on the Web yet? It's easy to get started with *Dummies 101*®: *The Internet For Windows*® *98* or *The Internet For Dummies*®, 5th Edition, at local retailers everywhere.

Or let us know what you think by sending us a letter at the following address:

...*For Dummies* Book Registration
Dummies Press
7260 Shadeland Station, Suite 100
Indianapolis, IN 46256-3945
Fax 317-596-5498

BESTSELLING BOOK SERIES FROM IDG